I0818436

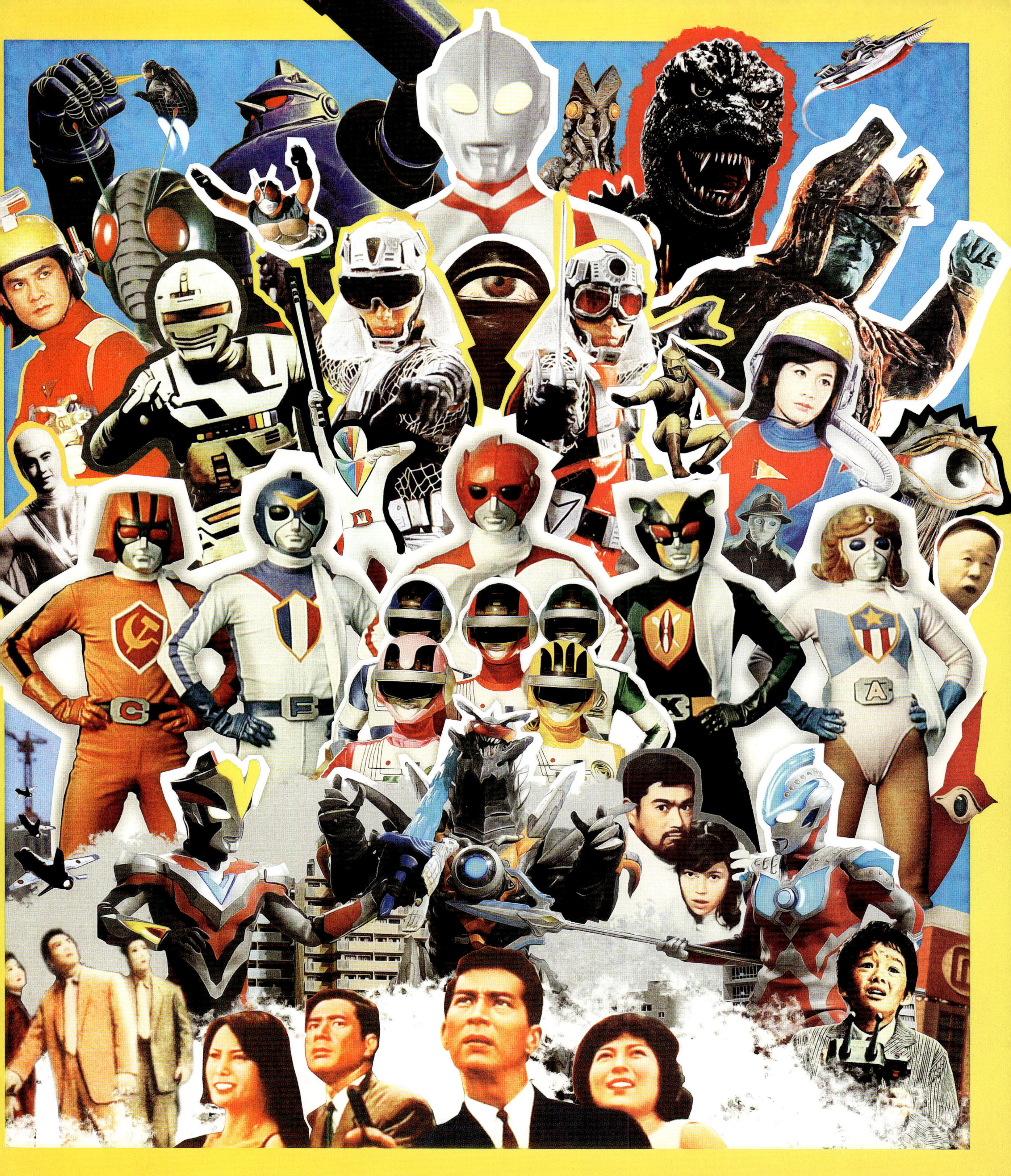

TOKUSATSU

A GUIDE TO KAIJŪ, SENTAI, AND JAPANESE SPECIAL EFFECTS FROM THEIR ORIGINS TO THE PRESENT DAY

CONTENTS

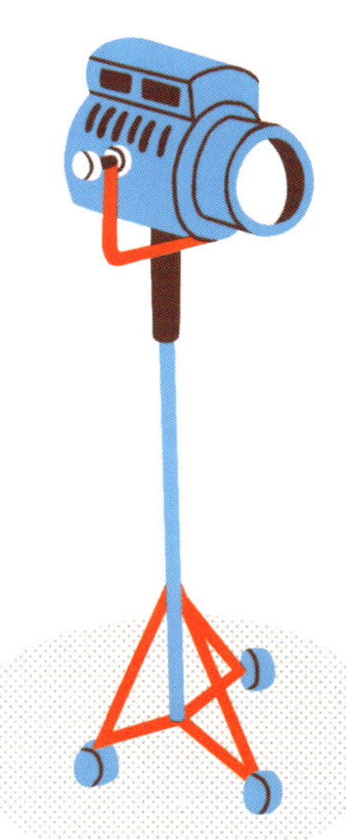

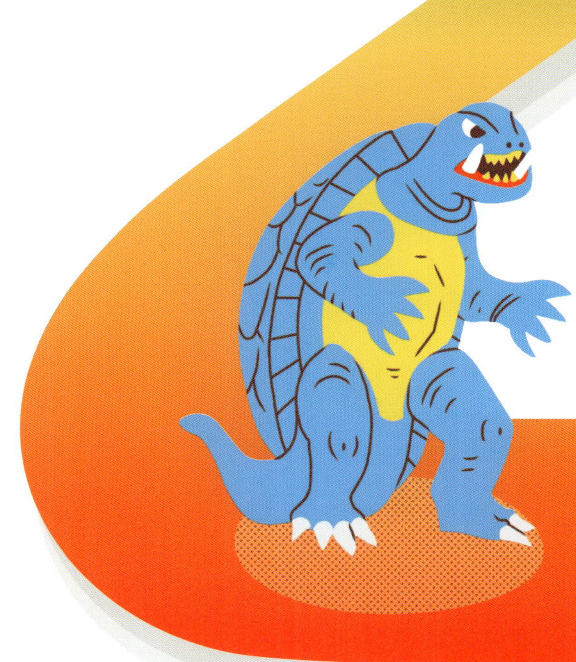

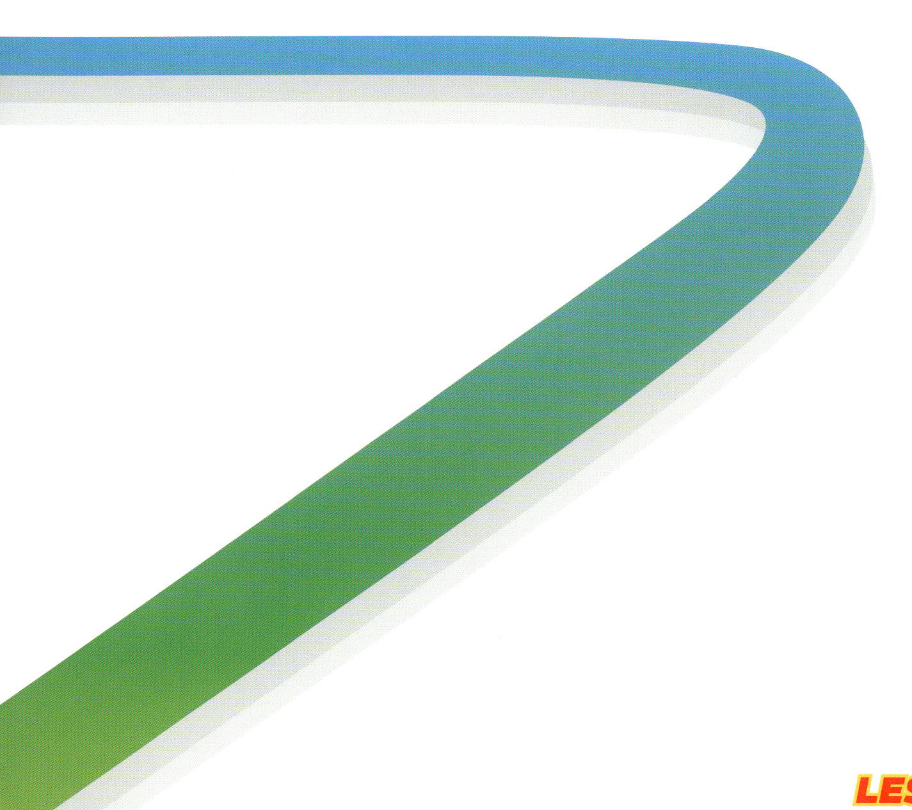

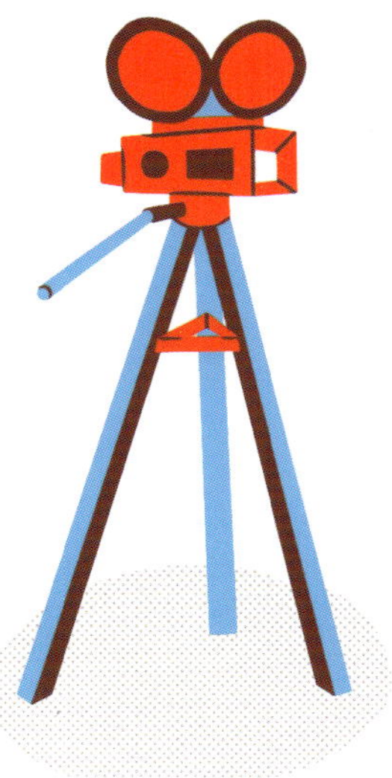

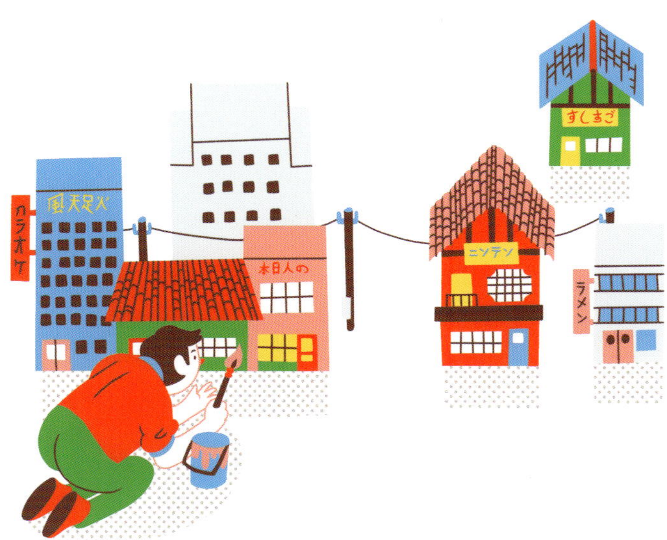

カラオケ

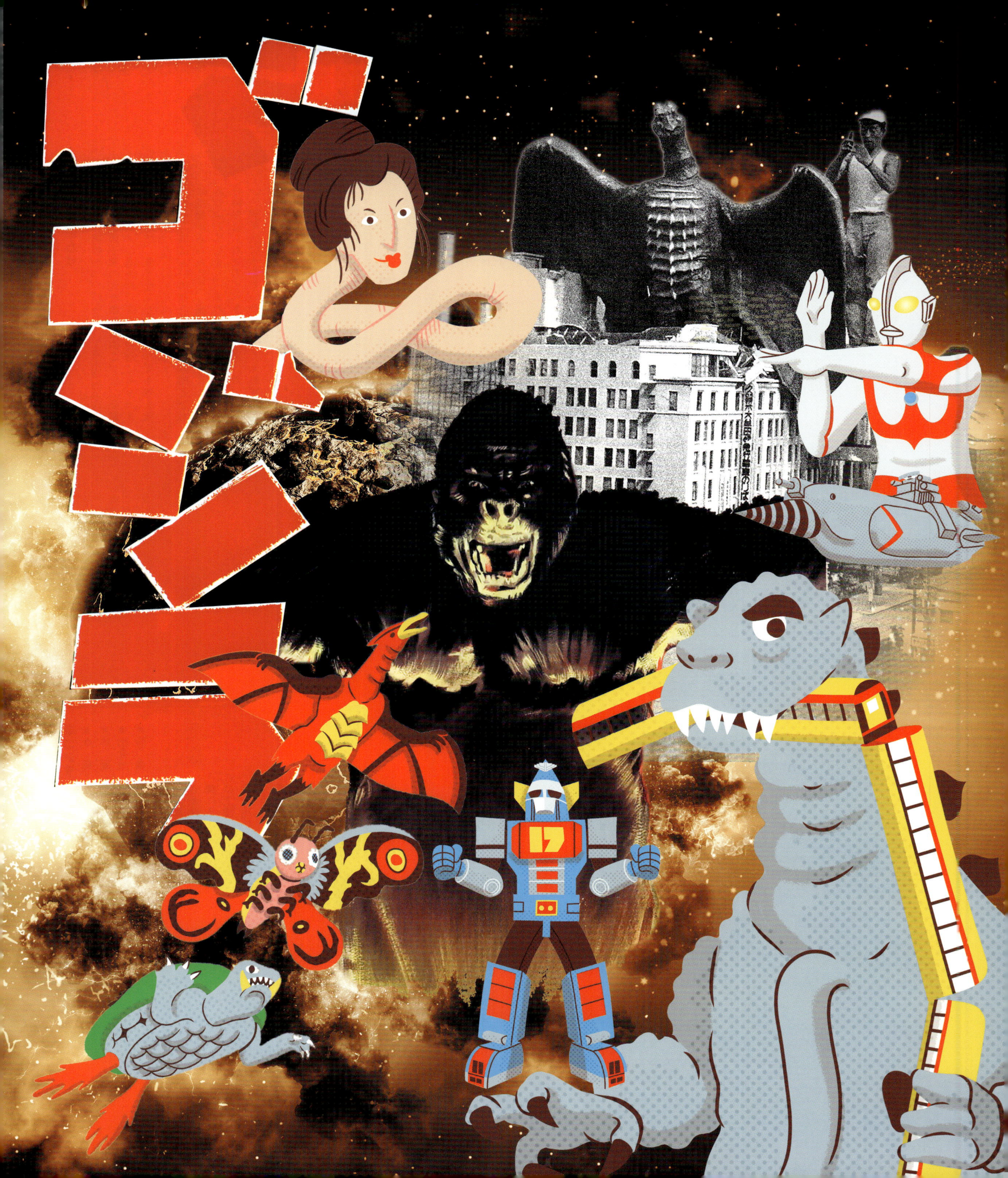
ゴジラ

INTRODUCTION

You may have never heard the word *tokusatsu* before, but we're willing to bet you know more about it than you think. First, let's talk etymology. *Tokusatsu* is the Japanese word for special effects. It is a contraction of *tokushu*, meaning special, and *satsuei*, or filming, and describes productions created primarily with just a simple camera. Used more broadly, *tokusatsu* refers to Japanese films and TV shows that are characterized by their special effects, resulting in a highly distinctive style. In the early days, special effects were achieved through costumes, makeup, miniature sets, and even explosives. Digital effects came into use later as technology advanced.

But does *tokusatsu* refer to any Japanese show that uses practical effects? There's no real consensus. The word is thrown around more freely in Japan, whereas the West perceives it as a uniquely Japanese style of cinema with specific filming methods and ways of creating fantastical worlds.

Tokusatsu certainly has no end of material when it comes to its storytelling. If you're looking to incorporate fantastical elements, science fiction, or over-the-top scenes into your film, *tokusatsu* is for you. As we will see, *tokusatsu* is distinct from yet complementary to the Western approach and a well-established part of Japan's cinematic culture.

When did *tokusatsu* first begin? Well, a smattering of special effects can be seen in early Japanese cinema, back when everything was still new. A prime example is *Jiraiya the Hero*, a silent short film directed by Shōzō Makino in 1921, inspired by a character from the classic *The Tale of the Gallant Jiraiya*. The film contained adventures and battle sequences that showcased early Japanese special effects, including a hero that could teleport, fly, and even transform into a giant toad. Though crude, such visual tricks constituted the first foray into the art.

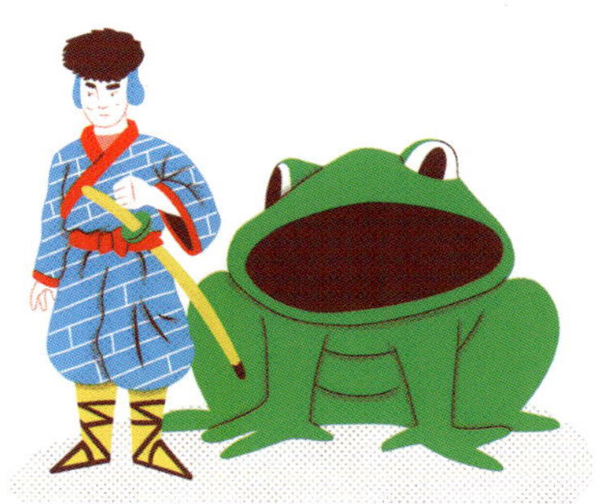

↑ **Above:** *Jiraiya, an early tokusatsu hero.*

↙ **Bottom left:** *Western films also influenced Japanese films.*

Around the same time, Western films like *The Lost World* (1925) and *King Kong* (1933), celebrated at the time for their groundbreaking special effects, inspired an entire generation of Japanese filmmakers. For years, *tokusatsu* was influenced by Western productions, traditional Japanese tales, and even the large-scale battle scenes depicted in war propaganda films made during World War II.

However, to experience a more mature form of the art of special effects as we know it today, we must leap forward to 1954, the year of that most iconic cinematic figure, Godzilla.

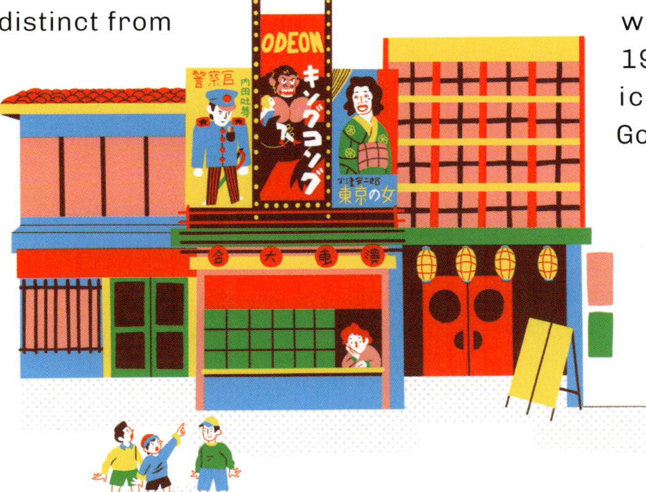

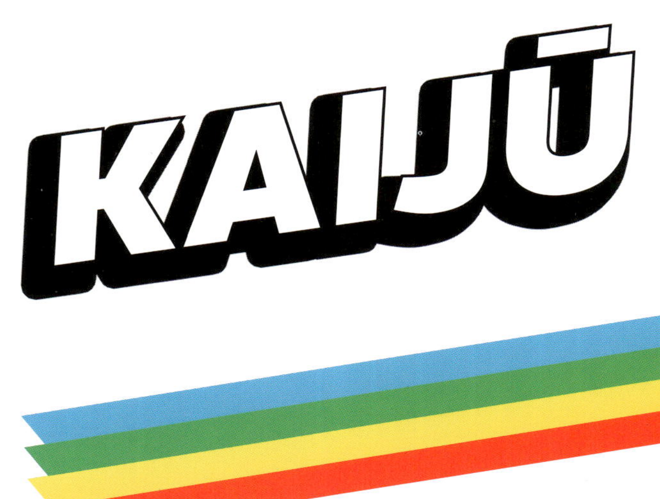

We can't talk about *tokusatsu* without mentioning aspects that are immediately recognizable even to the uninitiated. We're talking about two major categories likely to ring a bell: giant monsters and Japanese superheroes.

We mentioned King Kong, and giant monsters have truly flourished in Japan, leaving an indelible mark on popular culture, first in Japan and then worldwide. Everyone has heard of Godzilla and its franchise thanks to its widespread popularity, the cult status of its films, and its numerous Western adaptations. But where did Godzilla come from? What fueled our fascination with gigantic creatures and stories featuring a massive, living threat terrorizing an entire country or even the world?

It all starts with something called *kaijū*, literally "strange beast" in Japanese. The word first appeared in the nineteenth century and initially referred to creatures from fantastical tales. Over time, and under the influence of Godzilla, the term has evolved to signify a monster, one that may or may not be strange but that is, above all, humongous.

Yet *Godzilla* was not the first-ever *kaijū* movie. In the 1930s, there were several films that could be considered forerunners to what would become a genre in its own right in 1954. One notable example was *The Great Buddha Arrival* in 1934, a precursor to the giant monster concept and considered Japan's first cinematic attempt at it. The story is of a giant Buddha statue that comes to life. Although the film has been lost—the reel was reportedly destroyed during World War II—its legacy endures. In fact, without it, *Godzilla* may never have existed.

But the *kaijū* genre didn't truly gain traction until twenty years later, during Japan's period of economic, social, and cultural reconstruction. The American occupation of Japan ended in 1952, halting the monitoring and censorship of Japanese films and finally allowing Japanese cinema greater freedom

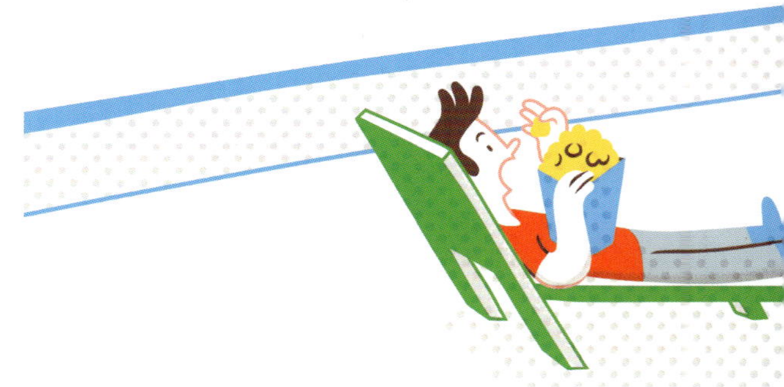

and latitude. The result was films that would rival those made by the former occupier.

Following the wave of war films, monster movies grew more popular. The United States saw a rise in films of all kinds, featuring everything from humanoid creatures to giant monsters. Examples include the aquatic monster from *Creature from the Black Lagoon* (1954), the giant dinosaur from *The Beast from 20,000 Fathoms* (1953) that wreaks havoc upon a city, and the giant invading ants from *Them!* (1954). These films harken back to the genre's origins, first inspired by *King Kong* (1933), and led to many imitators. The revival reinspired Japanese cinema in turn, prompting the legendary Toho studio to produce its own versions, led by the highly prolific Ishirō Honda. Thus, work began on *Godzilla* in 1954.

↓ **Below:** *Japanese theaters were inundated with giant monsters.*

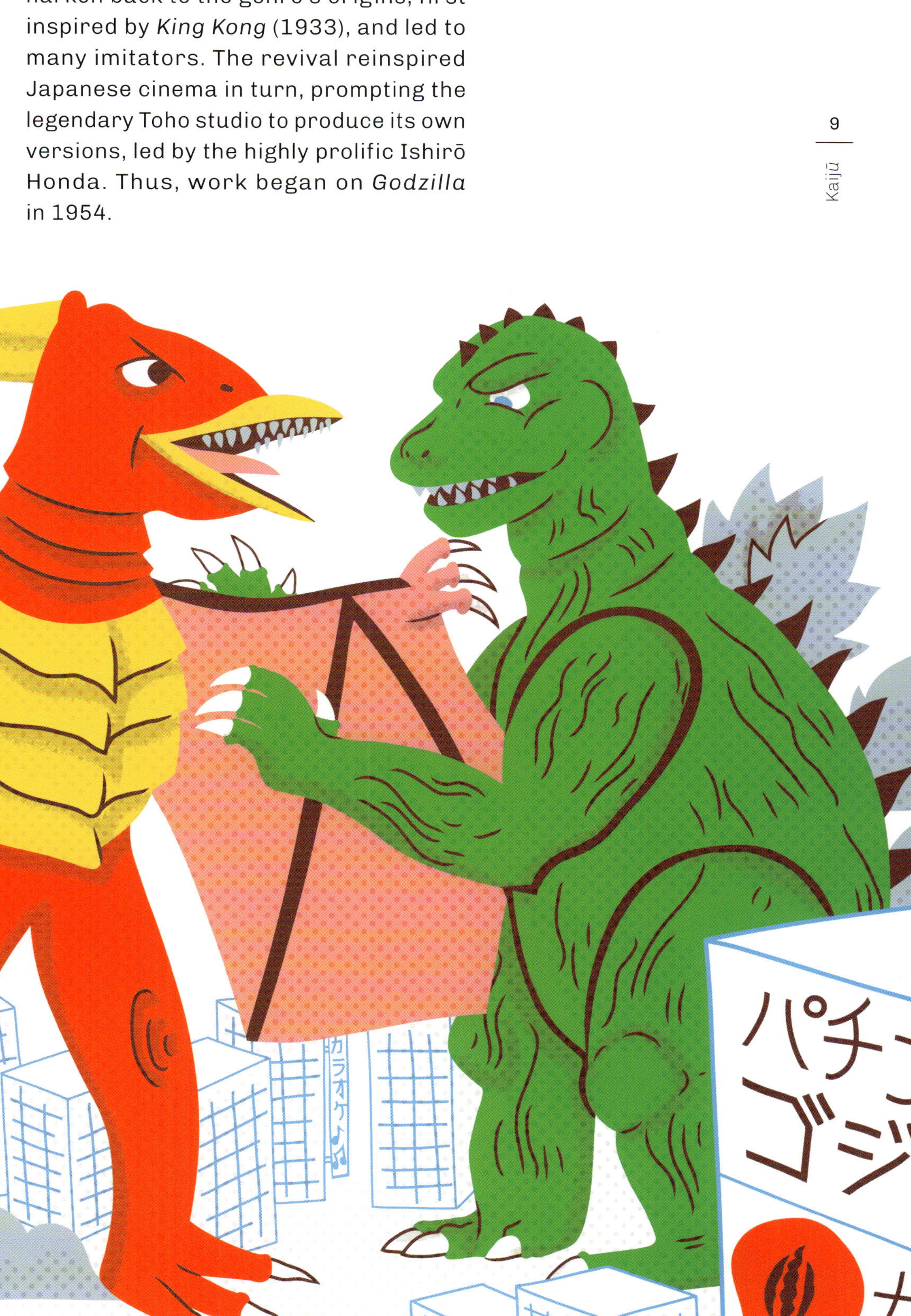

GODZILLA, KING OF ALL MONSTERS

ORIGIN STORY

The *Godzilla* project was originally conceived by Eiji Tsuburaya, Toho's special effects director. The initial story involved an octopus and used stop-motion animation, similar to *King Kong*. However, the amount of work required to animate the octopus would have been overwhelming—seven years of work (and eight arms!). The studio sought an alternative instead that would allow the film to be completed in under six months.

The original idea was scrapped. To cut down on work time, the octopus was swapped out for a giant lizard (inspired by *The Beast from 20,000 Fathoms*), and instead of animating it, the team opted to use an actor in costume. The name *Godzilla* is an amalgamation of *gorira* (gorilla) and *kujira* (whale). The new approach involved a costumed actor stomping through miniature sets designed to be destroyed, emphasizing the monster's destructive power.

The production was ambitious for its time but was carried by a dramatic storyline reflecting lingering fears of war in Japan. Godzilla is depicted as a creature of legend that stalks a port city on the fictional island of Odo, but that turns out to be very real. The monster is awakened by nuclear fallout from bombing near the archipelago. The creature's existence is hinted at and gradually confirmed as the story progresses, culminating in an attack on Tokyo. The city's destruction is slow, terrifying, and inevitable, much like

↓ **Below:** *Ishirō Honda, filmmaker and icon of the golden age of* tokusatsu.

↘ **Bottom right:** *The monster and storyline of* The Beast from 20,000 Fathoms *were both largely based on* Godzilla.

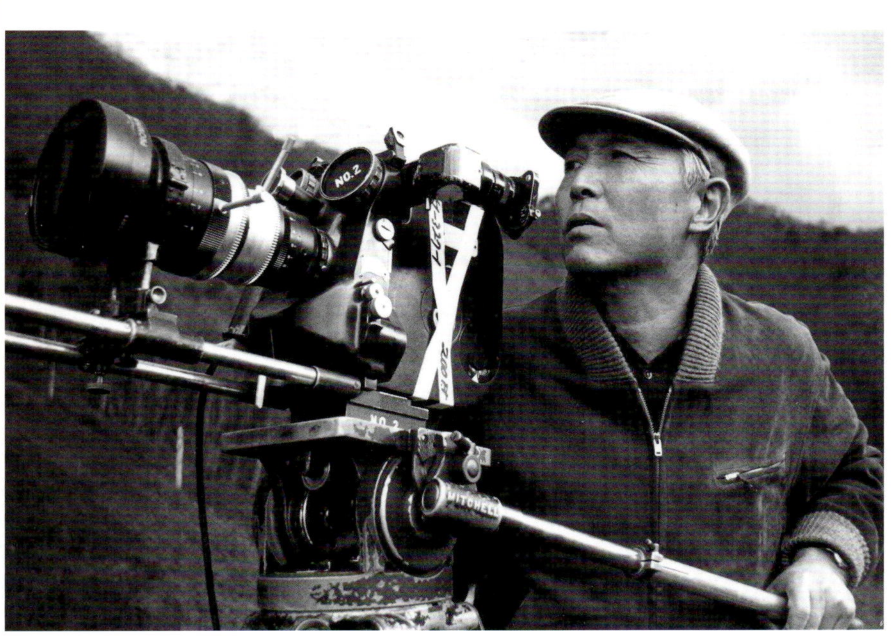

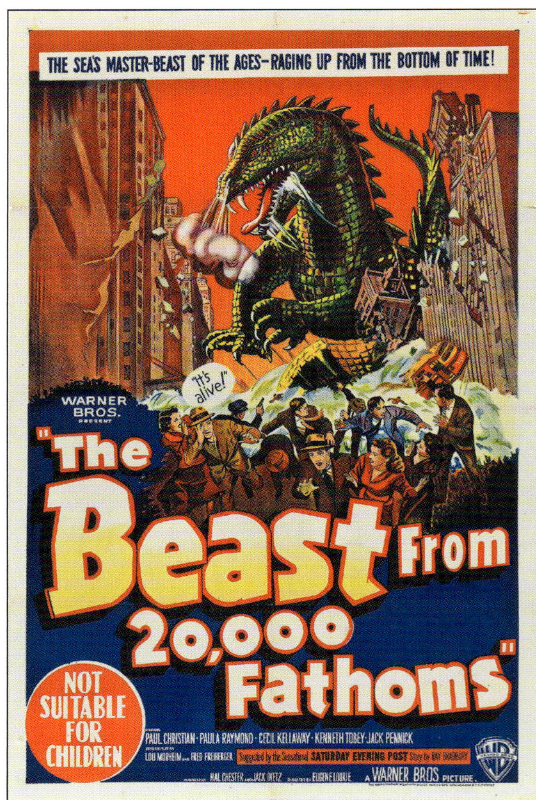

Godzilla itself—a metaphor for the fear of another nuclear catastrophe.

The filming process was challenging because the techniques being used were still brand-new. The character of Godzilla was played by Haruo Nakajima (1929–2017), who faced significant challenges due to the costume, which weighed over 220 pounds and was so hot it caused severe dehydration. It was also hard to maneuver amid the miniature sets. Despite these difficulties, Nakajima took the role extremely seriously. He developed a lifelike gait and gestures for Godzilla, even going so far as to visit a zoo to observe animals like elephants and bears for inspiration. Nakajima's efforts established the foundations of the profession of "suit actor," which refers to actors performing in costumes (specifically as monsters, and later as superheroes). More than mere stunt performers, suit actors bring life and personality to the creatures and superheroes they embody.

The film's overt political message, its advanced cinematic techniques, and its remarkable six-month completion time all combined to turn *Godzilla* into the cornerstone of modern *tokusatsu*. Though inspired by successful Western productions, the film was refined and reinterpreted through the lens of Japanese culture.

Toho soon produced a sequel. *Godzilla Raids Again* was released on April 24, 1955, a mere six months after the original movie. This time, instead of Honda, the film was directed by Motoyoshi Oda, another Toho stalwart, with Eiji Tsuburaya once again leading the special effects. The sequel sought to differentiate itself by introducing a second Godzilla, who battles a new *kaijū* called Anguirus.

Despite the promise of a fresh formula, the sequel was far less successful than the original. Some scenes made an impact on audiences (the war-inspired imagery continued to resonate, for instance), but the second film lacked its predecessor's powerful political message and the masterful direction that conveyed the weight and presence of massive monsters on-screen. It wasn't exactly a box office

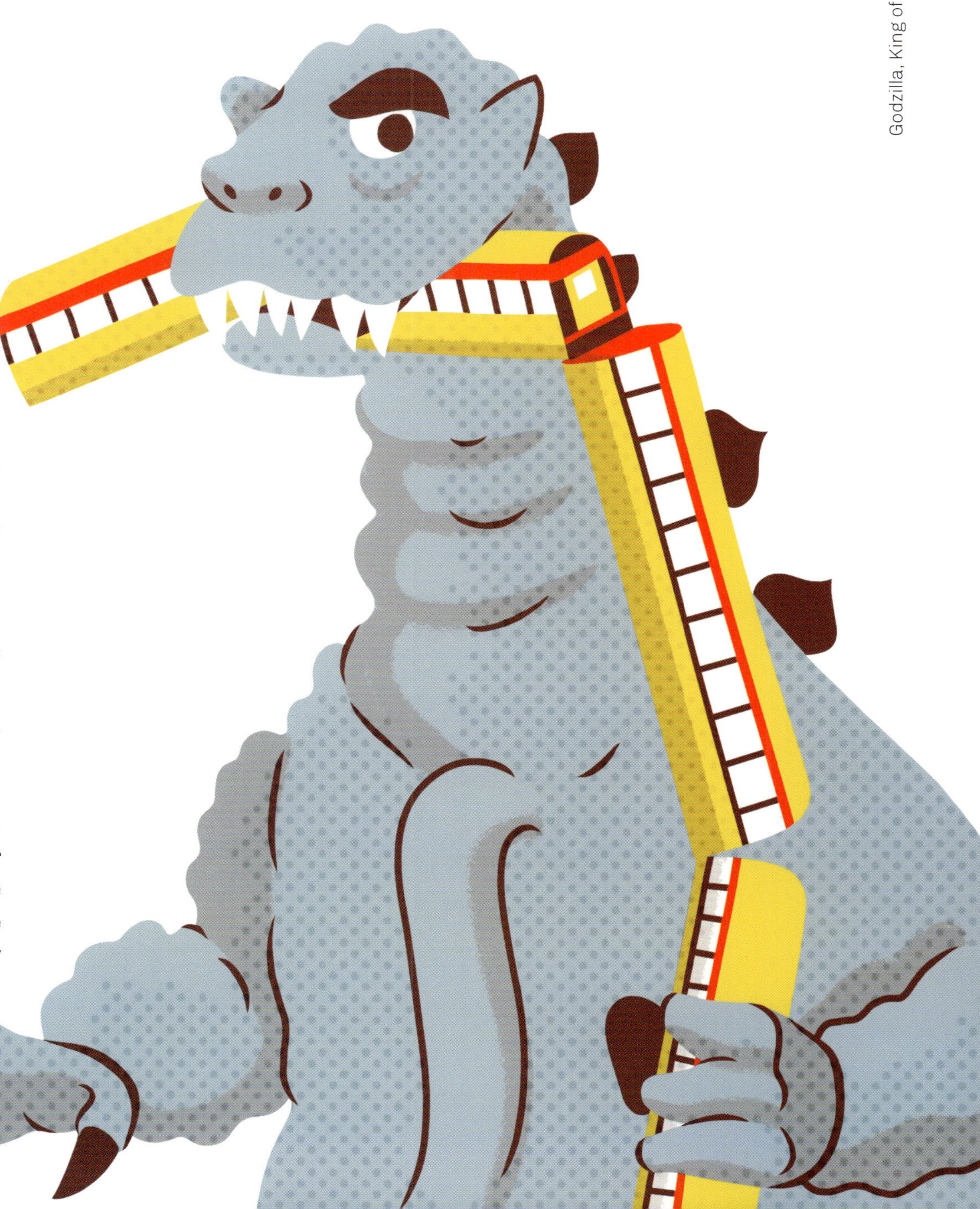

↓ **Below:** *One of Godzilla's favorite hobbies is snacking on trains.*

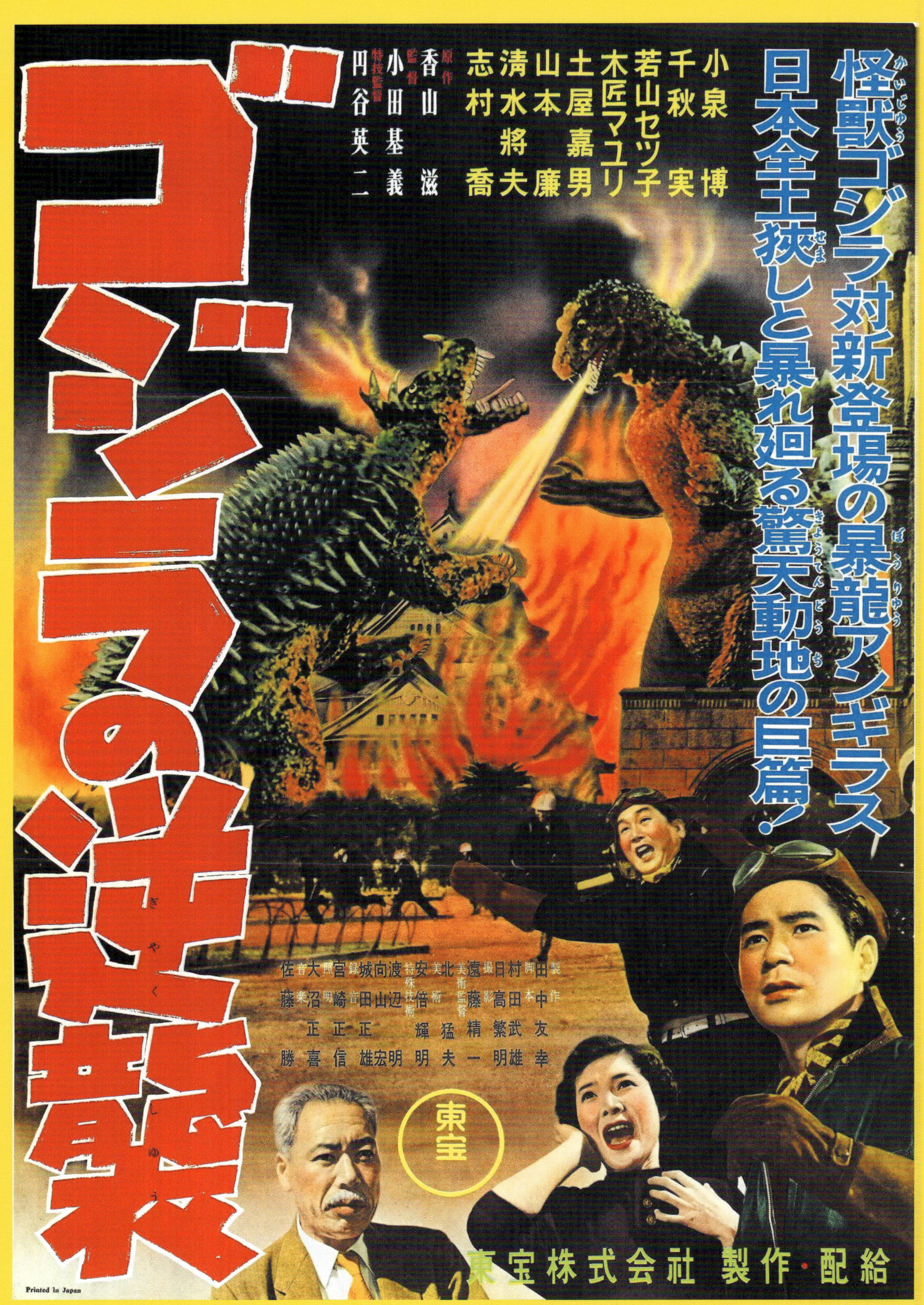

Right: *Japanese poster for the film* Godzilla Raids Again, *released in Japan in 1955 and in the United States in 1959.*

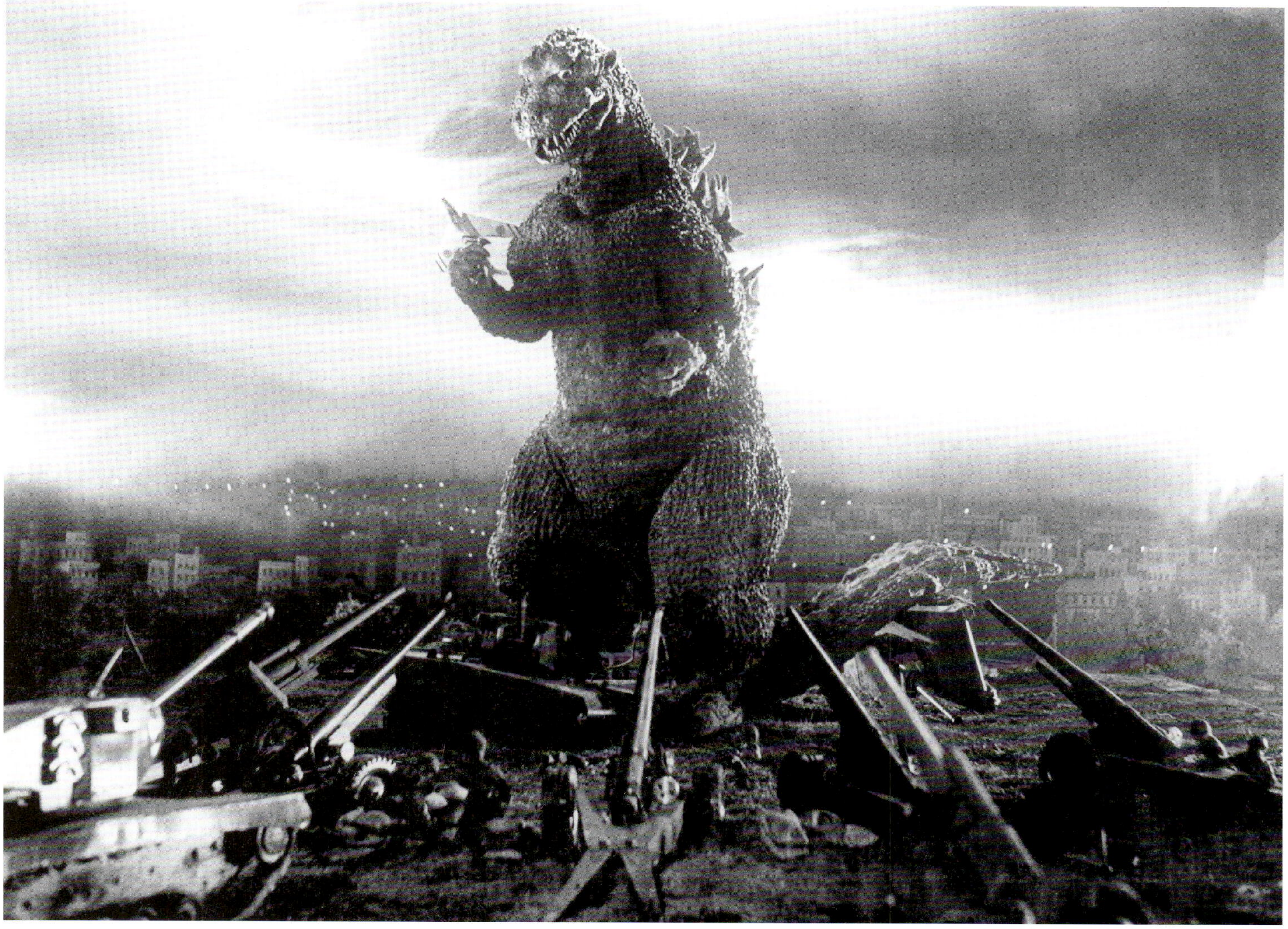

flop in Japan, but there would be no further sequels for some time. Instead, year after year, Toho churned out other films with giant monsters, different storylines, and more special effects, demonstrating the studio's growing mastery in the art. Finally, in 1962, Godzilla returned to theaters in a now-legendary showdown.

KAIJŪ TAKE OFF

In the early 1960s, Japan was in the midst of its "economic miracle," an era of rapid postwar recovery and growth. Economic prosperity, industrialization, and a rising birthrate fueled a cultural rise in manga, television, and cinema.

On August 11, 1962, Toho released *King Kong vs. Godzilla*. The film became a symbol of that era of prosperity, pitting Japan's iconic monster against the American cinematic legend of 1933. The film was originally intended to be made solely by the Americans, with King Kong battling a giant version of Frankenstein's monster. However, due to complications (the prohibitive cost of stop-motion animation and production disagreements), the project was passed off to Toho in Japan. This sparked the idea of a face-off between the two legendary

↑ **Above:** Godzilla *(1954)*

↓ **Below:** *At over 220 pounds, the Godzilla costume was exhausting to wear.*

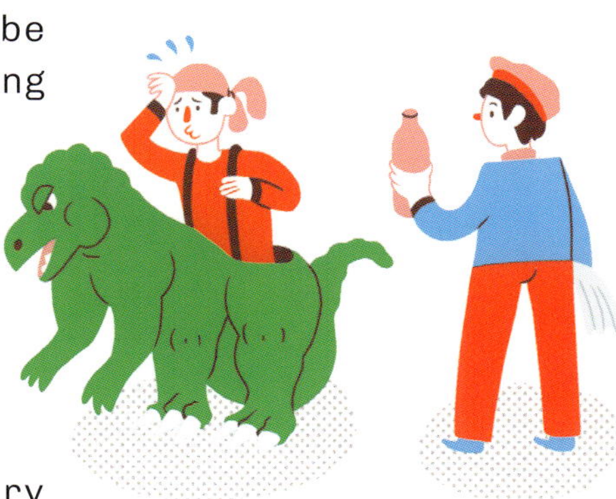

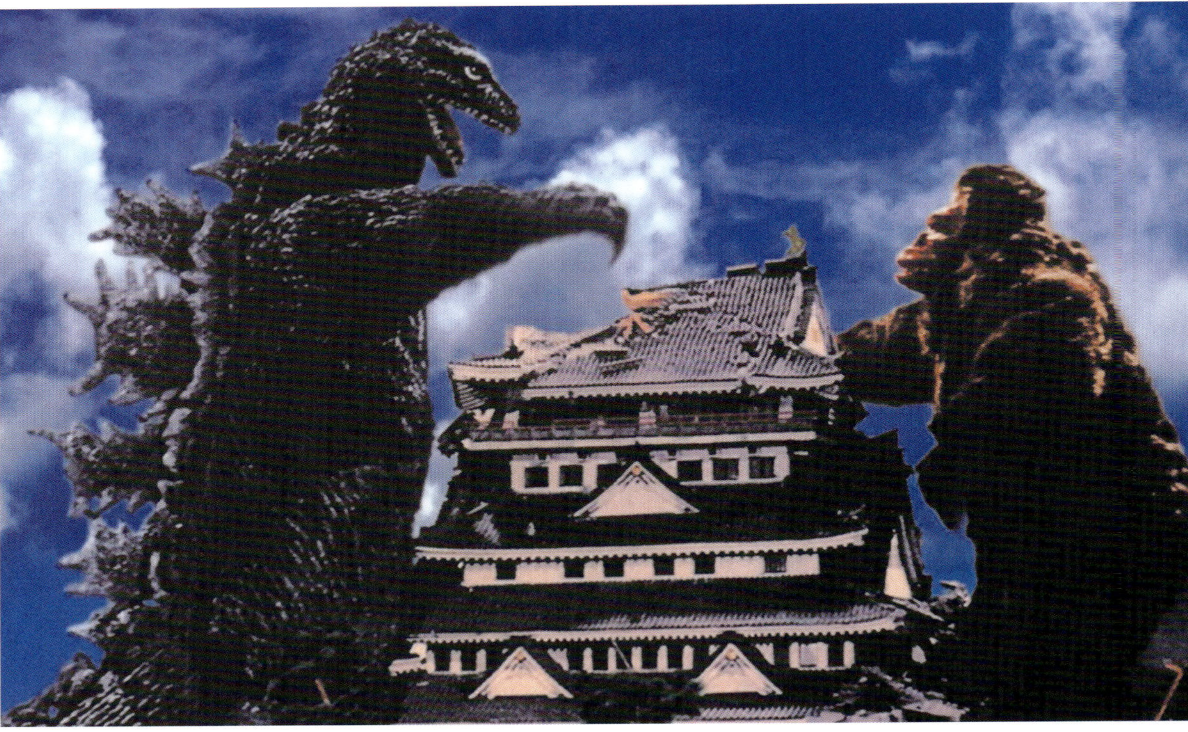

→ **Right:** King Kong vs. Godzilla *(1962)*

creatures. Toho was set to celebrate its thirtieth anniversary in 1962—the perfect opportunity to resurrect Godzilla, who had lain dormant since 1955. And what a triumphant return it was!

Directed by Ishirō Honda, the film adopted an unexpectedly humorous tone. The fear of nuclear devastation was pushed aside in favor of a critique of the burgeoning television industry and its marketing frenzy, all set against the backdrop of *kaijū* battles that tilted toward the comedic. The film was a smash success across Japan and remains a record-breaker in the franchise, drawing nine million viewers and cementing Toho's commitment to Godzilla for the next fifteen years.

Things moved quickly after that. The battle concept became a staple, with nearly each new installment featuring Godzilla fighting one or more new creatures. Among these were Mothra the giant moth, King Ghidorah the three-headed dragon, and the quirky Ebirah, a giant lobster.

But the franchise eventually fell victim to overexploitation. The tone of the movies grew lighter each year, eventually very nearly turning Godzilla into a children's hero. In 1967, Godzilla even had a son, Minilla, in *Son of Godzilla*. As the monster lost its original edge, ticket sales dwindled, reflecting waning interest. By 1966, Godzilla faced serious competition as TV

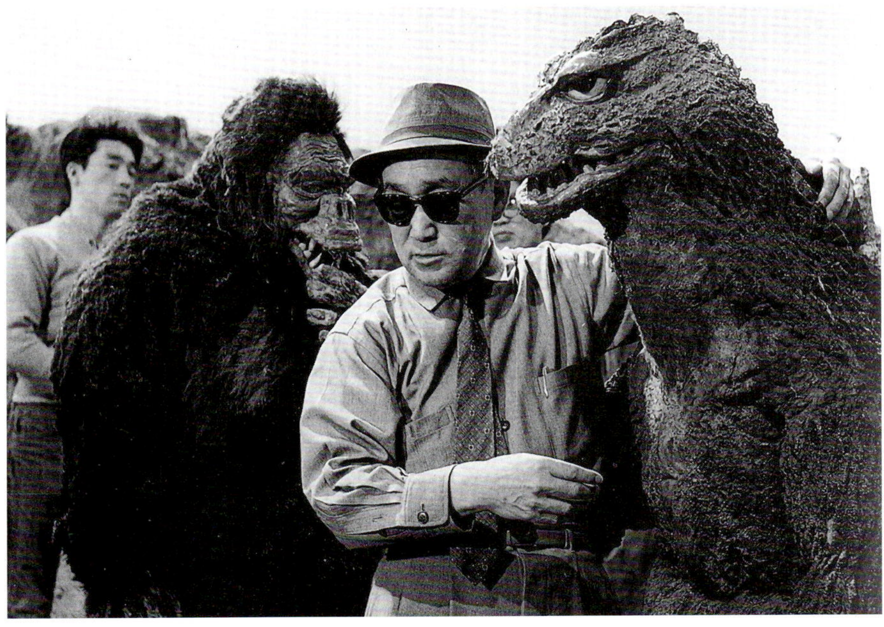

↓ **Below:** *Special effects director Eiji Tsuburaya chatting with King Kong and Godzilla during filming.*

superheroes hit the scene. While superheroes gained steady popularity, achieving a golden age in the 1970s when TV ownership skyrocketed, the *Godzilla* franchise made numerous attempts to maintain its audience.

In 1971, *Godzilla vs. Hedorah* was released, reprising the original film's darker themes by introducing a terrifying monster amid an environmental crisis. In 1973, *Godzilla vs. Megalon* introduced Jet Jaguar, a giant superhero-inspired robot. That same year, Godzilla even appeared in the TV superhero series *Zone Fighter*, lending a hand to the show's heroes—a lighthearted but ultimately minor crossover.

The final two attempts to rejuvenate the franchise came in the form of a new, charismatic antagonist, Mechagodzilla, a robotic version of the king of *kaijū*. First introduced in 1974's *Godzilla vs. Mechagodzilla* (directed by Jun Fukuda of *Ebirah, Horror of the Deep* fame in 1966), Mechagodzilla returned in *Terror of Mechagodzilla* (1975), with Ishirō Honda once again at the helm. The latter film presented Mechagodzilla as Godzilla's new adversary, with additional *kaijū* joining the fray. The story attempted to blend tragedy and human drama, featuring aliens and a scientist's daughter being used to control Mechagodzilla. Despite Honda's polished direction, the two films failed to make much of a splash. Toho understood the message and retired Godzilla from the big screen for many years to come.

HEISEI: NEW BEGINNINGS

In the early 1980s, Japan was just emerging from a decade of prosperity, during which art forms such as *tokusatsu* and animation gained a firm foothold, fueled by a surge in TVs in Japanese households. Animation thrived the most, dominating the TV, film, and even VHS markets. In contrast, *tokusatsu*

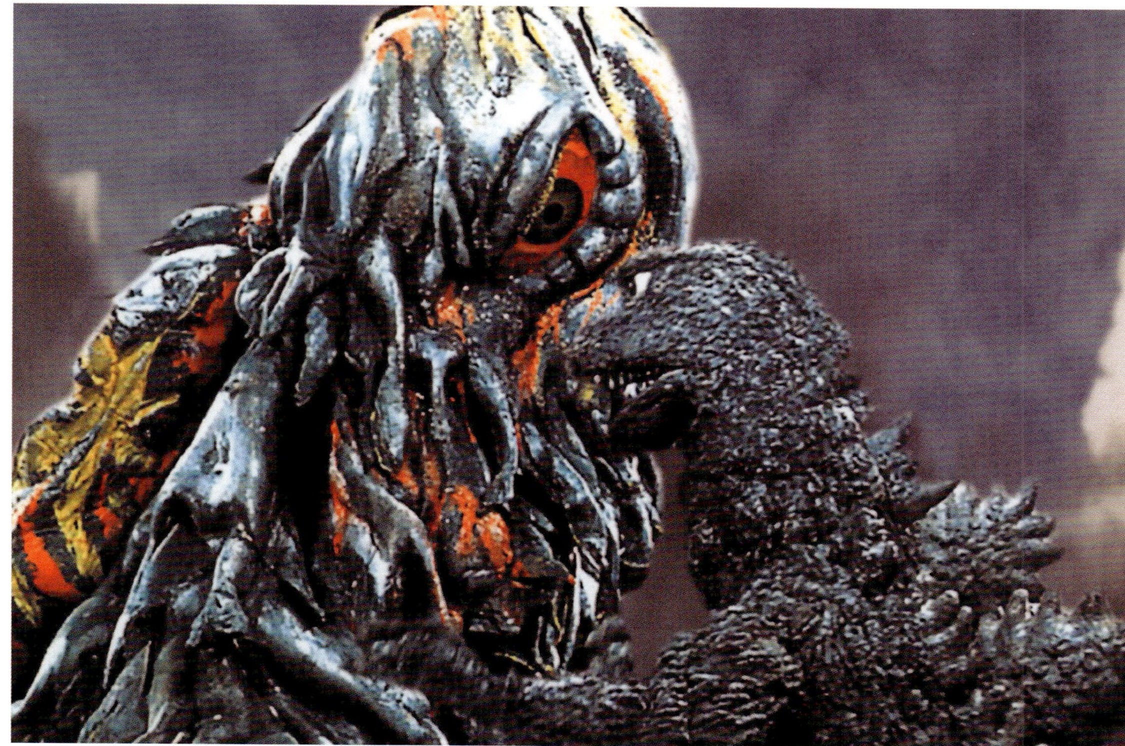

← **Left:** *Godzilla battles smog monster Hedorah in the film* Godzilla vs. Hedorah, *released in Japan in 1971.*

➔ Right:
Stills and a Japanese poster for the film Godzilla vs. Mechagodzilla *released in 1974.*

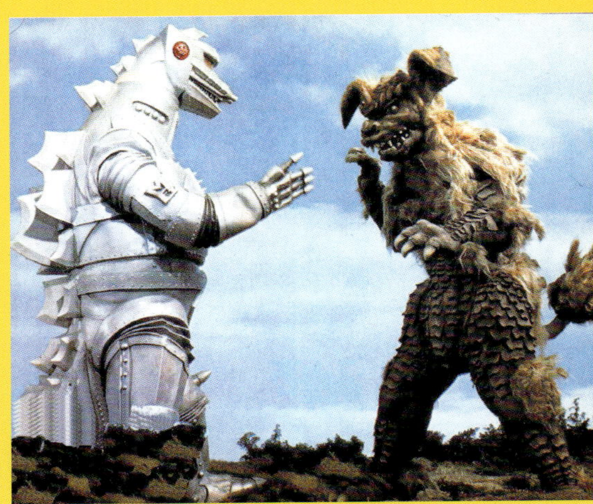

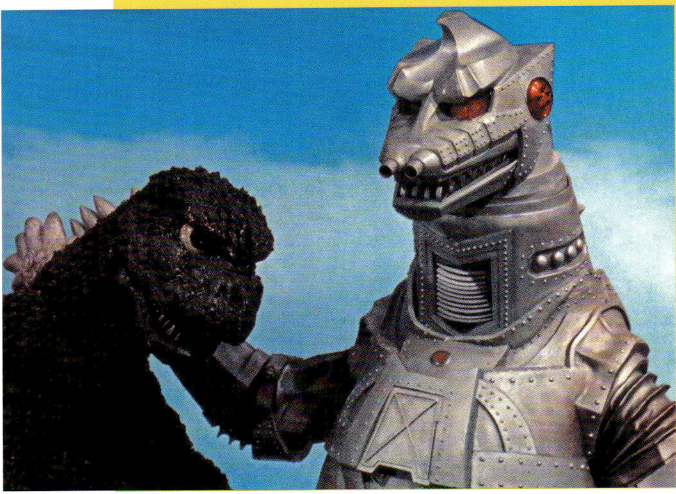

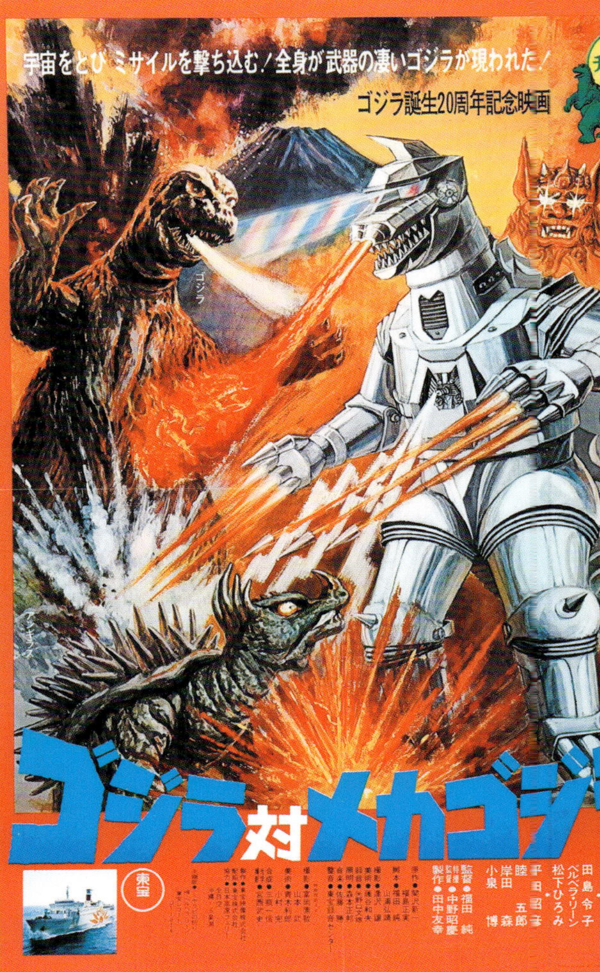

floundered somewhat in the face of such stiff competition, resulting in fewer shows and movies.

By 1984, fans had waited nine years for a new Godzilla film to hit the big screen, this time titled simply *Godzilla* in Japanese. Their patience was rewarded with a reboot that reignited the franchise. The movie served as a direct sequel to the 1954 original, set thirty years later, and tackled themes tied to the end of the Cold War, reviving the franchise's political relevance.

In terms of technology, the film achieved new heights. Director Kōji Hashimoto adjusted the relative scale of Godzilla and the cityscape. Skyscrapers towered over the monster to reflect Japan's postwar economic and social boom. Traditional *tokusatsu* techniques were refined, and innovations like animatronics added new layers to the monster's on-screen movements during close-ups.

Possibly to avoid repeating past missteps, producers took their time with the next film, *Godzilla vs. Biollante*, which premiered in 1989. The new installment shifted away from purely political narratives and adopted a more dreamlike tone, combining a story about a grieving father and his deceased daughter, psychic abilities, and a plant monster. Directed by Kazuki Ōmori, the ambitious movie introduced Biollante, Godzilla's latest adversary. The new monster had tentacles, each controlled by cables like a puppet, and crocodile-like jaws

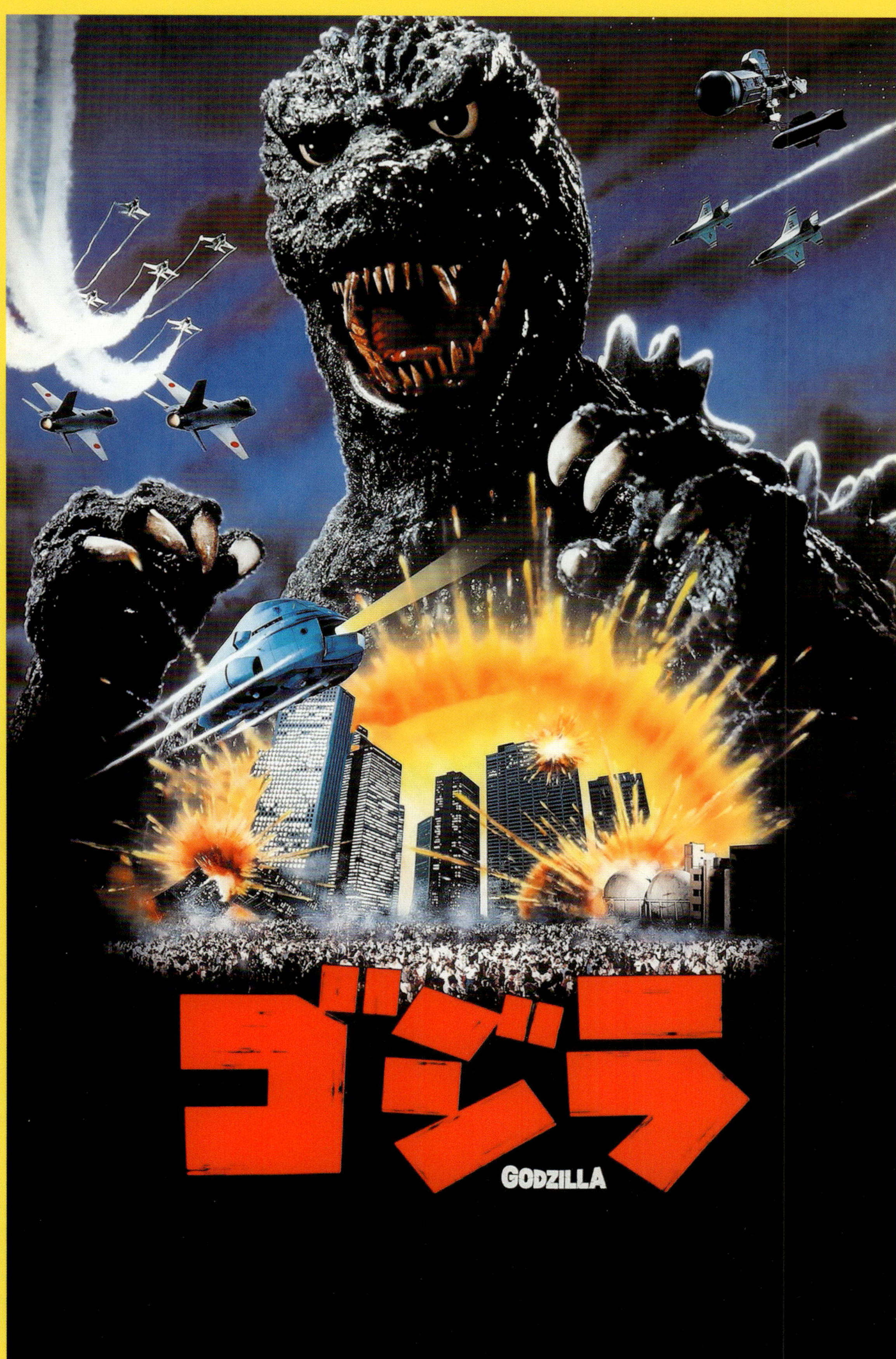

← **Left:** *Japanese poster for the film* The Return of Godzilla *(*Godzilla *in Japanese), released in Japan in 1984.*

↓ **Below, top:** *Japanese poster for the film* Godzilla vs. Biollante *(1989).*

↓ **Below, Bottom:** *Japanese poster for the film* Godzilla vs. Destoroyah *(1995).*

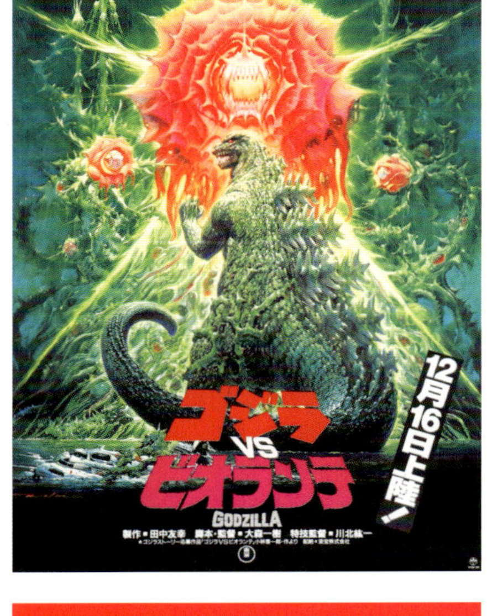

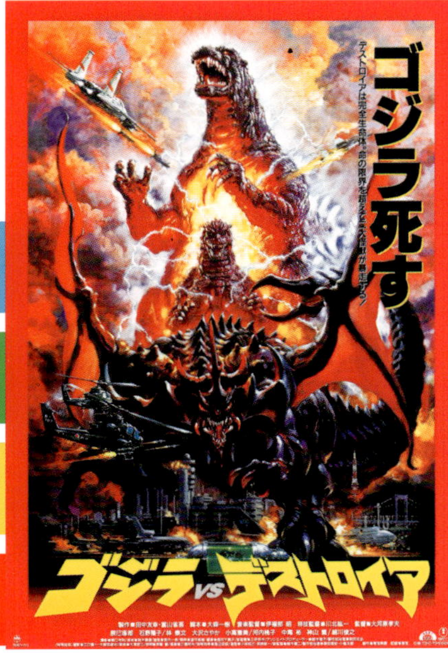

manipulated by an actor in costume. The result was a success that breathed fresh life into the franchise as it entered a new decade.

Tokusatsu cinema began taking off and flourished in the 1990s. A new Godzilla film was released every year between 1991 and 1995. Together with the two previous films, they form what is called the Heisei era series (referring to Japan's imperial period from 1989 to 2019). The seven-film narrative arc featured recurring characters, revived iconic monsters (King Ghidorah, Mothra, Rodan, and even a reimagined son of Godzilla), and explored colorful concepts such as time travel. It ended with a definitive conclusion to the series with *Godzilla vs. Destoroyah* (1995), Godzilla's final battle with Destoroyah (whose origins date back to events in the 1954 film), thus wrapping up the storyline. The end was fitting and coincided with an agreement for an American adaptation of *Godzilla* by Roland Emmerich to be released in 1998.

Critics weren't won over by the new version, however, though some enjoyed its criticism of the US military (portrayed dimly in the film) and nuclear testing and the depiction of the monster as a victim—a sharp turn away from the aggressive Japanese Godzilla. The drastically altered interpretation failed to resonate with many, especially Japanese audiences, prompting a new Japanese installment in 1999 to reclaim the franchise.

THE 2000S: WHAT'S NEXT FOR GODZILLA?

Toho revived Godzilla in 1999 with a new six-film series, kicking off the Millennium era. Instead of throwing out the baby with the bathwater, it took a simple but unconventional approach by making each film a standalone sequel to the 1954 original. Each had a different storyline—unlike the films of the Heisei era—and featured a new set of adversaries and new political themes adapted to contemporary contexts. Together, they provided a fresh take on the franchise, forming a new cornerstone forty-five years later.

Godzilla, Mothra and King Ghidorah: Giant Monsters All-Out Attack (2001; often abbreviated as *GMK*), directed by Shūsuke Kaneko, reimagined the same Godzilla as a mystical being animated by the spirits of those killed by Japan during World War II—reminders of a dark episode of Japan's history. This iteration of Godzilla faces off once again with Baragon, Mothra, and King Ghidorah, who embody Earth's three guardian deities.

Meanwhile, *Godzilla Against Mechagodzilla* (2002) and *Godzilla: Tokyo S.O.S.* (2003) formed a loose trilogy together with the 1954 original. This time, a modern Mechagodzilla is built on the skeleton of the first Godzilla to combat a newly emerged version of a monster named Kiryu. The series made Godzilla the enemy once more while also exploring the differences between the old and new Mechagodzillas.

The era ended with a bang. *Godzilla: Final Wars* was released in 2004 in honor of the franchise's fiftieth anniversary. Directed by Ryūhei Kitamura, the film encapsulated Godzilla's complete history in a single film, incorporating elements from its black-and-white beginnings, the vibrant 1960s, and the more serious tones of the 1980s and 1990s, alongside American influences. From storylines to characters, this grand tribute to a half-century of *kaijū* and science fiction had it all.

Godzilla: Final Wars received mixed reviews. Audiences loved the parade of

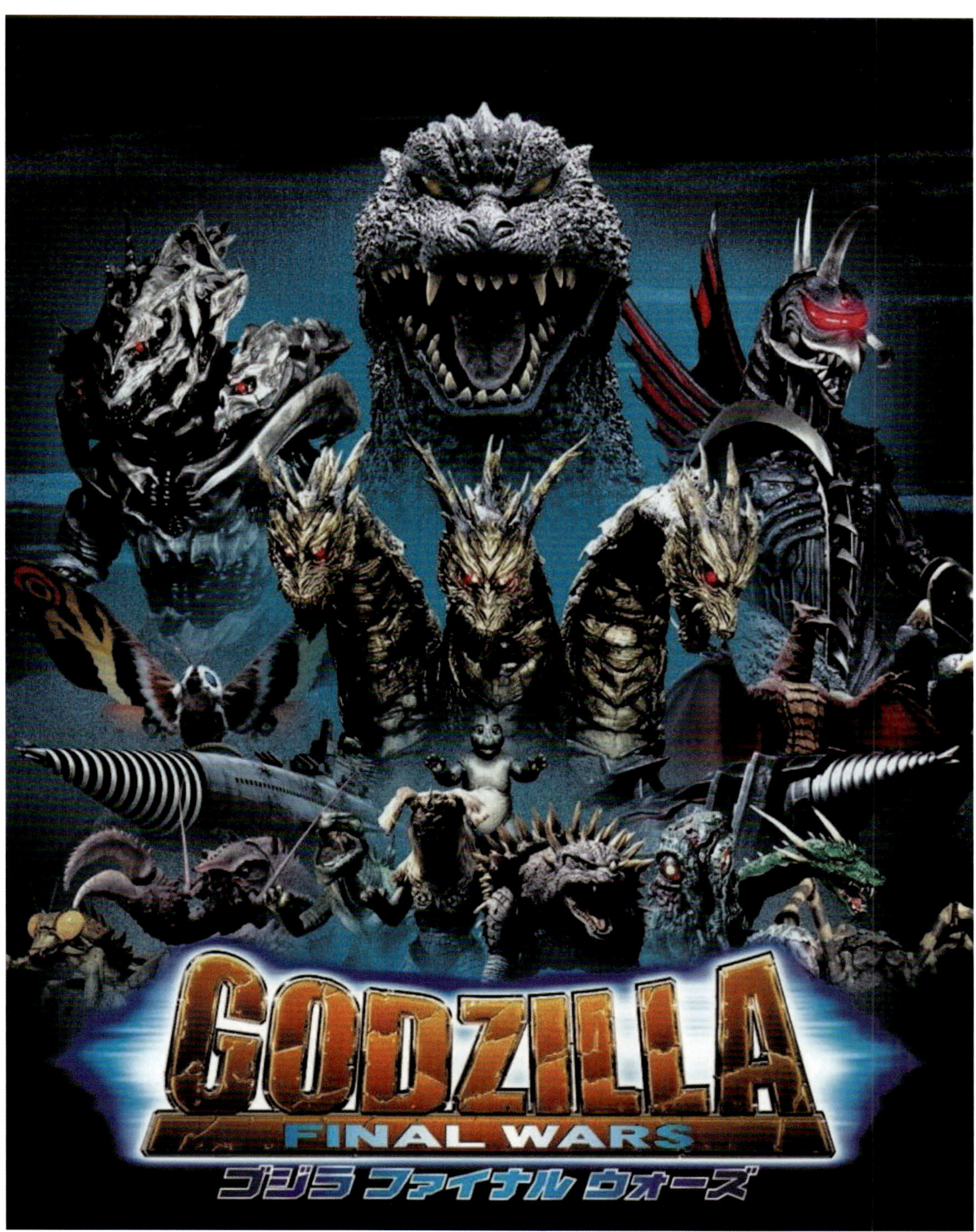

← **Left:** *Album cover for the soundtrack to the film* Godzilla: Final Wars *(2004).*

monsters and nods to the franchise as a whole, as well as to other Toho films. However, many derided the absurd plot, with its over-the-top direction and occasionally intentionally silly tone, which turned the film into a different kind of experience.

Unfortunately, even Japanese audiences were underwhelmed, and the colossal budget could not be recouped due to a resounding flop at the box office. This raised the question of whether *kaijū* films had run their course. It was a fair question, given the rising dominance of

American films and years of repeating the same formula of giant monsters and *tokusatsu* techniques.

Traditional *kaijū* films waned after 2004. They were seen more often in TV superhero series, which were popular at the time, or indirectly in parodies of the genre. With increasing competition from television, *kaijū* movies no longer seemed so essential. *Godzilla: Final Wars* may have revealed a sense of fatigue among Japanese audiences, who were turning toward big-budget American blockbusters. In any case, the film ensured that the franchise would be put on hiatus for the next twelve years.

RENAISSANCE

Like the 1954 film, *Shin Godzilla* was released amid the aftermath of a major disaster: the 2011 tsunami that struck Japan, crippling the Fukushima nuclear power plant and stirring controversy over the government's handling of the whole crisis. The film depicted a creature arriving in Tokyo Bay, initially

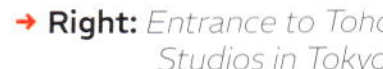

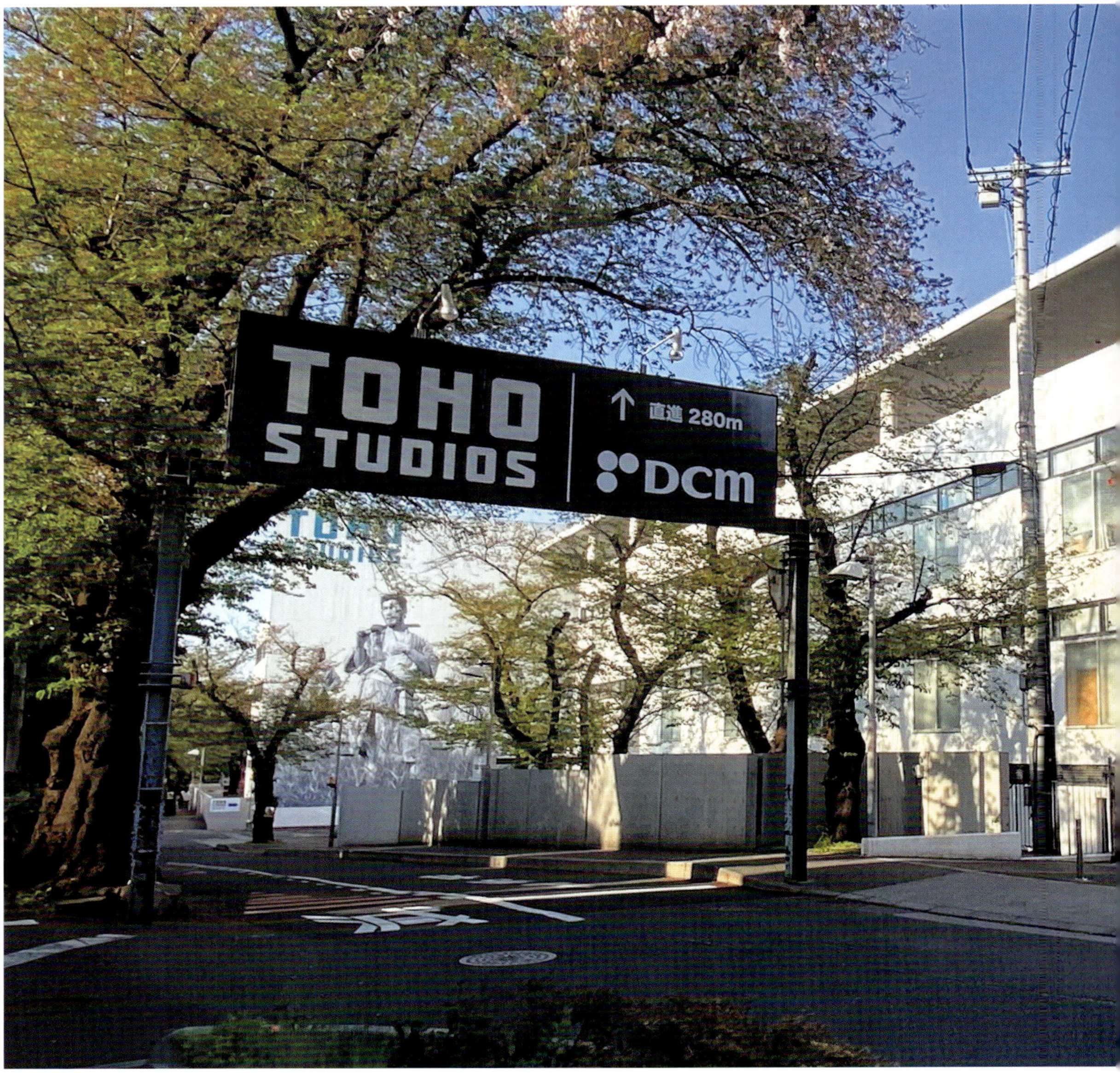

➔ **Right:** *Entrance to Toho Studios in Tokyo.*

in a crude, crawling form that gradually evolved into a towering titan that walked upright. Anno used the monster's threat as a metaphor to criticize the Japanese government's shortcomings, including its aging officials and their inability to make proactive decisions, resulting in disastrous crisis management. The biting political commentary made *Shin Godzilla* a particularly bold and successful film.

This resurgence also gave the franchise an opportunity to update its visuals. Monster suits were retired in favor of fully digital effects. The techniques may have evolved, but the legacy remained intact. Godzilla continued to be animated by a performer, though now using motion capture, a technology that translates an actor's movements into 3D space through sensors attached to the body. The monster's movements were crafted by Mansai Nomura, a renowned actor of *kyōgen*, a traditional Japanese theatrical art form that has historically influenced the way suit actors move. Thus, in a way, *tokusatsu* returned to its roots.

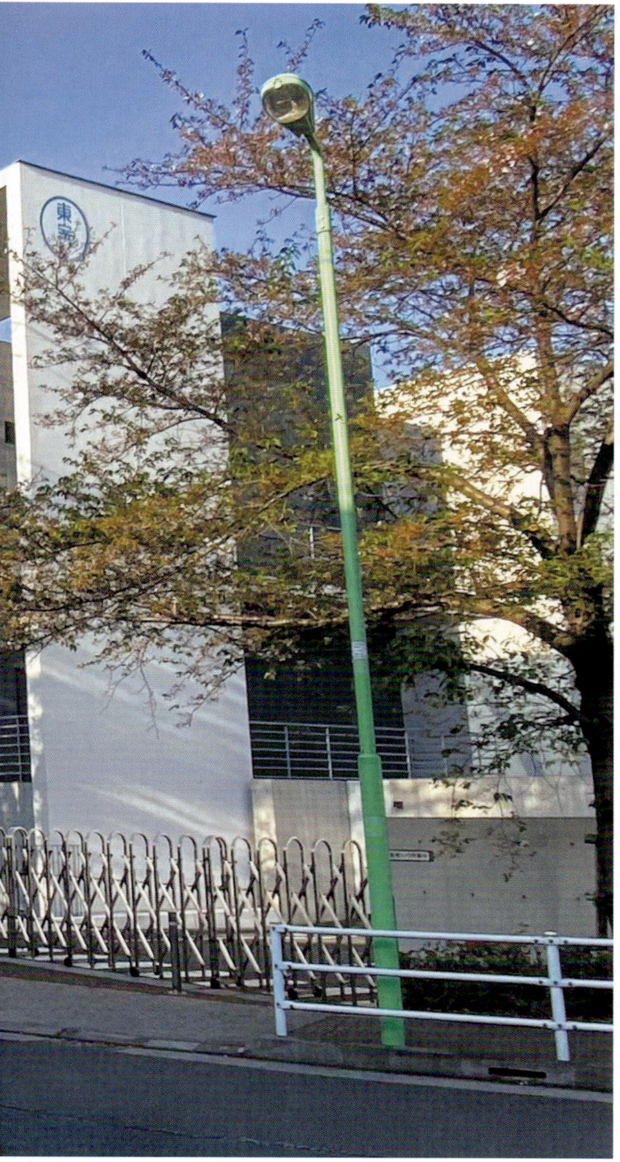

↓ **Below:** *Motion capture became a more common way to animate giant monsters.*

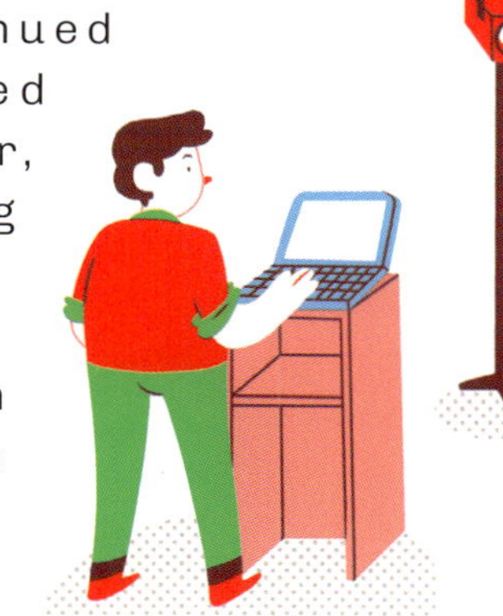

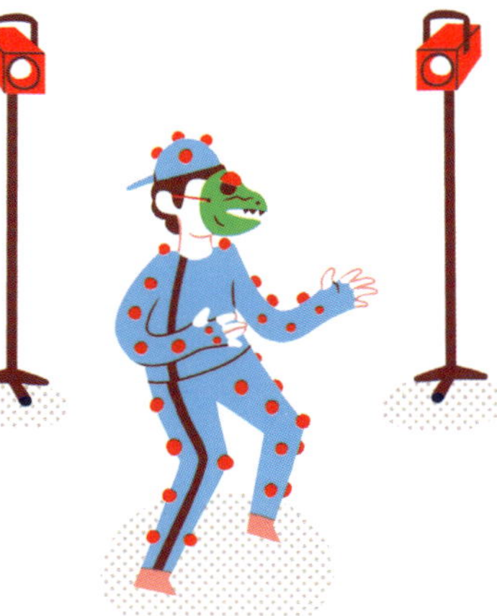

There were still a few scenes that used scale models, but most things were done digitally. The new methods allowed for striking visuals, delivering numerous innovative, memorable scenes for the franchise. An immense critical and commercial success, the film restored Godzilla's image in the cinematic landscape.

As the franchise expanded in the United States (most recently with *Godzilla x Kong: The New Empire* in April 2024), Godzilla also ventured into animation. In 2017 and 2018, three animated films premiered in theaters before being distributed globally via Netflix. Additionally, one animated series, *Godzilla Singular Point*, was released in 2021.

But the crowning achievement of the revival was Godzilla's return to live-action cinema in Japan with *Godzilla Minus One* in 2023. Directed by Takashi Yamazaki, the film diverged from recent productions. It was neither a sequel nor

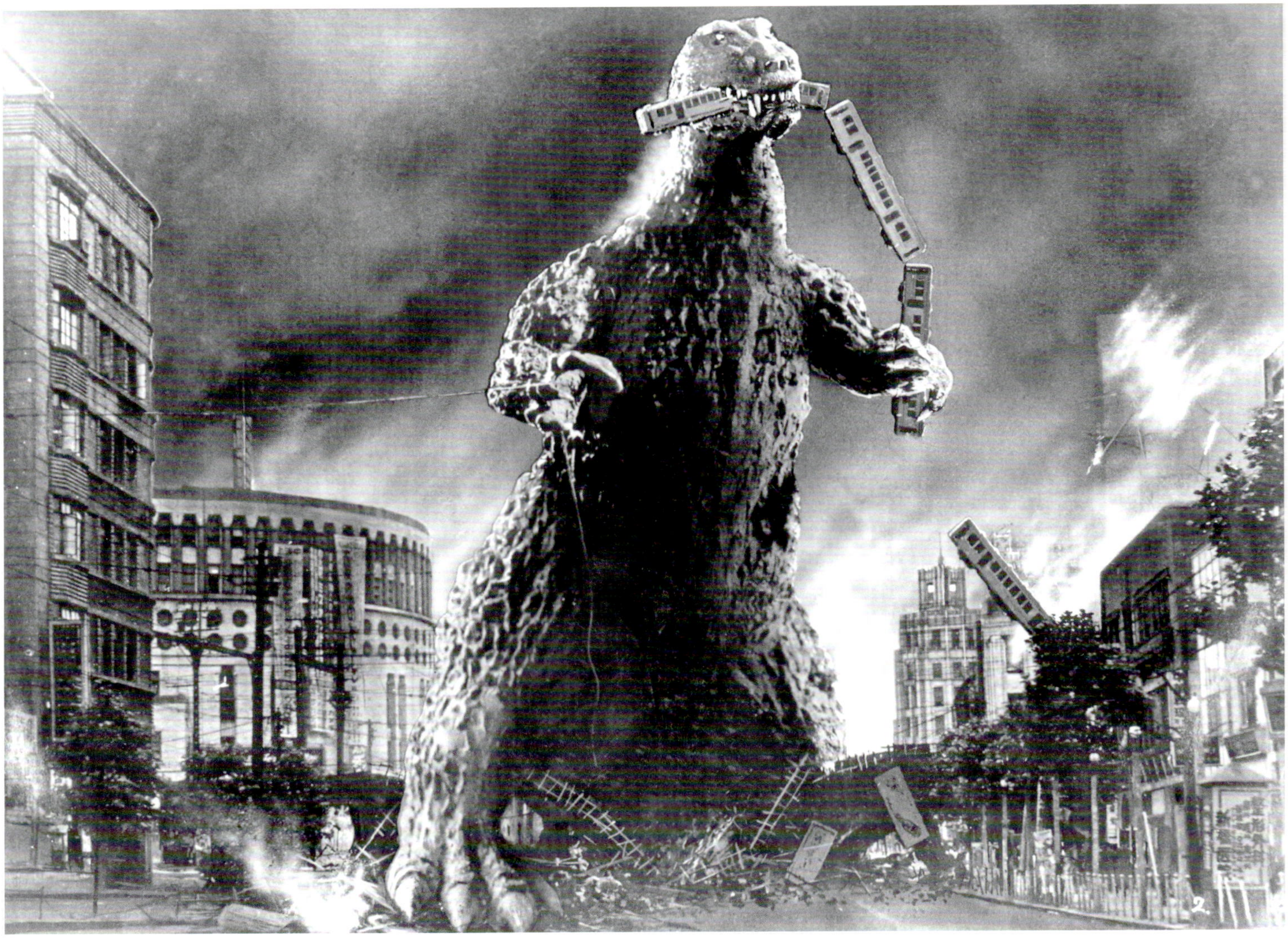

↑ **Above:** *Still from the 1954 film* Godzilla.

→ **Right:** *Special effects advanced by leaps and bounds between 1954 and 2023. Still from* Godzilla Minus One *(2023).*

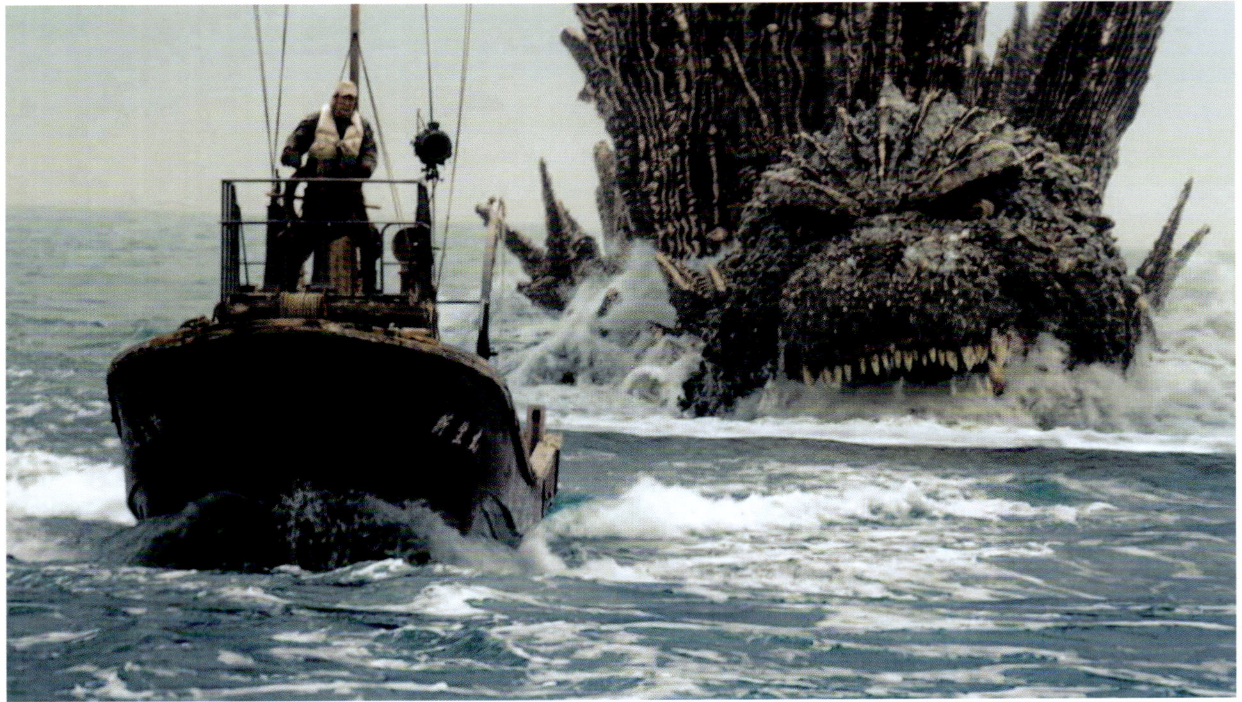

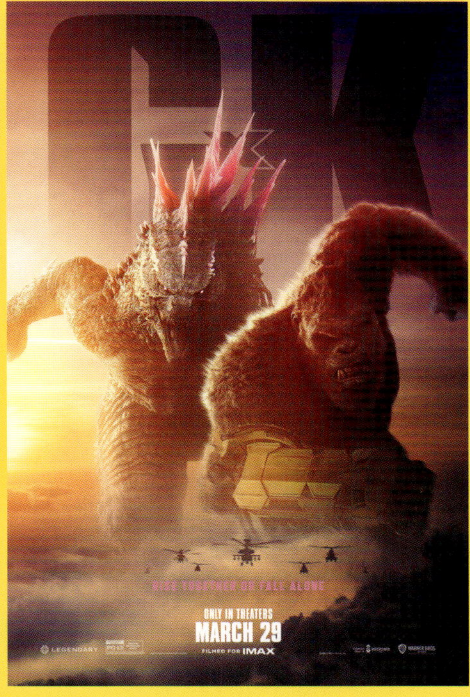

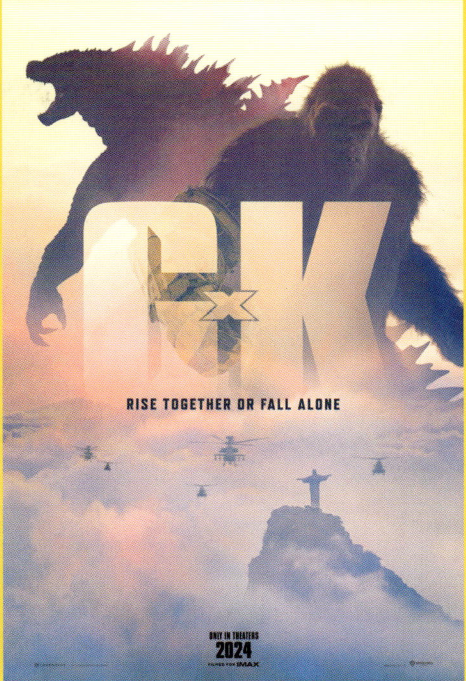

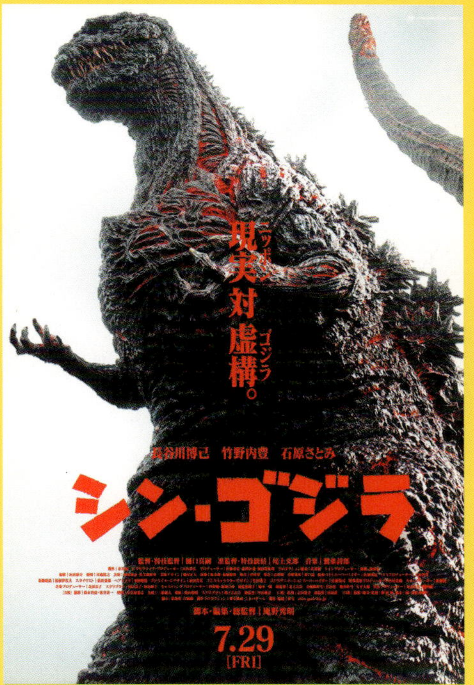

↑ **Above and right:** *Godzilla allies with King Kong in* Godzilla x Kong: The New Empire *(2023), an American spin-off.*

↗ **Far right:** *Godzilla, more terrifying than ever, in* Shin Godzilla *(2016).*

a remake, but instead offered a dive into postwar Japan in the late 1940s. The idea was to delve further than the 1954 original, depicting a still-crippled Japan struggling to rebuild while also facing the arrival of the creature.

This return to the franchise's roots proved exceptionally successful and emotionally resonant, leaving a lasting impression. In March 2024, *Godzilla Minus One* won the prestigious Oscar for Best Visual Effects to the surprise of all—including Yamazaki's technical team. Despite its limited global release, the film achieved widespread success, reaffirming the franchise's enduring vitality.

Godzilla is still being reinvented seventy years later, demonstrating through multiple art forms that the creature continues to captivate audiences and influence global cinema. However, Godzilla is not the only movie monster out there. Over the years, it has shared the spotlight with a number of rivals.

MONSTER COSTUMES

BRINGING KAIJŪ TO LIFE

The first challenge of crafting a physical *kaijū* is translating the initial design into a real-life, maneuverable object, sometimes even a giant puppet. First, the costume must be designed with the actor in mind. Measurements are taken, body proportions assessed, and parts of the costume are molded directly onto the actor, allowing the team to anticipate weight and movement constraints.

Next are the cosmetic aspects: skin texture, color, and additional features such as dorsal spines, wings, a tail, and, of course, the head. The molding stage is followed by sculpting, a specialty of Keizō Murase, an instrumental figure in monster costume design. Sculpting demands rigor and precision to make the costume believable, durable, and safe. In Japan, all these crafts are grouped under the term *zōkei*, which originally referred to the molding stage but now encompasses the entire process of fabricating monsters, superheroes, and other *tokusatsu* creatures.

But what would a stunning costume be without a convincing performance? Haruo Nakajima broke new ground as the world's first suit actor with *Godzilla*, and many others have since refined the craft. Over time, the costumes have become better designed, but they remain challenging to perform in. Vision, for example, has always been limited and continues to be so. Any trick to help actors navigate is welcome. Some costumes feature discreet holes in the monster's neck or even in the back of the throat to provide a small line of sight.

Bringing a *kaijū* to life also involves adopting improbable positions in bizarre situations. Playing a four-legged monster like Baragon or Anguirus might look amusing from the outside, but it's a difficult performance, especially given the actor's limited vision. Things grow even stranger with superhero *kaijū*, such as Pestar, the alien from *Ultraman* whose costume was so massive it required two suit actors.

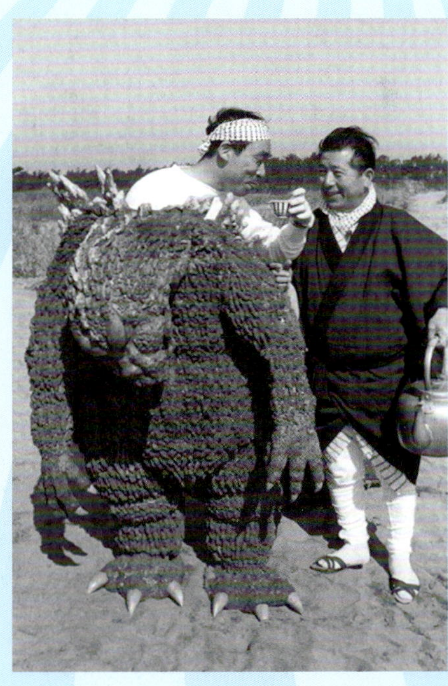

← **Left:** *Haruo Nakajima, the suit actor who played Godzilla from 1954 to 1972.*

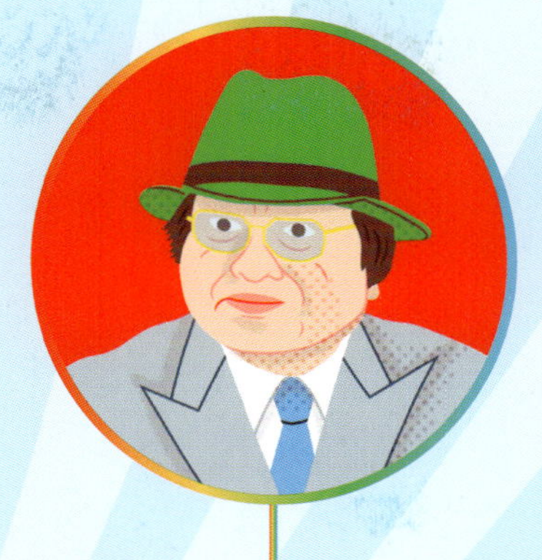

KEIZŌ MURASE (1935–2024)

As a costume designer, Keizō Murase played a key technical role in tokusatsu, transforming monster designs into costumes that actors could actually wear. He began his career at Toho, working on productions like *Varan the Unbelievable* (1958) before helping create iconic kaijū such as Mothra and King Ghidorah and even working for rival studios on characters like Gamera and Daimajin. Eventually, as he gained experience, Murase struck out on his own, founding several special effects studios (Ex Productions and Twenty). He passed away in 2024 at the age of eighty-nine.

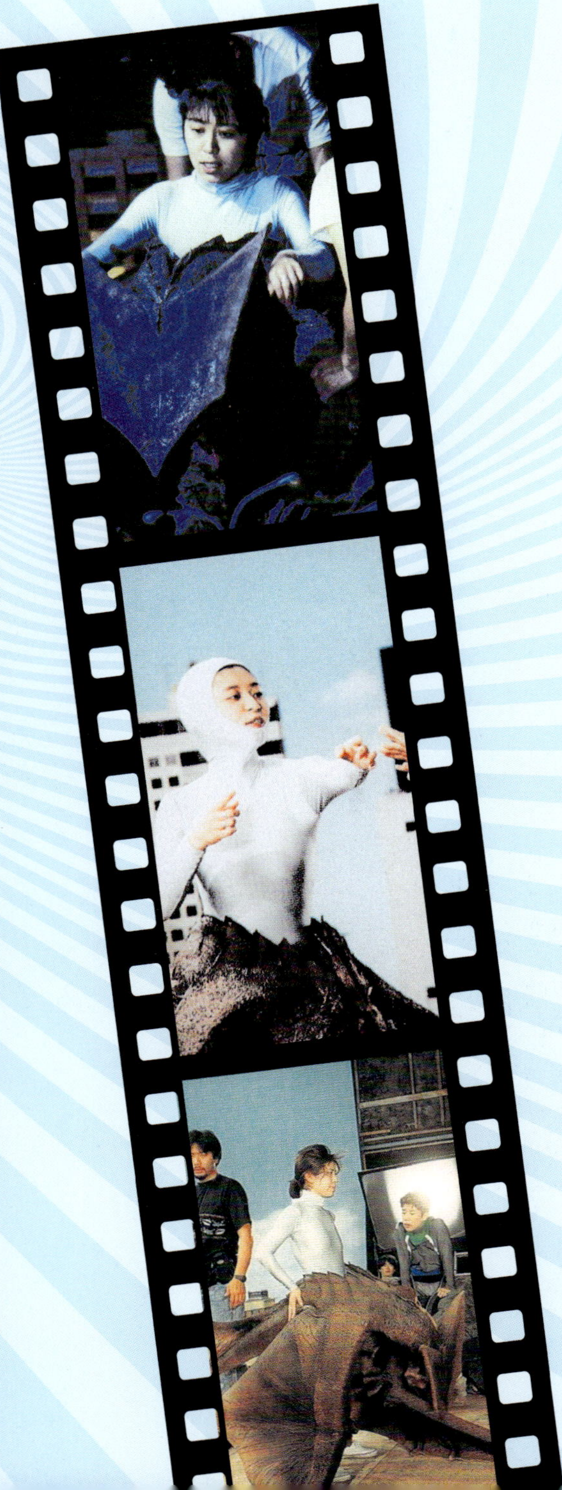

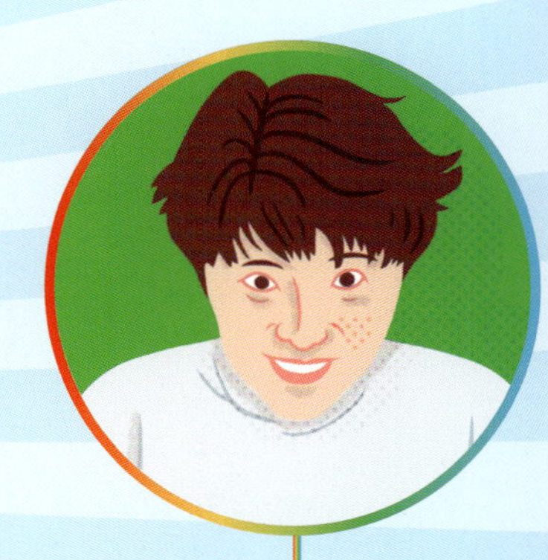

YŪMI KAMEYAMA (B. 1970)

Yūmi Kameyama is the first woman ever to play a kaijū. After spending years as a dancer, she transitioned to acting and eventually became a stunt performer. She was cast in *Gamera: Guardian of the Universe* (1995) as Gyaos, the winged antagonist of Gamera the giant turtle, becoming a trailblazer in the field. Other women actors followed, including Rie Ōta, who played Baragon in 2001 in *Godzilla, Mothra and King Ghidorah: Giant Monsters All-Out Attack*.

RODAN, MOTHRA & GAMERA: GODZILLA'S FRIENDS & FOES

↓ **Below, top:** *Japanese poster for the film* Frankenstein vs. Baragon *(1965).*

↓ **Below, bottom:** *Japanese poster for the film* The X From Outer Space *(1967).*

↘ **Bottom right:** *The proliferation of monster movies created demand for miniature sets.*

THE GOLDEN AGE OF GIANT MONSTERS

The success of *Godzilla* in 1954 didn't immediately drive Toho to produce numerous films centered on its flagship creature, but it did serve as the springboard for an entire genre: the giant monster movie.

Among the most notable films of the 1950s was *Sora no Daikaijū Radon* (1956), known simply as *Rodan* to international audiences, in which a species of giant *Pteranodon* emerges from the depths of a mine in a small Japanese village. The film remains impressive today, showcasing meticulously detailed scenes of destruction. With *kaijū* capable of leveling entire cities with a single wingbeat, it's no surprise that the visual effects were the work of Eiji Tsuburaya. Beyond its spectacle and occasional horror-like atmosphere, *Rodan* was a critique of rural Japanese society. Rodan is killed at the end, begging a question that would recur time and again in the genre: Who is the real monster here?

Rodan was a pioneer in its time, but the creature would never headline another film. Under Toho, Rodan crossed over into Godzilla's universe in 1964 in *Ghidorah, the Three-Headed Monster* and alternated between being Godzilla's enemy, rival, and ally. More recently, Rodan was reinterpreted in *Godzilla: King of the Monsters* (2019), as well as in the animated *Godzilla Singular Point* (2021).

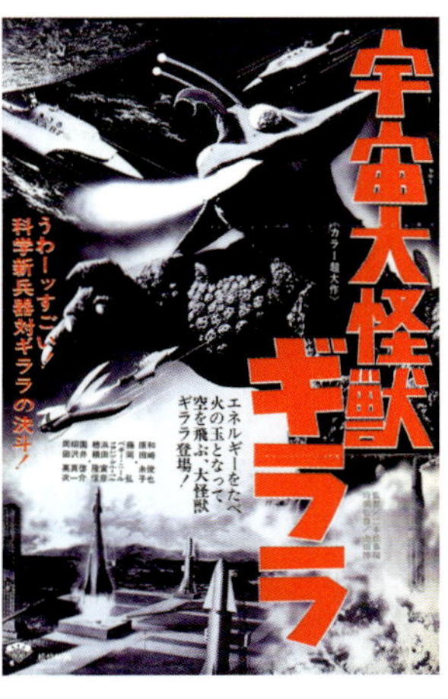

The 1960s ushered in a *kaijū* boom in Japanese cinema, fueled by the success of *King Kong vs. Godzilla* (1962). The genre exploded with creative variety. *Dogora* (1964) was equal parts heist film (involving the theft of precious jewels) and *kaijū* movie, complete with a giant space jellyfish who becomes caught up in the affair.

Frankenstein vs. Baragon (1965), or *Frankenstein Conquers the World* in the United States, offered a darker tone, reimagining Frankenstein's creature as an indestructible, living heart that is brought to Hiroshima by the Japanese shortly before the nuclear bombing. Fifteen years later, a strange, deformed boy is found on the streets, taken in, and studied. He becomes increasingly strange and monstrous as he grows, turning into a giant. Cast off by his family, he flees humans in fear. His journey ends in a battle against Baragon, a subterranean *kaijū*. A sequel followed in 1966, *The War*

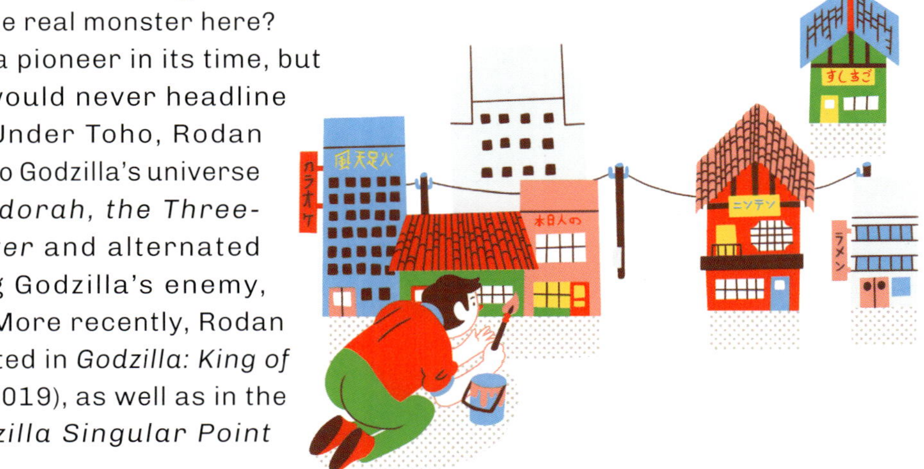

of the Gargantuas, featuring two new giant creatures who appear after the death of Frankenstein's monster. The one raised by humans is docile and peaceful, whereas the other, who raised himself, is wild and violent by nature. Thanks to humans and their actions, the two end up facing off.

At the time, every studio wanted its own giant monster. Nikkatsu produced *Monster from a Prehistoric Planet*, titled internationally as *Gappa: The Triphibian Monster* (1967). The name was an attempt to capitalize on the success of *Godzilla*, but Gappa was midway between an atomic dinosaur and a giant bird, and the plot revolved around *kaijū* parents searching for their child.

The X From Outer Space (1967) was a different style of film, a pure product of the kind of science fiction that was popular at the time. In the film, a space expedition to Mars brings back a strange substance that transforms into a giant destructive monster before scientists find a way to defeat it.

As the genre waned in the early 1970s, some studios resorted to trying anything and everything. Tsuburaya Productions, normally a television studio, branched out with *Daigoro vs. Goliath*, which debuted in 1972 with a rather unusual concept. Judge for yourself: Daigoro is a young *kaijū* taken in by humans after his mother was killed by the military. His diet becomes difficult for his adoptive family to manage, as they must provide him with ever-increasing amounts of food. The town's mayor eventually tries to get rid of him, sparking conflict between the monster's supporters and detractors when, to top it all off, another monster appears.

Daigoro vs. Goliath is the culmination of the *kaijū* genre. Daigoro's design is both endearing and off-putting. He behaves like a child, and the battles—ridiculous even for the time—only add to the absurdity. Then there's the giant toilet the humans build for Daigoro! The film is a delightful oddity that tries to appeal to young audiences at any cost, but it's still worth a gander for its quirky charm.

In many ways, the mania of the 1970s was also the genre's downfall. Audiences grew tired of the formula, unimpressed by attempts to revitalize it, and television's ruthless competition won out. Despite this somewhat lackluster ending, it was a true golden age that permanently shaped the Japanese perception of giant monsters.

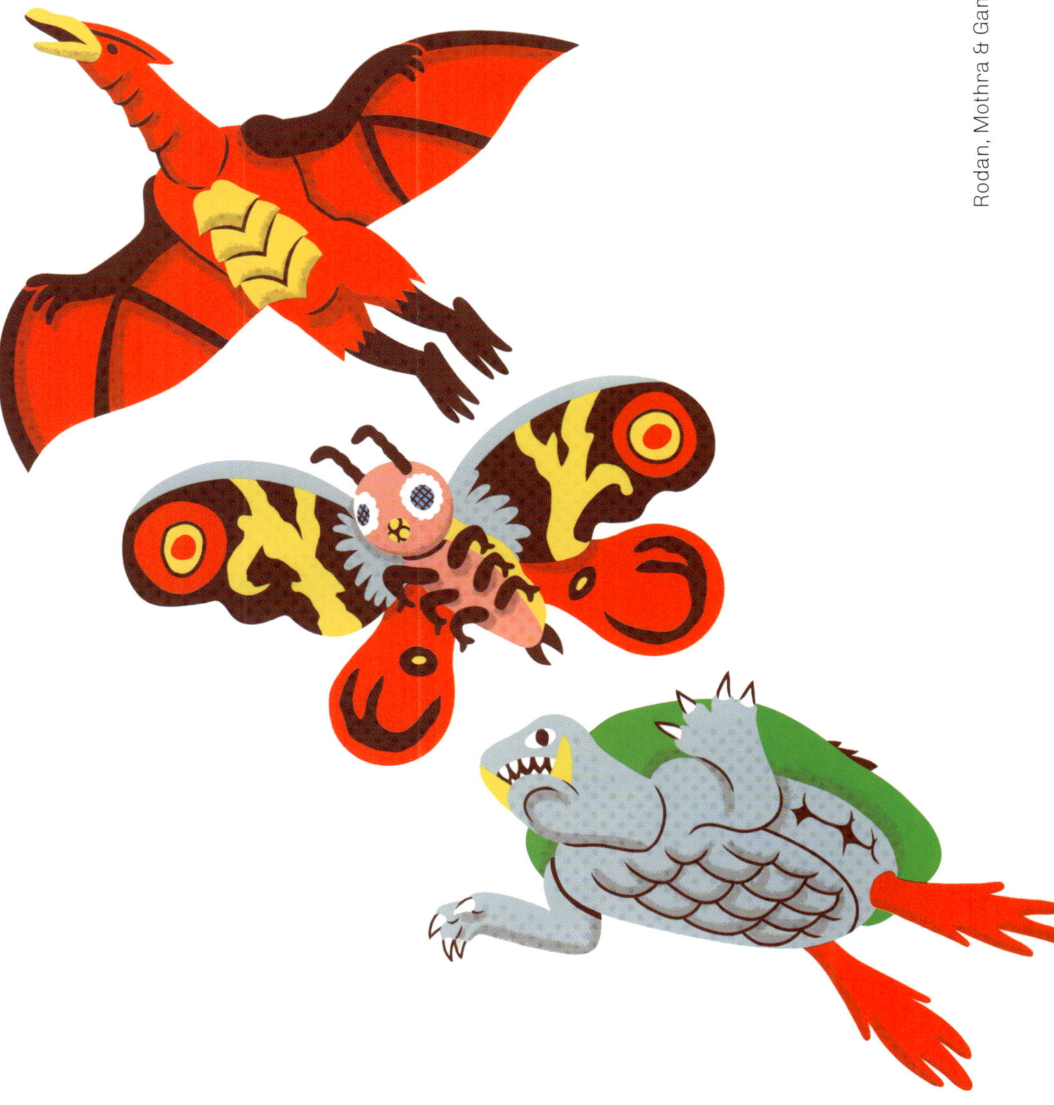

↓ **Below:** *Godzilla was soon joined by new kaijū.*

↓ **Left to right:** *Rodan, Mothra, and Gamera.*

MOTHRA, QUEEN OF MONSTERS

Mothra, another *kaijū* icon, received her own film in 1961, also directed by Ishirō Honda. This time, the approach was different. Mothra was a flying creature like Rodan but more fantastical and mysterious. She was protected by Shobijin, two fairylike guardians with a human appearance. Mothra is often associated with femininity and has a profoundly pacifist, albeit fiercely determined, nature. She is regarded as the queen of monsters.

In her first film, Mothra came from Infant Island, a fictional Pacific archipelago also affected by nuclear testing. Shipwrecked sailors discover the island, along with its unique flora and fauna, including a giant egg and the Shobijin who protect it. The fairies are taken back to Japan to be displayed as circus attractions. Sensing the disappearance of its guardians, the egg hatches, and the Mothra larva sets off to rescue the fairies from Japan. During the journey, the larva transforms into the gigantic, destructive moth we know today.

Right: *Mothra faces off against Godzilla in her second film* Mothra vs. Godzilla *(1964).*

Mothra distinguished herself immediately from her very first film. The traditional *kaijū* elements, including impressive scenes of destruction, were all present and accounted for, but unlike other *kaijū*, she was kindhearted. She was not inherently antagonistic toward humans but stood up to villains when they threatened her, her fairies, or nature itself. Like Godzilla—but in a complementary and more positive way—she is portrayed as a near-divine figure. This perception is enhanced by the cinematography and aesthetic choices, exemplified by the church setting of the film's finale. Her sole wish is to restore the balance between humanity and nature.

We saw this desire again in *Mothra vs. Godzilla* (1964), in which an egg laid by Mothra is swept away by a storm and ends up on an inhabited beach, catching the attention of unscrupulous people who see it only as a potentially moneymaking sideshow attraction. Godzilla, who hasn't been seen since his battle with King Kong, makes his return when he is drawn to the egg. This in turn attracts Mothra, who does everything she can to protect her offspring, even at the cost of her own life.

This is another of Mothra's characteristics: the notion of sacrifice, transmission, and even rebirth. Over the course of her various iterations, Mothra sometimes actually dies, often sacrificing herself for others. In 2001's *GMK*, Mothra gives up her own life to revive King Ghidorah to fight a possessed Godzilla. And the first film of the Rebirth of Mothra trilogy (1996–1998) focuses primarily on Mothra as well as her offspring, Mothra Leo, who goes on to become the

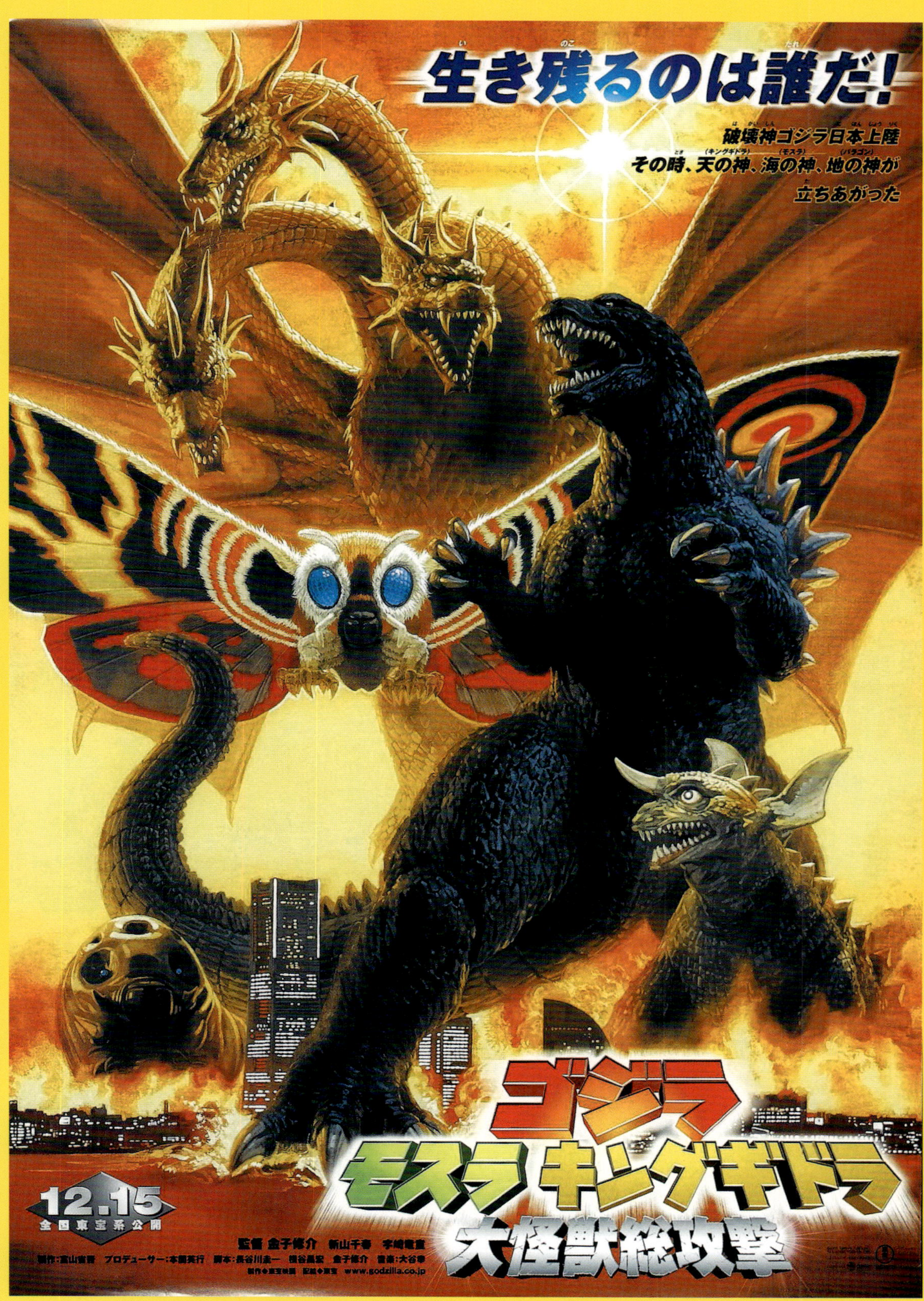

← **Left:** *Japanese poster for the film* Godzilla, Mothra and King Ghidorah: Giant Monsters All-Out Attack *(2001), in which Mothra plays a crucial role in defeating Godzilla.*

protagonist of the next two films after Mothra dies to save him.

This is how Mothra and her progeny and universe are generally depicted. She evolves both by bearing direct descendants and through perpetual reincarnation, as if Mothra were some sort of collective entity rather than a single monster. This is precisely what makes Mothra one of Toho's truly unique *kaijū*, a trait that Legendary Pictures retained in its reinterpretation of Mothra in its MonsterVerse.

GODZILLA'S ARCHENEMY

In the world of *kaijū*, Toho and Godzilla had many competitors, but the fiercest of them all was Daiei Film and its equally iconic monster, Gamera the flying turtle. However, Daiei didn't dive into the genre right away, despite its booming popularity in the early 1960s. Instead, the studio began with ghost films featuring *kaibyō*, supernatural cats of Japanese folklore. In 1956, Daiei dipped a toe into science fiction with *Warning from Space*, a story of alien invasion. In 1962, the company waded further into the *kaijū* genre waters with *Killer Whale*, the story of a giant whale terrorizing a small fishing village and a hero determined to defeat it—a Japanese take on the 1851 novel *Moby Dick*.

In 1964, Daiei attempted its first true *kaijū* film, *Giant Horde Beast Nezura*, which was to feature an army of giant rats and would be filmed using real live rodents. However, the project was scrapped because the studio was unable

↓ **Below:** *Japanese poster for the film Gamera, the Giant Monster (1965).*

↘ **Bottom right:** *American poster for the November 2023 video release of the film Killer Whale (1962).*

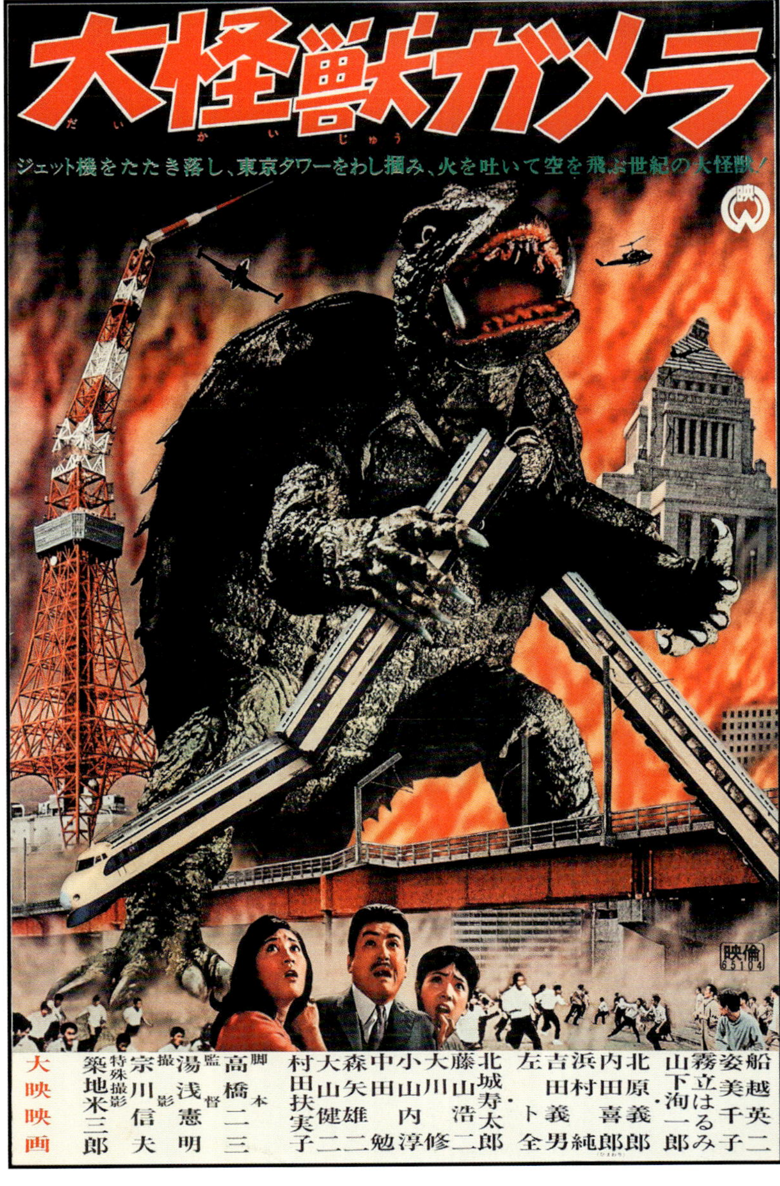

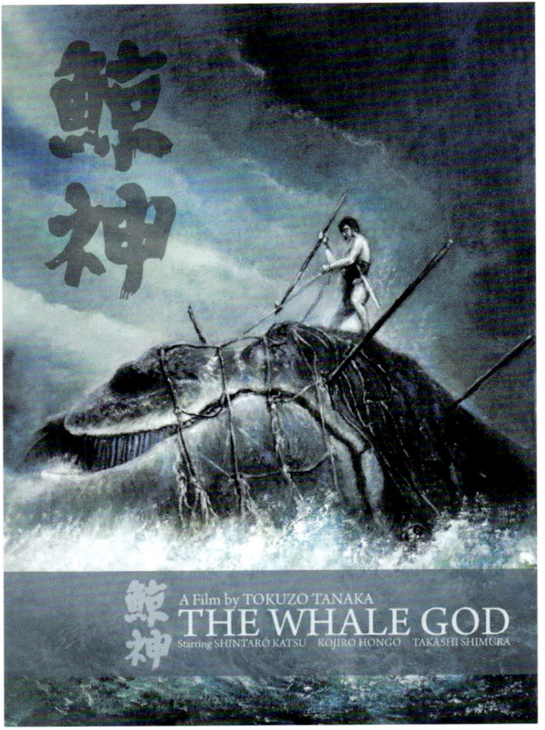

to contain the rats, resulting in fears of disease and infestation in the local area. Despite the setback and financial loss, Daiei remained determined and sought out a new approach.

The result was 1965's *Gamera, the Giant Monster*. Though it was released eleven years later, the film was clearly inspired by the 1954 version of *Godzilla* but with a more serious tone that was amplified by its decision to remain in black and white, unlike most other productions. Featuring a *kaijū* trapped in Arctic ice awakened by a nuclear bomb, the film's message was unmistakable. Daiei was trying to create its own flagship monster, a direct challenge to Godzilla.

From the start, Gamera was introduced as a fearsome, destructive *kaijū* with a signature move. It could retract its limbs into its shell, emit flames, and spin rapidly to launch itself into flight. Gamera's success the following year ushered it into the golden age of *kaijū* films, riding on the prevailing winds of the time, allowing it eventually to outpace Godzilla. Subsequent films quickly pivoted toward a younger audience, featuring child protagonists and pitting Gamera against its own roster of legendary foes, including Barugon, an ancient horned reptile (1966); Gyaos, which resembled a pterodactyl (1967); Viras, a squid-like space monster (1968); and Guiron, a *kaijū* with a head shaped like a massive blade (1969). Gamera's nemeses were marked by their wide-ranging diversity.

The studio quickly latched onto the "versus" format and turned out one film after another, firmly establishing Gamera in the collective Japanese imagination right alongside Godzilla. Gamera also became a protector *kaijū* and friend to children. The monster battled colorful enemies and even had its own ridiculously memorable moments, such as spinning around a giant metal bar like an Olympic athlete during a fight with Guiron.

Despite these efforts to remain relevant, Gamera struggled to captivate audiences, leaving Daiei unable to rely on the creature for long. Moreover, the studio itself faced financial difficulties. Even though Daiei produced a slew of films in the 1960s, including the extensive *Zatoichi* series about a blind swordsman, the studio was headed for collapse by the early 1970s and would never fully recover.

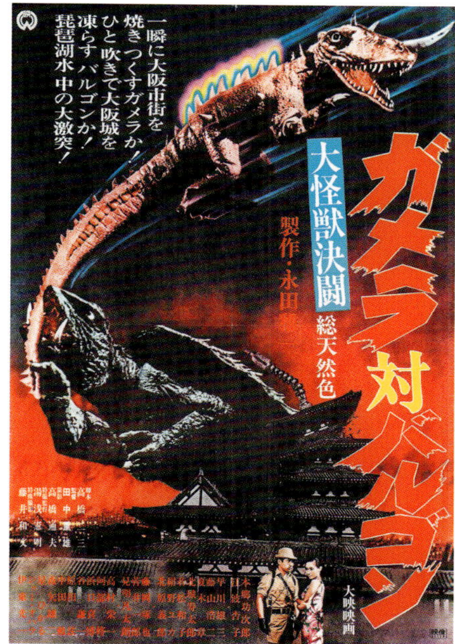

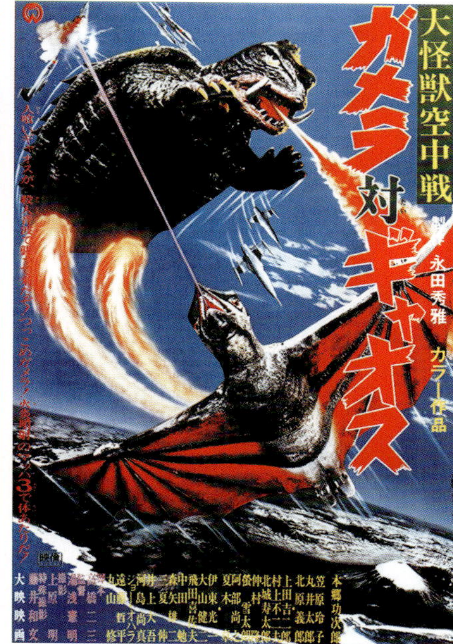

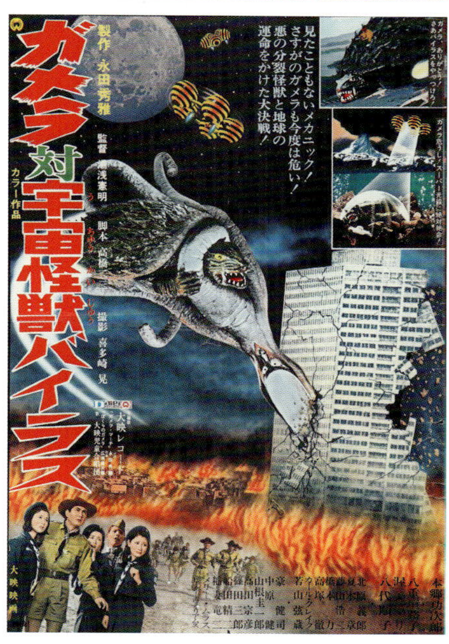

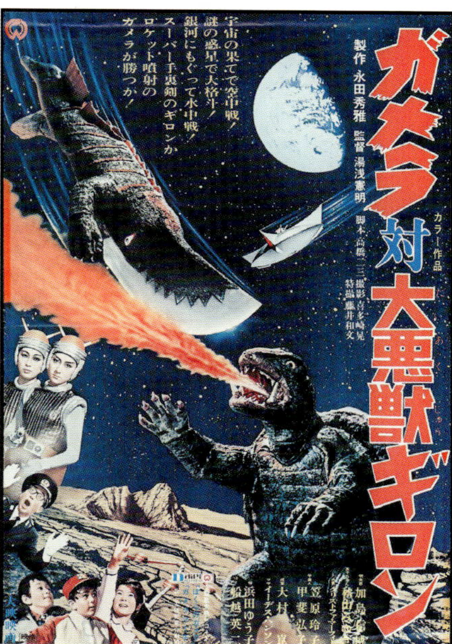

↑ Above: *Gamera and some of its enemies. Top from left to right: Japanese posters for the films* Gamera vs. Barugon *(1966) and* Gamera vs. Gyaos *(1967).*

↑ Bottom, from left to right: *Japanese posters for the films* Gamera vs. Viras *(1968) and* Gamera vs. Guiron *(1969).*

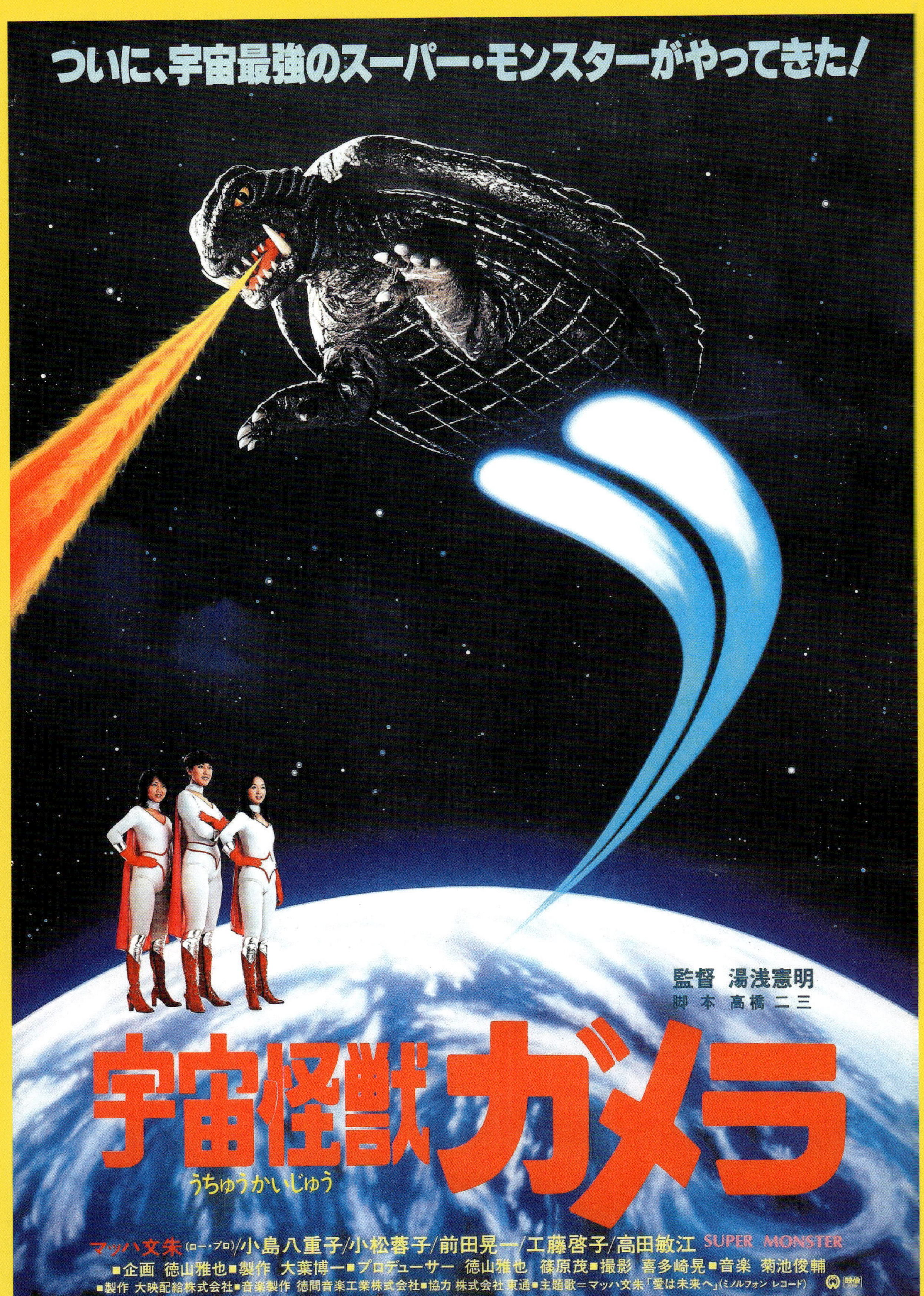

➜ **Right:** Gamera vs. Zigra (1971) contained every trope in the genre, including a child protagonist, an alien attack, and a kaijū battle amid stormy seas.

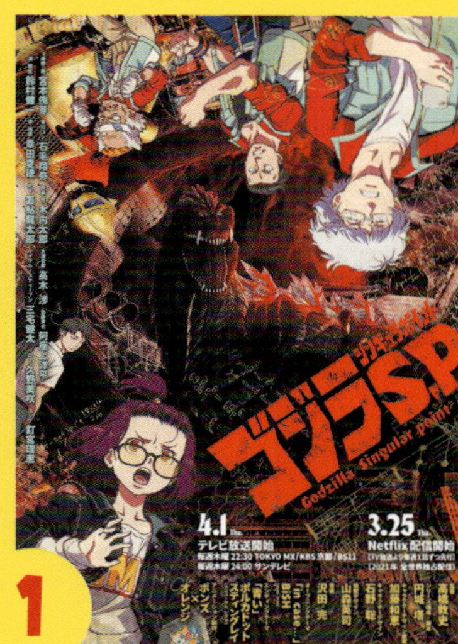

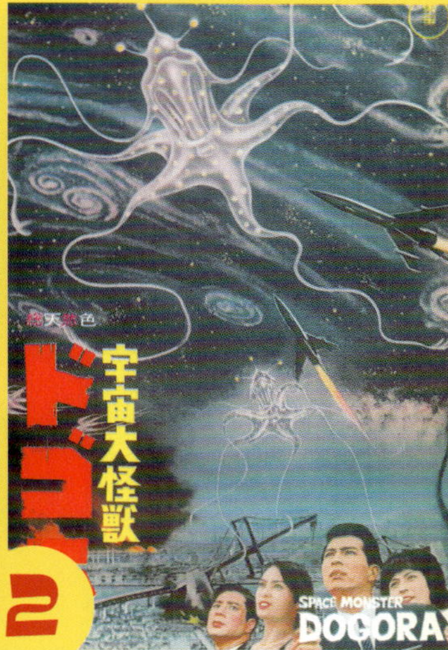

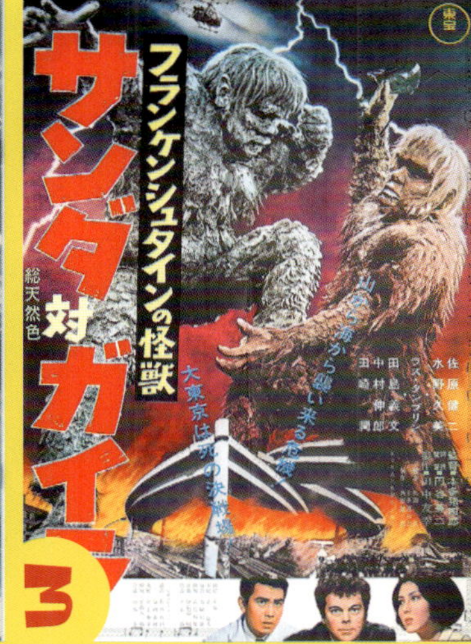

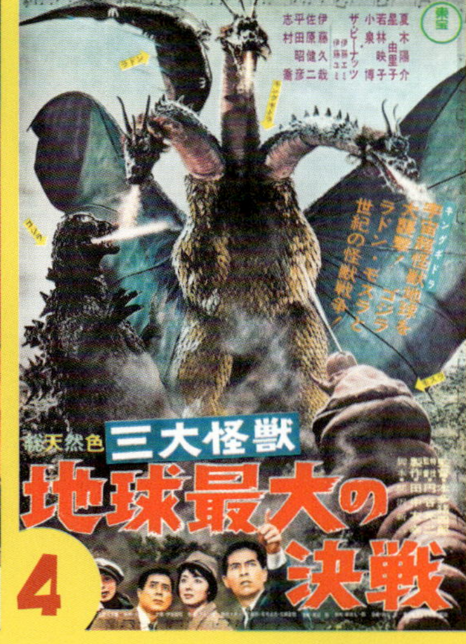

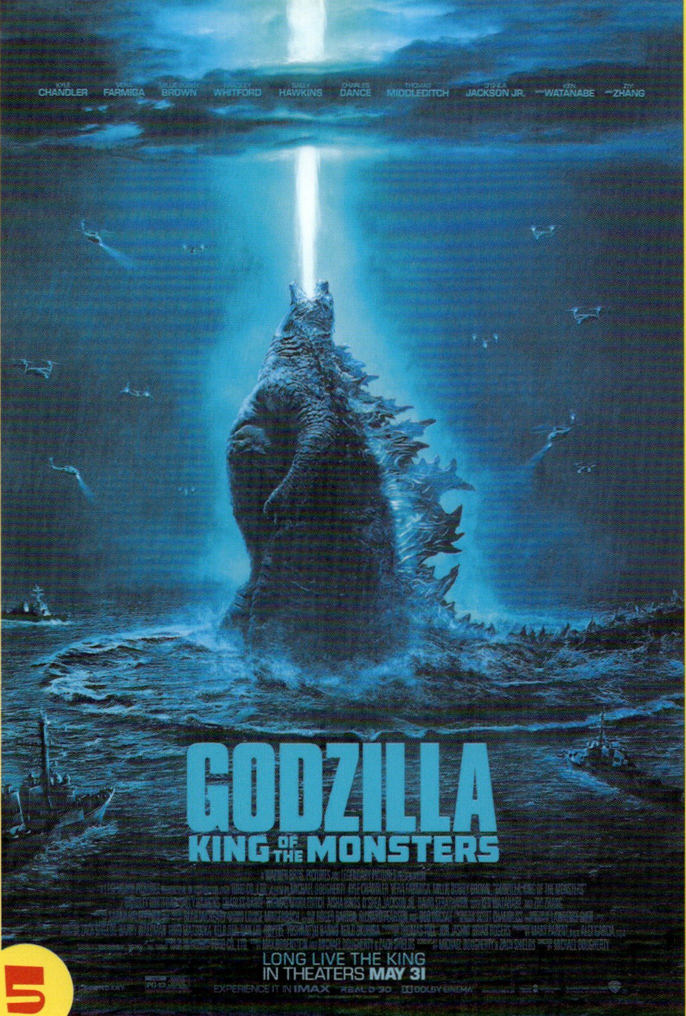

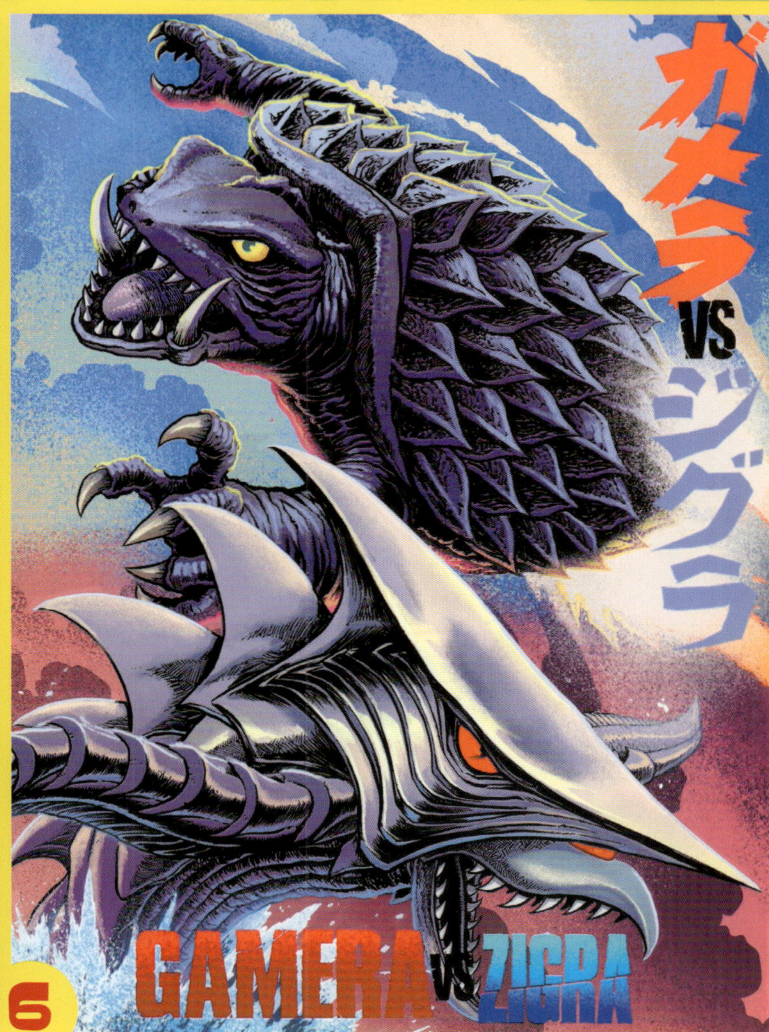

1. *Japanese poster for the anime series* Godzilla Singular Point *(2021).*

2. *Japanese poster for the film* Dogora *(1964).*

3. *Japanese poster for the film* The War of the Gargantuas *(1966).*

4. *Japanese poster for the film* Ghidorah, the Three-Headed Monster *(1964),* King Ghidorah's *first appearance in the Godzilla franchise.*

5. *American poster for* Godzilla: King of the Monsters, *the second film in the American series that began in 2014.*

6. *Illustration for the film* Gamera vs. Zigra *(1971) for the video release of the Gamera films by Arrow Video.*

KAIJŪ: LEGENDS AND MYTHS

↓ **Below:** *Japanese poster for the film* Return of Daimajin *(1966).*

↘ **Bottom right:** *Japanese poster for the film* Daimajin *(1966)..*

DAIMAJIN: HALF GOD, HALF KAIJŪ

Gamera wasn't the only *kaijū* that Daiei produced during the genre's golden age, though it did stand out for its originality. In 1945, Daiei's productions were split between two creative teams: Daiei Tokyo and Daiei Kyoto. Whereas Tokyo produced "mass market" works like *Killer Whale* and the *Gamera* series in the 1960s and 1970s, Kyoto opted for a more ambitious and prestigious approach. It was Daiei Kyoto that spearheaded the golden age of period films (*jidaigeki*), with classics like Akira Kurosawa's *Rashōmon* (1950).

In 1961, the Kyoto branch shot for the stars by creating the epic *Buddha*, inspired by grand American epics like *The Ten Commandments* (1956) and *Ben-Hur* (1959). The historical masterpiece explored Buddha's origins through the lens of divine representation via a giant statue. The theme carried over into 1966

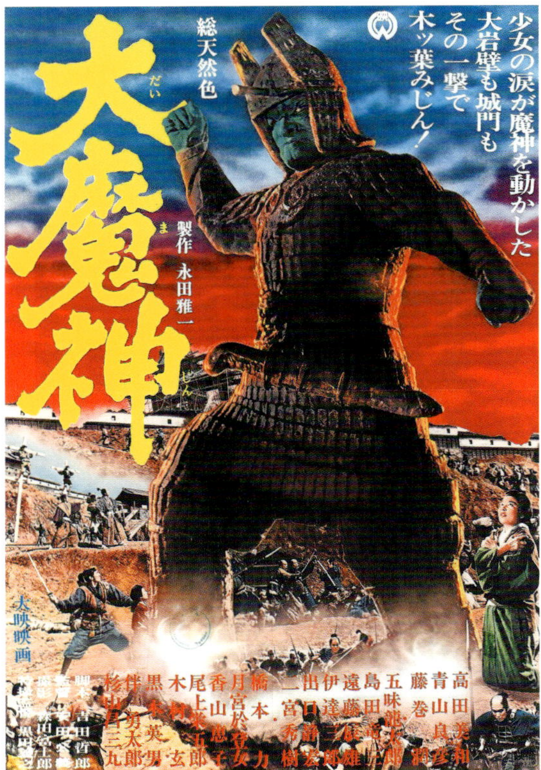

with the *Daimajin* trilogy. As if to prove the studio's determination, all three films were released in Japan within a year, an impressive feat even for the time. To achieve this, the three films were produced simultaneously by three different directors because each film was a standalone work. The first *Daimajin* was directed by Kimiyoshi Yasuda (creator of several *Zatoichi* films), the second by Kenji Misumi (who would later go on to make the wildly popular *Lone Wolf and Cub* series), and the third by Kazuo Mori (a versatile director of period dramas and samurai stories). In short, Daiei Kyoto played to its strengths, combining *jidaigeki*, its signature genre, with *kaijū*, which was peaking in popularity.

What made Daimajin unique was that he wasn't a monster. In all three films, Majin (*dai* simply means "big") was a giant statue that the local population viewed both as a divine protector and as a potential threat, should his wrath be unleashed. The plots often revolved around a village being invaded or village leaders being overthrown by violent, ruthless rival clans, awakening the god Majin to deliver judgment.

In *Daimajin*, released in April 1966, the main characters are forced out of their native village when the local lord is killed in a coup and a reign of terror begins under a new ruler. The heroes, some of whom are children at the start of the story, are forced to flee for a number of years but remain determined to reclaim their village when the time comes, even if it means awakening the god Majin to aid them.

In *Return of Majin* (August 1966), the second in the series, Majin resides on a central island, which various clans seek to seize, in a lake. In the third film, *Wrath of Majin* (December 1966), the setting shifts to snowy mountains, where a group of children are on a quest to rescue their families, who have been kidnapped and enslaved by a neighboring village lord. The iconic statue stands between the two opposing camps.

Although the narratives share similarities, they also serve as pretexts

↓ **Below:** *Daimajin emphasized the divinity of kaijū.*

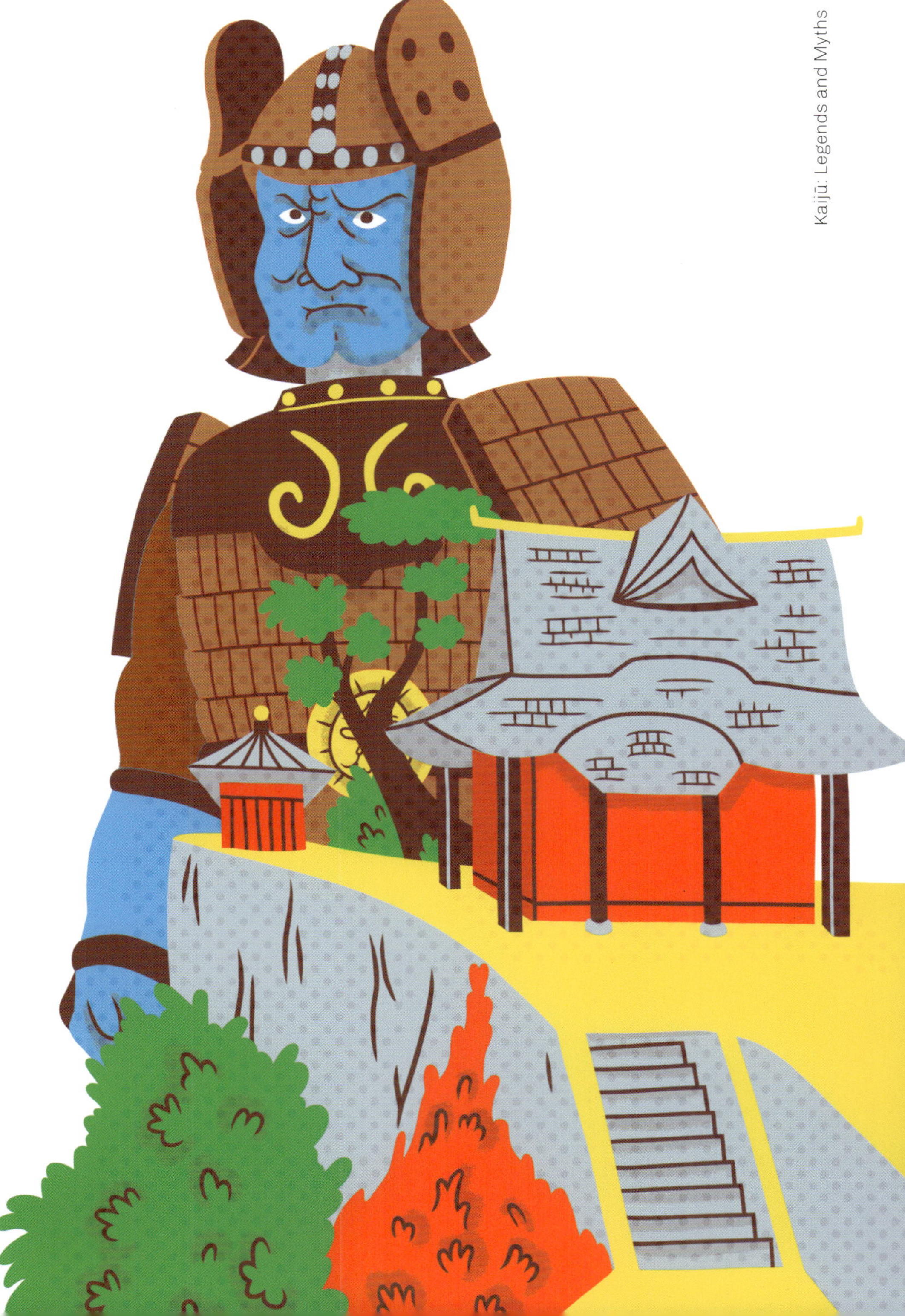

→ **Right:** *Japanese poster for the TV series* Daimajin Kanon *(2010).*

↓ **Below:** *Still from the TV series* Daimajin Kanon *(2010).*

↓ **Bottom left:** *Still from the film* The Ten Commandments *(1956) showing Moses parting the Red Sea.*

↘ **Bottom right:** *Still from the film* Return of Daimajin *(1966) showing Majin crossing a parted sea.*

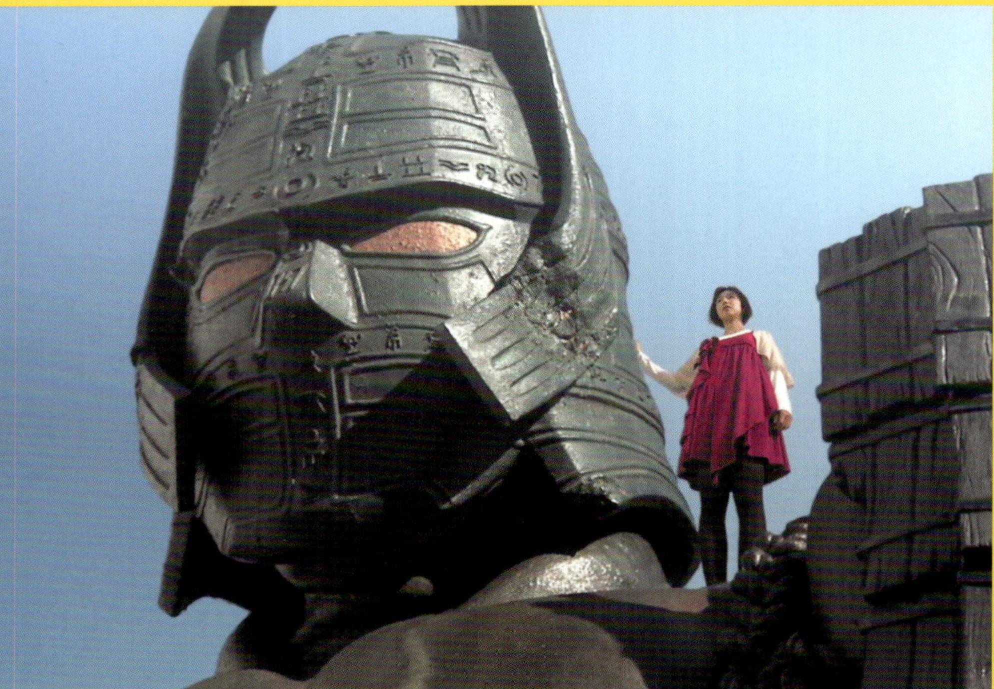

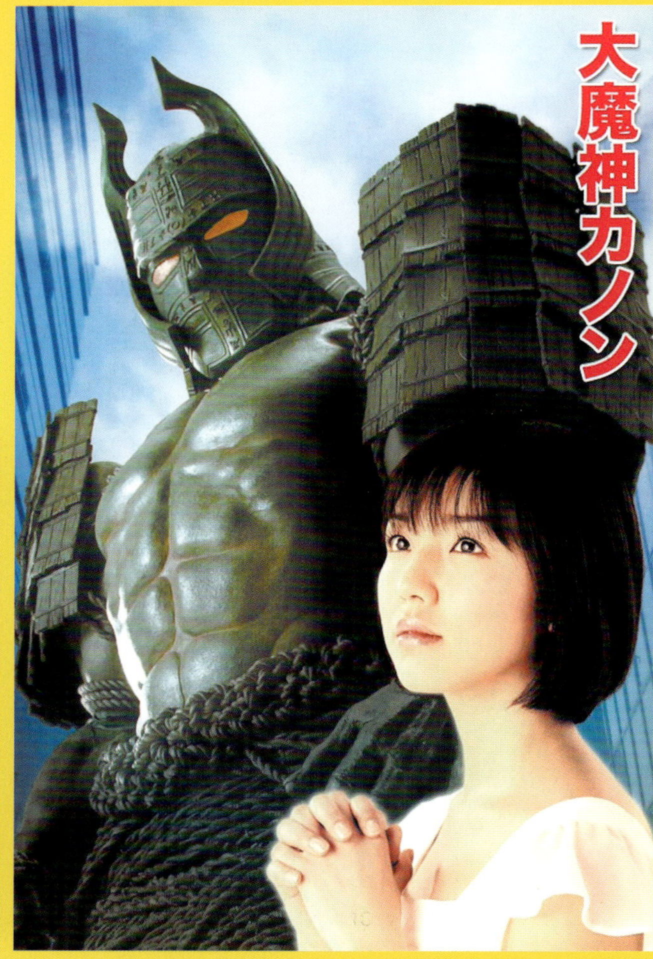

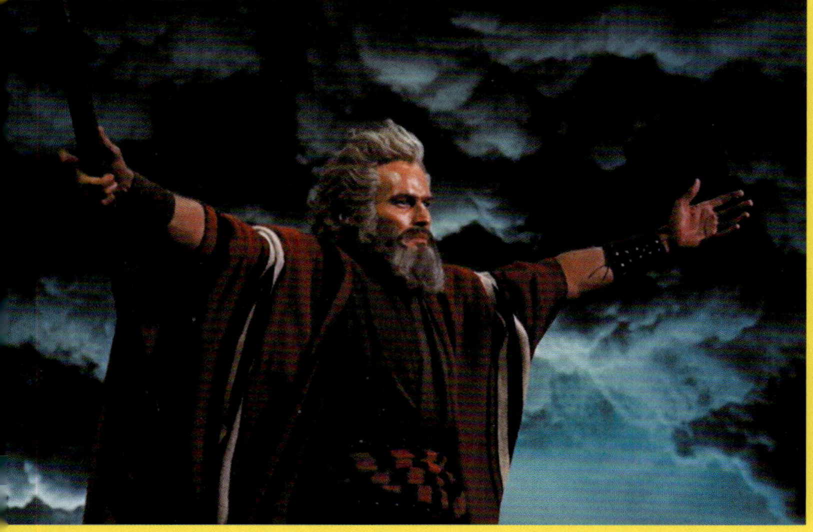

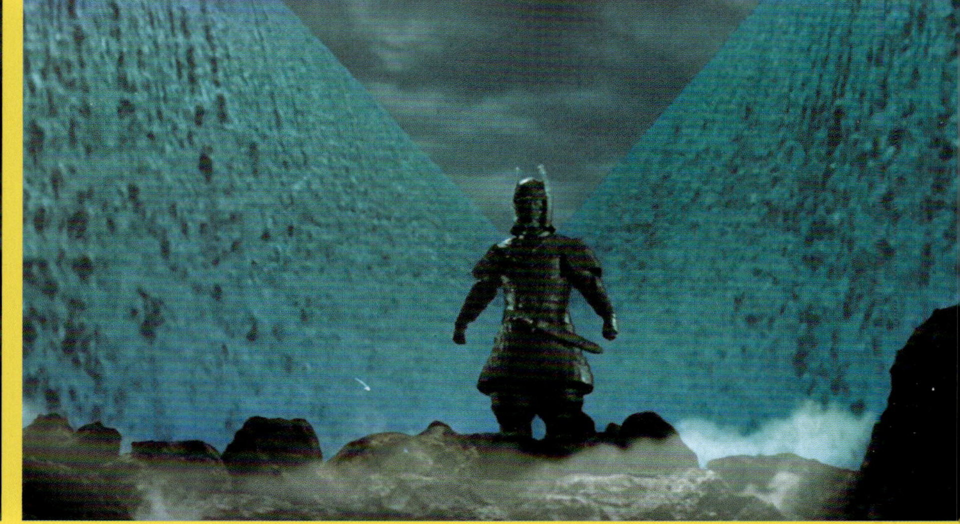

for showcasing a variety of landscapes and situations, highlighting the directors' talents, and emphasizing the presence of the sacred statue. At around fifty feet tall, Majin isn't quite in the same league as his *kaijū* peers, but he redefines the portrayal of size. Daiei spared no effort in making the statue imposing and its wrath terrifying, using unusual perspectives and striking cinematography to achieve this effect. Giant replicas of arms and legs were created on-set for key close-up scenes where desperate samurai attempt to fend off the statue's attacks. Other moments are striking for their framing, such as in the second film where Majin parts the lake like Moses in *The Ten Commandments* (1956).

Through its effective and intensive use of blue-screen compositing to insert Majin into wide shots, the intricate model work that enhances scenes of destruction, and the performance of Majin's suit actor, Chikara Hashimoto, *Daimajin* made a brief but impactful entry into the *kaijū* genre. The trilogy continued to explore the giant creature's duality as a terrifying and destructive yet also near-divine (or entirely divine, in this case) entity created to protect humanity from its own flaws.

Afterward, *Daimajin* took a well-deserved break. Despite rumors of a return to theaters in the 1990s and 2000s, particularly after Daiei was acquired by Kadokawa, Majin wasn't seen again until 2010, this time on television.

Daimajin Kanon, a twenty-six-episode *tokusatsu* TV series, took a radically different approach. Set in modern-day Japan, the story follows Kanon Mikazaki, a young woman aspiring to become a singer who returns to her hometown after a difficult breakup. Unbeknownst to her, her emotional struggles become central to a conflict involving various *yōkai* and demons, one that can only be resolved by awakening the stone giant Bujin (Majin's name in this version). Despite a few key scenes and Bujin's new muscular look, the series focuses less on action and spectacle and more on the main character's psychology, exploring her journey of self-recovery, during which she overcomes her depression and uses it as a means to move forward in her fight.

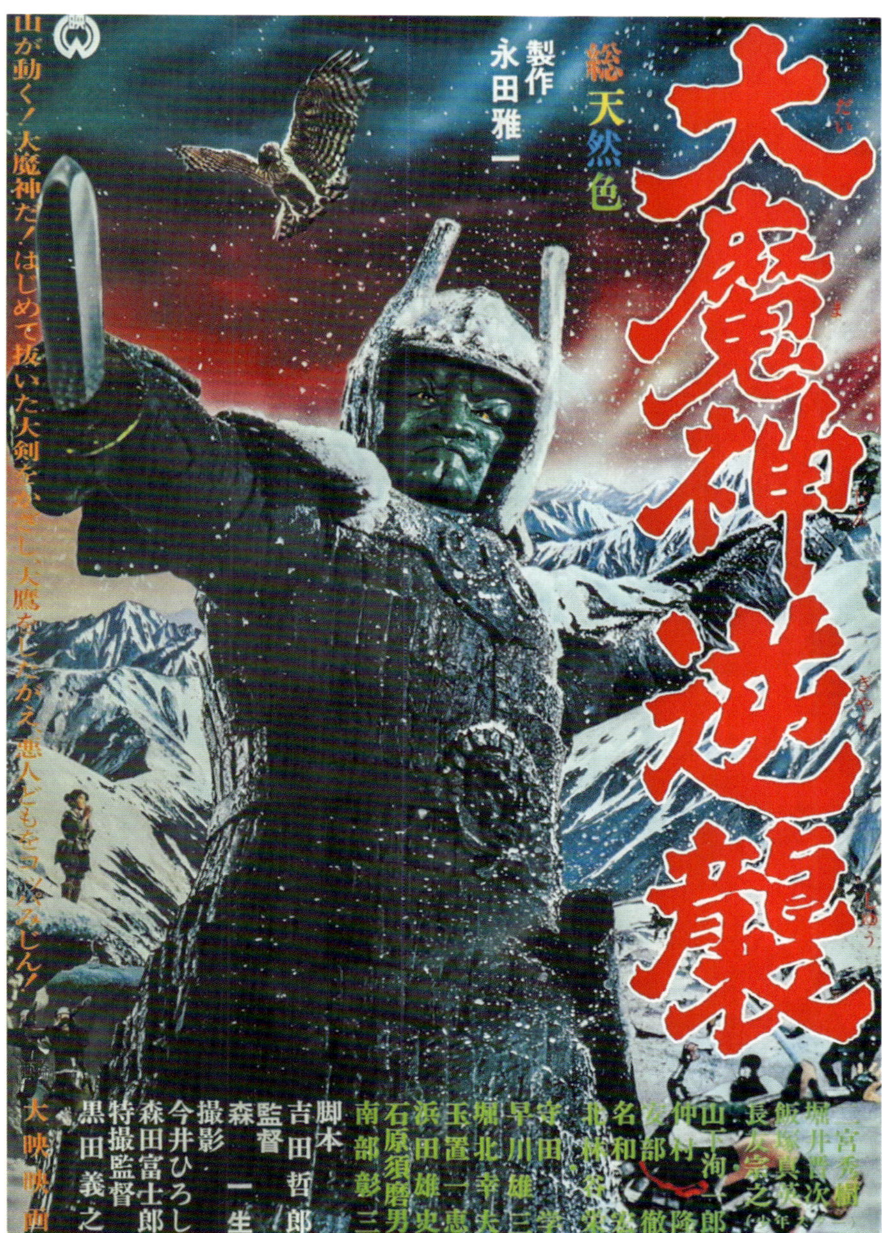

↑ **Above:** *Japanese poster for the film* Wrath of Daimajin *(also known as* Majin Strikes Again*) (1966).*

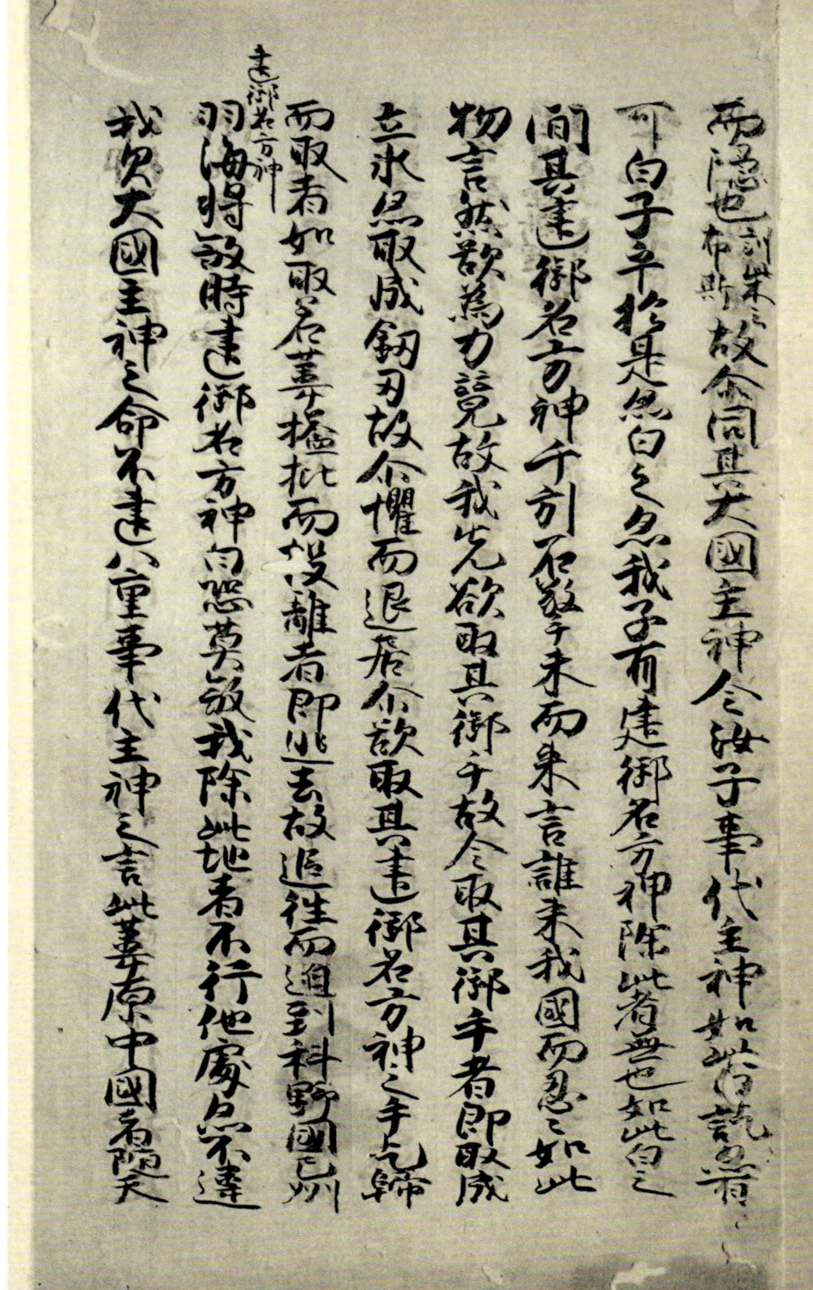

而隠也訓柴云布斯故爾問其大國主神今汝子事代主神如此白訖亦有
可白子乎於是亦白之亦我子有建御名方神除此者無也如此白之
間其建御名方神千引石擎手末而來言誰來我國而忍忍如此
物言然欲為力競故我先欲取其御手故令取其御手者即取成
立氷亦取成劔刃故爾懼而退居爾欲取其建御名方神之手乞歸
而取者如取若葦搤批而投離者即逃去故追往而迫到科野國之州
建御名方神
羽海將殺時建御名方神白恐莫殺我除此地者不行他處亦不違
我父大國主神之命不違八重事代主神之言此葦原中國者隨天

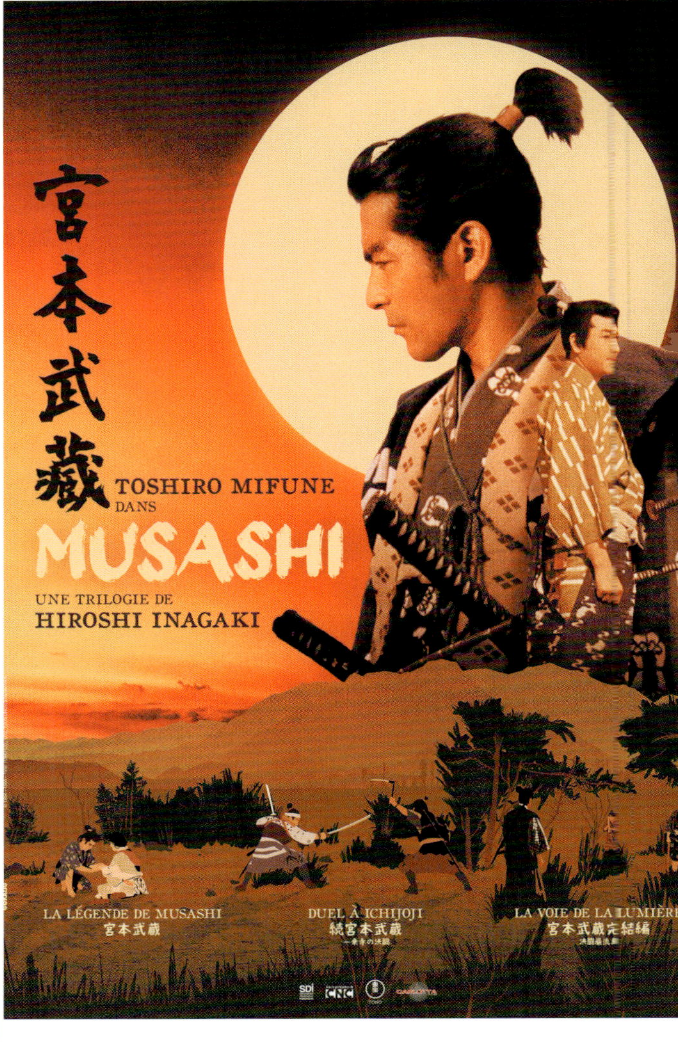

↑ **Above left:** *Reproduction of a page from* Kojiki.

↗ **Above center:** *French poster for the video release of the* Samurai Trilogy *by Carlotta Films.*

To this day, Daimajin remains a challenging character to bring to the screen due to its very nature: an unyielding, invincible stone giant with a mystical, divine essence. More recently, the statue made a comeback in a reimagining of the *Yōkai Monsters* trilogy—another classic Daiei series from the 1960s—reappearing as a formidable ally in the 2021 film *The Great Yōkai War: Guardians*, a testament to the statue monster's enduring presence in Japanese popular culture.

OROCHI THE DRAGON

Daiei wasn't the only studio adapting Japanese myths into *tokusatsu* films. In 1959, Toho created *Nippon Tanjō* (literally the birth of Japan, but titled *The Three Treasures* for the US release), an epic based on the *Nihon Shoki* and *Kojiki*, two eighth-century Japanese chronicles. As the original title suggests, the movie recounts the history of Japan and the founding of the Shinto religion through the character Yamato Takeru (played by

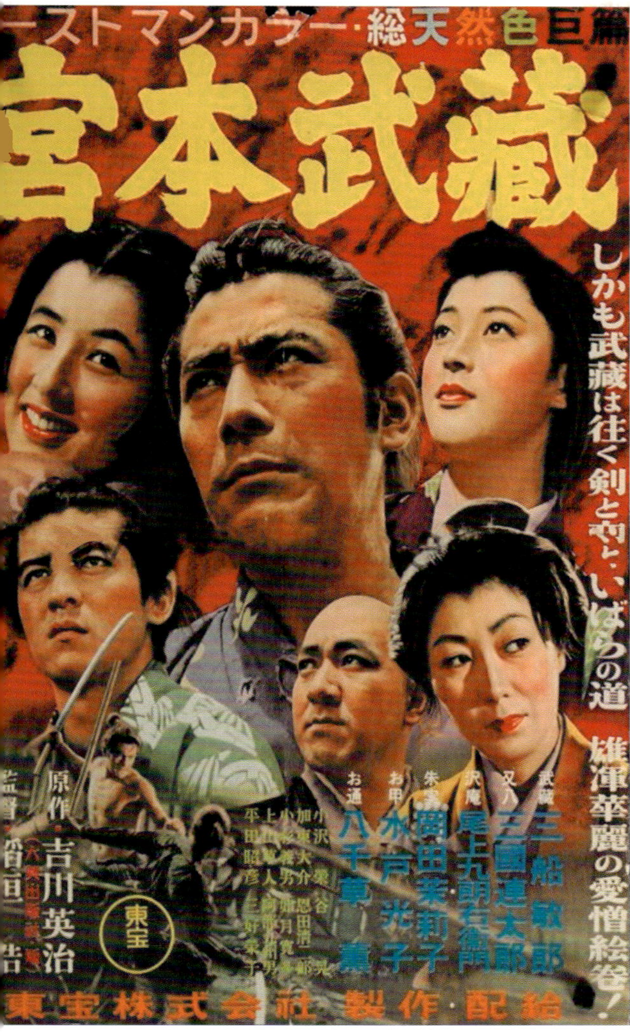

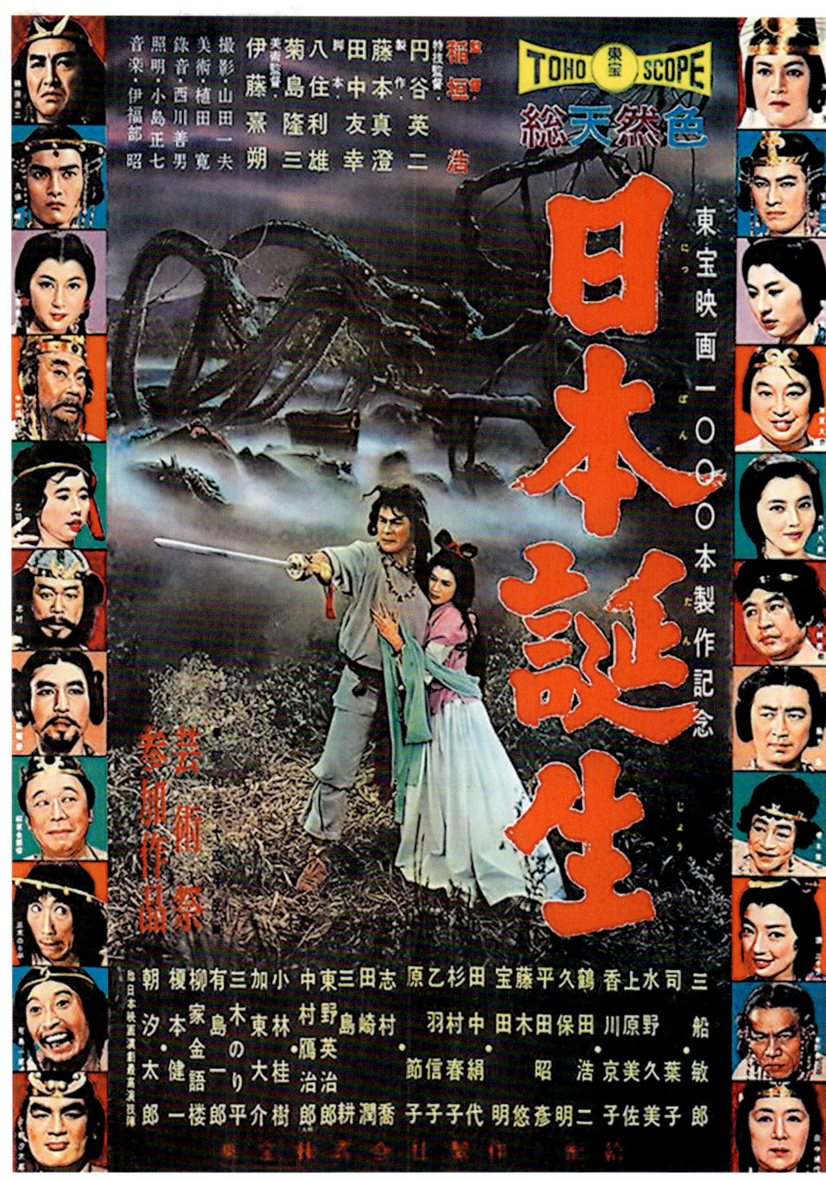

↑ **Above:** *Japanese poster for the film* The Three Treasures *(1959), in which director Hiroshi Inagaki made the leap from samurai tales to fantastical epics.*

the legendary Toshirō Mifune) and his battle against Orochi, the giant eight-headed dragon of Japanese mythology.

The film is known as one of the studio's most expensive productions, with a palpable ambition and unprecedented success. It was directed by Hiroshi Inagaki, another prominent figure at Toho alongside Ishirō Honda, known for his samurai films (particularly the *Samurai Trilogy* released between 1954 and 1956), and unsurprisingly, featured Eiji Tsuburaya on special effects. The film remains impressive even today, showcasing Tsuburaya's meticulous care in every scene, from the natural disasters (a volcanic eruption, a storm sweeping away ships, a flood sequence) to the confrontation with Orochi in an eerie lake.

As in the legend, the hero confronts the creature after luring and weakening it by making it drink buckets of sake. This is followed by a battle against a disoriented yet still tenacious creature. Though the on-screen animation techniques consisted of little more than manipulating the eight heads via a cable system, in their own way, they laid the groundwork for many other *tokusatsu* creatures, such as King Ghidorah in the *Godzilla* series and other variations on the mythological monster.

In 1994, the story was adapted anew for the big screen, this time with a more mainstream vision more in step with the times but with even more fantastical and *tokusatsu* elements. Simply titled *Takeru Yamato* in Japan and *Orochi, The Eight-Headed Dragon* in the United States (one highlighting the hero, the other focusing on the creature central to the plot), the film was released during a period of resurgence for giant monsters kick-started by the Heisei era of *Godzilla* and the *Gamera* and *Mothra* trilogies shortly thereafter.

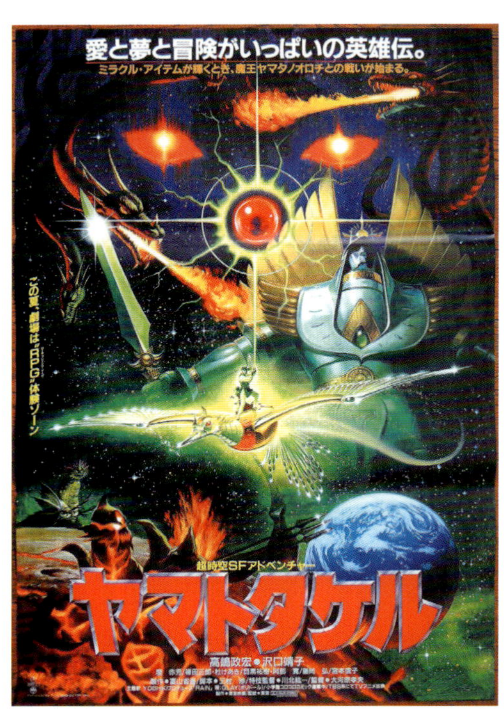

Orochi was directed by Takao Ōkawara (*Godzilla vs. Mothra* in 1992 and *Godzilla vs. Destoroyah* in 1995) and demonstrated Toho's range of mastery. Whereas the 1959 version was more akin to the grand historical epics of American cinema of the era, the 1994 film was a family-oriented tale full of adventure, monsters, and of course, abundant special effects—reminiscent of *Jason and the Argonauts* (1963) and *Clash of the Titans* (1981). In *Orochi*, the hero, Yamato Takeru, is accused of killing his own mother and is banished from the Yamato kingdom by order of his father, the king. To prove his worth and in an attempt to return to his people, he is tasked with defeating a rival clan and its leader. However, his journey soon becomes entangled with a far greater looming threat: the return to Earth of Tsukuyomi, the god of the Moon.

Drawing heavily from the original plot for many of its aspects, *Orochi* delivers a rich and varied adventure in which the hero traverses a variety of locations and faces numerous adversaries and fantastical creatures, from stone giants to tentacled sea *kaijū*. The pinnacle is undoubtedly the epic final battle, which is completely different and more spectacular than the previous film or even the legend itself. Yamato faces the dragon Orochi while riding on the back of a massive

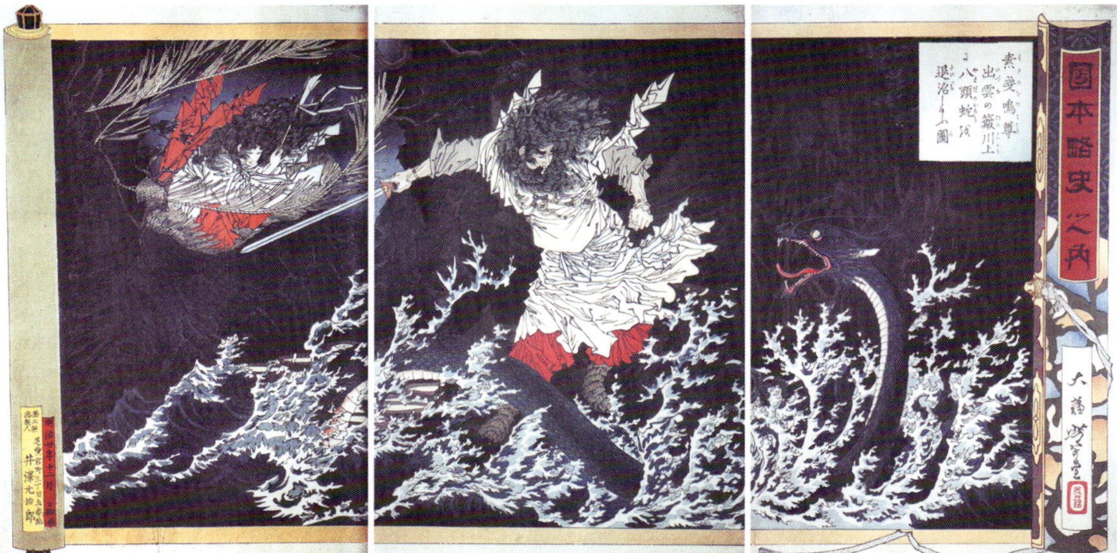

Above: *Japanese poster for the film* Orochi, The Eight-Headed Dragon *(1994).*

Right: *Print by artist Tsukioka Yoshitoshi depicting Susanoo battling Orochi, 1887.*

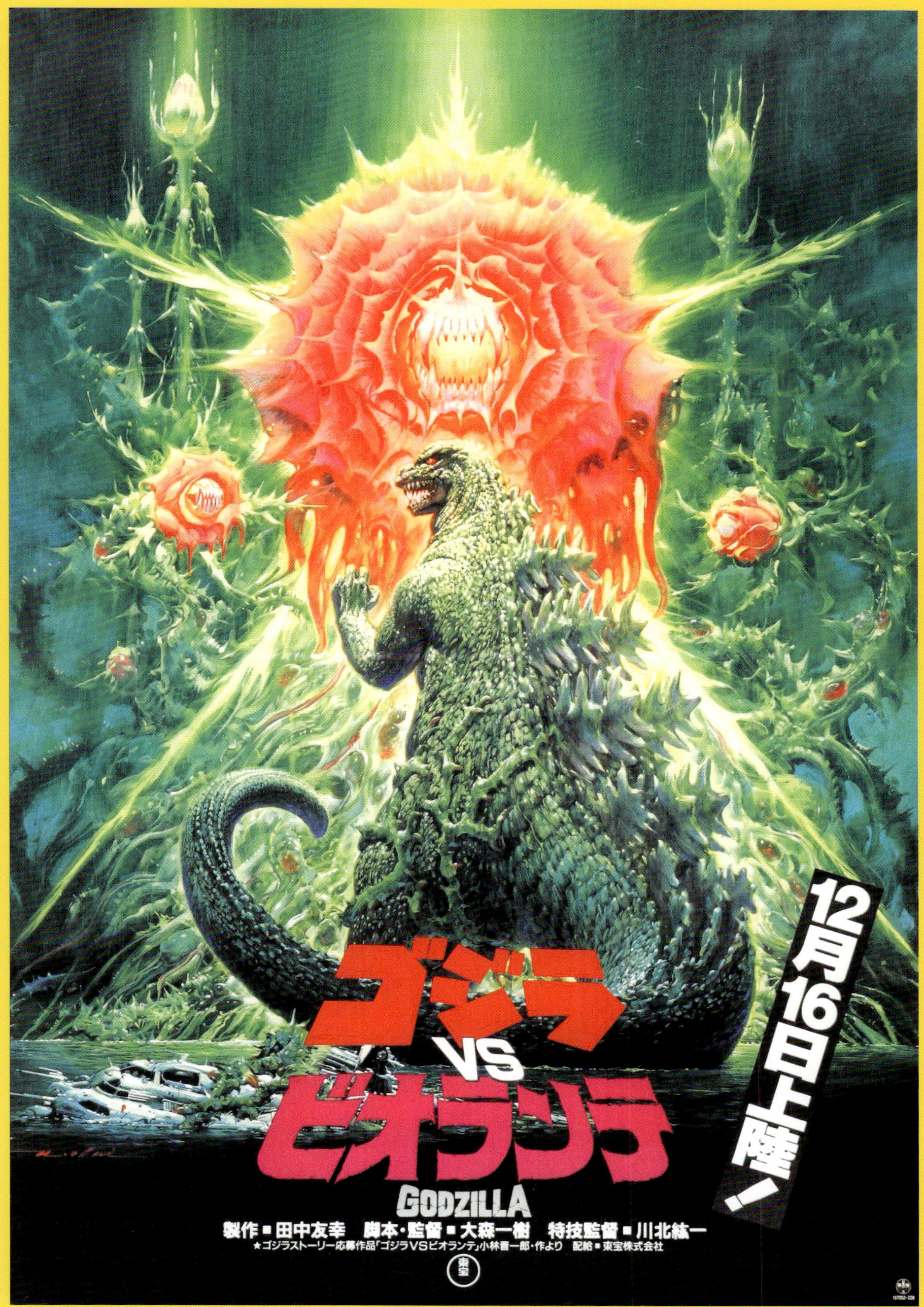

← **Left:** *Japanese poster for the movie* Godzilla vs. Biollante *(1989).*

golden bird, before summoning Utsuno Ikusagami, a colossal divine being reminiscent of giant heroes like Ultraman.

Kōichi Kawakita, whose résumé includes *Godzilla vs. Biollante*, handled the special effects. Animating Orochi presented an immense challenge. Each head was manipulated using cables, with some rigged to breathe enormous flames. For wide shots, the monster as a whole was shown with a massive, movable body. Despite its limited range of motion due to its impressive size, and because of the movie's fast-paced action, Orochi's design stands as one of the most complex among *tokusatsu* creatures.

Orochi remains firmly rooted in the modern Japanese imagination. In addition to the inevitable references across various media, the character appeared again in a new *tokusatsu* film in 2024 titled *Brush of the God*, directed by Keizō Murase. A renowned designer of *tokusatsu* monster suits since the 1950s, Murase made his directorial debut at the age of eighty-eight, adhering fully to the genre's traditional techniques. Once again, the monster was brought to life using an inspired blend of costumes, cables, and animatronics.

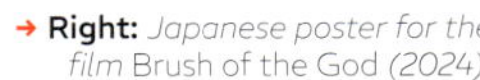

➔ **Right:** *Japanese poster for the film* Brush of the God *(2024).*

INSPIRATION FOR KAIJŪ

Tokusatsu draws from a wide variety of inspirations to build its worlds of giant monsters, from folklore to local mythology and even urban legends.

Another adaptation of legends and popular tales is the 1966 film *The Magic Serpent* by Toei studio. Directed by Tetsuya Yamauchi, the movie is loosely based on the adventures of Jiraiya, a famous ninja of Japanese folklore, which had already been adapted in 1921. Released forty-five years later during the golden age of Japanese cinema, *The Magic Serpent* delivers a sweeping epic that intertwines samurai (the director being well versed in the genre), fantasy, and giant monsters—a concentrated blend of every trope popular at the time.

The story follows the adventures of Ikazuchi-Maru, son of Lord Ogata and the sole survivor of the attack on his father's castle by Lord Daijō Yūki, assisted by his right-hand man, Orochimaru, who has the ability to transform into a giant serpent. On the run, Ikazuchi-Maru remains in hiding for several years and trains in the art of *ninjutsu* under his mentor and surrogate father, Dōjin Hiki. A twist of fate leads to Dōjin Hiki's death at the hands of Orochimaru, and with his dying breath, he teaches Ikazuchi-Maru a technique that allows him to transform into a giant toad. Adopting the name Jiraiya, he vows to avenge all who died under Daijō's orders and to kill Orochimaru.

The film is an excellent representation of *tokusatsu* and the techniques of that

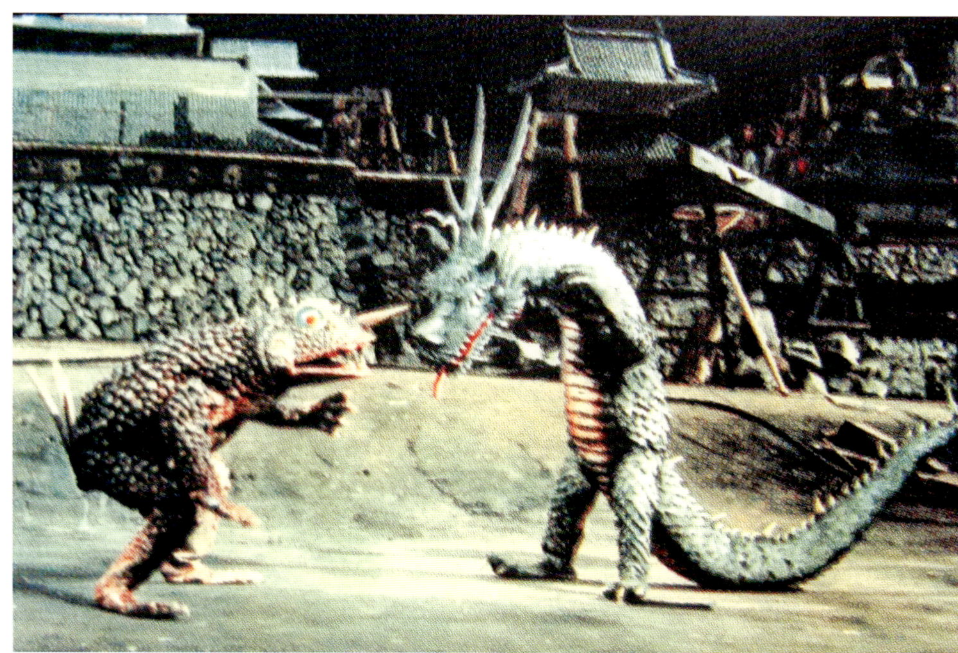

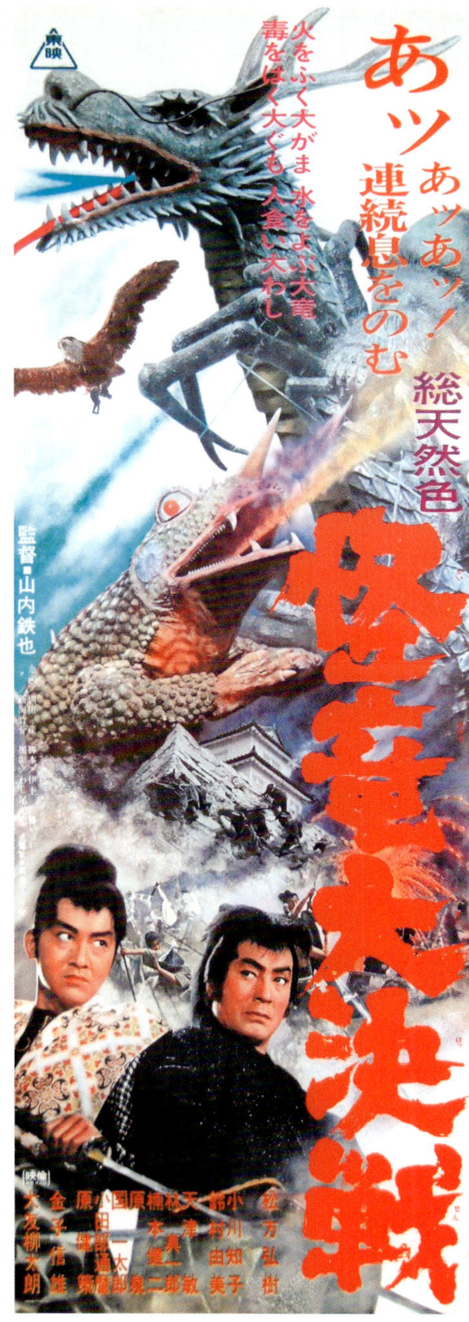

era, just before the start of the superhero craze. With dazzling ninja battles, magical techniques, and fights between a giant toad, spider, and dragon, it remains an inventive production that has held up over time.

Interestingly, the movie even had a French release at the time, albeit in a dubbed and very loosely adapted version. The Japanese title for *The Magic Serpent* could have been translated as "The Great Battle of the Magical Dragon" but instead became *Les Monstres de l'Apocalypse* (Monsters of the Apocalypse). This reflects a practice common in France at the time of importing Japanese films and marketing them as something entirely different through titles and posters created for local audiences.

To study the bizarre nature of *kaijū* rather than their sheer size, we must look back to a time before the 1960s, the genre's golden age. Mere months after the release of the second *Godzilla*, other types of giant monsters began to appear on-screen, such as with the release of *Half Human* in August 1955, a Japanese interpretation of the abominable snowman, the mythical beast that inhabits snowy mountains. The creature was nowhere near as massive as Godzilla, as the *kaijū* genre was still in its infancy and its tropes and clichés had not yet crystallized.

The film was made by Toho by the old dynamic duo, director Ishirō Honda and special effects genius Eiji Tsuburaya. The story takes place in the mountains of Japan where several disappearances have occurred. An investigative journalist interviews people who claim to have survived attacks by some kind of humanoid creature. Through flashbacks, we learn that the monster and its offspring were discovered during a mountain expedition, but attempts to drag them back to civilization for purposes of exploitation quickly turn tragic.

However, the film had a darker side. Though the abominable snowman is a globally recognized legend, and the movie

↖ **Above left:** *Film set of the battle between the movie's two kaijū.*

↑ **Above right:** *Japanese poster for the film* The Magic Serpent *(1966).*

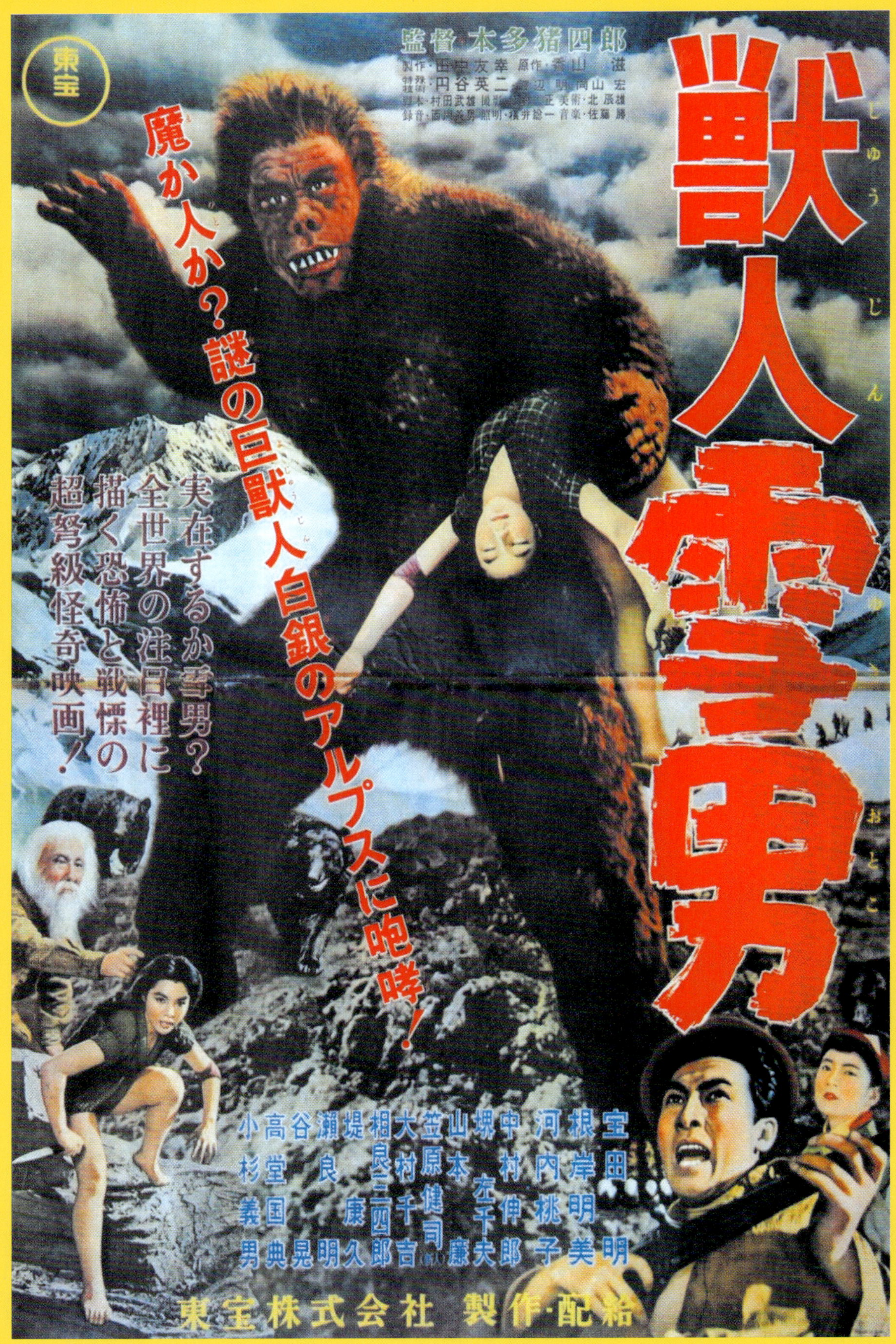

➔ **Right:** *Japanese poster for the film* Half Human *(1955).*

blends aspects of both the monster and horror genres—much like Western productions did with the monsters of Universal Studios—the Japanese version touched a nerve that would ultimately prove fatal for the picture's future. The story focuses not only on the creature but also on the mountain people isolated far from Japanese society, though not by their own choice. Such people are referred to as *burakumin*, a group historically discriminated against in Japan due to social and cultural origins that trace back generations. The discrimination continues today and remains a sensitive topic.

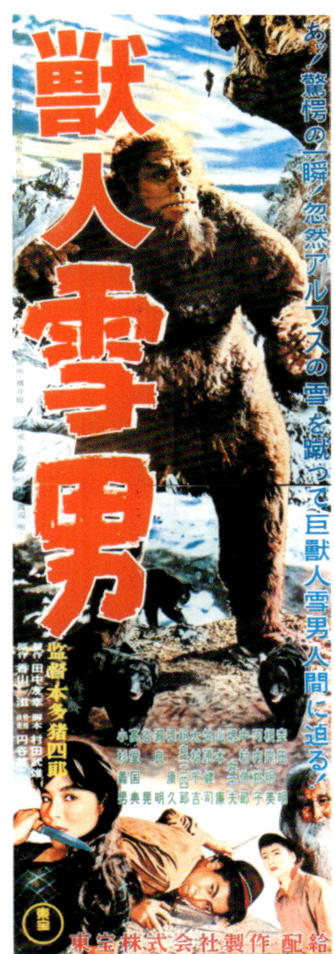

In Honda's film, the mountain-dwellers are a clear reference to the *burakumin*, who are negatively portrayed as poor, uneducated, almost savage, and violent. Although the film was released in 1955, Toho made the enormous decision several decades later to permanently ban the film's distribution for video or cinema release, an act of radical self-censorship in response to the film's unflattering message regarding the *burakumin*.

Half Human was not one of Honda's best works nor one of the best in the genre. Though it had some redeeming qualities—including certain special effects and the creature's design—it would never transcend its status as a minor work. At best, it is intriguing for its concept and its place in Toho's history of monster films, but ultimately it remains an insignificant *tokusatsu* curiosity.

← **Left:** *Japanese poster for the film* Half Human *(1955). To this day, the film is banned from distribution.*

SPECIAL EFFECTS: CREATING THE SPECTACULAR

THE ILLUSION OF SIZE

When making a monster appear larger than life, miniature sets and models play as important a role as the monsters themselves. It takes a true artisan to craft a set that meets all the requirements. It must look like a dense city with finely detailed buildings but also be fragile enough to shatter easily when a monster crashes into it. A particular level of precision is needed so that Godzilla can tear through power lines, Rodan can send hundreds of roof tiles flying with a single flap of its wings, and Gamera can destroy an entire port area.

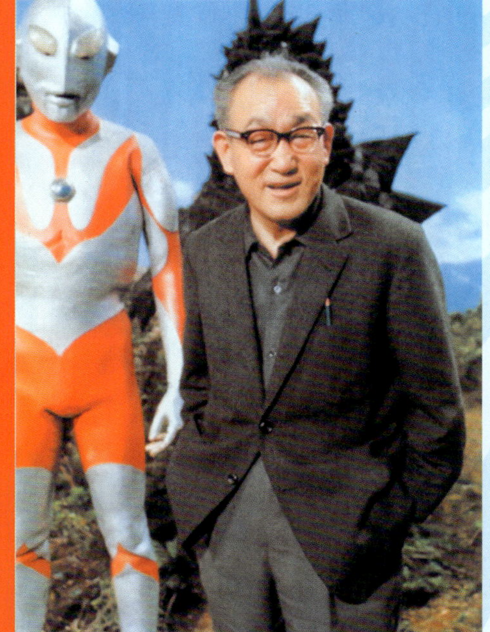

In addition to *zōkei* (modeling), *sōen gishi* is another special effect specialty that encompasses a variety of crafts that all contribute to the unmistakable *tokusatsu* aesthetic. These "mechanical effects technicians" (the literal translation) handle numerous aspects, including one of the most iconic, the art of explosions. This involves taking actors (who may or may not be in costume) and positioning them perfectly in relation to sets and props destined to go up in smoke. Buildings, mountains, and even vehicles might vanish in a perfectly timed explosion.

Then there are weather effects to control, which can include torrential rain, floods, snowstorms or sandstorms. There are also specialists responsible for manipulating creatures not played by actors, almost like puppeteers, and others who maneuver off-camera parts of the costume that the actor can't control, such as wings or tails. The pinnacle of this type of special effect is a *kaijū* made of an empty costume physically propelled by the scene's action and manipulated in midair by cables.

The meticulous work is elevated by the talent of the camera operators, who employ low-angle shots and ground-level framing and sometimes shoot between a monster's legs to create a contrast in scale in relation to the set. The action can be filmed directly on a miniature set or even from inside a building to enhance the sense of size and for greater impact. These techniques continue to evolve, as in recent years with the use of miniature cameras like the GoPro, enabling unprecedented, dynamic shots that bring the action closer than ever.

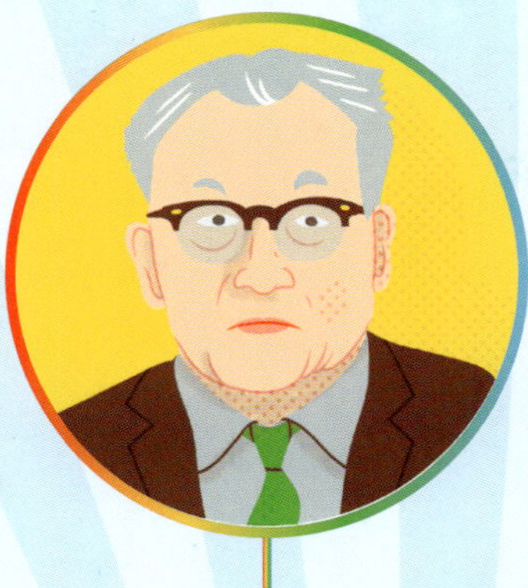

EIJI TSUBURAYA (1901–1970)

Eiji Tsuburaya is considered the god of special effects for his massive influence. An enthusiast of miniatures since childhood, he worked for studios like Nikkatsu in 1919 and Shochiku in 1925 before joining Toho in the 1930s, where his work in special effects left a lasting impact. The 1954 version of *Godzilla* gave him the boost he needed to found his own studio, Tsuburaya Productions, in 1963. He passed away at only sixty-eight years old but left an indelible mark on the industry.

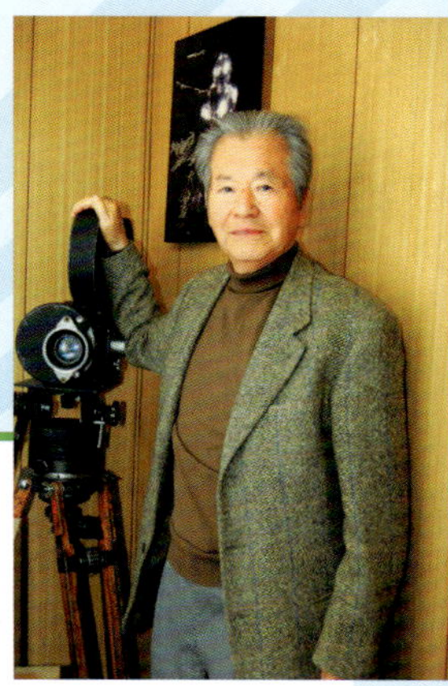

SPECIAL EFFECTS LABORATORY

Following in Tsuburaya's footsteps, special effects director Nobuo Yajima founded Tokusatsu Kenkyūjo (literally, special effects laboratory) in 1965, a studio dedicated to creating special effects scenes for movies and TV shows for studios such as Toei. He worked on franchises that included *Kamen Rider* and *Super Sentai*. The studio is still active today, working to keep its technical knowledge alive and maintain a *tokusatsu* touch in its creations, miniatures, effects, and explosions.

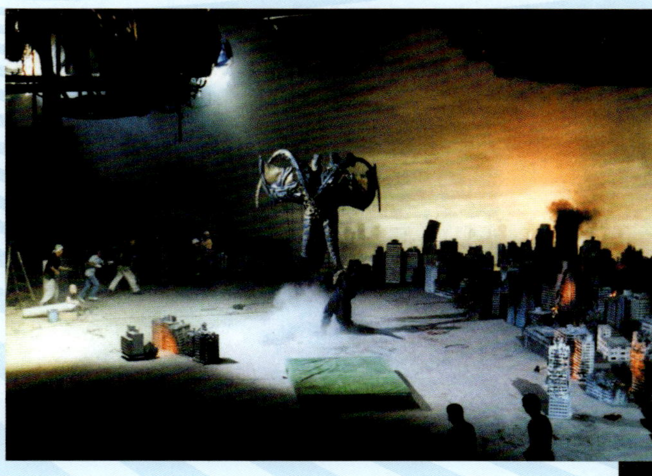

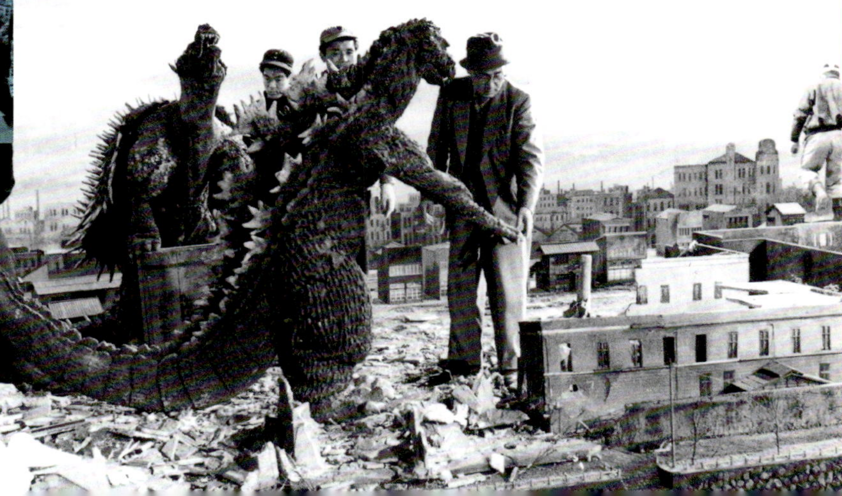

↗ **Above right:** *Nobuo Yajima, another major figure in Japanese special effects.*

↑ **Above:** *Set of* Godzilla: Final Wars *(2004).*

→ **Right:** *Eiji Tsuburaya on the set of* Godzilla Raids Again *(1955), standing between the film's two kaijū.*

← **Opposite:** *Eiji Tsuburaya with Ultraman, the superhero who changed everything.*

NEW MILLENNIUM, NEW KAIJŪ

MODERN KAIJŪ: A HUMOROUS TAKE

After the failure of *Godzilla: Final Wars*, a chill seemed to settle over the *kaijū* genre of movies. Although there was the odd standout here and there, including *Gamera the Brave* (2006), the industry found itself in a peculiar new era, one where humor and self-parody began creeping into the genre. After fifty years, some tropes and genres had been so overplayed and assimilated into Japanese culture that they had become a source of amusement. Comical *kaijū* films were nothing new, but after 2004, it felt as if the struggling genre needed to lighten the mood to recapture its past glory.

Big Man Japan (2007) kicked off the trend, led by comedian and television star Hitoshi Matsumoto. The film takes the tropes of giant superheroes like Ultraman and *kaijū* and sticks them in a mockumentary format. The plot features Masaru Daisatō, the tired heir of a long line of giant superheroes, struggling to reconcile his family legacy

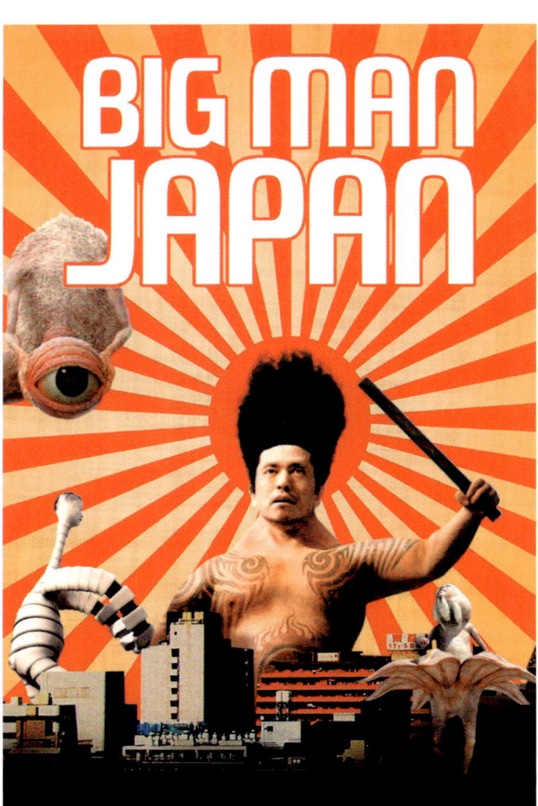

→ **Right:** *International poster for* Big Man Japan *(2007).*

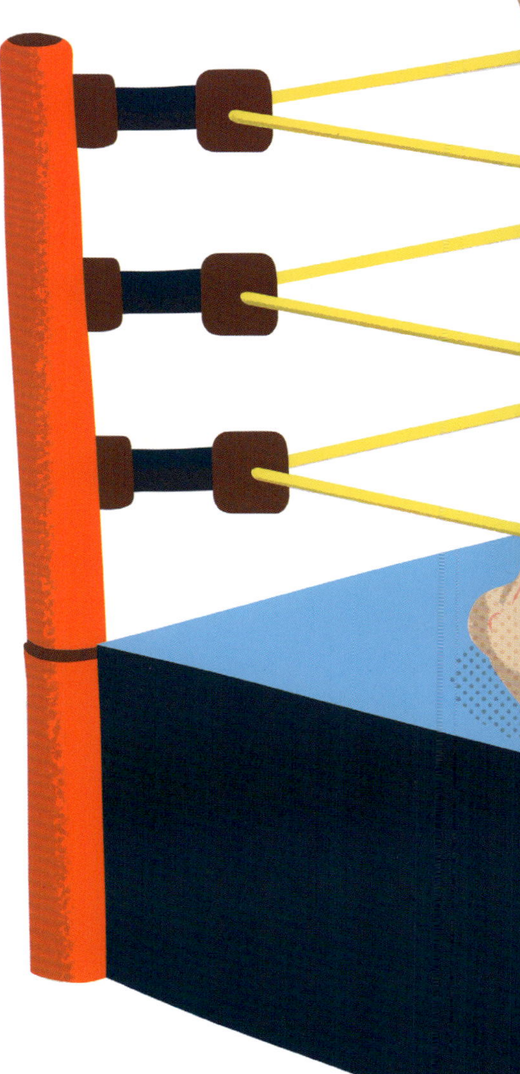

with modern Japan while searching for a successor. As always, Japan is constantly under attack by *kaijū*, but in this film, the creatures are more bizarre and unsettling than ever. Whereas *tokusatsu* taught us to expect strange and colorful designs, *Big Man Japan* embraced CGI to create a host of grotesque, disturbing, and funny monsters, such as a baby *kaijū* that must not be awakened, a hopping eyeball, and a tentacled creature with a conspicuous bald spot—a clear break from anything the genre had seen at the time. The film is relentlessly funny yet carries a poignant message about Japan's aging society and outdated traditions.

↓ **Below:** *With Godzilla on the sidelines, other monsters battled for the spotlight. (From left to right: A titan from* Attack on Titan*, Masaru Daisatō from* Big Man Japan*, and Nezura the kaijū rat made by Daiei).*

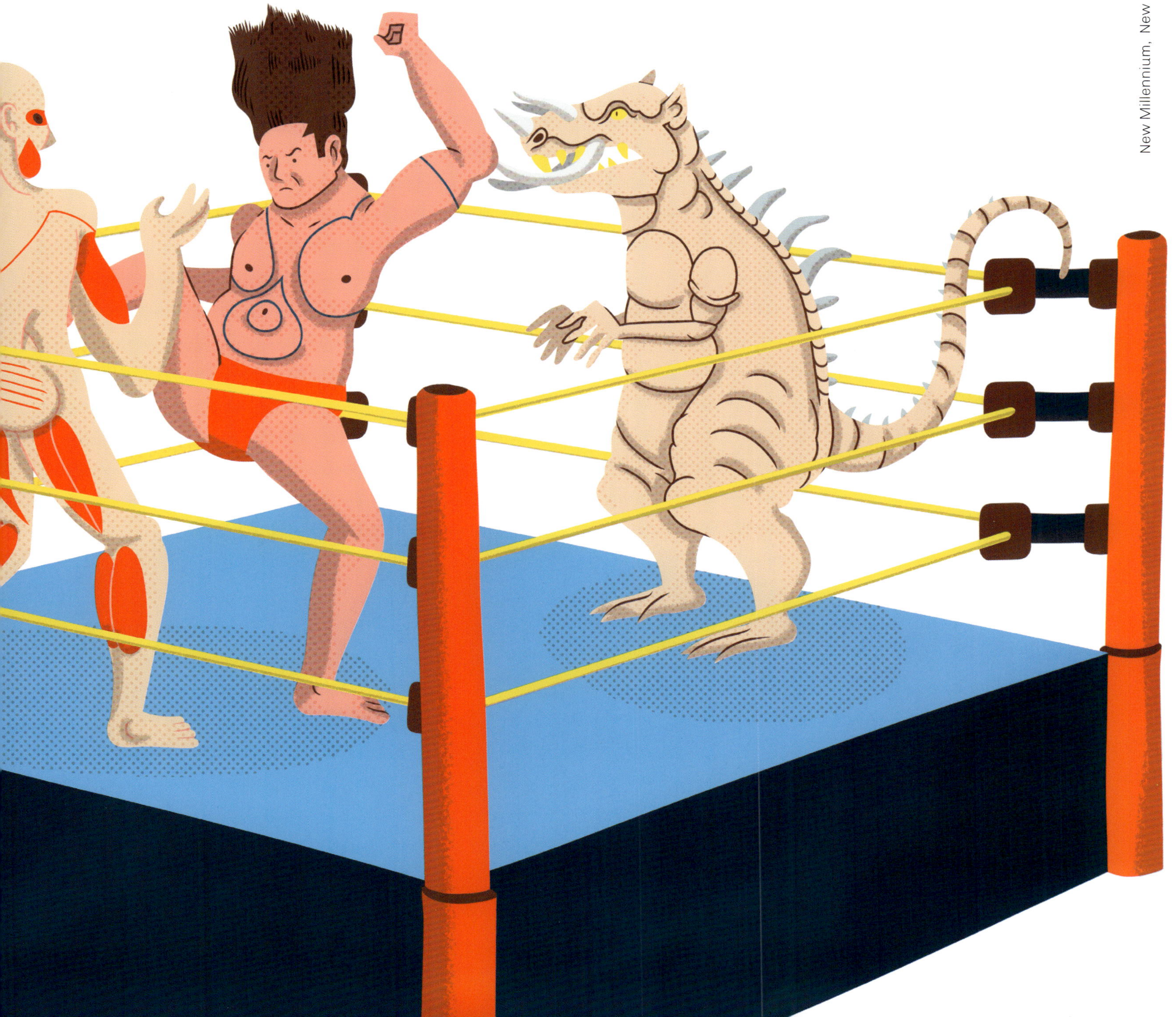

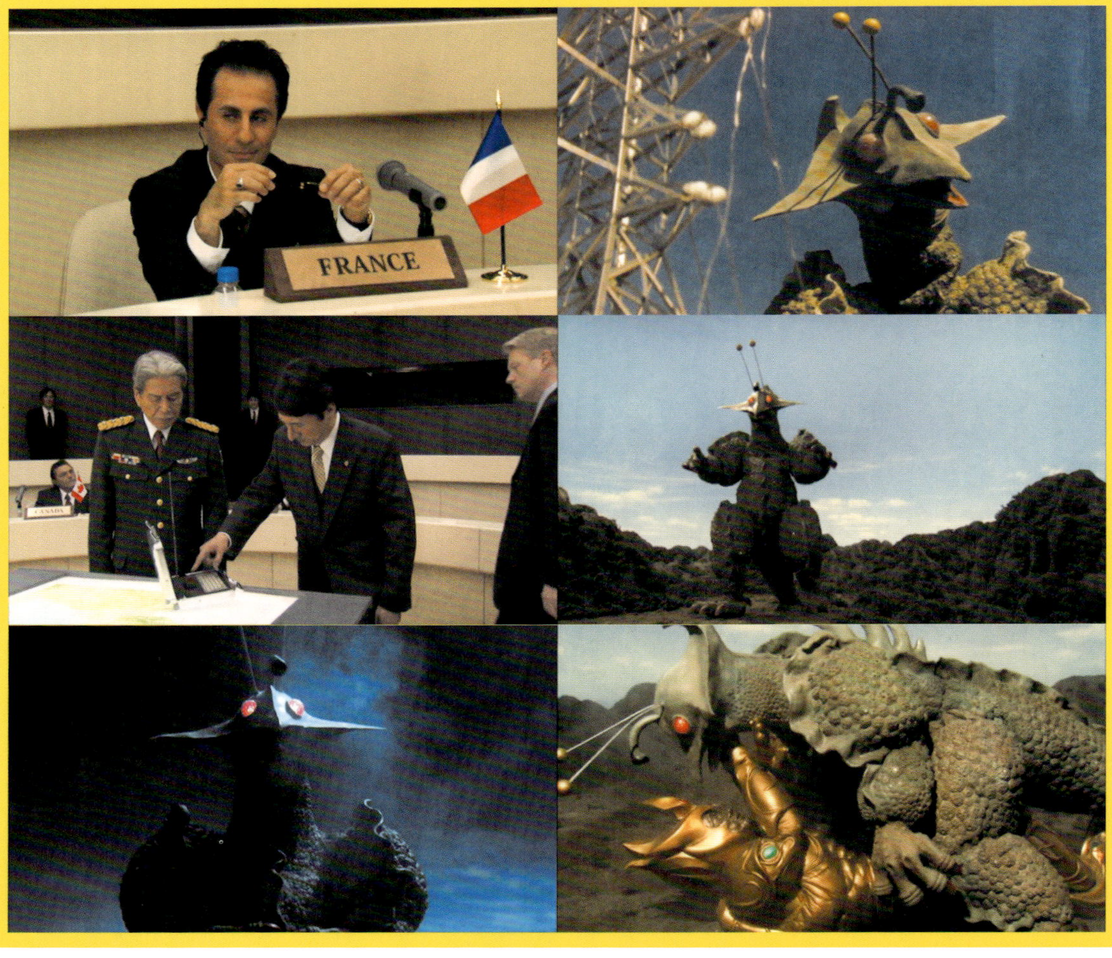

→ **Right:** *The film* Monster X Strikes Back: Attack the G8 Summit *(2008) combines kaijū humor and a critique of international (and Japanese) politics.*

A more satirical approach followed a year later with *The Monster X Strikes Back: Attack the G8 Summit* (2008), directed by Minoru Kawasaki. It resurrected the 1967 *kaijū* Guilala in a pastiche where the monster attacks Japan during a G8 summit, the political forum where government leaders gather to discuss the future of the world. Kawasaki asks the question: How would they react to such a monster? From there, he plays with *kaijū* tropes, leading to absurd reactions from the eight nations, which he then uses to deliver biting political satire, including a humorous caricature of former French president Nicolas Sarkozy, played by actor Kourosh Amini.

Kawasaki started out in the late 1980s with independent (some might say amateur) films before capitalizing on his growing fame to delve into *kaijū* cinema, as well as other genres, in the 2000s, with his unique use of absurd, goofy humor and often intentionally outdated techniques. Within the realm of *kaijū*, he addressed the aftermath of Fukushima in *Earth Defense Widow* (2014), staged improbable battles between a wrestler and *kaijū* in *Kaijū Mono* (2016), and offered solutions to world hunger by cooking up tasty *kaijū* in *Monster Seafood Wars* (2020).

Gradually, the irreverence for *kaijū* took hold far and wide. In 2009, NHK, one of Japan's largest television networks, produced the short film *Geharha: The Dark and Long Haired Monster*. It served as a heartfelt, amusing, yet deeply

series, most notably the *Ultraman* franchise. Over the years, he mastered the art of capturing and creating the illusion of size. Whereas the young Pikadon is played by animatronic characters, the grand finale plunges viewers into a quintessential *kaijū* scene featuring classic techniques that include a turtle in a costume and an impressive miniature city that serves as a playground for the action.

Taguchi shared his perspective on CGI in a behind-the-scenes featurette for the film. “It would have looked more realistic if we had used CGI for the whole thing,” he said, “but our method, using *tokusatsu* and miniatures . . . adds a bit of charm, which ultimately makes it more interesting.” He added, “If we had made the movie with CGI, it would have been a completely different film. I truly think we made the right choice.”

Taguchi declared in no uncertain terms that his visual choices for the project were deliberate, striking a balance between realism and the creative freedom offered by distinctly Japanese techniques. He aptly concluded by saying, “In this film, we thoroughly enjoyed taking full advantage of everything that *tokusatsu* has to offer.”

This lighthearted vision that has permeated *kaijū* cinema since the mid-2000s evinces a continued deep affection for *tokusatsu* and all its techniques, revealing that there is always a generation ready to carry on its legacy in all its forms.

MANGA AND TOKUSATSU: KINDRED SPIRITS

The key ingredients to *tokusatsu* productions in the challenging post-2004 era of today are passion and a readiness to take risks, as well as an awareness of the evolving technologies around us. And sometimes, in order to move forward, we must take stock of all that has been achieved.

In the summer of 2012, Hideaki Anno organized an exhibition at the Museum of Contemporary Art in Tokyo entirely dedicated to the art of *tokusatsu*, showcasing numerous costumes, set pieces, and other objects used in past productions of the genre. The goal was to celebrate *tokusatsu* and highlight its importance in Japanese culture, even as CGI loomed large. The crowning moment of the tribute was a ten-minute *tokusatsu* film titled *Giant God Warrior Appears in Tokyo* made by Studio Ghibli. It was written by Anno, directed by Shinji Higuchi, produced by Toshio Suzuki, and made possible by the technical team at Tokusatsu Kenkyūjo, a studio specializing in *tokusatsu*-style special effects.

In another connection to Hayao Miyazaki’s studio, the plot is based directly on the god warrior creature from

↓ **Below:** *Japanese poster, photograph from the Museum of Contemporary Art in Tokyo, and still from the short film* Giant God Warrior Appears in Tokyo *(2012).*

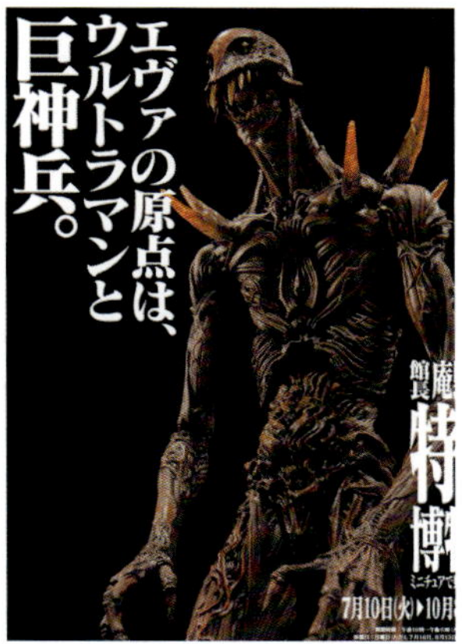

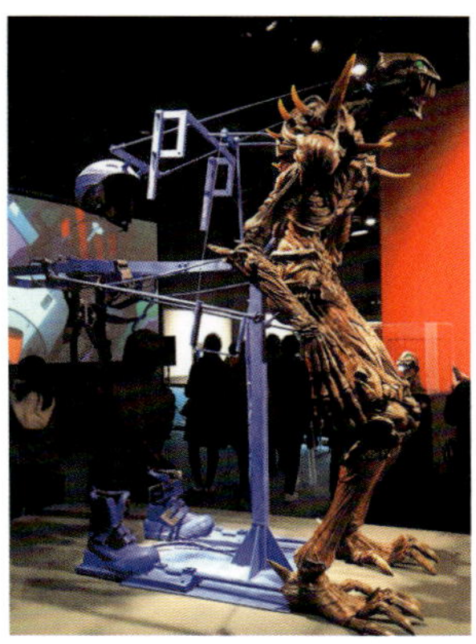

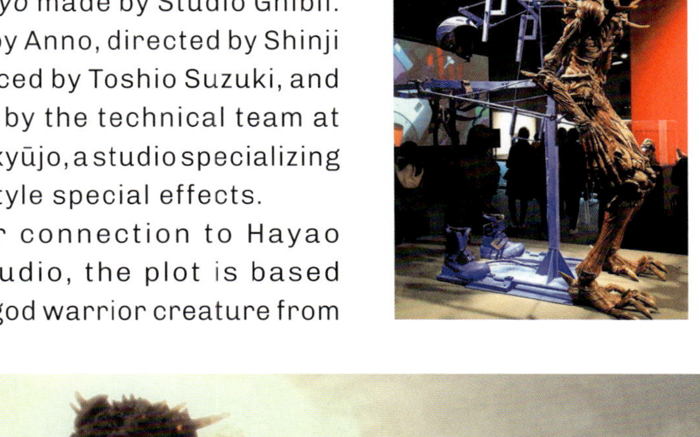

the manga and anime *Nausicaä of the Valley of the Wind* and is set in modern Japan. Its title perfectly encapsulates the premise of an impending apocalypse following an invasion of Tokyo by the infamous warriors.

The movie's triumph lies not only in its complex, detailed, formidable *kaijū* but also the monster's acting and movements. In a display of technical prowess, the giants were actually life-sized puppets. Instead of using wires to manipulate them from above, a puppeteer was dressed head to toe in a blue-screen suit, which was connected to the back of the puppet by a metal structure and several carefully placed cables. The puppet and its master thus moved simultaneously, with the puppet replicating the actor's movements when an arm was raised, the head tilted or legs moved in a walking motion. Thanks to the blue-screen suit, the puppeteer could be digitally erased in the final rendering. The film was masterfully done and became Studio Ghibli's first—and, to date, only—live-action production.

Because manga and anime are the main driving forces of Japanese pop culture, it's no surprise that *tokusatsu* occasionally draws inspiration from them—and vice versa—and even adapts their stories. When it comes to the giant monster genre of the 2010s, one memorable work that lent itself well to a *tokusatsu* adaptation was Hajime Isayama's renowned manga *Attack on Titan*.

In 2015, two films directed by Shinji Higuchi, as well as a three-episode miniseries, were released just two months apart. The project was initiated by Higuchi himself, who was enthralled by the early volumes of the manga and saw its potential for the big screen. The adaptation deliberately focused only on the initial premise of the original story and quickly veered off toward a different ending. However, the project offered plenty in return, thanks to Higuchi's skillful re-creation of the manga's despairing

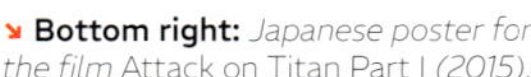

Bottom right: *Japanese poster for the film* Attack on Titan Part I *(2015).*

Bottom left: *Promotional photo of the cast of the* Attack on Titan *films. Liberties were taken with some of the heroes' weapons.*

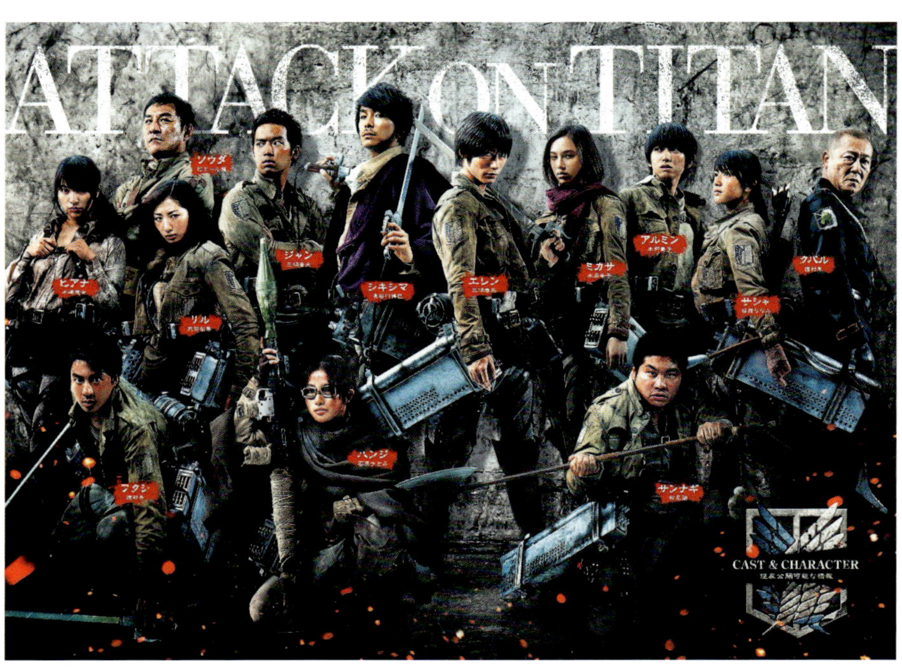

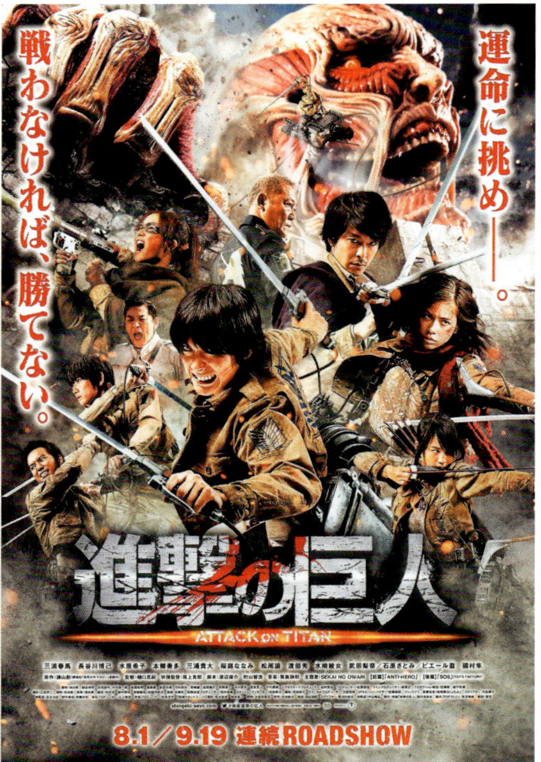

world and his aesthetic choices, which set it apart.

The movie exemplifies both *tokusatsu* and *kaijū*, the essences of which were evident even in the manga's pages. The Titans remain as grotesque and unsettling as ever, played by actors in costumes and intricate makeup. The Colossal Titan, towering two hundred feet tall in the story, was played by an enormous puppet operated by multiple crew members in blue-screen suits. Many action scenes featured models and other miniatures that could be destroyed in an instant.

The films allowed Higuchi to show off the best "traditional" *tokusatsu* techniques at a time when digital effects had already become dominant elsewhere, resulting in a visually striking project that swam against the current and proved that Japanese cinema was still a force to be reckoned with.

It is of particular interest in light of *Shin Godzilla*, released the following year, also directed by Higuchi. As mentioned previously, *Shin Godzilla* embraced the use of CGI, making Higuchi's *Attack on Titan* films his swan song of "old-school" *tokusatsu* productions. Yet they also form the perfect transition between the two approaches. As for the mournful scenes of cities devastated by Titans and the grief-stricken humanity depicted in *Attack on Titan*, Higuchi himself has stated that *Shin Godzilla* couldn't have attained the technical and aesthetic achievements that it did if he hadn't been able to experiment with special effects in *Attack on Titan*.

The *Attack on Titan* films suffer from being an adaptation of a manga that was unfinished at the time, forcing the team to improvise a self-contained ending, but they are a necessary milestone in Higuchi's filmography. They paved the way for him to reach new heights in his subsequent works, from *Godzilla* to *Shin Ultraman* in 2022.

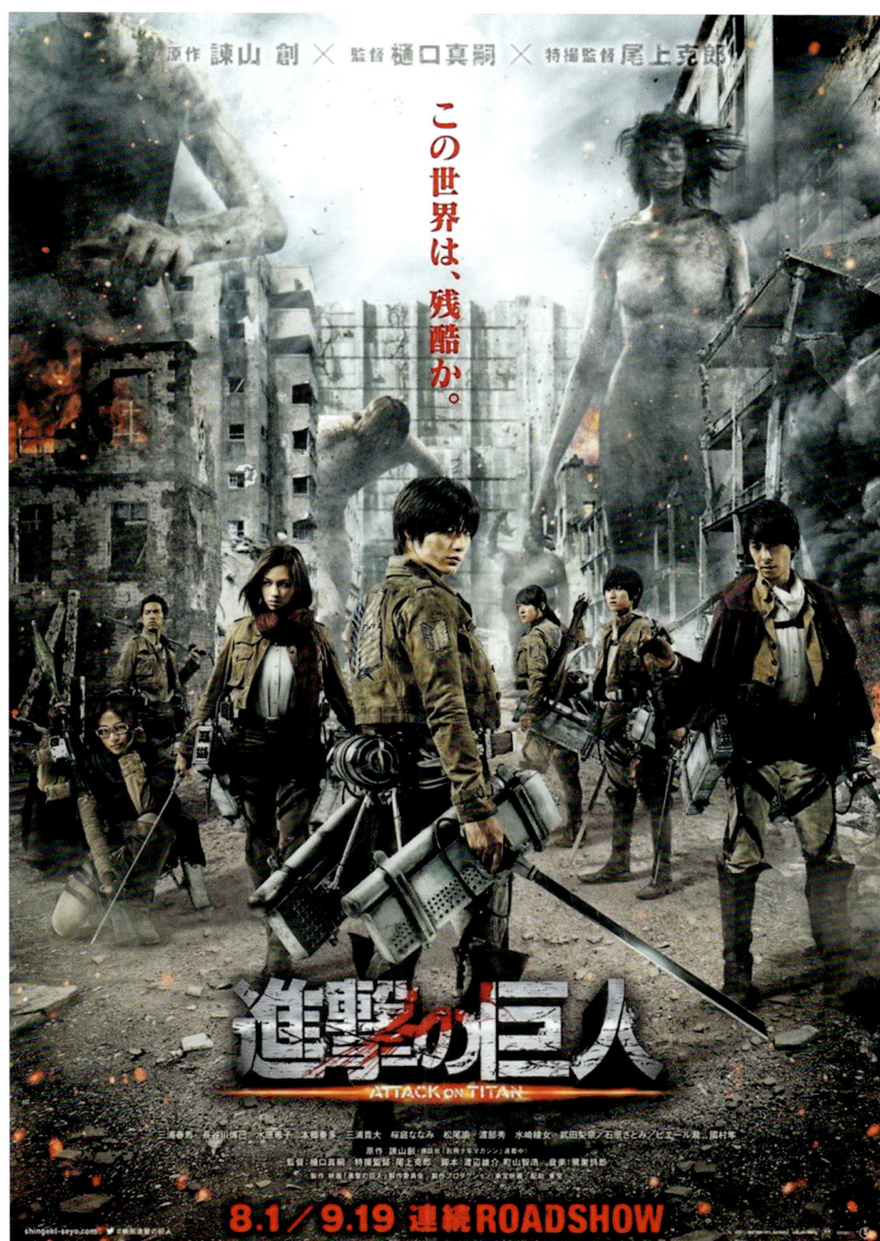

↑ Above: *Japanese poster for* Attack on Titan Part I *(2015).*

↓ **Below:** *Japanese poster for the film* Howl from Beyond the Fog *(2019)*

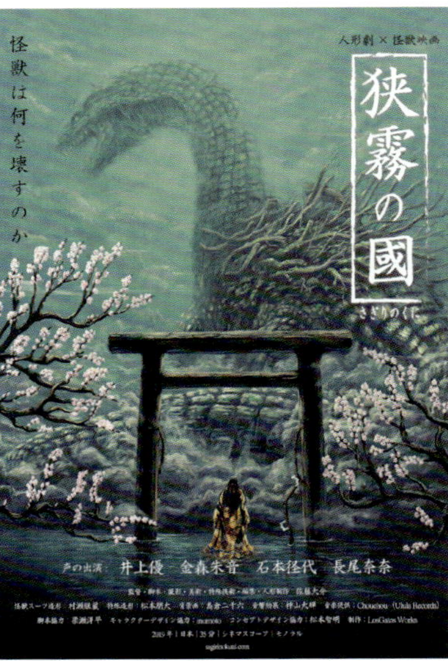

THE RISE OF INDIE STUDIOS

The *kaijū* genre may not be as prominent today as it was in its original form—as defined by its golden age, when so many pure cinema classics were born—but its fascination with giant creatures is more relevant than ever in the global pop culture landscape. Its tropes are now ubiquitous, its influence is undeniable, and most excitingly, there is a new generation of fans eager to expand on the stories. This brings us to a young yet highly promising studio named 3Y Film.

Founded in 2015, Studio 3Y Co. Ltd. specializes in audiovisual work for film and television, from marketing to video editing. One of its directors, Hiroto Yokokawa, created 3Y Film, a division dedicated solely to filmmaking. After producing a series of short student films to establish its credentials, Yokokawa embarked on the studio's first major project and no small feat: *The Great Buddha Arrival*, released in 2018.

The title evokes that forerunner to *kaijū* films, the aforementioned 1934 film of the same name—and that's no coincidence. Despite 3Y's status as an independent film studio with modest resources, Yokokawa and 3Y Film delivered a deftly constructed hybrid, turning the original film into a documentary about the urban legend of a Buddha statue near Tokyo in the 1930s that supposedly could come to life. More than a mere remake, the film drew from historical events (referencing the now-lost original film) and added the traditional hallmarks of a traditional monster movie.

Bolstered by its critical success, 3Y Film followed up in 2021 with *Nezura 1964*. Once again, the studio paid homage to forgotten *tokusatsu* films, this time presenting a fictionalized, lighthearted version of the story behind *Giant Horde Beast Nezura*, which was intended to be Daiei's first *kaijū* film—the one involving a giant rat—that famously failed. The medium-length film revisits the story while attempting to replicate the filming techniques of the era, including humorous sequences where live rats, guided by mirrors reflecting light through miniature cityscapes, refuse to cooperate. Behind-the-scenes footage shown in the film's closing credits reveals that the attempts were never truly successful, forming a perhaps unintentional meta commentary.

After a detour in 2022 with *Ghost-Cat Rhapsody*, a nod to the studio's ghost-cat films of the 1950s, Daiei returned to *kaijū* in October 2023 with a new production, *Hoshi 35*. The project was a crowdfunded original work, not an adaptation of a past franchise, and served as a tribute to 1990s *kaijū* films, embracing their style and themes. The film follows Mizuno, a geologist, and Yukari, a journalist, who are conducting research at the foot of Mount Amami when they stumble upon a village's horrifying tradition of sacrificing young women to appease the Great Star Beast, a supposed creature from the heavens.

Between these movies and a few other short films, the studio has proven passionate about the genre and seems destined for a bright future. In general, and particularly in recent years, *kaijū* productions have served up plenty of surprises, especially the ways in which the genre has been explored thus far: revivals of past eras, comedic angles, and unique aesthetics.

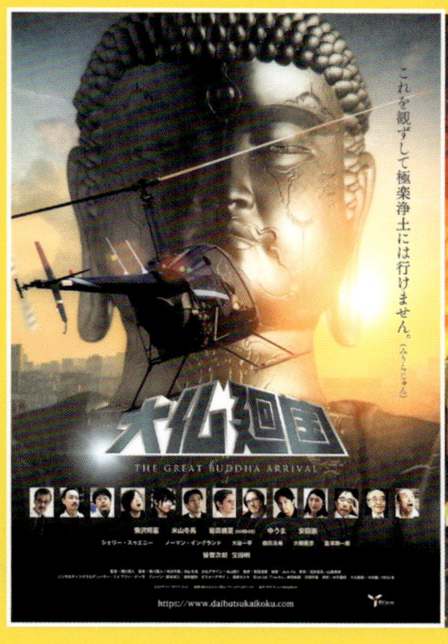

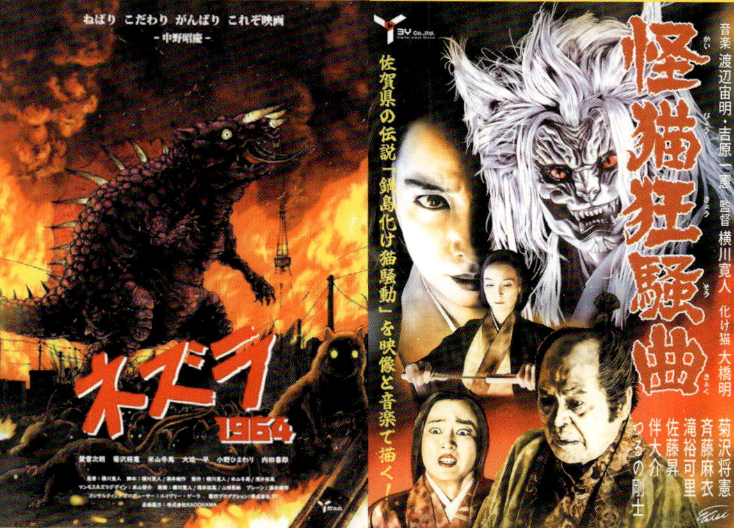

← **Left:** *Productions by 3Y Film. From left to right:* The Great Buddha Arrival *(2018),* Nezura 1964 *(2021), and* Ghost-Cat Rhapsody *(2022).*

Of the most recent examples, one movie stands out as proof positive that *tokusatsu* still has much to offer outside of major blockbusters. *Howl from Beyond the Fog* (2019)—directed by Daisuke Satō, who also directed *Hoshi 35*—takes a more poetic and intimate approach to *kaijū* storytelling, even in its very format, which uses puppets for the human characters and a traditional monster suit for the creature.

In a much lighter vein, two quirky films were released in 2022. *Yuzo: The Biggest Battle in Tokyo*, directed by Yoshikazu Ishii, tackles the sensitive subject of COVID-19 through the lens of a humorous *kaijū* film. Meanwhile, *What to Do with the Dead Kaijū?*, whose bigger budget was still relatively small for the genre, uses humor to address a long-ignored question: What does one do with a *kaijū*'s corpse after it has been defeated?

The monster movie genre continues to inspire filmmakers, and the sensational success of *Godzilla Minus One* suggests that the momentum is unlikely to slow down anytime soon. Could we be entering a new golden age? Though that remains to be seen, what's clear is that there is a generation ready to rise to the challenge, one that is intimately familiar with another equally significant pillar of the *tokusatsu* genre: superheroes.

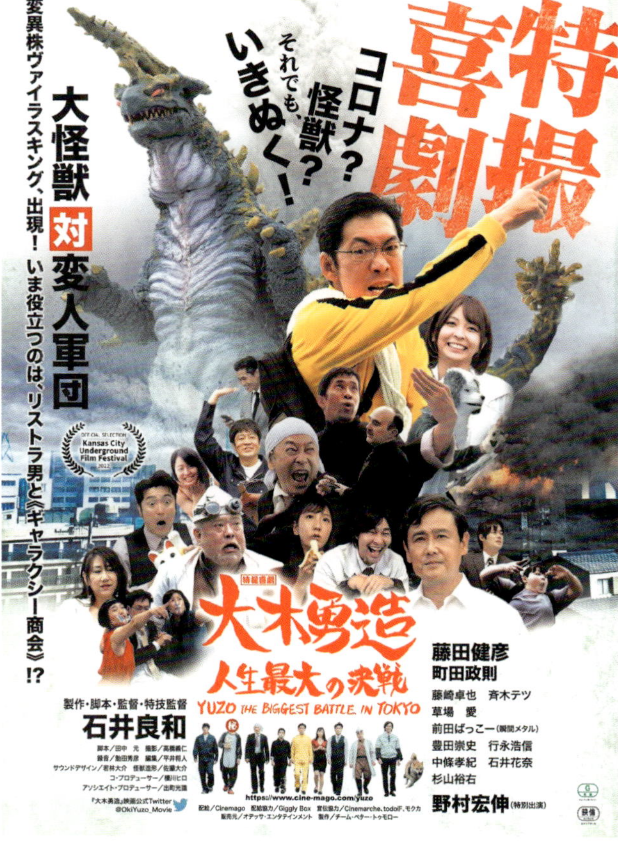

↓ **Below:** *Japanese poster for the film* Yuzo: The Biggest Battle in Tokyo *(2022), a kaijū film shot during the COVID-19 pandemic.*

SUPERHEROES

By now, you should have a clearer idea of what *tokusatsu* represents. But as you've likely understood, the term also describes Japanese superheroes, another subgenre that quickly became dominant and established the genre's rules, and which we've mentioned several times due to their immense influence. But what makes a superhero Japanese instead of Western or even American? Are they really so different?

We discuss them here for a very specific reason. Superheroes are integral to *tokusatsu*. Though superhero stories are also found in other media, such as manga and anime (*My Hero Academia*, *One Punch Man*), they live primarily on-screen, whether big or small. Whereas American superheroes were born out of, and continue to thrive in, comic books, in addition to TV and theaters, Japanese superheroes are primarily *tokusatsu* characters.

Compared to American superheroes, their Japanese counterparts are distinguished by their ability to unabashedly embrace visuals and abilities that seem outlandish by Western standards. Only *tokusatsu* can deliver, in earnest, giant superheroes wearing multicolored costumes inspired by a variety of sources and capable of transforming into improbable objects.

A prime example of the genre's vision is the concept of a team where each member is represented by a dominant color and owns a robot that can combine with others to form an even larger one. From the Western perspective, such concepts and ideas are often treated as peculiarities, with humor or irony, emphasizing their eccentricity. But for *tokusatsu* creators and enthusiasts, it is simply the norm.

Japanese superheroes are also shaped by an entire visual, physical language inspired directly by *kabuki*, Japan's most expressive theater tradition. *Kabuki* has been around for centuries and focuses heavily on spectacle, from extravagant, colorful costumes to exaggerated acting and spectacular set designs one might be tempted to call special effects. *Tokusatsu* heroes are essentially a modern version of *kabuki*, evident in the way they face off with enemies, their combat style, and their habit of striking a pose upon victory. Though things may have evolved over time, *tokusatsu* heroes have kept up these traditions, which remain quite unique. It's their way of standing out, and ultimately, it's what makes the shows so appealing.

Below: Super Sentai, *the biggest tokusatsu franchise of all time.*

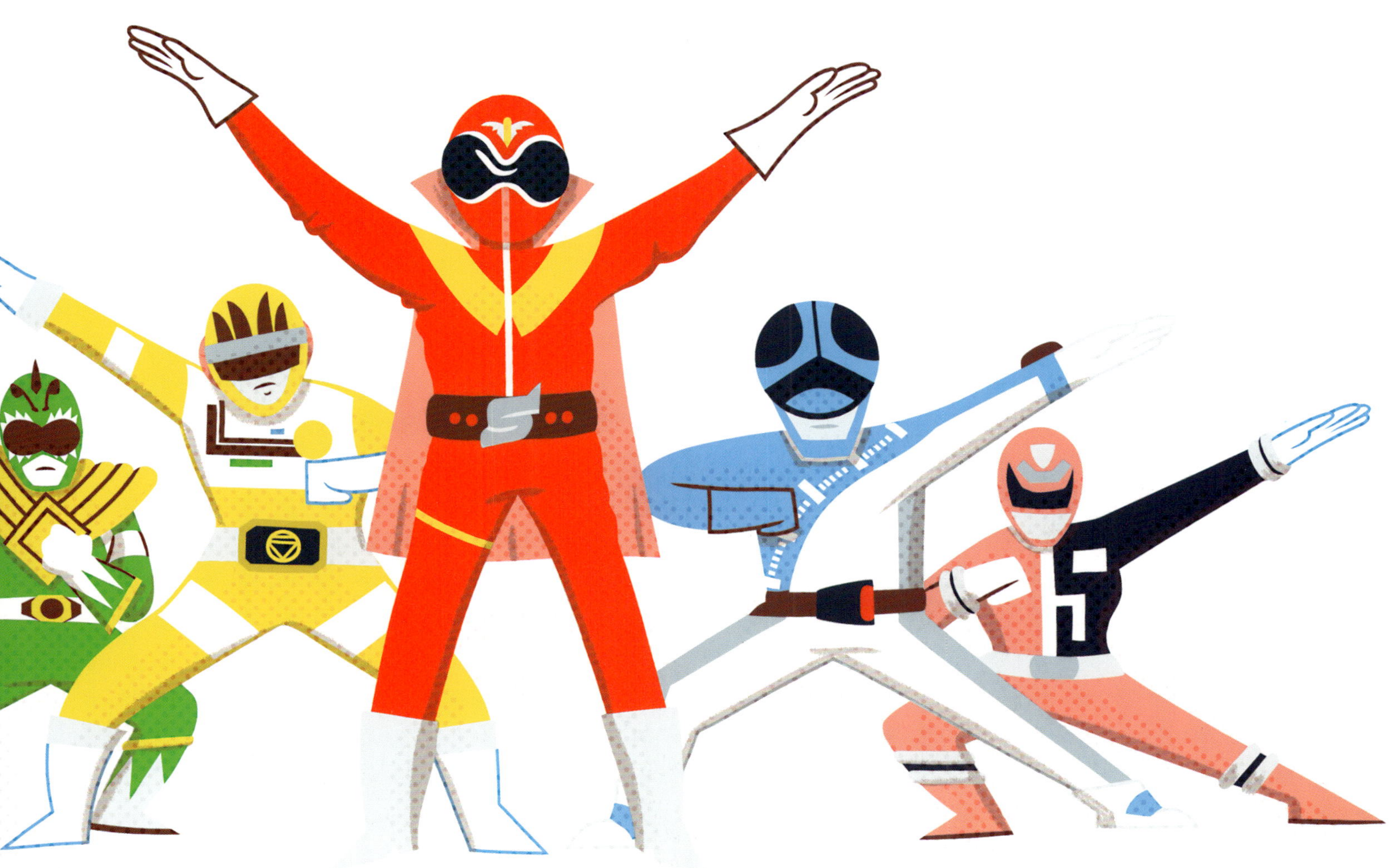

PRE-1966: SUPERHEROES IN BLACK AND WHITE

THE EARLY DAYS OF THE SMALL SCREEN

To understand the origins of Japanese superheroes, we need to travel back in time nearly a hundred years, before superheroes became associated with TV and movies.

The first superhero recognized as such by Japanese audiences was created in 1931 by Takeo Nagamatsu. He was named Ōgon Bat (literally, the Golden Bat) and was a hero of *kamishibai*, a form of street theater where a storyteller would narrate tales accompanied by a series of illustrations. Remarkably, Ōgon Bat predates figures better known in the West, including Superman (1938) and Batman (1939), by several years. Though not yet considered *tokusatsu*, the seeds of the genre had been planted.

Despite his intimidating appearance, Ōgon Bat found an audience among children, enabling him to remain popular even through the difficult war years. The character appeared in various formats outside of *kamishibai*, though his first true *tokusatsu* adventure came in 1966 thanks to Toei. By then, however, other heroes had already claimed the spotlight.

Inspired by the success of superhero serials[1] in the West, Japan began creating its own series, including *Super Giant*, introduced in 1957. Resembling Superman in many ways, Super Giant became the first true superhero of the big screen, starring in nine films between 1957 and 1959.

Television sought its own thrilling programming. TV was a fledgling medium in 1953 and couldn't hope to rival celluloid productions. The strategy had to be reformulated. In 1958, Kōhan Kawauchi created Moonlight Mask, a masked vigilante akin to Batman or Zorro, though more down-to-earth and not yet a full-fledged superhero. His adventures occasionally included fantastical elements, but Moonlight Mask was primarily a vigilante without superpowers. Armed only with his fists, a couple of guns, and a motorcycle, he captured the imagination of Japanese audiences like never before.

The TV series was produced by Senkosha, whereas its movie adaptations were made by Toei. This spurred the creation of similar superheroes, such as 1959's Seven Color Mask, who was capable of multiple transformations. These early works lacked the traits we now associate with Japanese superheroes, but they laid the initial foundation for the genre and presaged what was to come in 1966.

In a way, 1966's Ōgon Bat marked the end of an era and a transition to a period of new superheroes steeped in modern science fiction. With the advent of color productions and larger-than-life storytelling on the small screen, the stage was set for the arrival of *Ultraman*.

1. Films released in theaters in multiple short installments, much like TV shows later.

↓ **Below:** *Early tokusatsu superheroes won over new audiences, thanks in part to television. From left to right: Seven Color Mask, Moonlight Mask, and Ōgon Bat.*

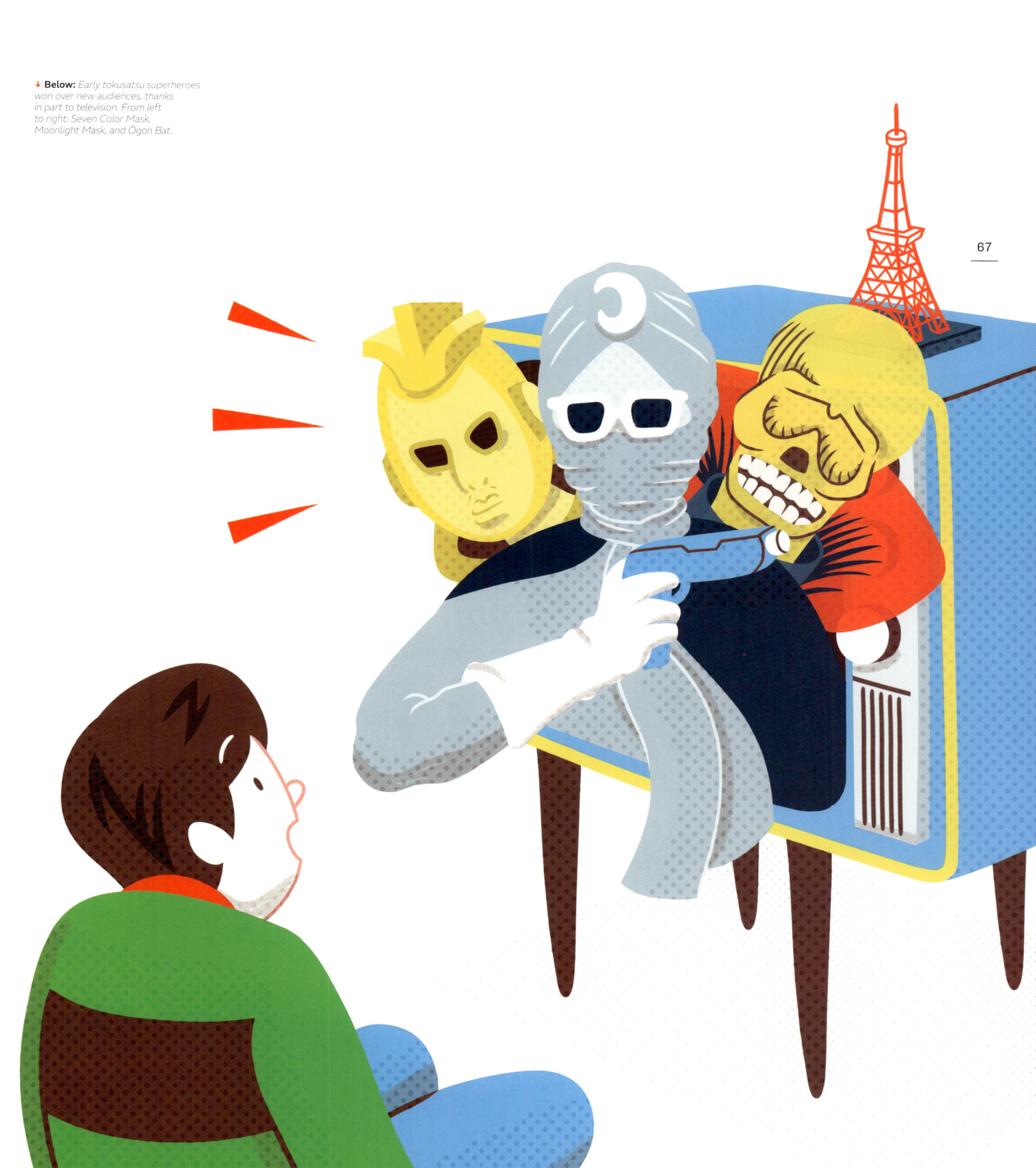

ULTRAMAN: THE GIANT WITH THE BLINKING LIGHT

THE GENESIS

Having worked on numerous projects for Toho, Eiji Tsuburaya decided to found his own company, Tsuburaya Productions, in 1963. The company started off doing work for other studios, but by 1966, its focus had shifted to making its own *tokusatsu* productions. This was a pivotal year for *tokusatsu* and particularly for the superhero genre, with the rise of the *kyodai hero* or "giant heroes."

But first, there was *Ultra Q* in January 1966, a TV series spotlighting *kaijū* but no superheroes. It was Japan's answer to *The Twilight Zone*, an American TV series featuring standalone episodes with bizarre, sometimes morally ambiguous tales. *Ultra Q* was the studio's opportunity to bring giant monsters to television, a format previously deemed too expensive. Its immediate success spurred Tsuburaya to push further.

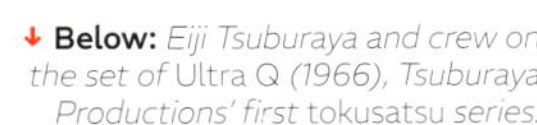

Below: *Eiji Tsuburaya and crew on the set of* Ultra Q *(1966), Tsuburaya Productions' first* tokusatsu *series.*

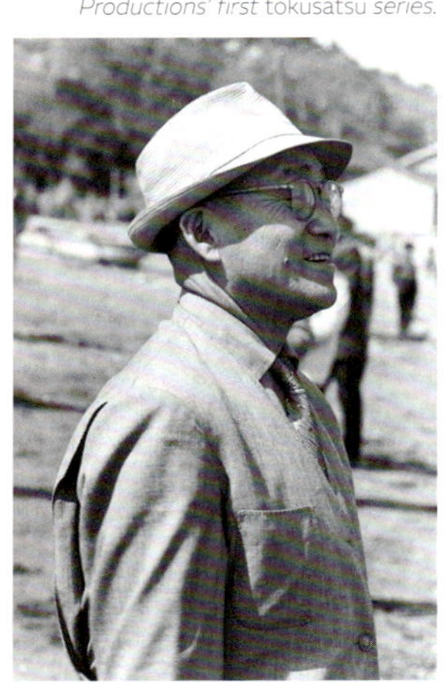

Originally, *Ultra Q* included plans for an alien with a sleek, humanoid design. Though unused in the show, the alien was redesigned and eventually received its own show. By July 1966, the modified alien had become Ultraman, an extraterrestrial that crashes on Earth while chasing a space creature. To survive Earth's atmosphere, Ultraman merges with Shin Hayata, a pilot he injures during his fall. This fusion lets Ultraman switch between human form, working as part of the Science Patrol investigating alien threats, and his usual form, a *kaijū*-fighting giant over a hundred feet tall.

In each episode, the storyline allotted a specific amount of screen time to action. A light on Ultraman's chest blinked whenever time was running out before he had to revert to his human form, also helping establish the time limit.

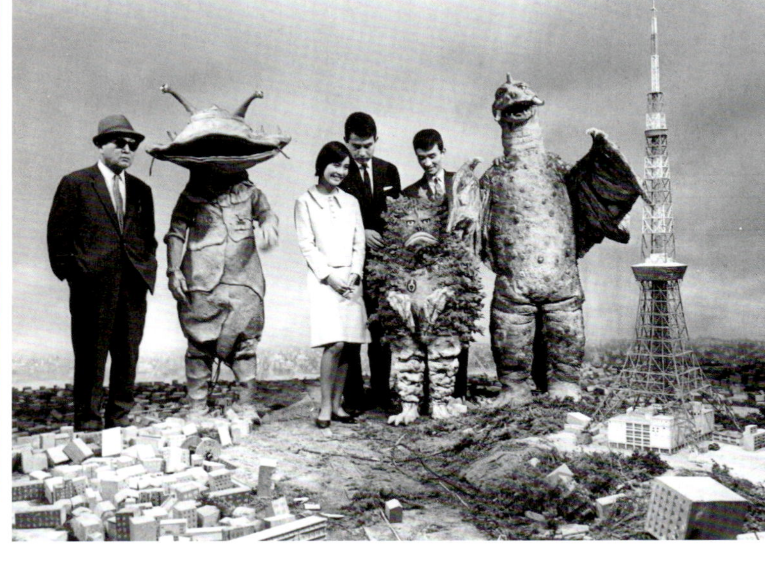

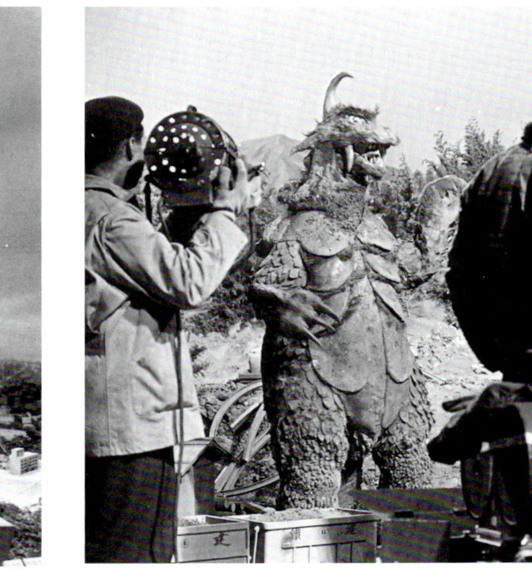

A revolution was underway. For the first time, in the same year and through two different series, audiences could watch *kaijū*, science fiction, and fantastical superheroes (as opposed to the more human heroes of black-and-white series) on television rather than in theaters, a shift that contributed to a decline in ticket sales.

The series entrenched and built upon the formula established by *Ultra Q*, with a new monster in every episode and a multitude of ways to tell stories and play with science fiction and a variety of themes. Sometimes, the plot was presented in a very straightforward manner. A monster appears out of nowhere, and only Ultraman can stop it. Other times, it was humorous, like in the episode where a *kaijū* has the power to distort reality. They could also be more serious or even moving, raising questions about humanity's impact on the aliens.

The following year, Tsuburaya raised the stakes with *Ultraseven*, a series in the same vein but featuring a new superhero. The formula was refined, introducing new concepts like "pocket *kaijū*" that superheroes could carry in capsules—a concept that directly inspired the *Pokémon* franchise. The quality of the screenwriting made many of its episodes iconic.

← **Left:** *A beta capsule, seen in the first series, which gives Ultraman his ability to transform.*

↓ **Below:** *Ultraman's iconic stance when shooting his famous Spacium beam to kill kaijū.*

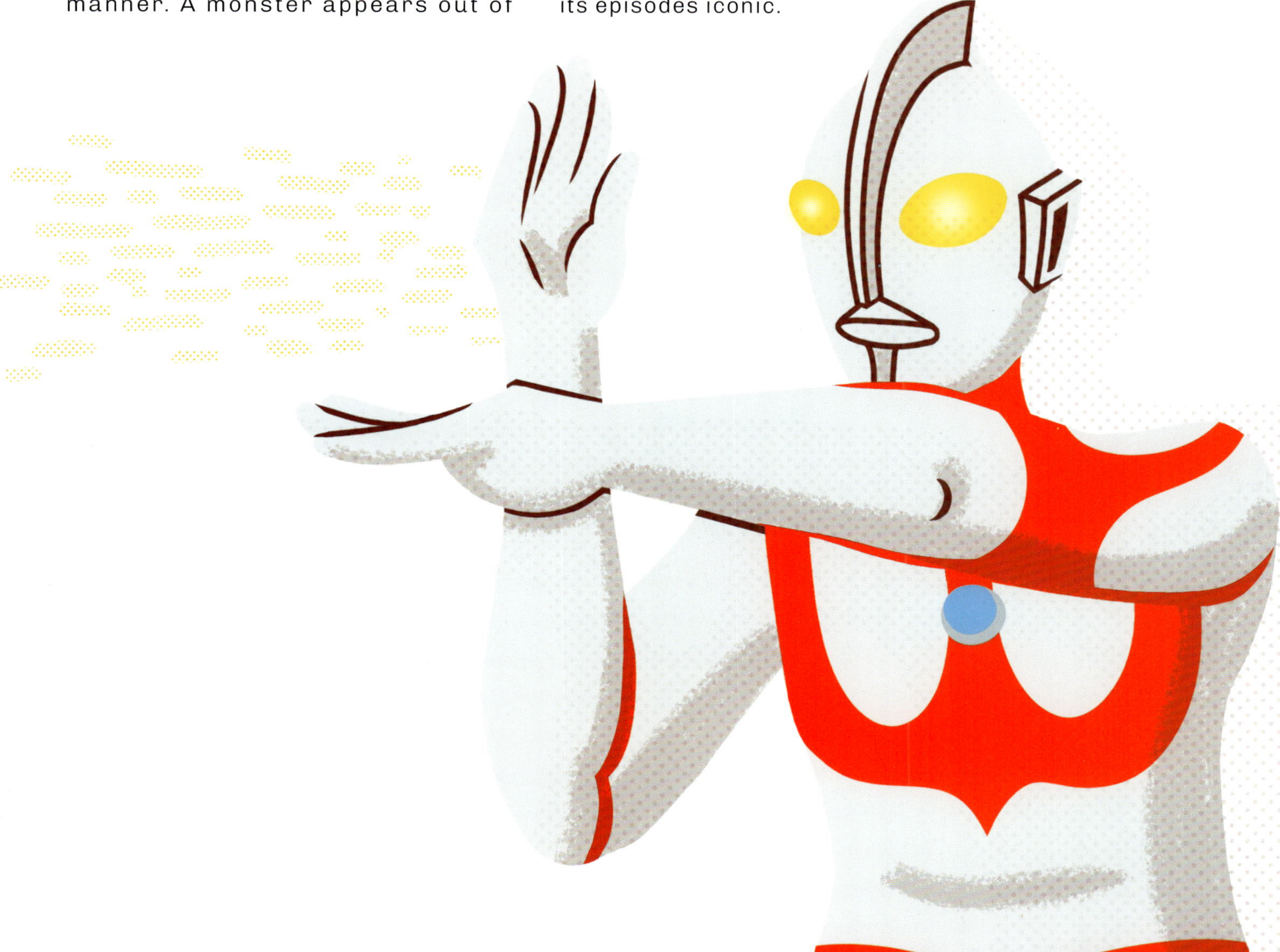

↓ **Below:** *Ultraman and the blinking chest light indicating imminent danger.*

However, these series remained as costly as they were ambitious. After *Ultraseven*, Tsuburaya shelved giant superheroes to explore other approaches to science fiction with series like *Mighty Jack* and *Fight! Mighty Jack*, both released in 1968, though they proved to be less popular. Eiji Tsuburaya passed away in

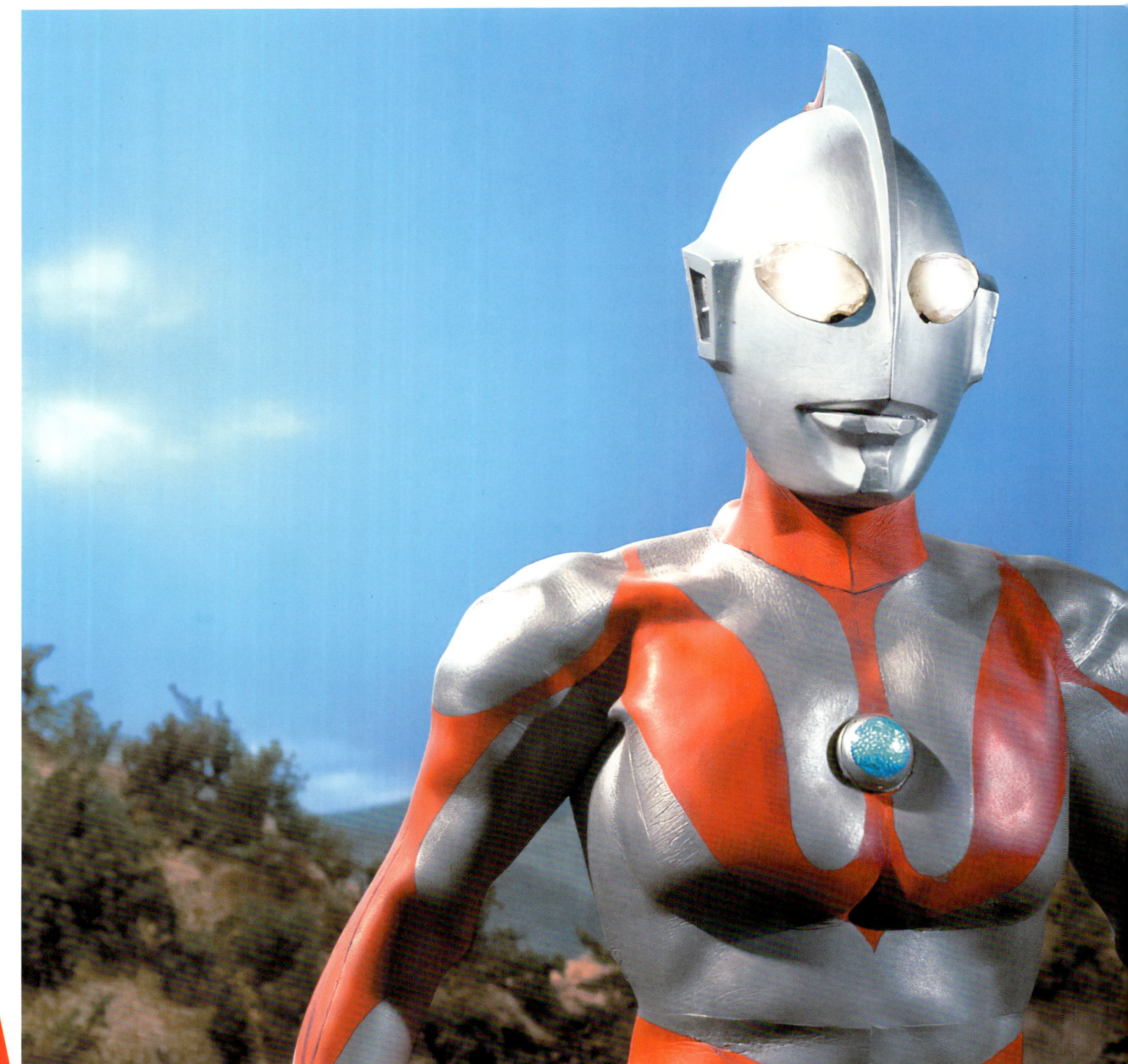

1970, prompting the studio to rethink its direction for the years ahead.

THE PANTHEON

The 1970s brought significant changes to superheroes as households began adopting televisions. TV networks demanded content, and *tokusatsu* leaped at the opportunity. *Ultraman* made a tentative return in 1970 with the peculiar *Ultra Fight*, consisting of 196 episodes averaging three minutes each. Half were compilations of Ultraman and Ultraseven battles with running sports commentary, while the rest were low-budget new footage. The series backed off of its original superhero concept as much as possible, enabling the studio to stay afloat long enough until the boom in television occurred.

Ultra Fight achieved notable success and paved the way for *Return of Ultraman* in 1971, which marked a true new entry in the franchise with 51 episodes and a return to the twenty-four-minute format. It was a turning point for an entire generation (frequently cited by Hideaki Anno as a key influence) and rekindled the franchise's former glory.

An important detail for what follows: With its new hero capable of transforming into Ultraman Jack, the series eventually reintroduced Ultraman and Ultraseven as companions who come to the aid of Ultraman Jack. This concept laid the groundwork for what we now call a shared universe, a feature that would soon become central to the franchise. *Ultraman Ace* (1972), *Ultraman Taro* (1973), and *Ultraman Leo* (1974) were all given the title Ultraman before their individual given names, and together they formed the Ultra Brothers, a team of superheroes.

Ultraman Ace introduced a new dynamic with two protagonists, a man and a woman who merged to become a single giant superhero. The series

Below: *American poster for a film consisting of compilations of clips from the series* Mighty Jack *(1968).*

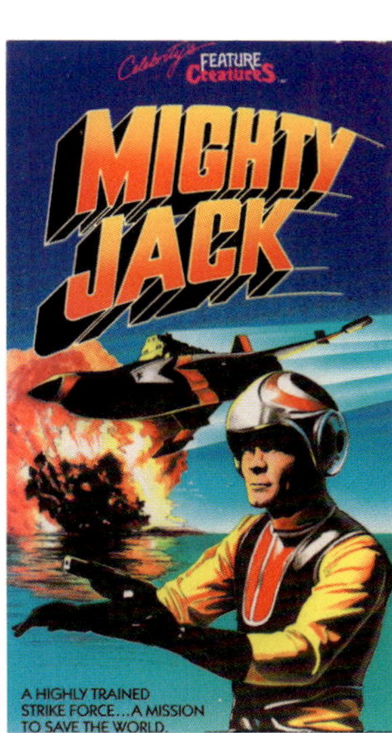

Below: *Eleking, an iconic* kaijū *from the series* Ultraseven *(1967).*

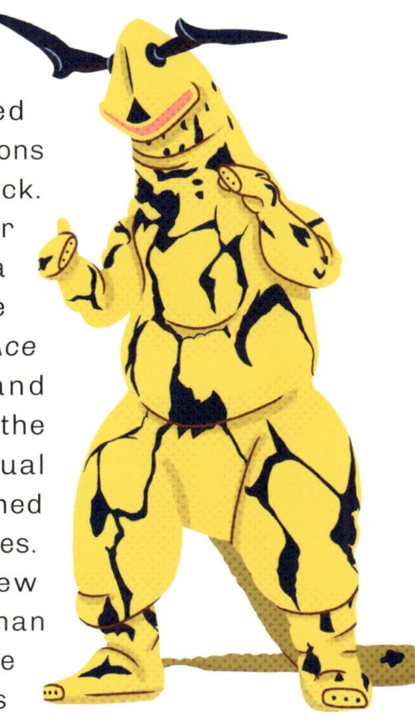

→ **Right:** *Two promotional images for* Ultraman 80 *(1980).*

↘ **Center:** *Ultraman Taro battling the mortar* kaijū.

↓ **Below:** *Ultraman Jack in* Return of Ultraman *(1971) and his human alter ego, Hideki Gō.*

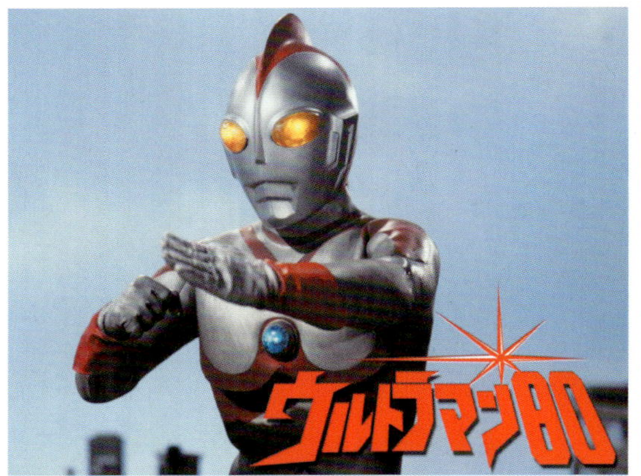

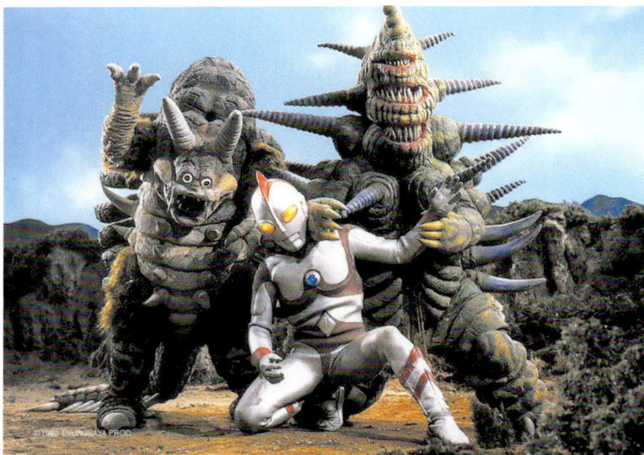

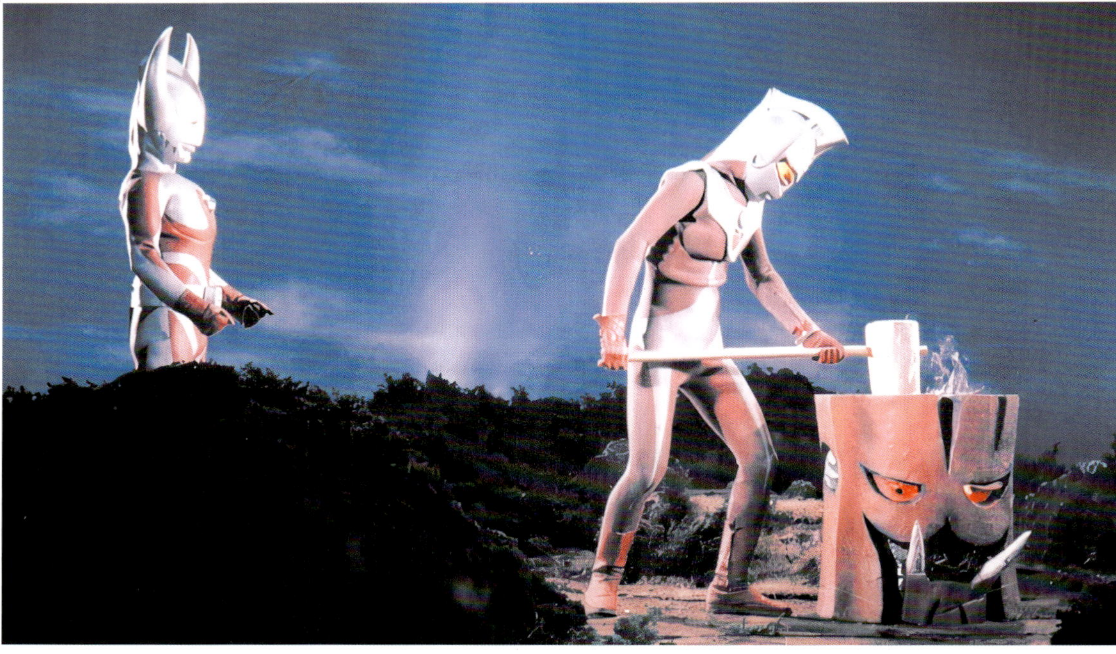

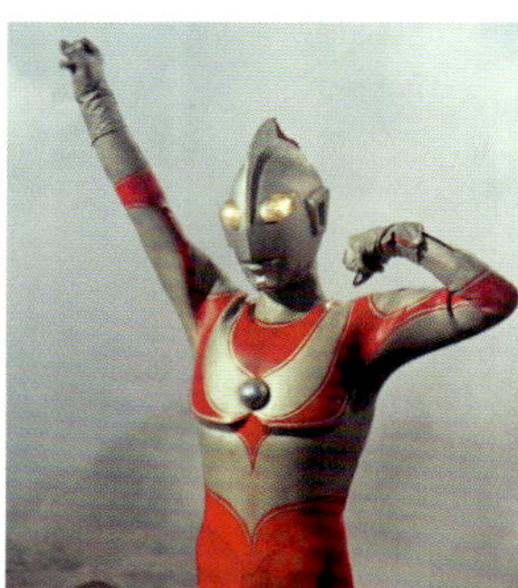

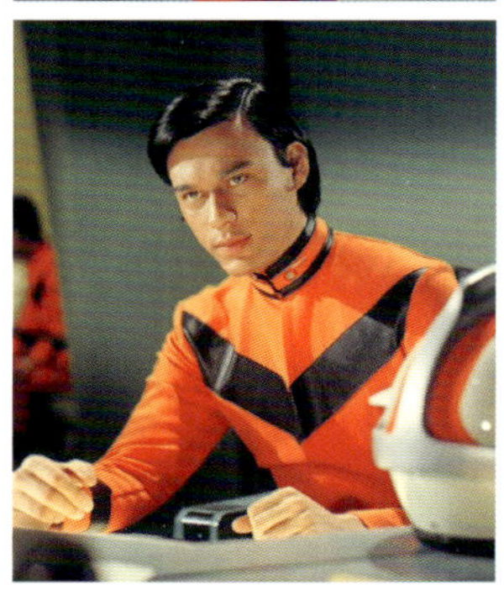

also featured a mix of highly whimsical episodes (such as one in *Ultraman Taro*, where he battles a *kaijū* inspired by the traditional Japanese mortar used for making mochi, a rice flour confection) and others that expanded on the shared universe by including all the Ultraman heroes introduced so far.

Eventually, the formula began to lose steam. Under the added pressure of squabbles within the Tsuburaya family over how to manage the franchise, Ultraman was ultimately sidelined for a few years. The character reappeared in the animated series *The Ultraman* in 1979, then returned to *tokusatsu* with *Ultraman 80* in 1980, this time not as a member of a scientific or military organization but as a schoolteacher—a deliberate choice made in an effort to restore the reputation of the teaching profession during a period when Japanese youth were becoming increasingly disengaged from school. However, the series failed to resonate and remains a minor entry in the franchise. Tsuburaya didn't quite know what to do with it and put the franchise on hold for nearly fifteen years.

Well, not entirely, because in 1983, Tsuburaya produced *Andro Melos*, a low-budget spin-off. Instead of boxing matches in an arena, it offered a small-scale space adventure of Ultramen in battle armor

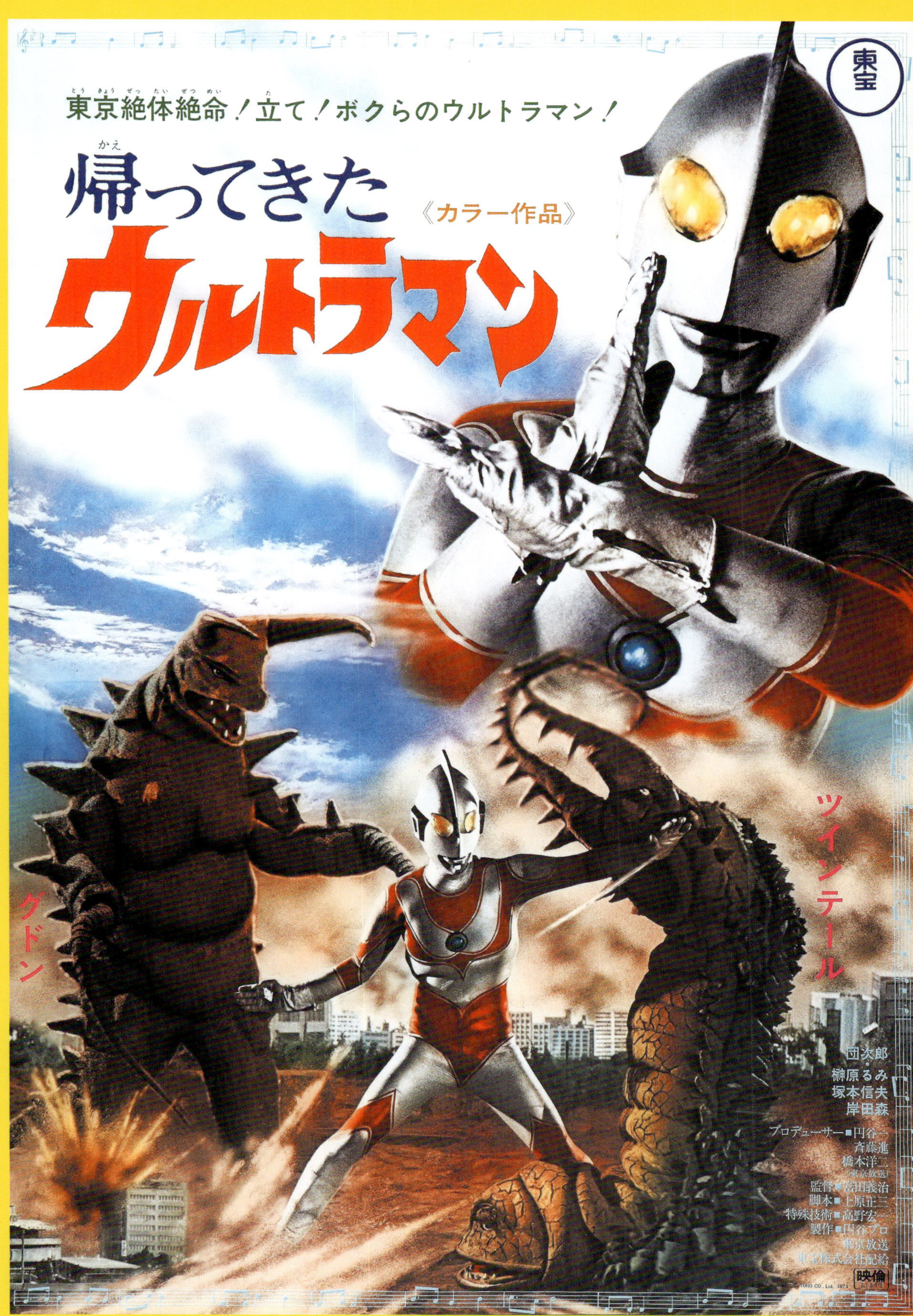

Left: *In the 1970s, several tokusatsu TV series compiled clips into movies for special screenings. Shown is the Japanese poster for the first film based on* Return of Ultraman *(1971).*

fighting a new threat. The whole production operated on a shoestring budget. All scenes were filmed in-studio, with no outdoor shots, and the short five-minute format was a clear indication that the forty-five-episode series was meant to serve as a stopgap measure.

It wasn't until 1996 that Ultraman returned in much better form. In the meantime, the franchise was kept alive through side projects, including animated series and films, notably *Ultraman: The Adventure Begins*, released in 1987 in collaboration with American studio Hanna-Barbera.

THE BIG COMEBACK

Tsuburaya Productions had been churning out innovations since the 1990s. Bolstered by its modest experience with animation through *Ultraman: The Adventure Begins*, the studio ventured outside Japan once more with *Ultraman: Towards the Future* and *Ultraman: The Ultimate Hero*.

Ultraman: Towards the Future was an Australian production filmed in English with local actors. It was first released in 1990 on the Japanese home video market before airing on Australian television in 1992. It was a low-budget series, with Australia's often-barren landscapes proving helpful for the setting. The series consisted of only thirteen episodes and was (indirectly) followed by *Ultraman: The Ultimate Hero*, an American production, in 1993.

For both series, production was reportedly difficult at times due to a lack of experience on the English-speaking side and the challenges of long-distance communication with Japan. Although a few Japanese experts in the genre managed to visit the sets, including Shinji

↑ **Above:** *Andro Melos, the superhero from the eponymous 1983 series and an integral part of the Ultraman universe.*

↓ **Below:** Ultraman: The Adventure Begins *is an American-Japanese joint animated film from 1989 and an attempt to export the Ultraman concept.*

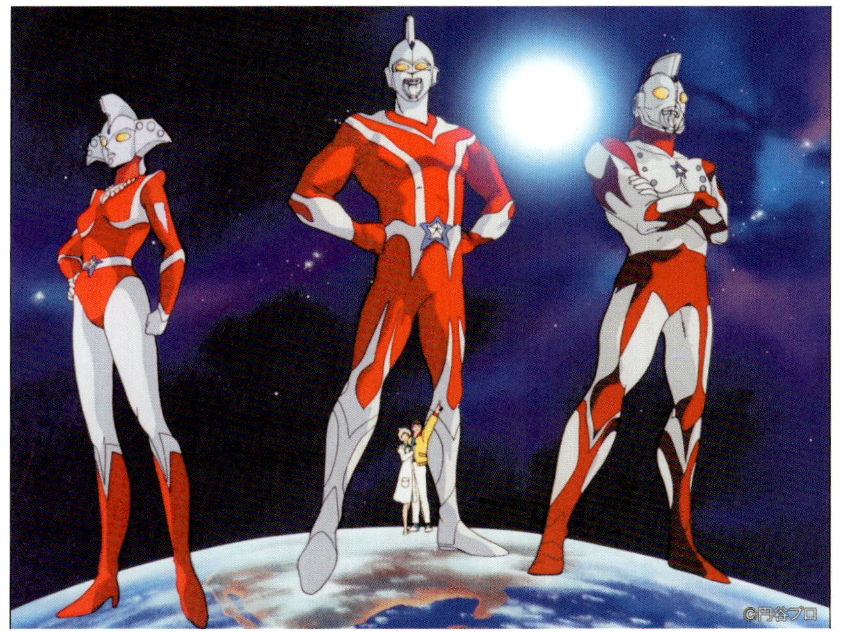

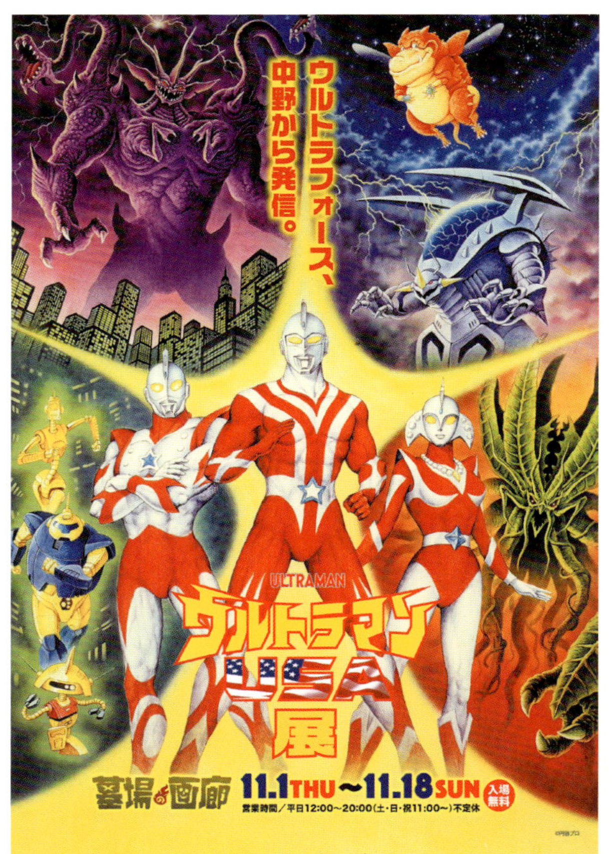

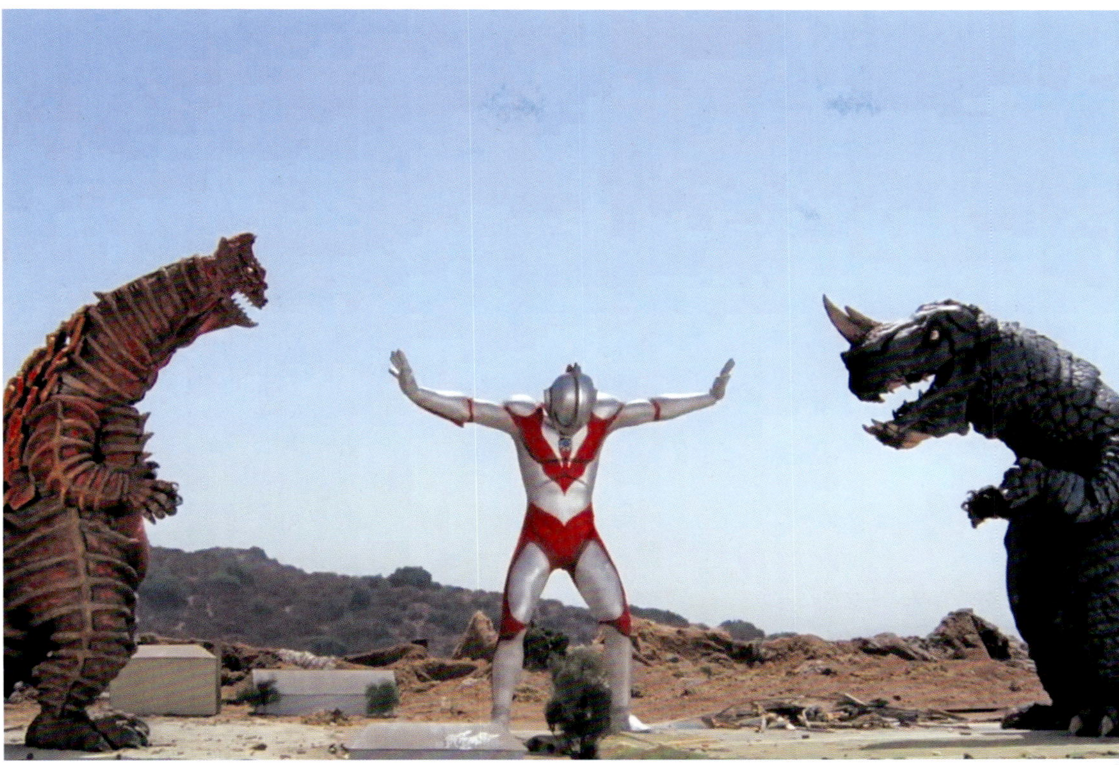

← **Left:** *Still from* Ultraman: The Ultimate Hero *(1993).*

↓ **Center:** *Ultraman Tiga enters the arena fist-first.*

↙ **Bottom:** *Over the years, Ultraman's transformation items became increasingly elaborate and majestic. Below is the item from* Ultraman Tiga *(1996).*

Higuchi's visit to the set of *The Ultimate Hero*, the English-speaking teams often worked in isolation, facing numerous challenges in costume management (choosing materials and ensuring the functionality of the final build), set construction (creating believable miniature cities), and special effects.

For *Ultraman: The Ultimate Hero*, the final result speaks for itself. There were thirteen episodes produced, but despite being filmed in English for the American market, the series was released exclusively in Japan.

In 1996, for Ultraman's thirtieth anniversary, the franchise made a true comeback in grand style. It began modestly with the highly eccentric film *Ultraman Zearth*, a parody homage in which the hero transforms using a toothbrush. However, it was *Ultraman Tiga* that marked the franchise's triumphant return. The series is still considered a classic of the franchise to this day.

Breaking away from the past and earlier productions, *Ultraman Tiga* offered a fresh start. The team was comprised of Tsuburaya's finest talents and delivered a generous series filled with breathtaking moments of bravery, pure Japanese science fiction, and particularly endearing characters. Its success propelled Tsuburaya and the *Ultraman* franchise toward new horizons. *Ultraman Tiga* was followed by *Ultraman Dyna* (1997) and *Ultraman Gaia* (1998), which solidified the formula and still stand today as a cornerstone of the genre and a perfect gateway for newcomers.

In 2001, *Ultraman Cosmos* achieved new heights with a sixty-five-episode series and a slightly different angle for its superhero, who was characterized by his blue suit. This Ultraman

↓ Below from left to right: *American poster for* Ultraman Zearth *(1996) and the Japanese poster for* Ultraman Cosmos: The First Contact *(2001).*

resolved most conflicts in a more peaceful manner. The series emphasized compassion as a central theme, even though combat remained inevitable in order to adhere to the conventions of the genre.

In 2004, the franchise raised the bar even higher. *Ultraman: The Next* became the first true Ultraman feature film created specifically for theaters. Previously, most films were simply compilations of clips from TV series. The movie adopted a more mature tone and introduced an Ultraman with a more organic design. The story was a reinterpretation of the franchise's core themes. In the plot, Shunichi Maki is a soldier and young father who encounters an Ultraman pursuing a *kaijū* that has fled to Earth. The narrative was engaging and also allowed the technical team to experiment with new technologies, such as motion capture. For instance, during some flying sequences, a figurine attached to a stick was maneuvered amid a simple cardboard city model and scanned by multiple cameras to record its movement in 3D. After processing, the final result was sequences never before seen in the franchise, showing a hero soaring freely through the skies. Though the scenes now appear antiquated, they were a milestone in the franchise's transition to digital technology.

That same year, *Ultraman Nexus* flipped many narrative conventions on their heads. The main character is not the one who transforms into Ultraman, and

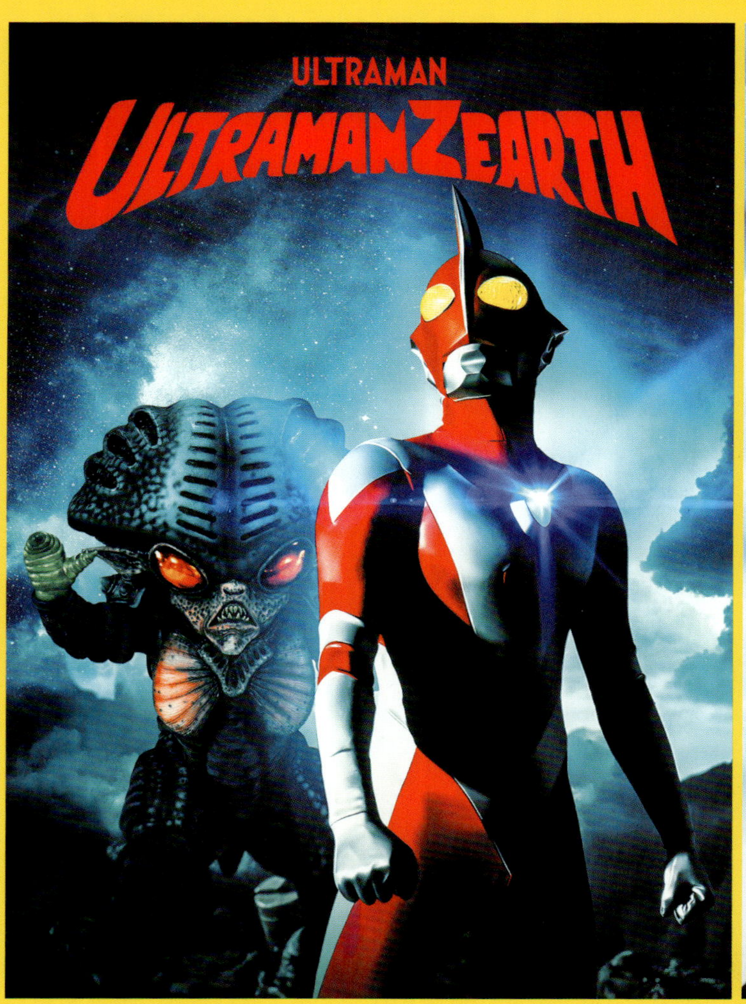

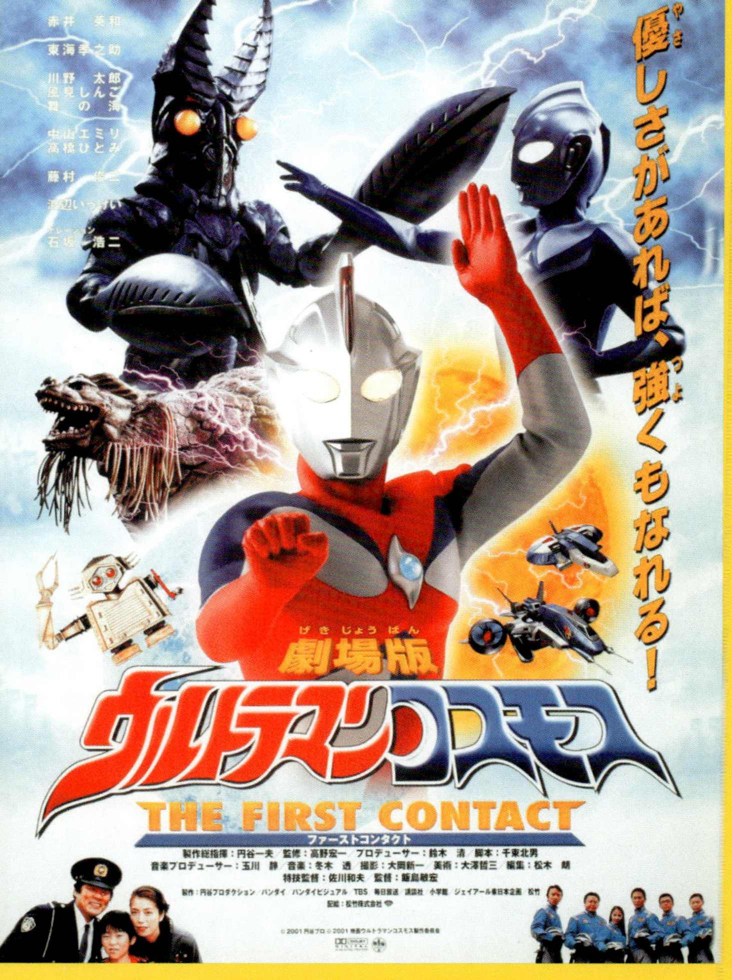

the hero himself is relegated to an almost supporting role. This bold approach led to weak commercial performance, with only thirty-seven episodes produced. However, over time, the series gained a cult following on the strength of its narrative.

As the years passed, Tsuburaya continued to evolve, which was reflected in the series. *Ultraman Mebius* (2006) celebrated the franchise's fortieth anniversary with the return of several well-known characters. *Ultraseven X* (2007) became the first series explicitly aimed at adults, featuring a darker tone—much different from the series' usual optimism—and a limited thirteen-episode run.

The "end" of the era was marked by the *Mega Monster Battle: Ultra Galaxy* series (two seasons, in 2008 and 2009), which were Ultraman shows in which Ultraman himself rarely appeared. Instead, the focus was on *kaijū* battles, designed to promote a card-based arcade game. The concept extended an idea first introduced in *Ultraseven* in 1967, that of deploying "pocket monsters" in battles. The franchise had come full circle, paving the way for a vibrant new chapter in its history.

HALCYON DAYS

In 2009, the *Ultraman* series soared to new heights with the film *Mega Monster Battle: Ultra Galaxy Legends—The Movie*. Behind this lengthy title lies a film with a dual purpose. On one hand, it serves as a conclusion to the *Mega Monster Battle* series. On the other, it aims to be a grand ensemble film celebrating the *Ultraman* universe in spectacular fashion. In simple terms, think of it as a sort of Japanese *Avengers*, where a group of superheroes assembles to face a shared adventure and common threat.

The film took the *Ultraman* universe to outer space and made it accessible to new viewers by briefly reintroducing all the essential elements of its mythology. The result was a full-throttle, exhilarating spectacle directed by Kōichi Sakamoto, a former *tokusatsu* stuntman who became a skilled choreographer and director of action scenes. Sakamoto's work is notable for its Hong Kong style of using props in fight scenes in creative ways and employing wires for exaggerated leaps. The movie marked his first project with Tsuburaya, one of many eventual collaborations.

The following year, a direct sequel was released in theaters, *Ultraman Zero: The Revenge of Belial*, written and directed by Yūichi Abe, a veteran of the franchise. Zero, a character introduced in the previous film, embarked on his first standalone adventure in a feature film that matched the quality of its predecessor. The movie offered a galactic road trip with bold aesthetic choices.

These two films also signaled a temporary pause for the *Ultraman* TV series. While Zero continued his adventures through a series of direct-to-video releases, fans had to wait until 2013 for *Ultraman* to return to television and reclaim his role as a primarily TV-based icon. Tsuburaya Productions had always been plagued by management issues, and some of its acquisitions and other internal changes in the late 2000s influenced the studio's choice of content formats (series, films, direct-to-video, etc.).

Ultraman Ginga (2013) consisted of only eleven episodes, and its sequel,

Below: *Ultraman Zero transforms using an item resembling a pair of futuristic sunglasses.*

Ultraman Ginga S (2014), produced sixteen. In 2015, the modern formula began to take shape—a structure that remains largely unchanged today—with *Ultraman X*. The studio found a happy medium by limiting the series to twenty-five episodes, sometimes accompanied by a concluding film. This format eliminated the need to fill nearly fifty-two weeks of television, creating breathing room in order to deliver a more refined series.

At the same time, the *Ultraman* series now fully embraces the shared universe concept while remaining accessible. Each series features its own superhero or superheroes, but others occasionally make appearances within the storyline. Ultraman Zero, for example, has lived up to his name by becoming a recurring figure in various series over the years, indirectly overseeing this new direction.

This more structured, stable approach is supported by a significantly enhanced and well-managed merchandising strategy (with Bandai still on board), a tack that has proven successful. Tsuburaya has regained its footing. Though the studio has faced financial turbulence more than once, occasionally teetering on the brink of bankruptcy, it has always bounced back by making the right moves at the right time, reestablishing itself as a heavyweight in the *tokusatsu* industry.

↓ **Below:** *Still from the film* Ultraman Zero: The Revenge of Belial *(2010), in which multiple Ultramen are assembled.*

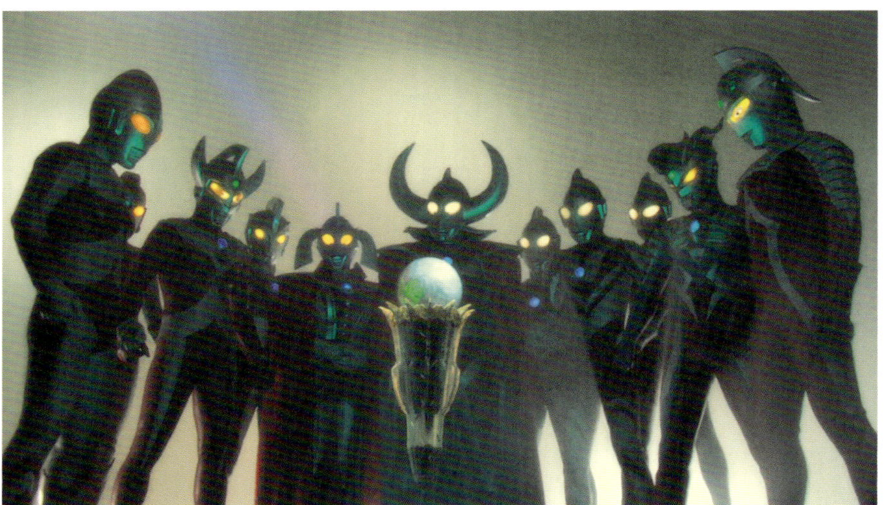

The release of *Shin Ultraman* in 2022 stands as proof of its resurgence. With Hideaki Anno as the writer and Shinji Higuchi as the director, *Shin Ultraman* offered audiences a stunningly modernized reinterpretation of the original 1966 series in the form of a polished blockbuster. This kind of ambitious project would have been unthinkable a decade earlier, serving as a powerful symbol of a studio brimming with confidence.

Much like *Shin Godzilla*, *Shin Ultraman* embraced fully digital effects while maintaining a balance between innovation and the *tokusatsu* heritage. For example, Bin Furuya, the original suit actor for *Ultraman* in 1966, reprised his role at nearly eighty years old, this time through motion capture technology—a fitting tribute to the actor known as the man who transformed into Ultraman.

Shin Ultraman includes small details and Easter eggs for devoted fans, but it never loses sight of its role as a true superhero film, filled with heroism and the optimism that defines Ultraman. It also contains a profound message about humanity and its capacity for self-transcendence.

For nearly a decade, the *Ultraman* franchise has been experiencing what could be considered a new golden age. Fifty-eight years after its inception, and despite a few rough patches, *Ultraman* has firmly cemented its status as a beloved icon and a major representative of Japanese pop culture.

The franchise is even going global. Since 2020, new TV series have been released for free worldwide on YouTube with subtitles. In 2024, the American animated film *Ultraman: Rising* was released on Netflix, and Marvel has even published dedicated *Ultraman* comics. Is *Ultraman* finally gaining recognition? Could it finally achieve widespread popularity in regions where it remains largely unknown? Only time will tell, but all signs point to a bright future ahead.

← **Left:** *Japanese poster for the film* Shin Ultraman *(2022).*

↓ **Below:** *The modern version of Ultraman's Spacium beam still holds true to the original in* Shin Ultraman *(2022)*

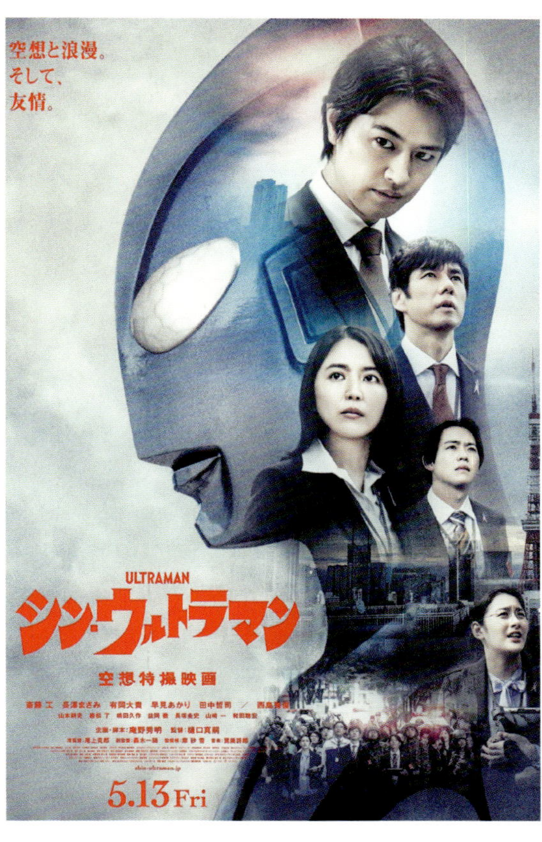

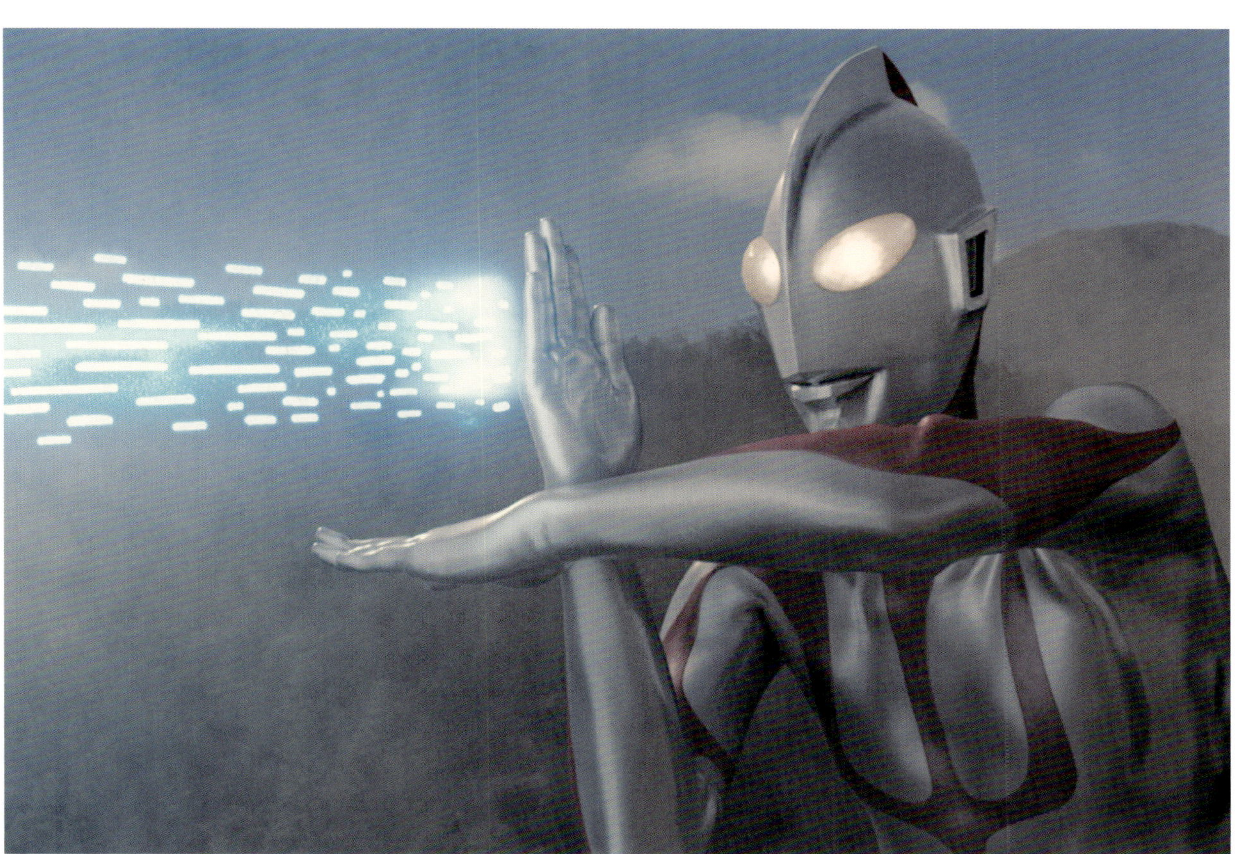

KAMEN RIDER: THE MASKED MOTORCYCLIST

THE BIRTH OF AN ICON

While *Ultraman* was winning over audiences, competitors scrambled to create their own flagship series. Toei had dabbled in *tokusatsu* in the 1960s, with *Moonlight Mask* in theaters and a few successful TV series (*Giant Robo*, *Captain Ultra*), and was still searching for its golden goose in TV *tokusatsu*.

The studio teamed up with Shōtarō Ishinomori, a manga artist and disciple of Osamu Tezuka, known for works such as *Cyborg 009* (1964). The goal was to conceptualize a new superhero that could compete with Ultraman. Ishinomori proposed building on his "one-shot" (standalone) manga *The Skull Man* (1970), which depicted a dark, tormented, human-sized skeleton creature. Toei rejected the idea, fearing it was too dark for their young audience. Ishinomori went back to the drawing board and contemplated various superheroes, including one inspired by a grasshopper, an insect that fascinated him in his youth. This turned out to be just the ticket. Toei approved the grasshopper character, threw in the iconic motorcycle, and named it Kamen Rider.

Thus, *Kamen Rider* was born as both a TV series and a manga (created simultaneously by Ishinomori himself).

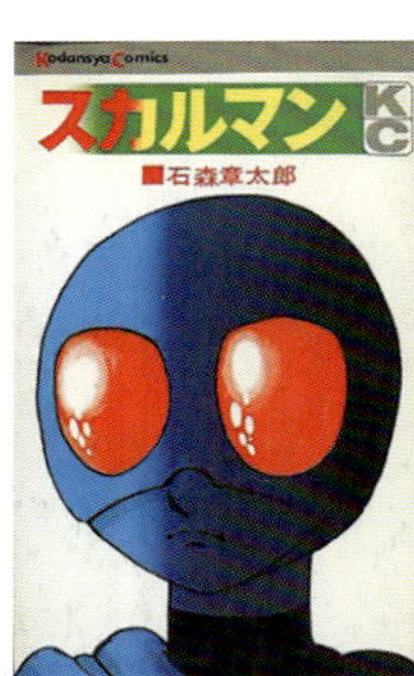

Above: *Japanese cover of the manga* The Skull Man *(1970).*

Right: *French cover of the manga* Cyborg 009 *(1964).*

Far right: *Hiroshi Fujioka, the main actor to play Takeshi Hongō the Kamen Rider since 1971.*

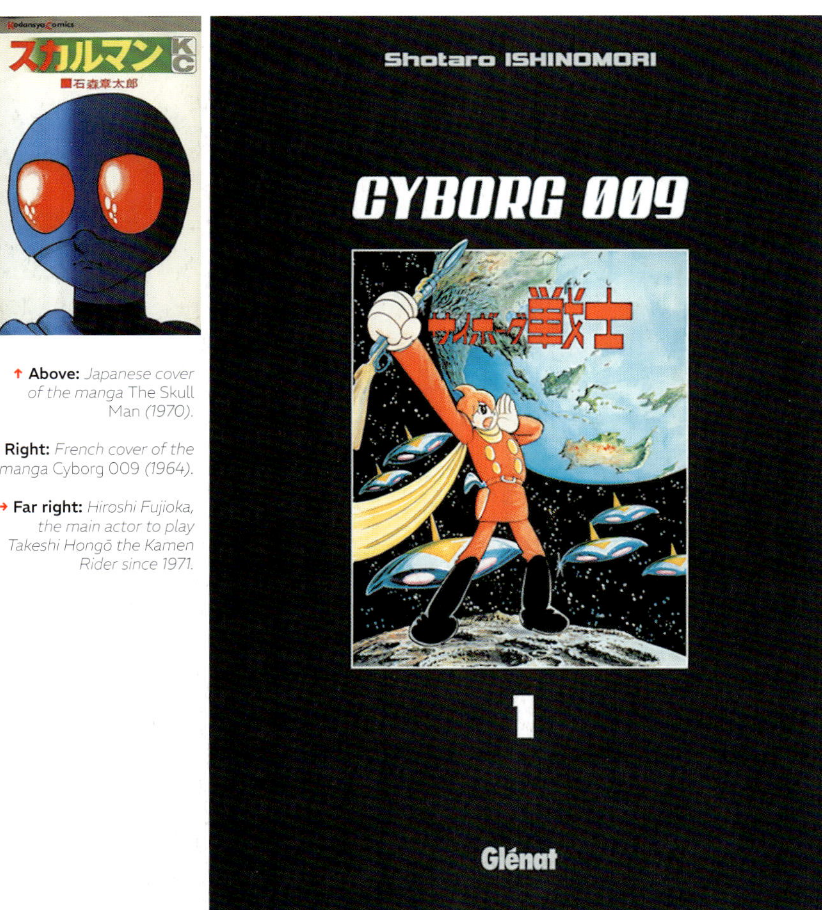

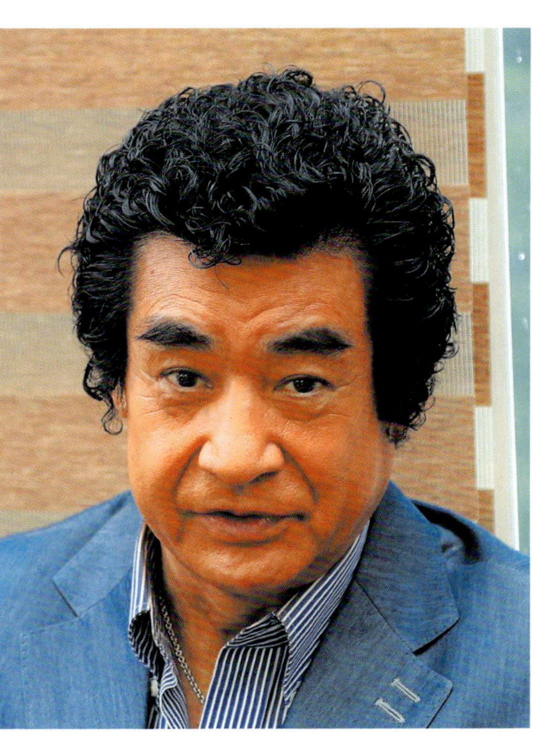

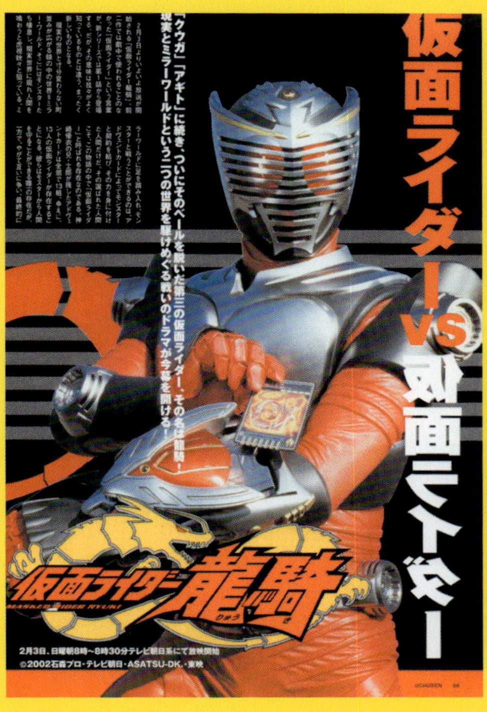

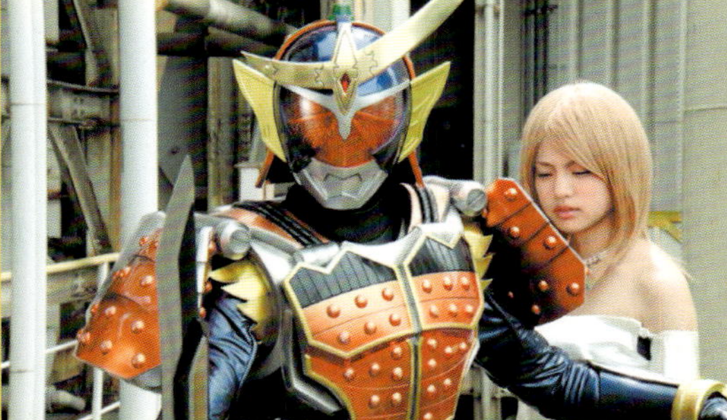

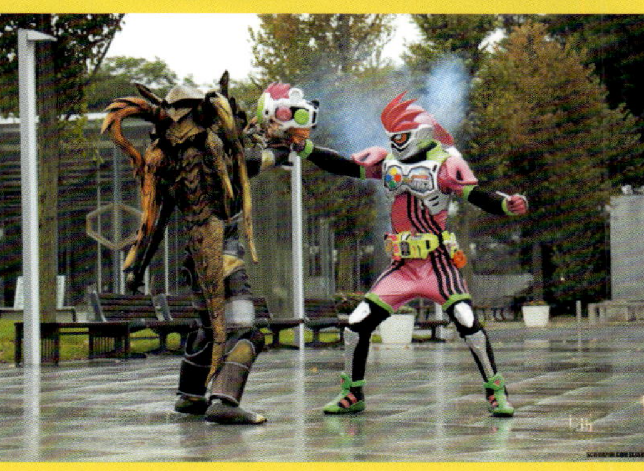

← **Clockwise from left:** Kamen Rider Ryūki *(2002)*, Kamen Rider Gaim *(2013)*, *and* Kamen Rider Ex-Aid *(2016)*.

FIFTY YEARS AND COUNTING

In 2019, Japan changed emperors, marking the start of the Reiwa era. *Kamen Rider* commemorated the event in its own way with a return to its roots in *Kamen Rider Zero-One*, released that same year. More in tune with contemporary issues, the series revisited the transhumanism theme of the original 1971 series by presenting a world where humans and Humagears (android assistants) coexist. Some of the androids begin to develop their own consciousness, raising questions about the system, sometimes through violent means.

This classic sci-fi theme, previously explored in *tokusatsu* series like *Robot Detective* (1973), was revisited in 2019 with a modern perspective on human-machine relationships, ethical abuses of technology, and the recognition of androids as legitimate, conscious members of society. This adds remarkable depth to the story.

In addition to the start of the Reiwa era, the *Kamen Rider* franchise celebrated its fiftieth anniversary in 2021. Despite disruptions caused by the COVID-19 pandemic, the franchise, like the rest of the *tokusatsu* genre, remained resilient

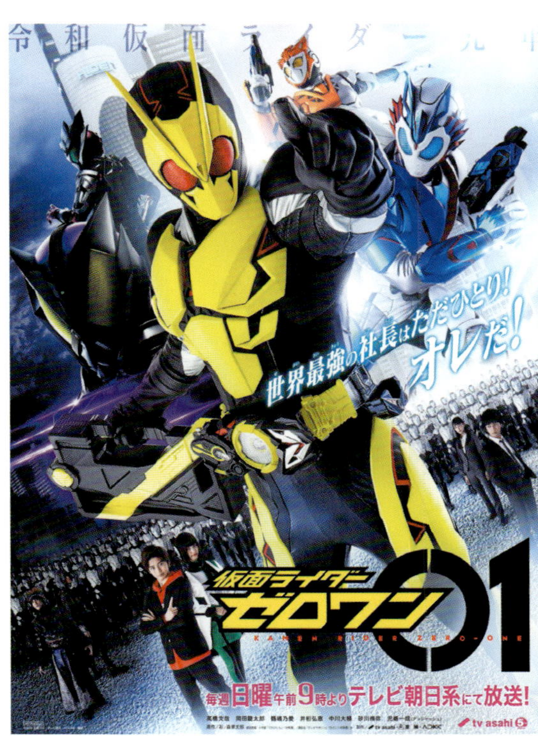

↙ **Below:** Kamen Rider Zero-One *(2019)*.

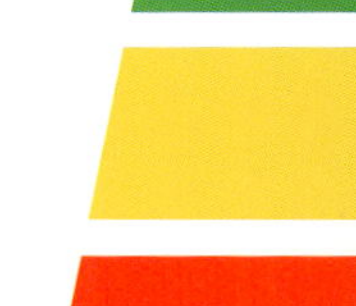

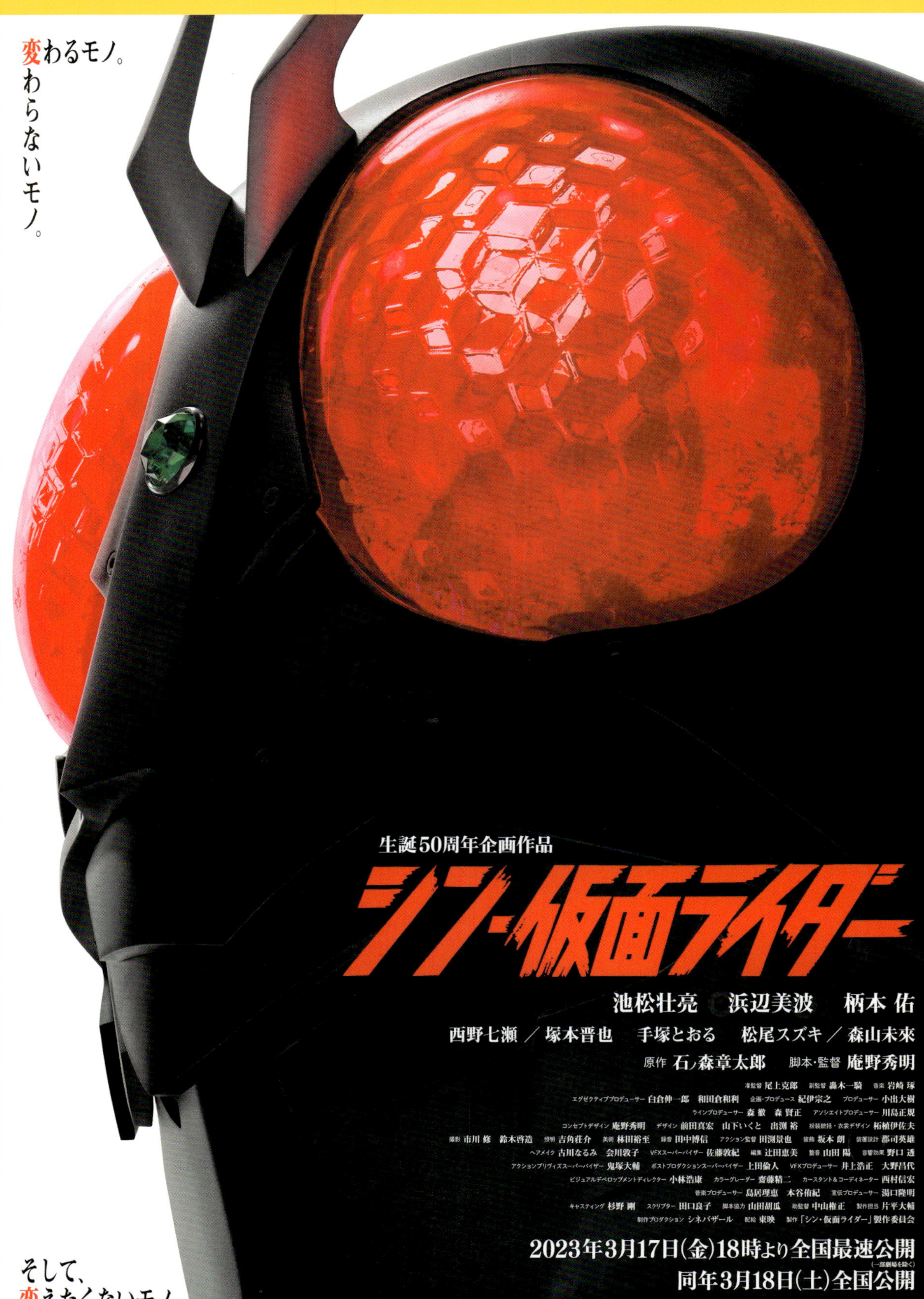

➜ **Right:** *Japanese poster for* Shin Kamen Rider *(2023).*

giant robot often associated with *Super Sentai* had yet to be invented.

At the time, the expression *Super Sentai* (and what it would later come to represent) did not yet exist, and the building blocks necessary to create a franchise of the caliber of *Kamen Rider* had not been assembled. Nevertheless, with its eighty-four episodes, *Gorenger* laid the groundwork for many of the subgenre's defining elements, including the exaggerated team introductions during battle sequences, inspired by *kabuki* theater. As their foes stood silently by, each superhero would introduce themselves by their superhero name (emphasizing their color), strike a pose, and punctuate the moment with an iconic explosion in the background. Team introductions became a staple of the franchise, an integral and cathartic ritual performed during climactic scenes.

After nearly two years on air, the series was succeeded by *J.A.K.Q. Dengekitai* (1977), which had less success, running for "only" thirty-five episodes. Though still lacking a robot, the aesthetic had begun to shift, with the team's theme inspired by playing cards. The four members were the Ace of Spades, Jack of Diamonds, King of Clubs, and Queen of Hearts. Unfortunately, ratings were lackluster as the series struggled to find its footing amid an era chockablock with *tokusatsu* shows to choose from. In an attempt to boost ratings mid-season, Big One, a new team member, was added to kick-start the cast's chemistry and pique viewers' interest. The character was played by Hiroshi Miyauchi of *Kamen Rider V3* fame. This was no accident. Despite his flashy appearance both before transformation (a white tuxedo) and after (white suit and rainbow helmet), the series failed to achieve the same level of success. The final piece of the puzzle was still missing. It would come in the form of unexpected influence by a

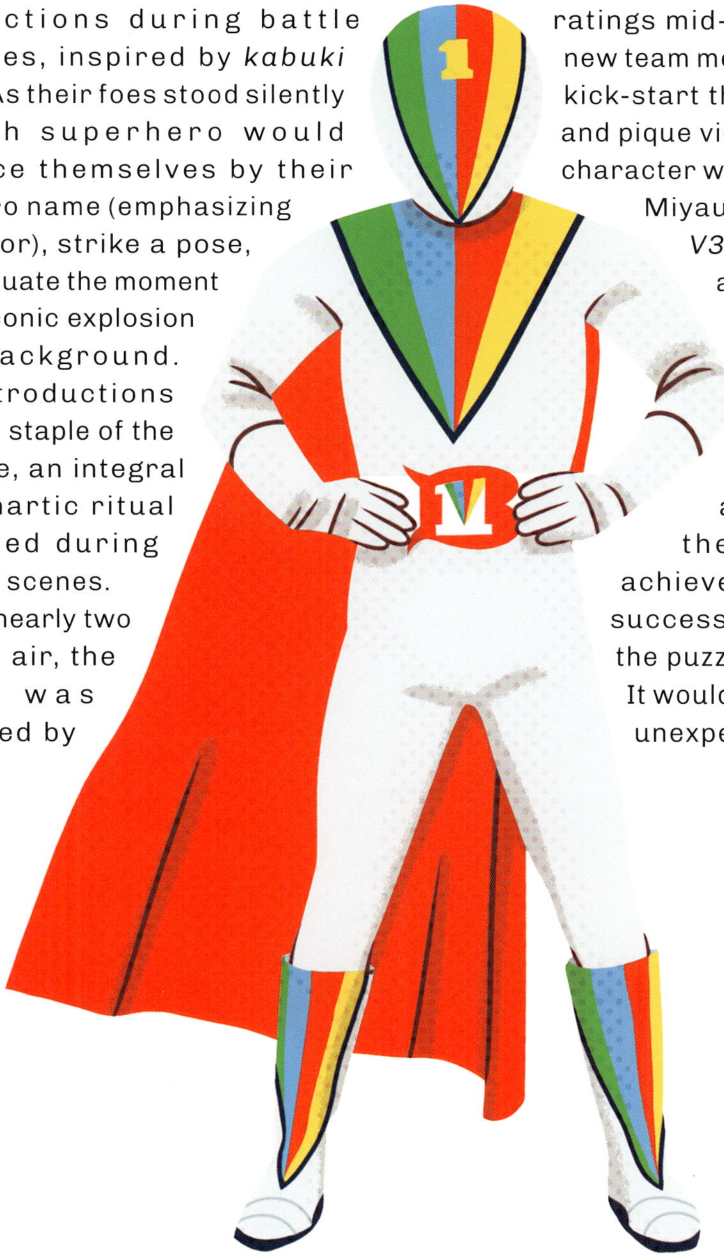

Below: *Big One, leader of the J.A.K.Q.* sentai.

➜ **Right:** *Magazine page dedicated to Spider-Man.*

➘ **Far right:** *Cover from the Japanese DVD edition of the series Spider-Man (1978).*

➜ **Below:** *Boxed play set containing Spider-Man and his robot sidekick, Leopardon.*

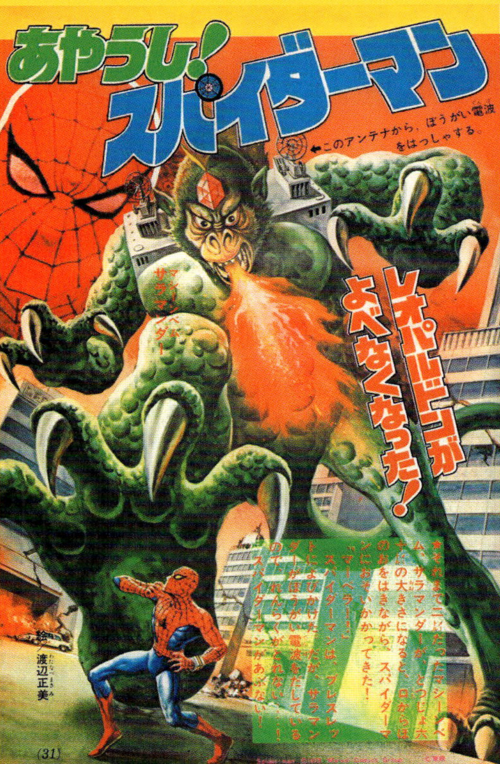

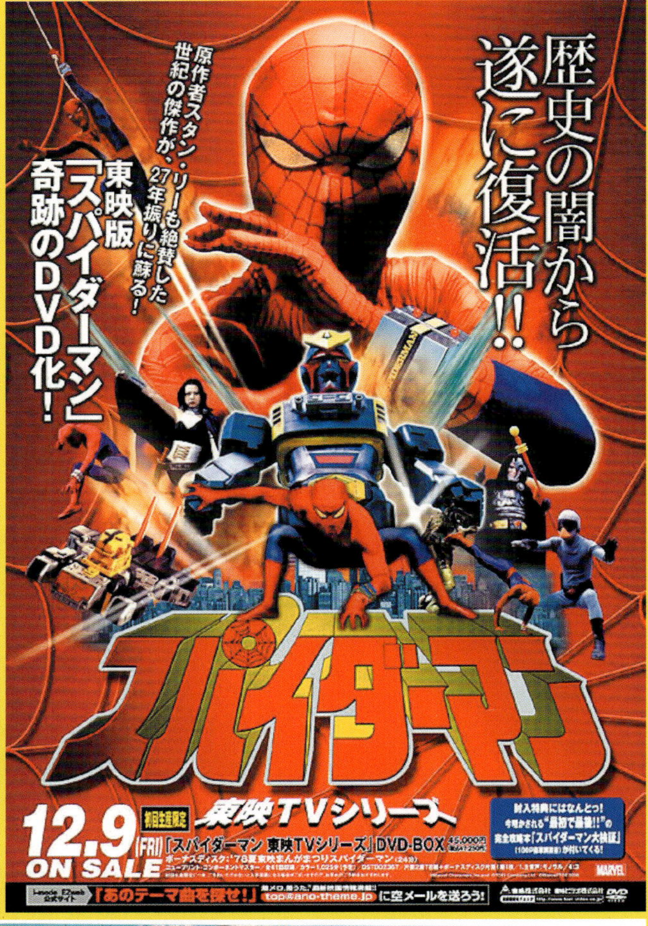

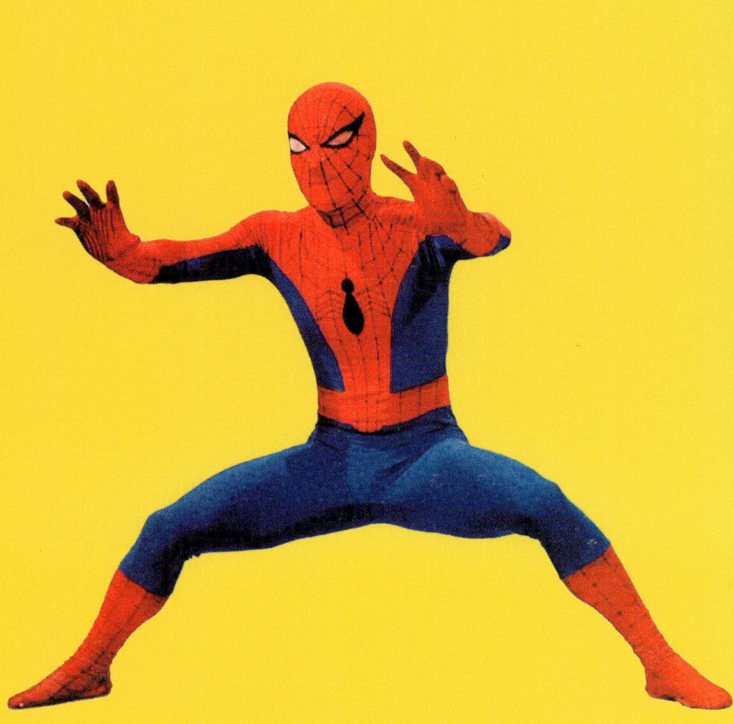

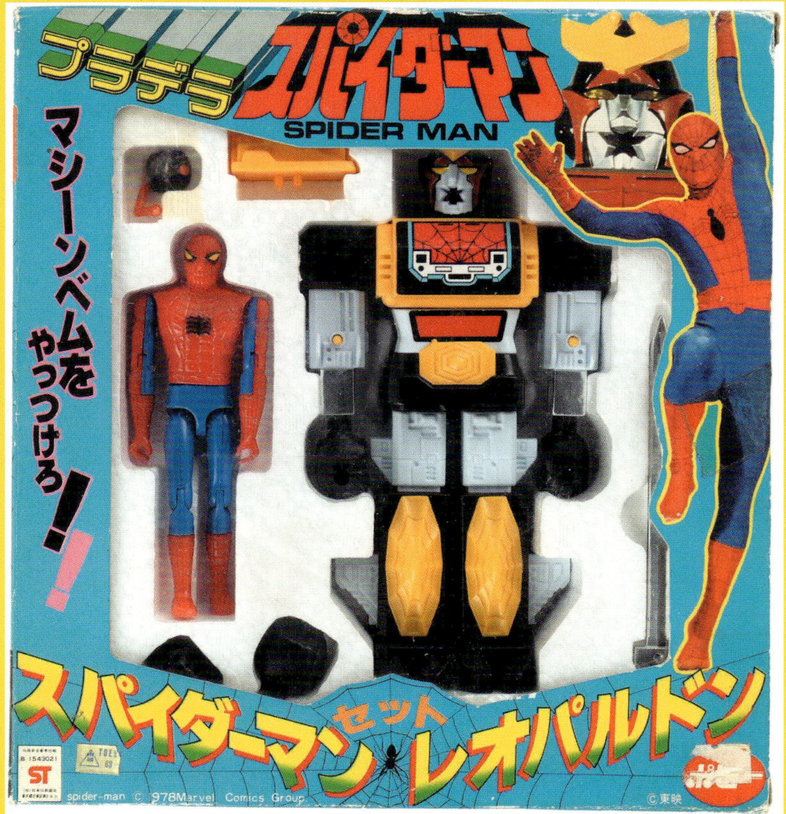

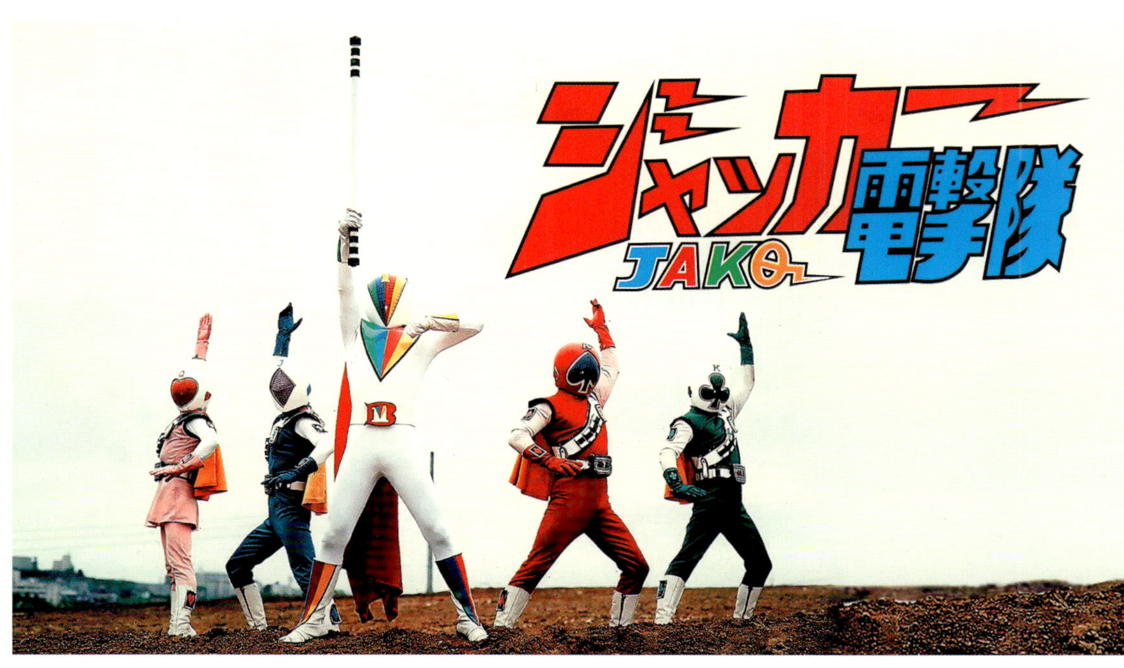

Left: *Despite the addition of Big One, the J.A.K.Q. series experienced limited success.*

Below: *America was represented in Battle Fever J by the pink Miss America.*

certain American superhero that would trigger a roaring comeback for *sentai*.

ROBOTS AND SPIDERS

To understand how *sentai* became "super," we must take a detour to discuss Spider-Man, another well-known superhero experiencing his own revival. In the 1970s, Marvel Comics was looking for ways to expand beyond comics and the local, or even Western, market. One of its ideas was to partner with Toei to develop several live-action series featuring its superheroes to introduce them to the Japanese landscape, which at the time had little to no appreciable comic book culture. The aim was to create something localized for Japanese audiences to promote the Marvel brand (with Stan Lee's approval, of course).

The first step in this endeavor was a *tokusatsu Spider-Man* series in 1978, which filled the TV slot left by the conclusion of *J.A.K.Q. Dengekitai*. Beyond its appearance, this version of Spider-Man had little in common with the original. Instead of Peter Parker, the journalist, there was Takuya Yamashiro, a young motocross rider. Though his powers also originated from a spider, Takuya's spider was extraterrestrial. Takuya could don his costume by transforming via a bracelet, and he had a gadget-equipped car and, most notably, Leopardon, his transformable robot.

Marvel made significant adaptations to suit the Japanese market. The masked, motorcycle-riding hero that used a robot that could grow to enormous size to fight monsters was essentially an amalgamation of everything popular at the time: *Kamen Rider*, *Giant Robo*, and even animated series like *Mazinger Z* and

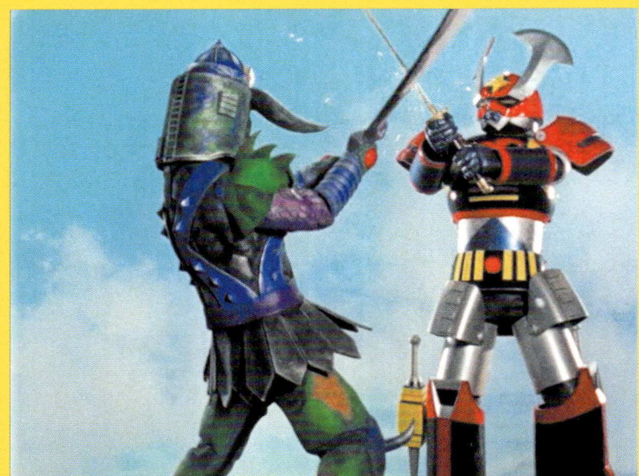

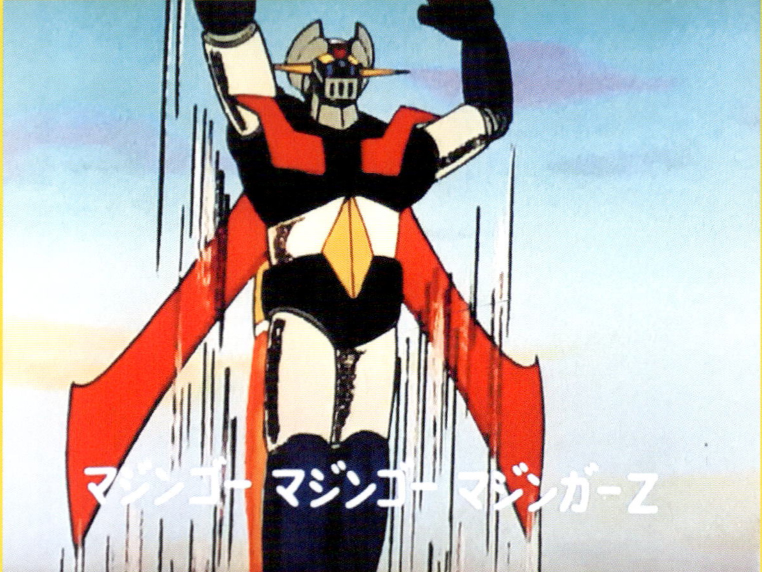

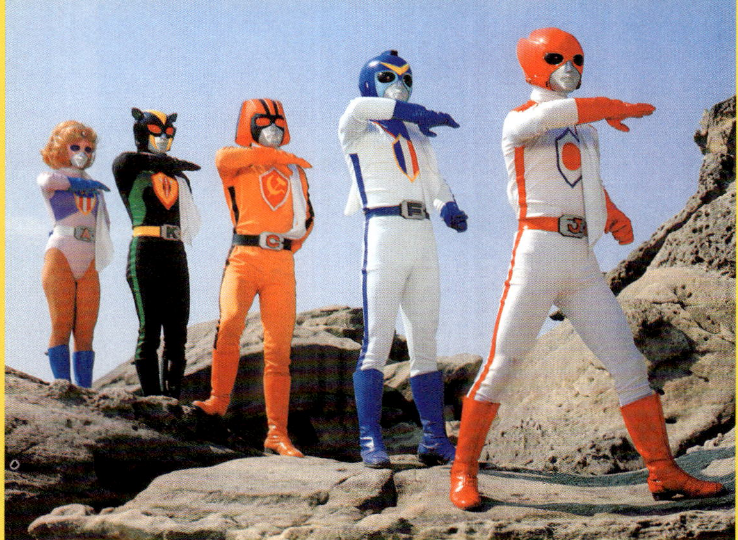

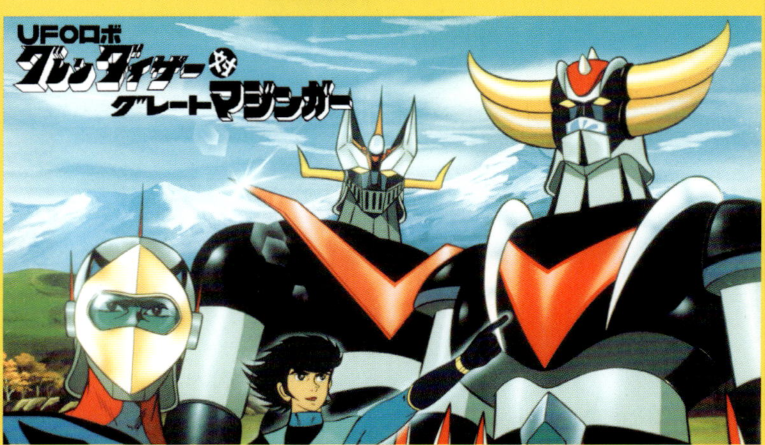

↑ **Above:** *Capitalizing on the major success of Japanese anime and Spider-Man,* sentai *finally introduced its own giant robot while maintaining the colorful team of superheroes.*

Voltes V. The result, in keeping with the genre's conventions, was successful and left a small mark in the history of *tokusatsu*.

However, for Marvel, the situation was more complicated. In essence, although liked and endorsed by Stan Lee, the series failed to convince the rest of Marvel's leadership, who saw no commercial potential outside Japan. Consequently, the agreement between Marvel and Toei ended quickly, even though a Japanese *Captain America* series had been considered. But all was not lost. The early concepts of the project evolved into a team of five superheroes representing various countries and cultures. This resulted in the third *sentai* series, *Battle Fever J*, released in 1979.

The series revived what had become a *sentai* franchise and sought to evolve it by incorporating successful elements directly inspired by *Spider-Man*, particularly the giant robot. In this first attempt, the robot was unique and arrived on the battlefield via a dedicated transport ship—an idea that effectively energized the concept and continued to develop. With the series' success, *sentai* shows became popular again and were produced annually, with around fifty episodes per series. Notably, the use of robots continued to change and grow.

Toy manufacturer Bandai (among others) became involved in the creative process of *tokusatsu* series for Toei. The company's input carried weight in discussions on concepts and designs, particularly if it could boost profits through merchandising, a crucial component of a series' success. Despite what might seem like a controversial practice, the partners managed to strike a balance, ushering the *sentai* genre into an era of prosperity.

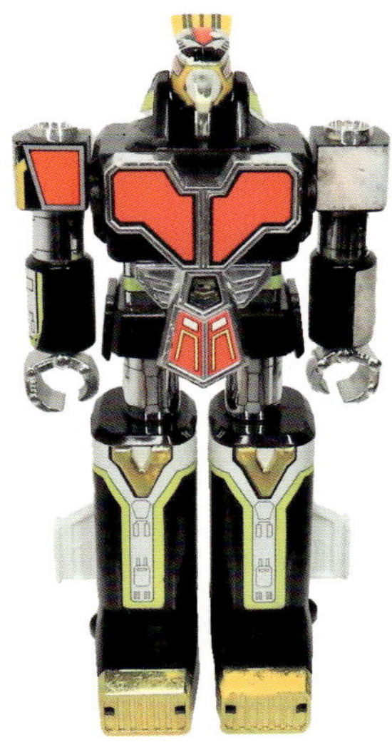

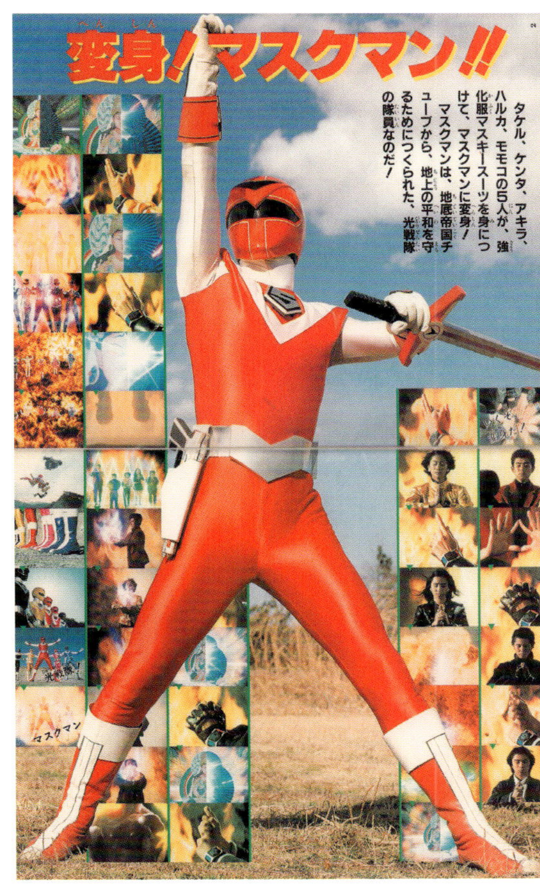

← **Left:** *Double-page magazine spread dedicated to* Hikari Sentai Maskman *(1987).*

↙ **Far left:** *Jet Garuda robot toy from the series* Chōjin Sentai Jetman *(1991).*

↓ **Below:** *Giant robots were played by specialized actors. Shown is the robot from* Denshi Sentai Denjiman *(1980).*

The concept was further refined. Robots grew ever more present, with team members having their own vehicles (or even their own robot in some series) that they could combine with other members' vehicles (a process called *gattai* in Japanese) to form a giant robot. The term *Super Sentai* didn't appear until the 1990s, when Toei redefined its franchise more broadly, turning it into a brand name, a Toei property, and almost a subgenre of its own, with a trademark colorful team, combat vehicles, and most importantly, a unified giant robot as the centerpiece.

The formula quickly gathered steam with several high-quality series from the 1980s. It's hard to deny the impact and quality of shows like *Choudenshi Bioman* in 1984, *Hikari Sentai Maskman* in 1987, and *Choujyu Sentai Liveman* in 1988. The reformulation showcased the full potential of the *tokusatsu* subgenre through group dynamics, thrilling action emphasizing the giant size of the robots, and storylines that were more clever and more sophisticated than they might initially appear. This quality persisted into the 1990s, with *Chōjin Sentai Jetman* in 1991 being one of the most popular entries even today. It's considered a true classic, celebrated for its characters, twists, and nuanced storytelling.

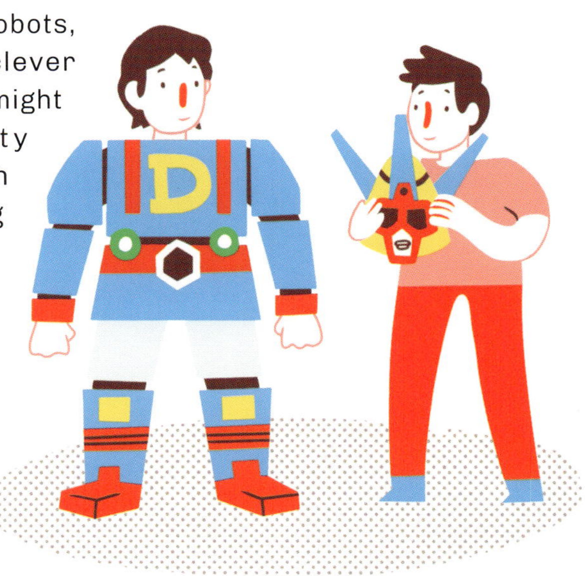

Toei managed to stabilize its franchise, turning it into an influential work in the world of *tokusatsu* (and beyond) and inspiring others to replicate its success. The word *sentai* became strongly

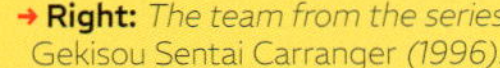
Right: *The team from the series* Gekisou Sentai Carranger *(1996).*

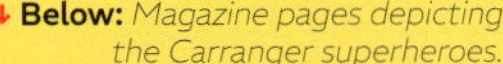
Below: *Magazine pages depicting the Carranger superheroes.*

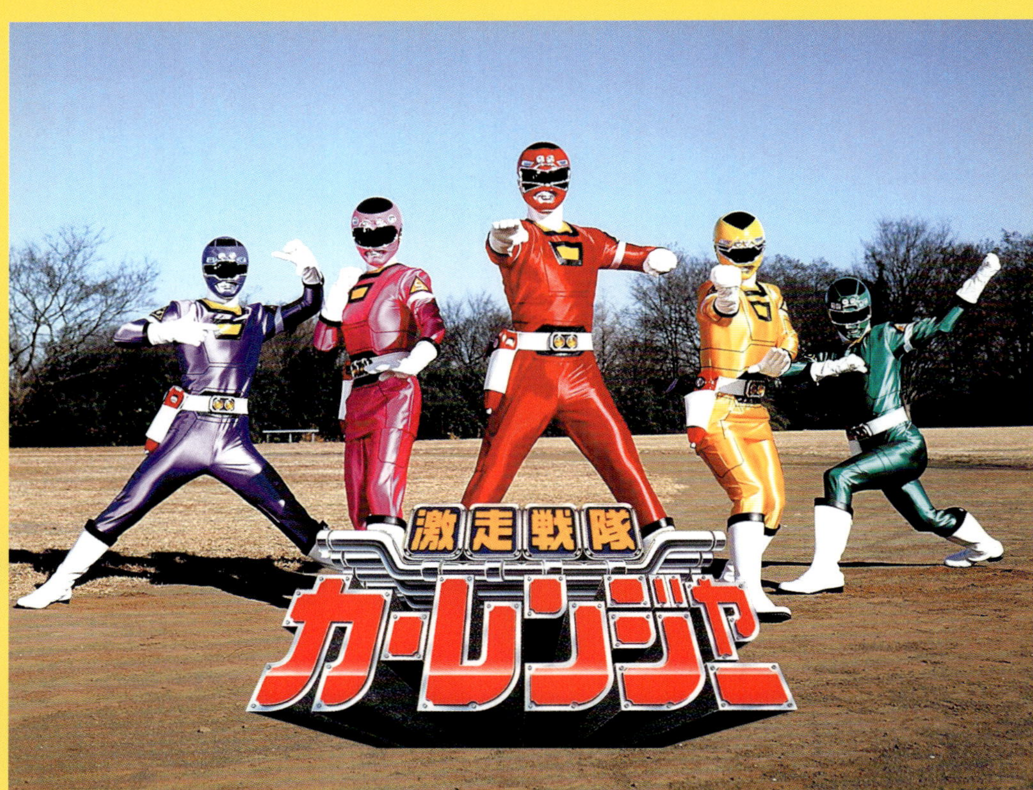

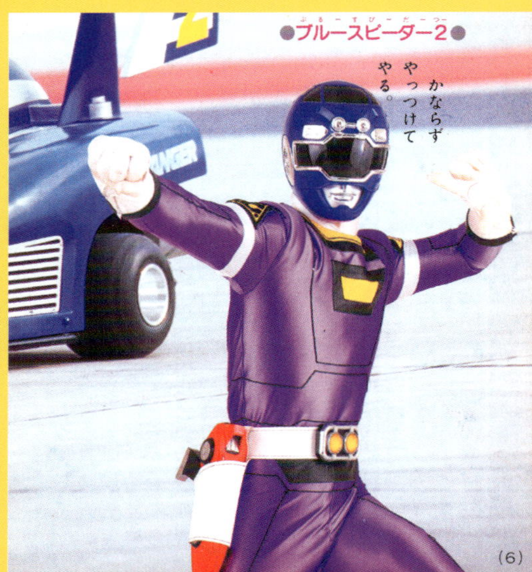

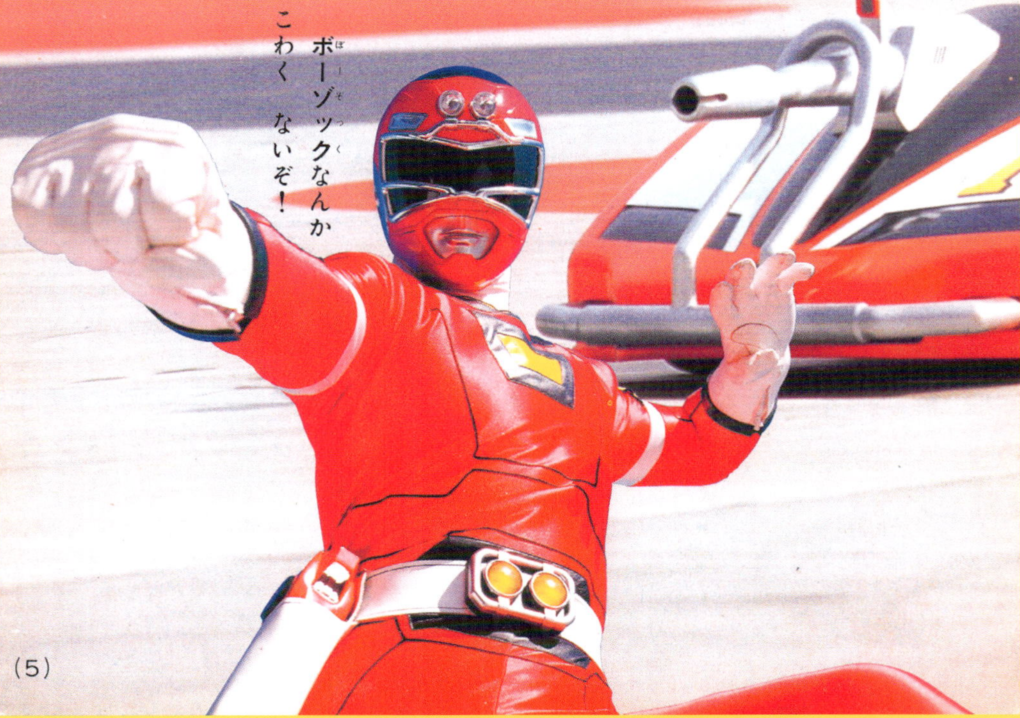

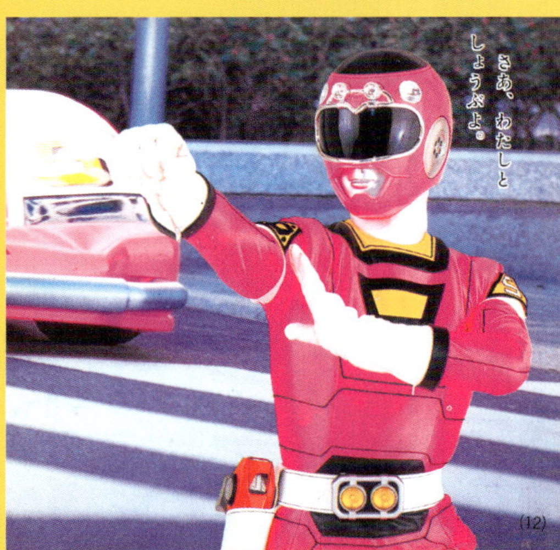

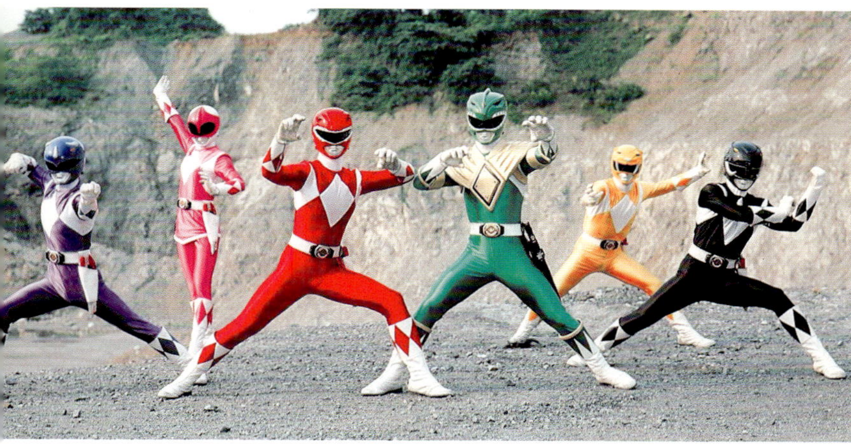

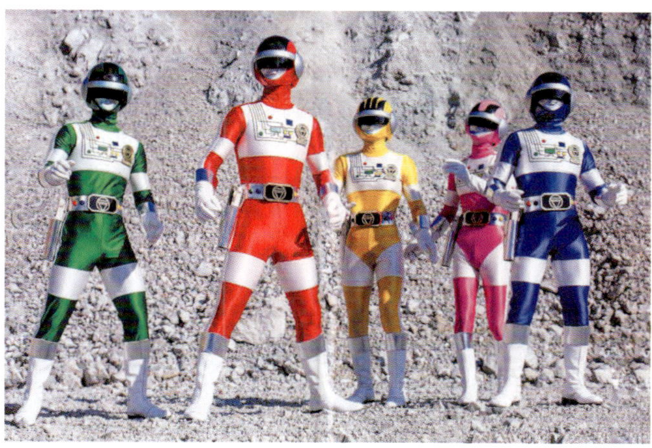

associated with Japanese superheroes, iconic visual elements (such as the colorful team), and above all, Toei's signature formula featuring a transformable giant robot. In short, Spider-Man may not technically be a (super) *sentai*, but he likely rescued the genre from obscurity, ultimately helping it become the standard-bearer of Japanese superheroes, right alongside *Kamen Rider* and *Ultraman*.

SUPER SENTAI: THE BEDROCK OF JAPANESE SUPERHEROES

A new era began quietly in 1992 with the release of *Kyōryū Sentai Zyuranger*, the first *Super Sentai* series to adopt the theme of dinosaurs and other prehistoric creatures. The story focuses on five warriors who lie dormant for millions of years until they are awakened in the present day to combat the resurrection of Bandora the witch. Using their medallions, they become the Zyurangers, warriors capable of piloting Guardian Beasts, giant mechanical creatures that can come together to form a massive robot.

If the visuals seem familiar, it's likely because they remind you of another series launched the following year by producer Haim Saban, *Mighty Morphin Power Rangers*, which reused footage and costumes from *Zyuranger*. This did not stop *Super Sentai* from continuing to thrive.

Creating a *Super Sentai* series required only a few key elements: a central theme on which to build the superheroes' designs and robots, a broader outline on which to structure the story, and an annual production cycle of fifty action-packed episodes. For example, *Gekisou Sentai Carranger* (1996), created for the franchise's twentieth anniversary, reinvented the genre through self-parody, humor, and affection for its own tropes, using cars and automotive themes as its motif. Superheroes, robots, and even alien antagonists were depicted comically in this motorized world.

Though many storylines in the series drew on the theme of extraterrestrial threats, Toei consistently found ways to innovate. *Denji Sentai Megaranger* (1997) explored technologies emergent at the time (in particular, a fascination with virtual spaces), *Kyuukyuu Sentai GoGoFive* (1999) tackled large-scale rescue operations with a serious tone, and *Mirai Sentai Timeranger* (2000) ushered in the new millennium with a time-traveling squad

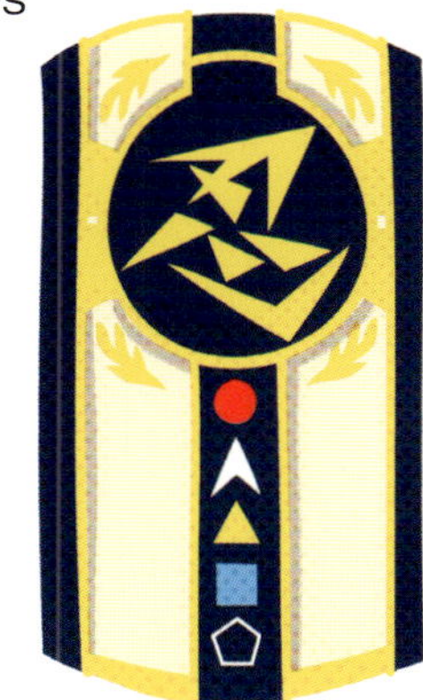

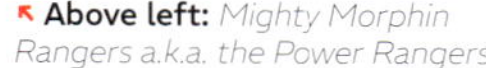

↖ Above left: *Mighty Morphin Rangers a.k.a. the Power Rangers.*

↑ Above right: *The superheroes of* Choudenshi Bioman *(1984).*

↓ Below: *The Doron Changer, which* Kakurangers *(1994) use to don their ninja suits.*

→ Right: Ninja Sentai Kakuranger *(1994).*

↓ Below: Denji Sentai Megaranger *(1997).*

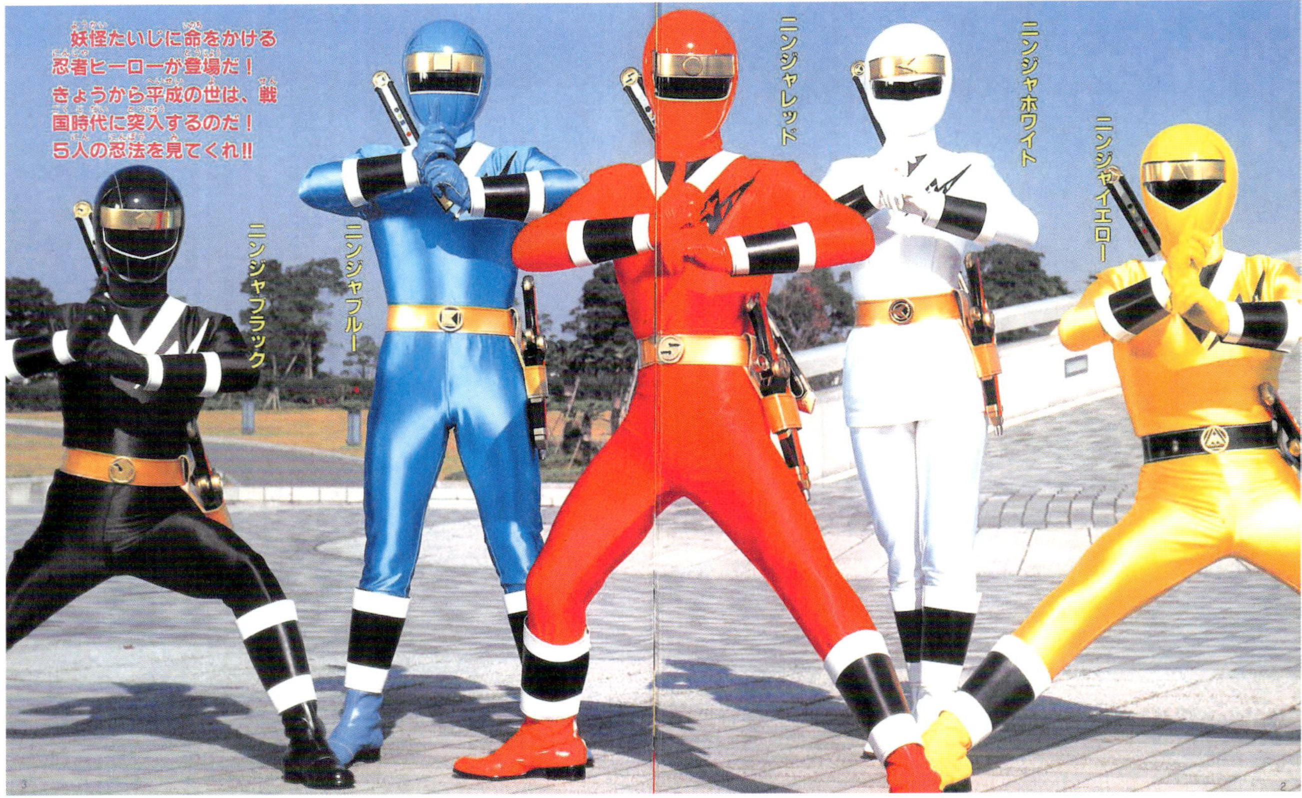

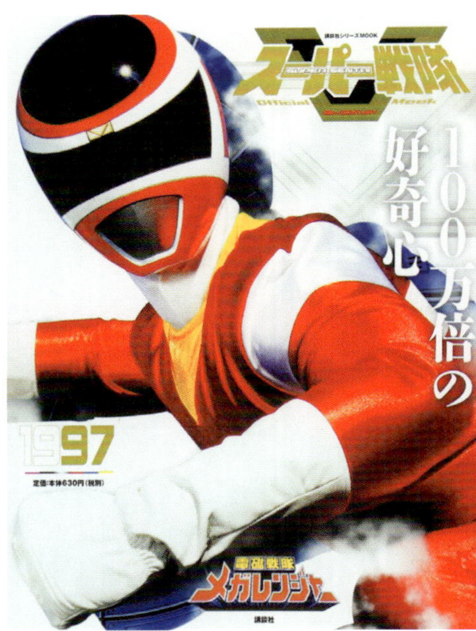

capturing temporal criminals. The latter, akin to *Kamen Rider Kuuga* for its quality and popularity, was indicative of the franchise's robust health.

Over time, each series introduced its own special touch: larger teams, more robots, and countless new combinations to diversify group dynamics. Bandai played a significant role in driving these additions, influencing themes and motifs to enhance merchandising potential. Despite these "constraints," Toei consistently maintained a balance to deliver high-quality series.

For Western audiences, these fantastical concepts, quirky monsters, and oversized robots may come across as cheesy. Yet it is precisely these elements that have cemented the identity of *Super Sentai* and secured its place in Japanese popular culture. Highlights include the *Men in Black*–like atmosphere of *Tokusou Sentai Dekaranger* (2004) and its space cops, the homage to Hong Kong cinema in *Jūken Sentai Gekiranger* (2007), and the rich, intricate storytelling of *Samurai Sentai Shinkenger* (2009), a heartfelt tribute to samurai-themed series intertwined with *tokusatsu* over the years.

However, the early 2010s came with some challenges, pushing Toei to seek new ways to revamp the franchise.

CONTINUING EVOLUTION

Super Sentai encountered some obstacles in the 2010s but nonetheless continued to pump out excellent series for both new viewers and longtime fans. The year 2011 marked the franchise's

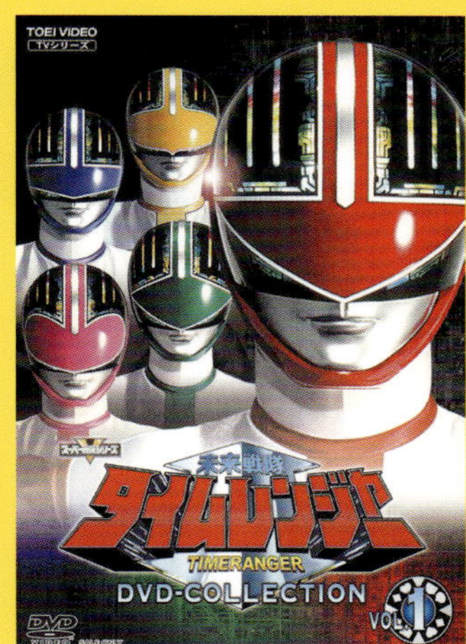

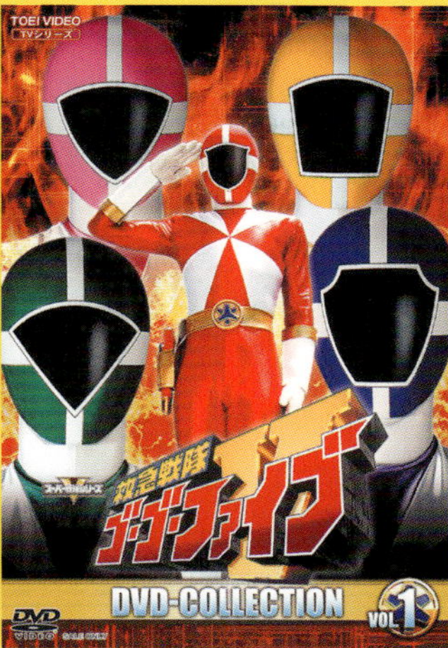

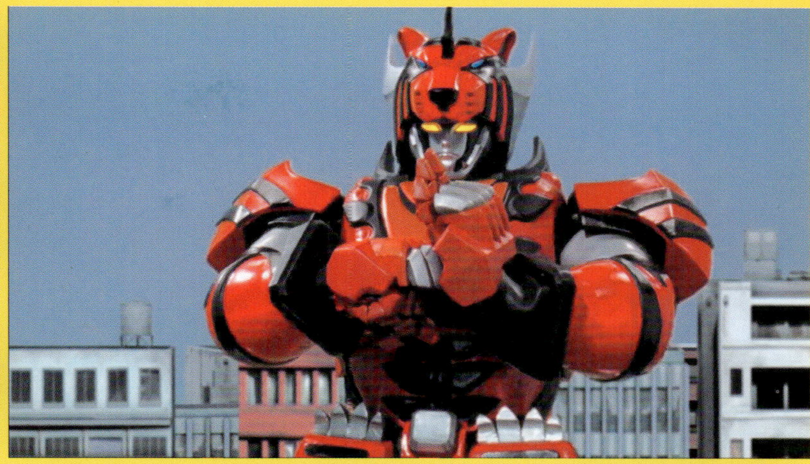

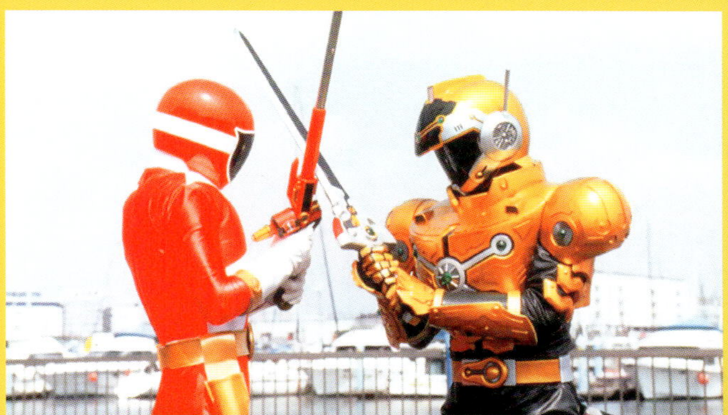

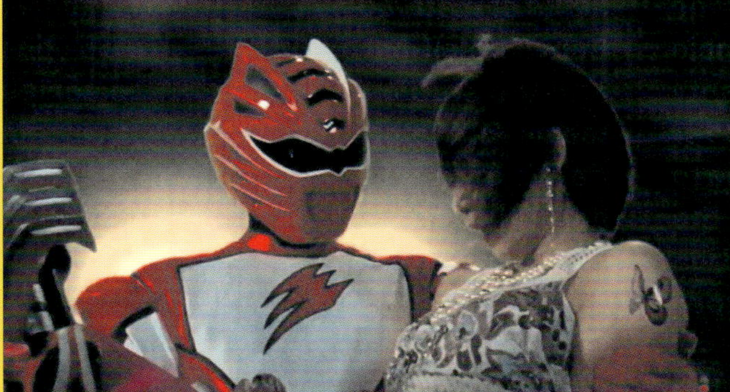

Clockwise from top left: *Covers from the Japanese DVD editions of the* Mirai Sentai Timeranger *(2000) and* Kyuukyuu Sentai GoGoFive *(1999) series; stills of the robot and Blue Ranger from* Jūken Sentai Gekiranger *(2007); the team from* Mirai Sentai Timeranger *(2001); the team from* Tokusou Sentai Dekaranger *(2004), reprising their roles in 2024 for a film celebrating the 20th anniversary of the original series;* Jūken Sentai Gekiranger *(2007); and* Kyuukyuu Sentai GoGoFive *(1999).*

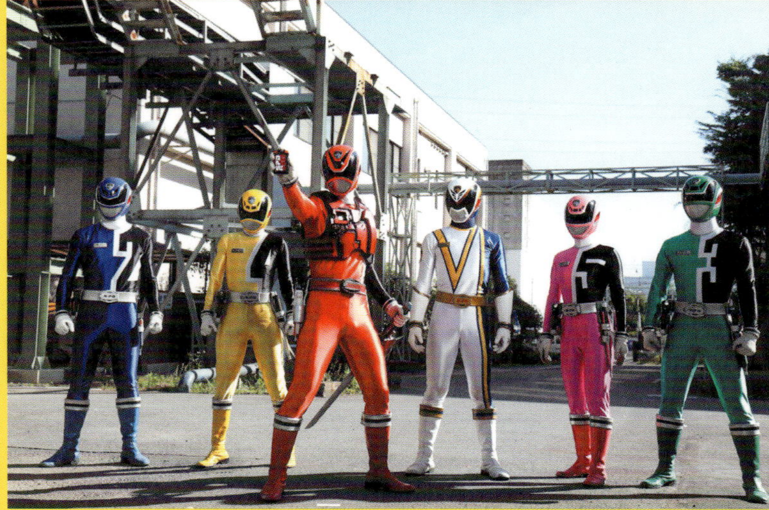

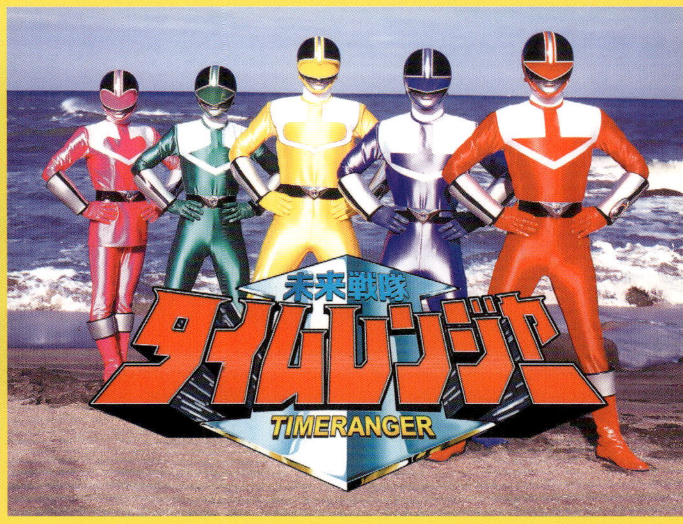

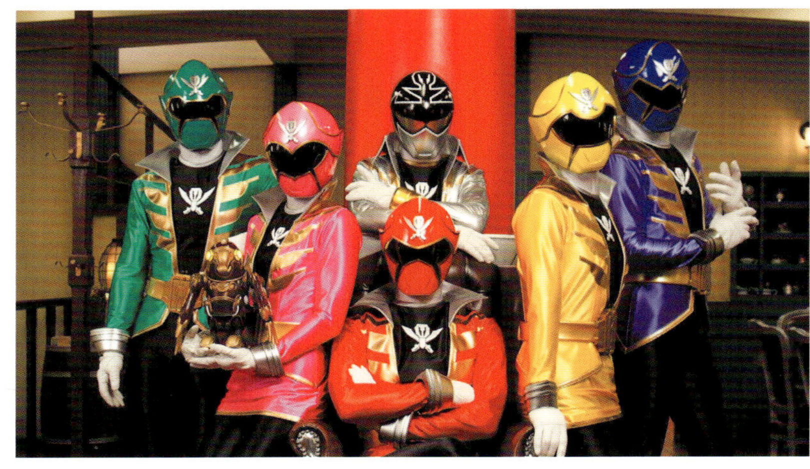

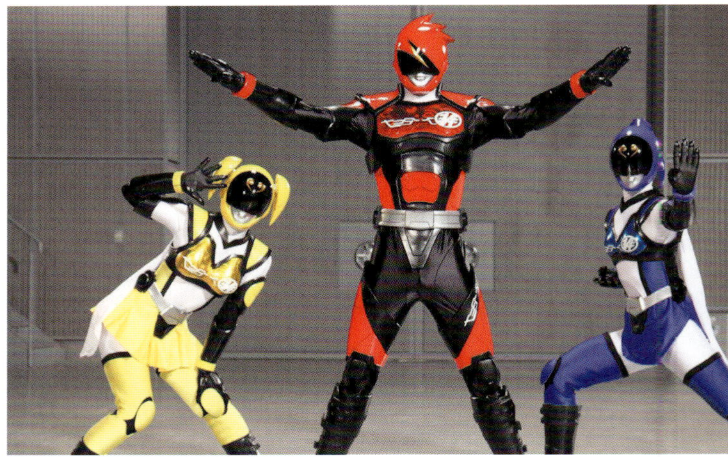

↑ **Above left:** *Space pirates from* Kaizoku Sentai Gokaiger *(2011).*

↗ **Above right:** *The unofficial team from* Unofficial Sentai Akibaranger *(2012).*

↓ **Below**: *The Gaburevolver from* Zyuden Sentai Kyoryuger *(2013), a weapon and transformation item.*

thirty-fifth anniversary, the perfect opportunity to create a series celebrating the franchise in all its forms. The result was *Kaizoku Sentai Gokaiger*, which featured space pirates, complete with a pirate ship, with the ability to transform into previous colorful warriors and use their powers. The series created an opportunity to bring back numerous former actors and their characters, from simple cameos to episodes that, nearly twenty years later, felt like epilogues to past series. *Gokaiger* remained accessible to all while uniting generations within the same show and is universally recognized as a passionate love letter to the *Super Sentai* legacy.

In a different vein, aimed less at the usual target audience and more at long-time fans who were all grown up, Toei surprised everyone with *Unofficial Sentai Akibaranger* in 2012 and 2013, running for two seasons of thirteen episodes each. The series takes viewers into the sometimes-bizarre streets of the *otaku* (a term for fans of Japanese pop culture) district of Akihabara in Tokyo, where we follow the adventures of Nobuo Akagi, himself an *otaku* and *Super Sentai* fan. He is recruited along with two others to form the unofficial squadron named Akibaranger (hence the title) to defend the district.

However, though Nobuo initially believes everything is just part of a film shoot, the monsters they face seem all too real, and the boundary between reality and what he knows about *Super Sentai* becomes increasingly blurry. The show dives headlong into wild, often cheeky humor, full of love for the *Super Sentai* franchise and frequently pushing the limits of meta-commentary on the genre. Between self-parody of the genre's tropes and the studio producing it, the series teems with references requiring a certain depth of knowledge, but it remains a delightfully offbeat, heartfelt celebration of *Super Sentai*.

In its regular series (that is, the non-anniversary editions), the franchise kept adding more and more elements into the mix to compensate for occasional declines in popularity, particularly in the face of a thriving *Kamen Rider* and a resurgent *Ultraman*. Standouts include series like *Zyuden Sentai Kyoryuger* (2013) and its dinosaur theme, and *Uchū Sentai Kyuranger* (2017) and its space opera theme, which featured unprecedentedly large teams of eleven and twelve members, respectively—a number unmatched to this day. Throughout the decade, the franchise delivered series that reminded viewers why it was so beloved, including *Ressha Sentai ToQger* (2014), which

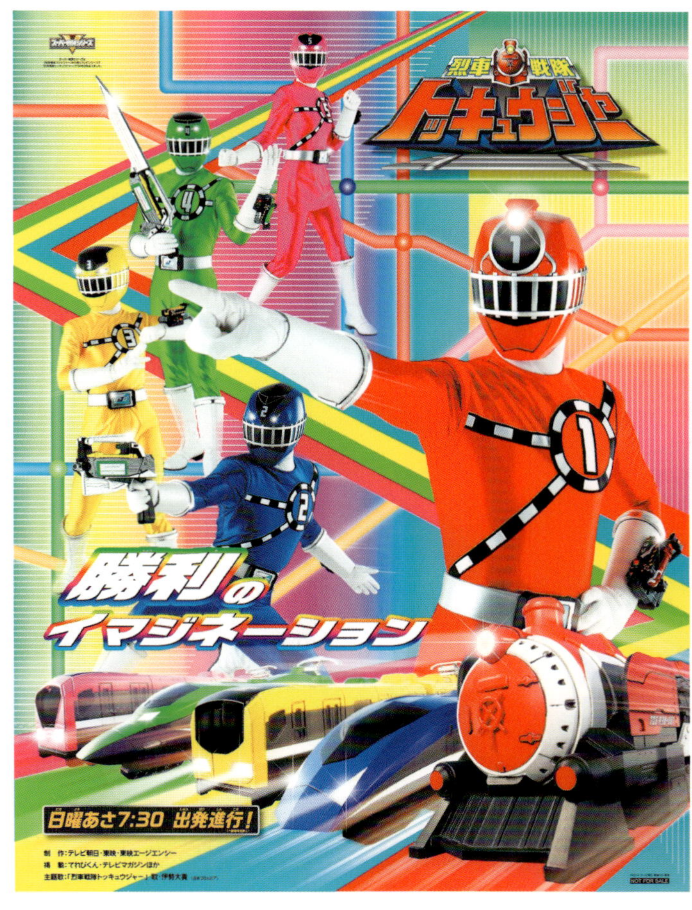

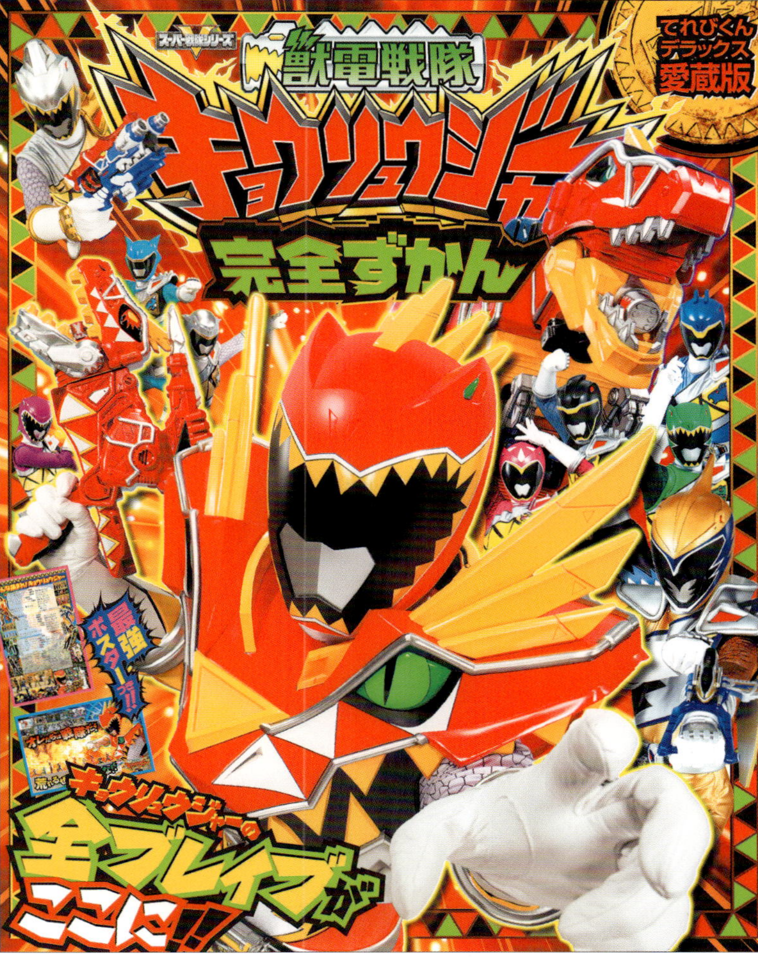

↖ **Above left:** Ressha Sentai ToQger *(2014) featured trains heavily.*

↑ **Above right:** *Dinosaurs made a comeback in* Zyuden Sentai Kyoryuger *(2013).*

celebrated the power of imagination, childhood, and one of Japan's great passions, trains. The series is a classic of its time.

In recent years, the franchise's technology and narratives have undergone significant transformations, resulting in some unusual outputs. *Kikai Sentai Zenkaiger* (2021) boldly introduced a team comprised almost entirely of robots and no humans (and thus no visible actors). The robots themselves transform into giant robots. The following year, *Avataro Sentai Donbrothers* (2022) completely upended how *sentai* stories are told, with a perpetually scattered and dysfunctional team and an entirely unpredictable storyline. It also broke new technical ground. Some of the superheroes, once transformed, were no longer actors in costumes but fully CGI characters, enabling never-before-seen changes in scale.

One of the most significant advancements occurred in 2023 with *Ohsama Sentai King-Ohger*, an ambitious series set in a world divided into kingdoms ruled by kings and queens and rife with rivalries, alliances, and conspiracies. The series combined chivalric and steampunk imagery with insect-themed robots, resulting in striking visuals. Toei went even further by using LED wall technology for the first time, a technique famously pioneered by Disney's *The Mandalorian* that uses a giant, curved screen to create highly realistic digital backdrops. Though not quite as sophisticated, the innovation

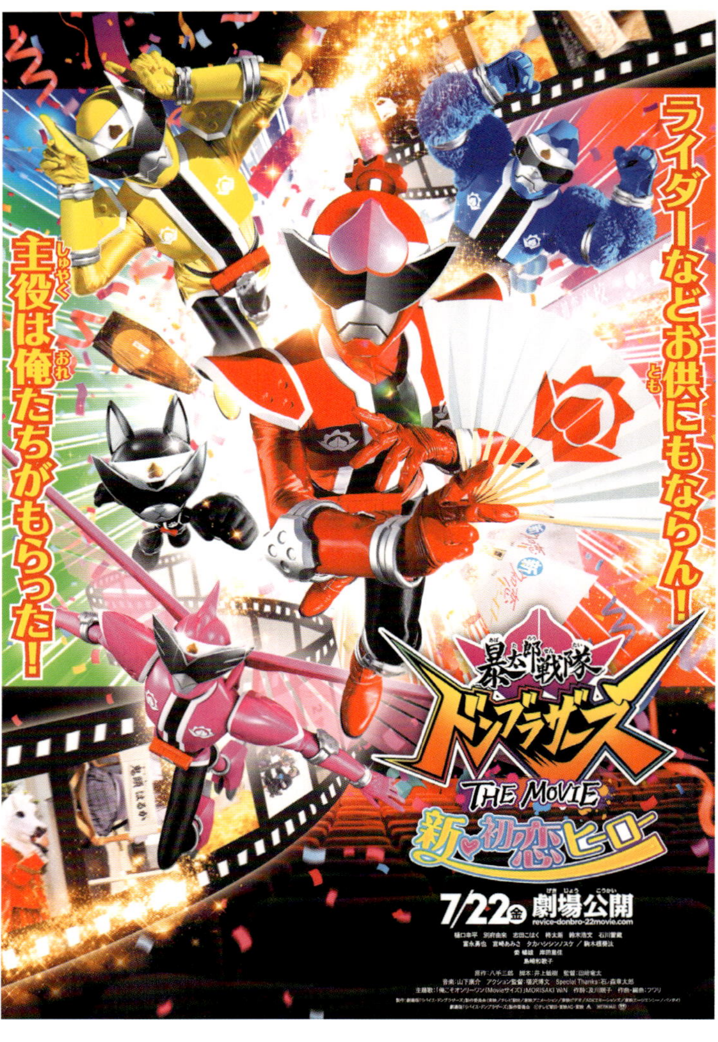

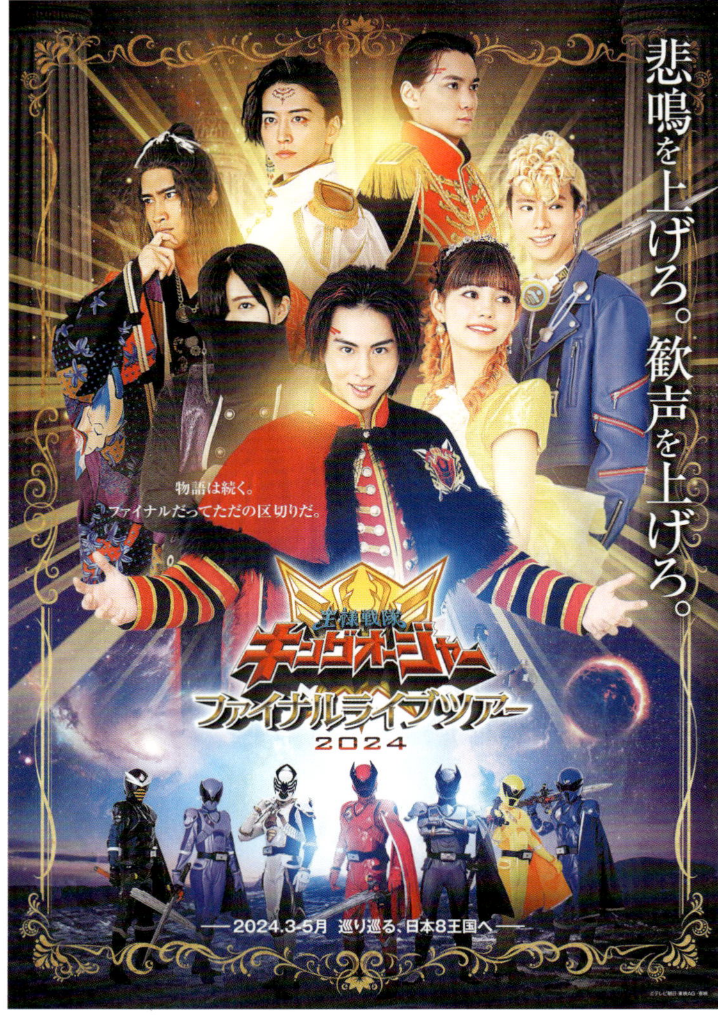

↑ **Above:** Avataro Sentai Donbrothers *(2022) (above left) and* Ohsama Sentai King-Ohger *(2023) (above right). After their initial run, the series were reborn as films and live shows.*

introduced genuine novelty and hinted at exciting possibilities for the future.

With its undeniable cultural impact, distinctive style, and unparalleled ability to constantly reinvent itself while staying on air continuously since 1979, *Super Sentai* has firmly established itself as a cornerstone of Japanese superhero franchises. However, one thing remains elusive: true global recognition. In 2023, Toei's veteran producer Shinichirō Shirakura announced Toei New Wave 2033, a comprehensive strategy to expand its superhero franchises internationally over the next decade. With the simultaneous decline of *Power Rangers*, the future may be brighter—and more colorful—than ever for the return of Japanese superheroes to Western audiences.

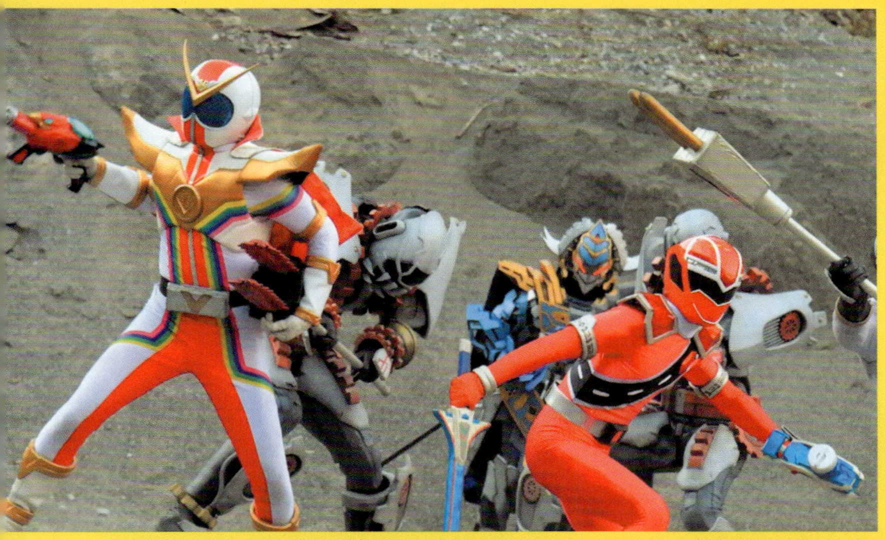

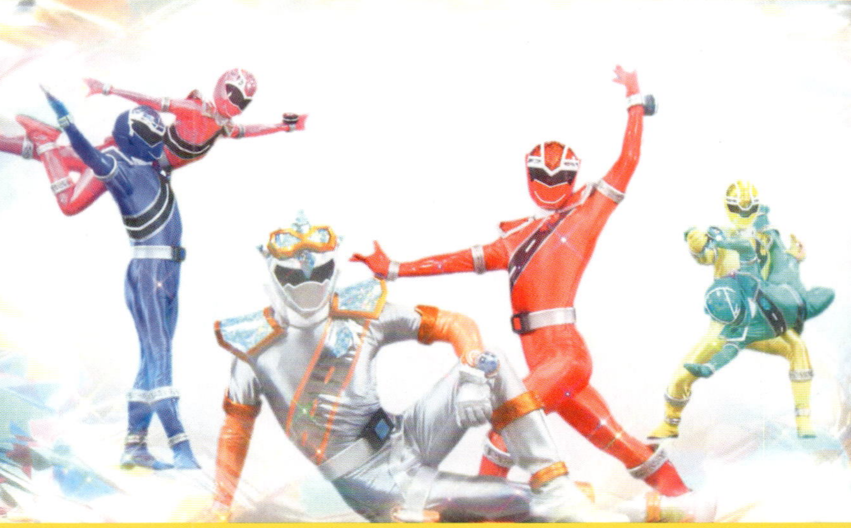

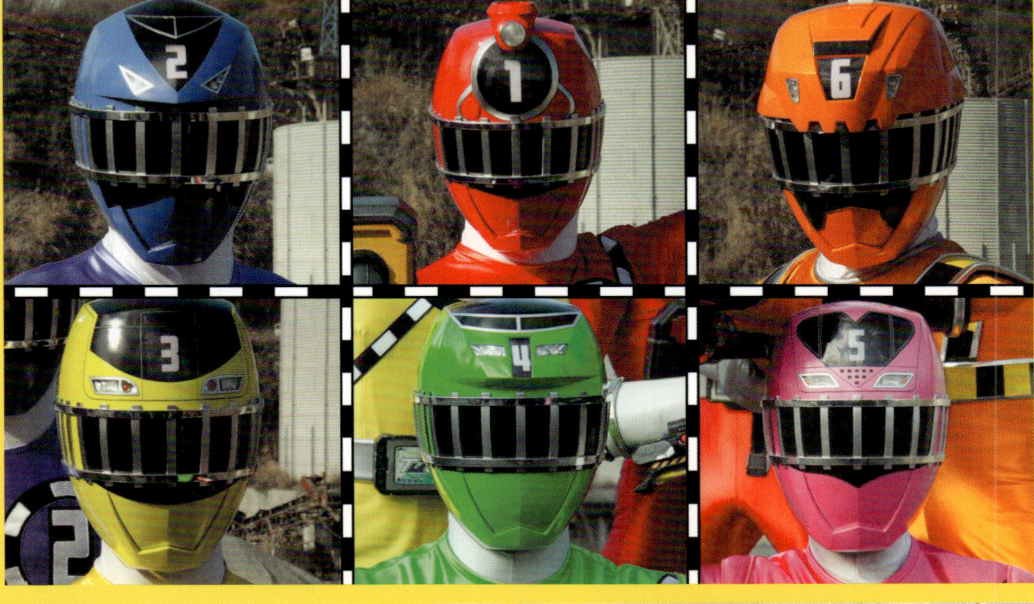

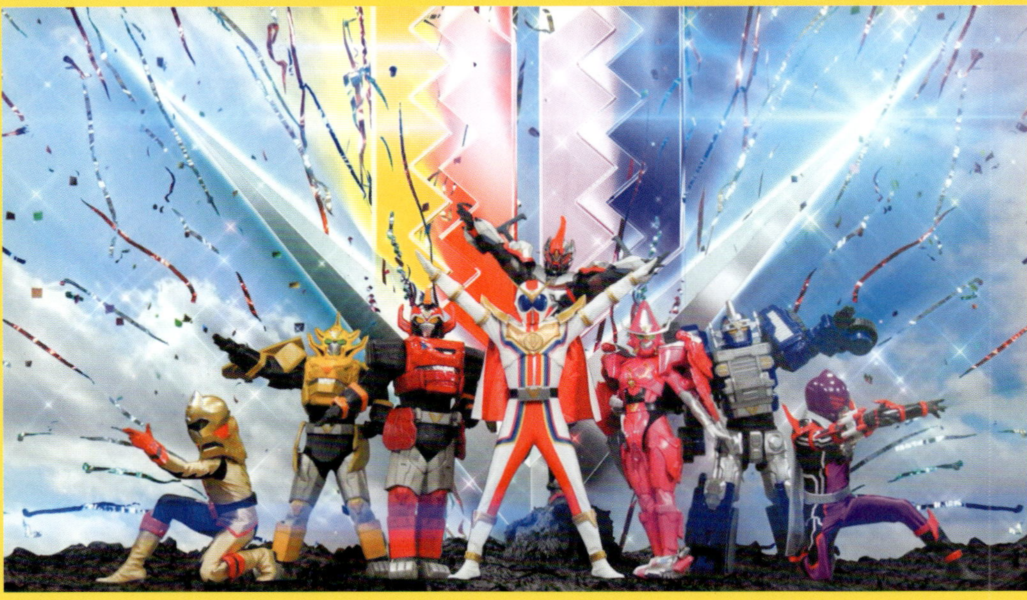

↖ **Above left:** *The team from* Mashin Sentai Kiramager *(2020).*

↑ **Above right:** *Sentai series cross over regularly. Shown is a crossover between Zenkaigers and Kiramagers, sentai from 2020.*

← **Left:** *One unusual ability of ToQgers was their power to switch colors, symbolizing trains switching rails at railroad junctions.*

↙ **Below:** *Still from* Kikai Sentai Zenkaiger *(2021).*

METAL HERO: SUPERHEROES OF STEEL

THE SPACE SHERIFF TRILOGY

Today, Toei's heroes are primarily represented by *Super Sentai* and *Kamen Rider*. However, *Metal Hero*, another of its franchises, enjoyed its own significant success once upon a time, though it has not endured. *Metal Hero* emerged as the successor to the wave of 1970s superheroes, effectively stepping in to replace *Kamen Rider* during a period when it was struggling to remain relevant. The first cornerstone of the new franchise was the iconic *Space Sheriff Gavan* in 1982.

The arrival and unprecedented success of *Star Wars* deeply influenced science fiction worldwide, and *tokusatsu* was no exception. In *Space Sheriff Gavan*, the main character hails from space, transforms into a justice warrior made of metal, wields a laser sword, and commands a massive spaceship along with other futuristic vehicles. His mission brings him to Earth to thwart the attempted invasion by Makuu, a criminal space organization led by Don Horror.

Gavan's name is a deliberate homage to the beloved French actor Jean Gabin, the hero of a new era. Gavan was played by Kenji Ohba, primarily a stuntman and suit actor at Toei (aside from a stint as the Black Warrior in *Battle Fever J*) before taking on what would be his first leading role. This turned out to be a key ingredient in the show's success, the palpable energy in scenes featuring an untransformed superhero, driven by its lead actor. In the

→ **Right:** *Covers for the Japanese Blu-Ray and DVD editions of the series* Space Sheriff Gavan *(1982).*

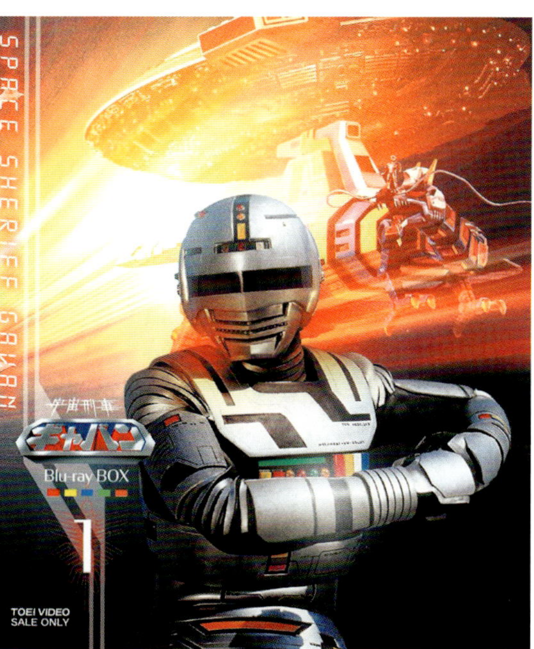

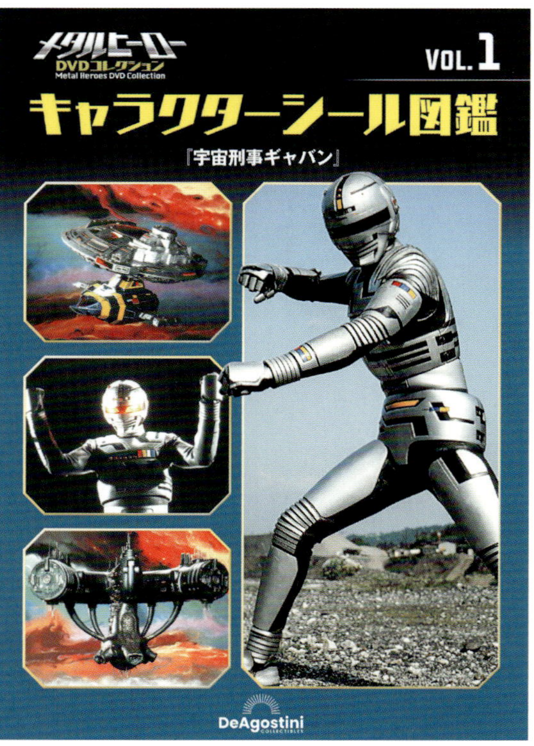

1970s, non-costumed lead actors would sometimes fight on-screen, but such scenes were usually brief, quickly transitioning to the superhero transformation, allowing a more experienced stuntman to perform in costume, paired with the typical array of special effects.

But in *Gavan*, Ohba's superhero is capable of executing the most daring stunts and moves even before donning his iconic silver suit. Ohba performed explosive chase scenes and improbable jumps entirely on his own, without a stunt double. This shift highlights advancements in *tokusatsu* stunt training in the 1970s (and in Japanese action films in general), improvements that were fostered by organizations like the Japan Action Club (renamed Japan Action Enterprise in 1996) and significantly beefed up the quality of uncostumed action scenes.

The series was highly dynamic and action-packed and even experimented with visual effects in battle sequences where the superheroes had transformed.

↓ **Below:** Metal Hero *and its space vigilantes. From left to right: Spielvan, Gavan, and Jaspion.*

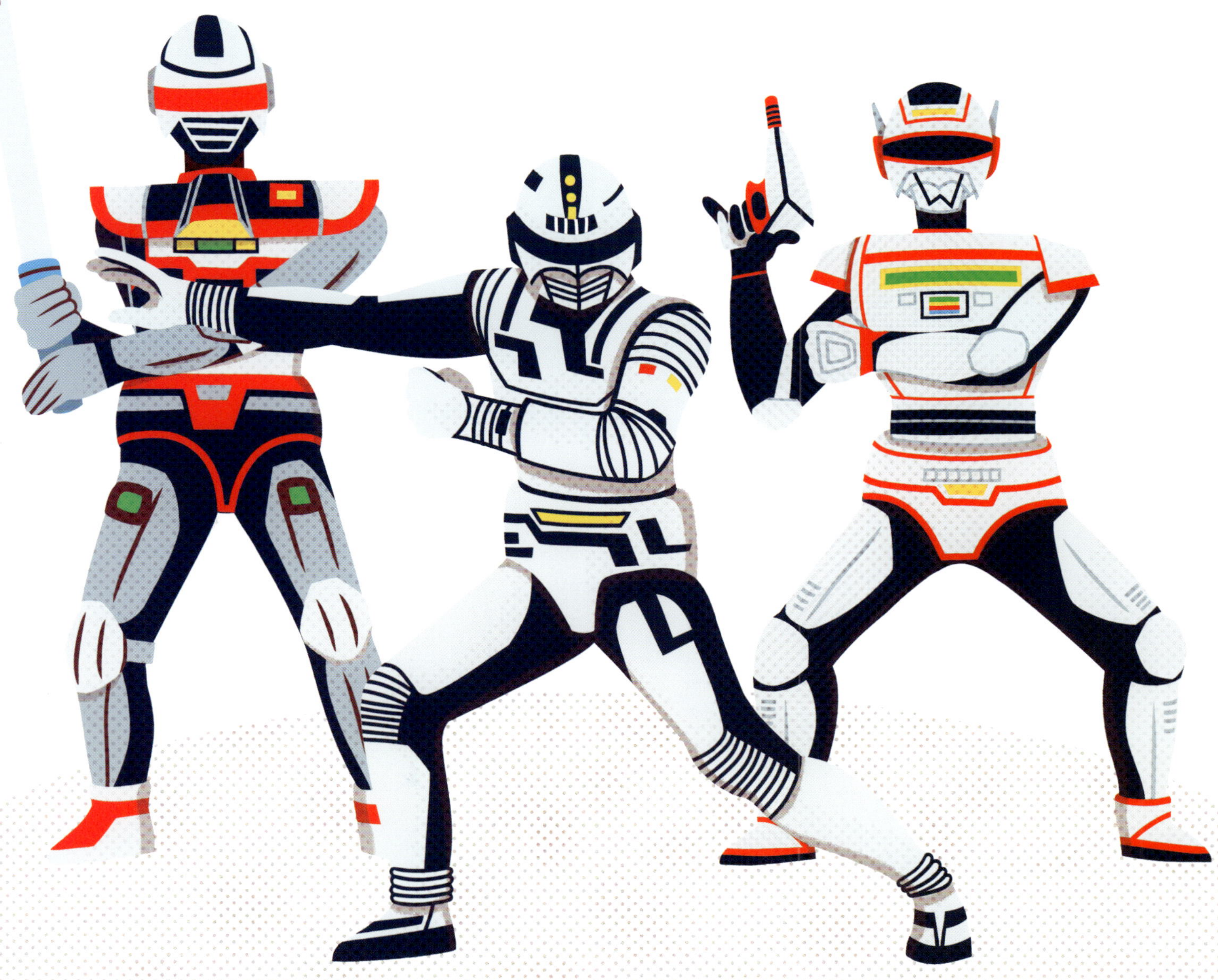

➜ **Right:** *Magazine spread for the series* Space Sheriff Gavan *(1982).*

➜ **Below:** *Saibarian, one of Gavan's vehicles.*

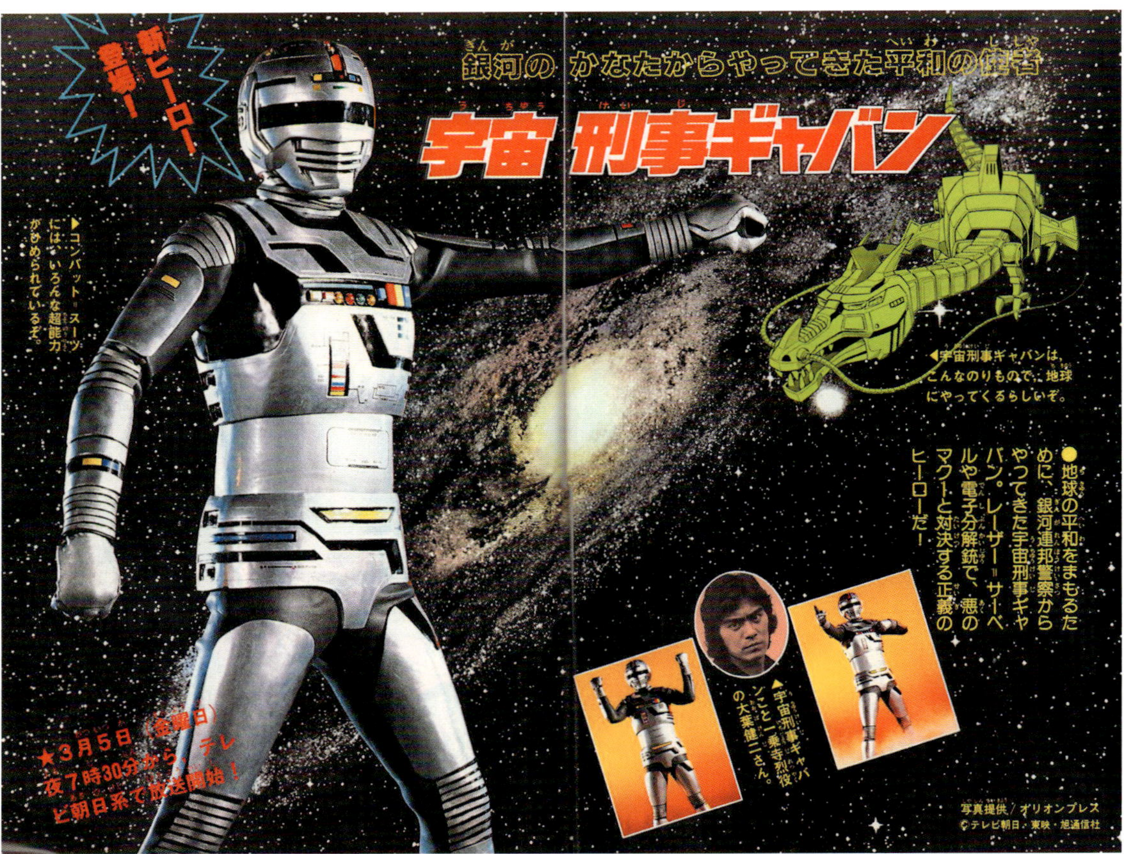

When Gavan confronts members of Makuu, he is often transported to an alternate dimension that looks noticeably different from the typical Earth settings (and the usual natural backdrops of *tokusatsu*). The scenes feature ethereal, almost psychedelic environments, created using matte painting, a large painted backdrop used in live-action scenes to simulate a surreal, deep-space landscape.

Gavan had a lot to recommend it for its time. It featured a hero performing acrobatic stunts in civilian form, a charismatic superhero with inventive battles, and, as a bonus, his ship, the iconic *Dolgiran*. In essence, it cherry-picked the best parts of science fiction and inserted them into *tokusatsu*.

The series was followed directly by *Space Sheriff Sharivan* (1983) and *Space Sheriff Shaider* (1984), completing what is now known as the *Space Sheriff* trilogy. Like *Kamen Rider* in its time, each series can be viewed as a continuation of the previous one, directly related but introducing a new hero in each story.

Sharivan dazzled with his shiny red armor, whereas Shaider sported a brilliant blue suit. The formula remained largely unchanged—a warrior of justice armed with a laser sword (though its technical challenges made frequent appearances difficult)—but the studio refined the concept, particularly the way in which the heroes' ships transformed. Shaider's ship transforms into a giant gun, which he then wields from a distance.

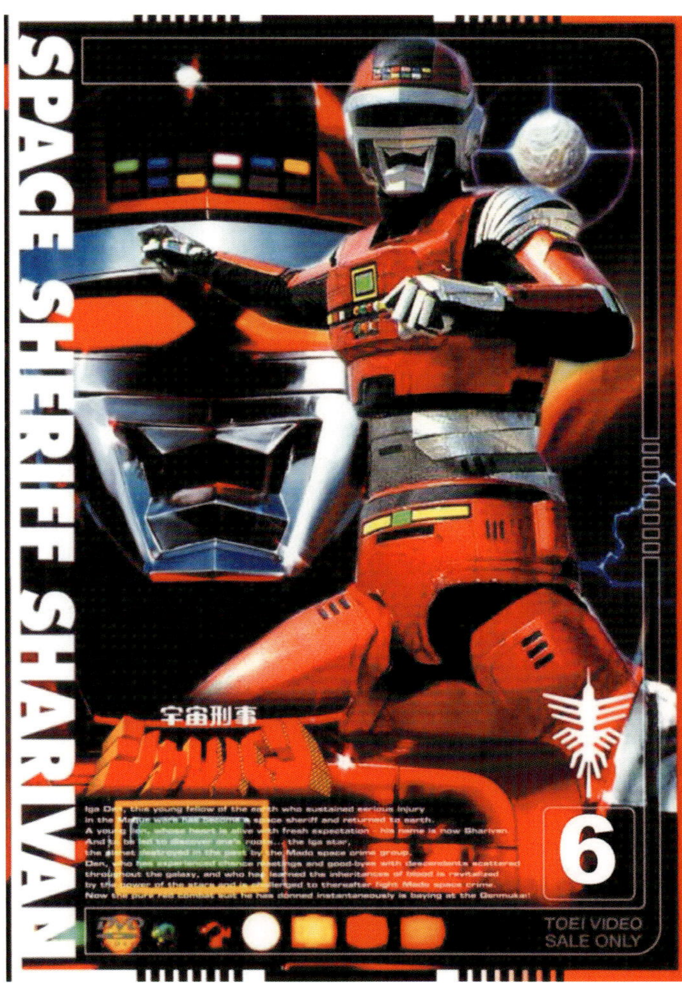

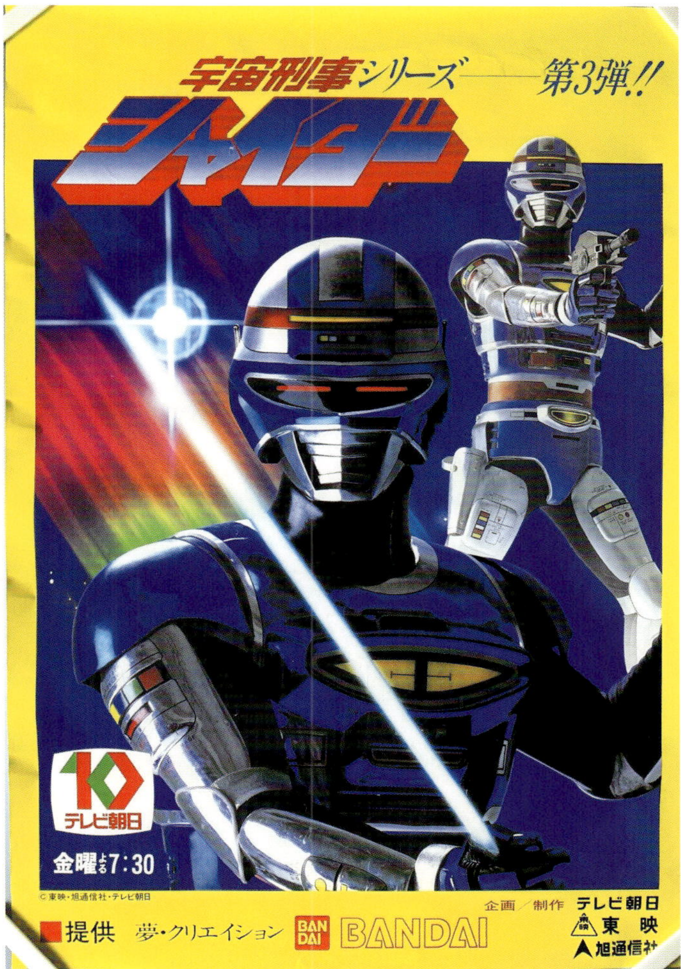

Above left: *Japanese DVD cover for* Space Sheriff Sharivan *(1983).*

Above right: *Promotional poster for* Space Sheriff Shaider *(1984).*

The trilogy also introduced female characters accompanying each hero. They didn't transform into superheroes themselves, but they frequently provided crucial support.

Even today, Gavan and his companions remain iconic among 1980s superheroes, both in Japan and internationally. But ultimately, regardless of the country, the fact remains that the trilogy introduced an entire generation to the world of *tokusatsu*. In Japan, it marked the end of the creative frenzy of the 1970s, whereas in other countries, it heralded an opening to Japanese media. The *Metal Hero* series became a foundational entry point for many—a cornerstone of the franchise that would later unveil even more surprises.

CHANGING COURSE

With its *Space Sheriff* trilogy in place, Toei was able to confidently launch the *Metal Hero* franchise. But instead of merely copying and pasting the formula with slight variations each year, the franchise gradually introduced changes, some radical, in tone and universe.

Rather than direct sequels, more spiritual continuations emerged with series like *Jaspion* (1985) and *Spielvan* (1986). Despite similar appearances and basic concepts, the two series are in no way related to the *Space Sheriff* series and instead follow their own paths. In spirit, they are closer to the *Super Sentai* series of the same period, emphasizing

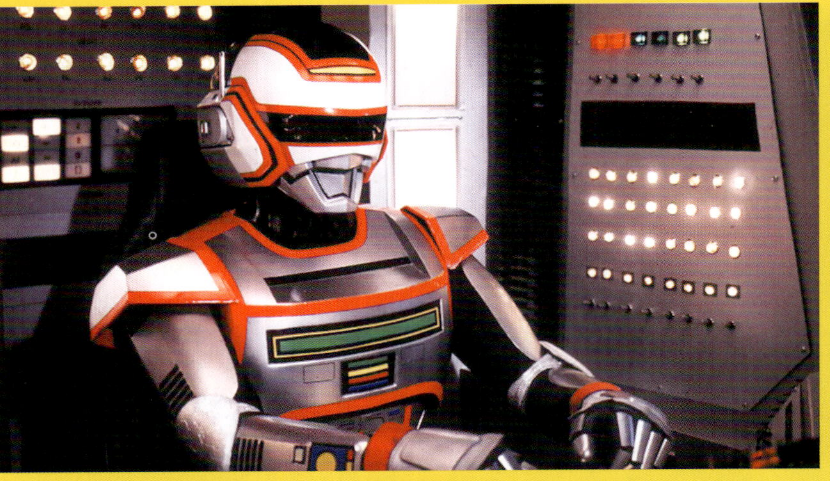

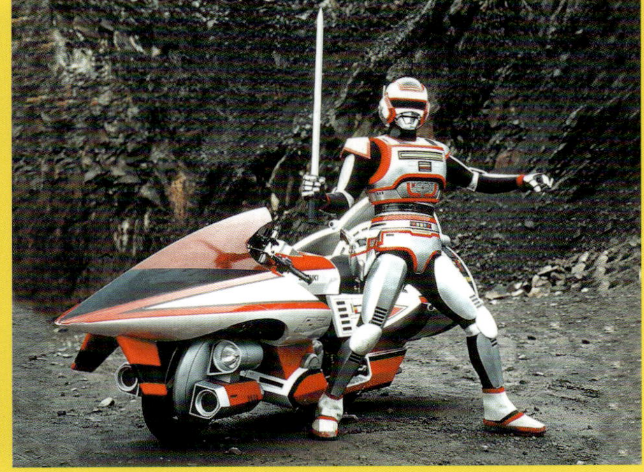

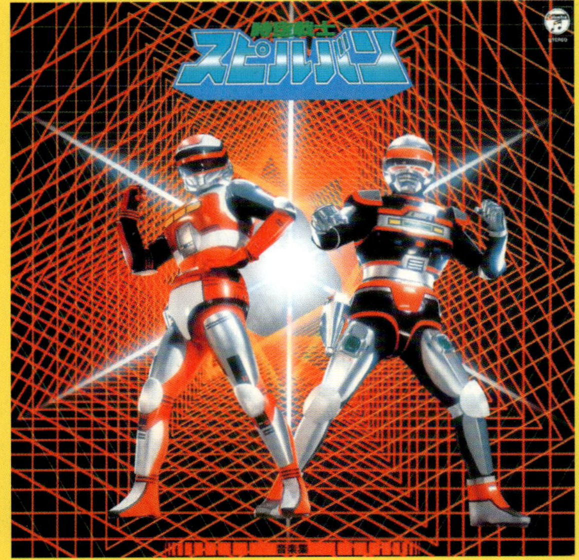

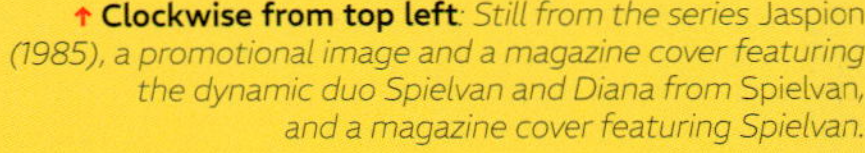

↑ **Clockwise from top left**: *Still from the series* Jaspion *(1985), a promotional image and a magazine cover featuring the dynamic duo Spielvan and Diana from* Spielvan*, and a magazine cover featuring* Spielvan.

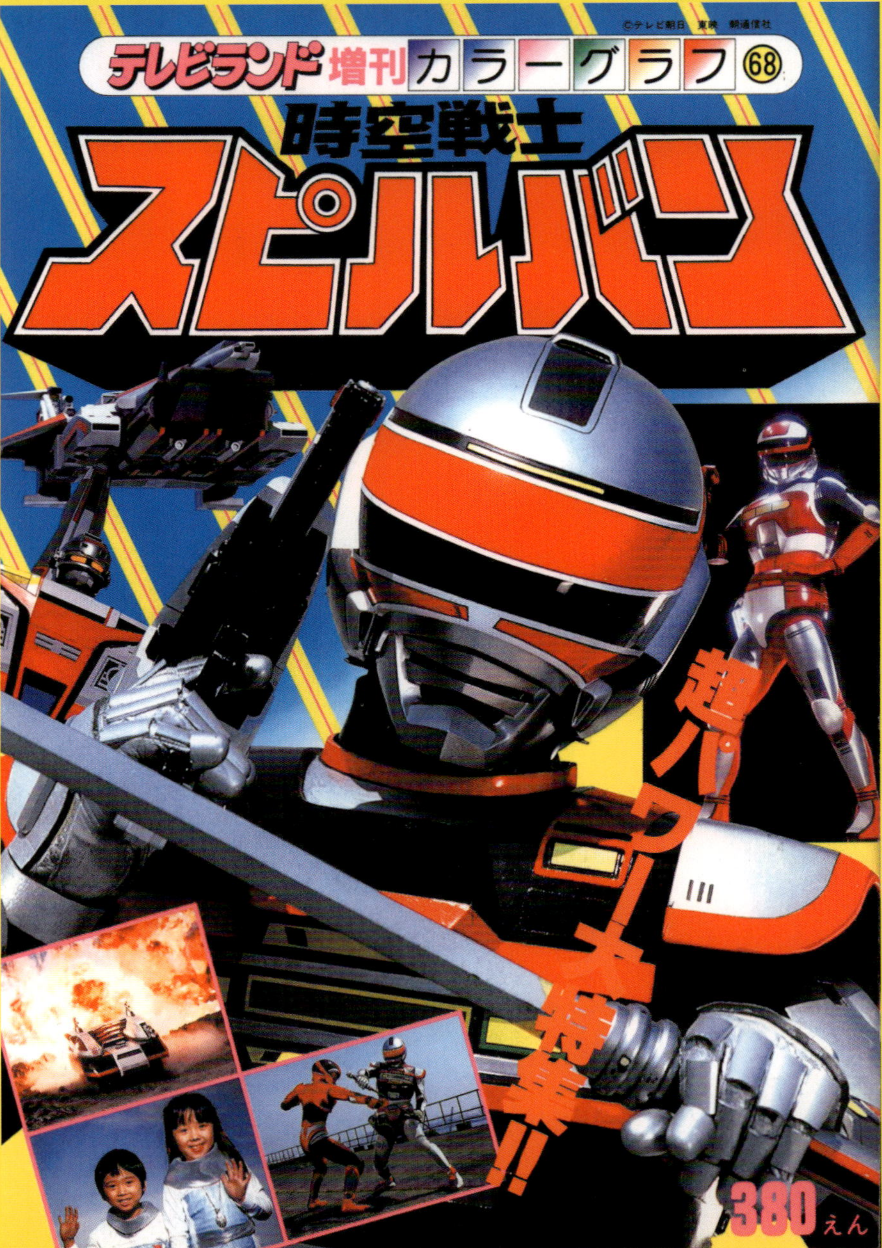

variations on a theme rather than strict continuity.

The absence of *Ultraman* on television left a gap, which *Jaspion* attempted to fill by highlighting battles with and against giants. These featured the hero's spaceship transforming into a mighty steel-fisted robot and monsters arriving on Earth. The series seemed to ride the wave of *Super Sentai*, which was gaining popularity with its engaging formula. The tone was also lighter, with Jaspion as a laid-back hero, accompanied by Anri, his clumsy android sidekick, and Miya, an alien creature reminiscent of Chewbacca from *Star Wars*.

Overall, the connection to *Star Wars* was even stronger than before, especially in the beginning when Jaspion traveled across space for his adventures. However, the narrative eventually forced them to return to Earth, likely a practical solution to the technical challenges of producing a space opera in an action-heavy series.

This approach set the stage for *Spielvan* (1986), which involved Spielvan and Diana, survivors of their planet's destruction by the Waller Empire, fleeing to Earth. The series introduced a continuous storyline revolving around the duo's origins and families. It combined familiar elements—heroes, giant robots—with a noteworthy innovation: the introduction of a female superhero on par with the usual male protagonist. Diana, played by stuntwoman Makoto Sumikawa, was portrayed as a true field combatant, equally effective in civilian and armored forms. She was later joined by Helen, the hero's sister, who could also transform. This dynamic brought a fresh, new perspective to such series that was all too rare at the time.

Choujinki Metalder (1987) returned to the premise of single, solitary hero with a uniquely complex nature. Unlike *Kamen Rider*, who is part human and part machine, Metalder is a pure android, entirely mechanical. Named Ryūsei Tsurugi by his creator, he uncovers his true nature and origin: He is an android created by a scientist in the image of his son, who died as a *kamikaze* during World

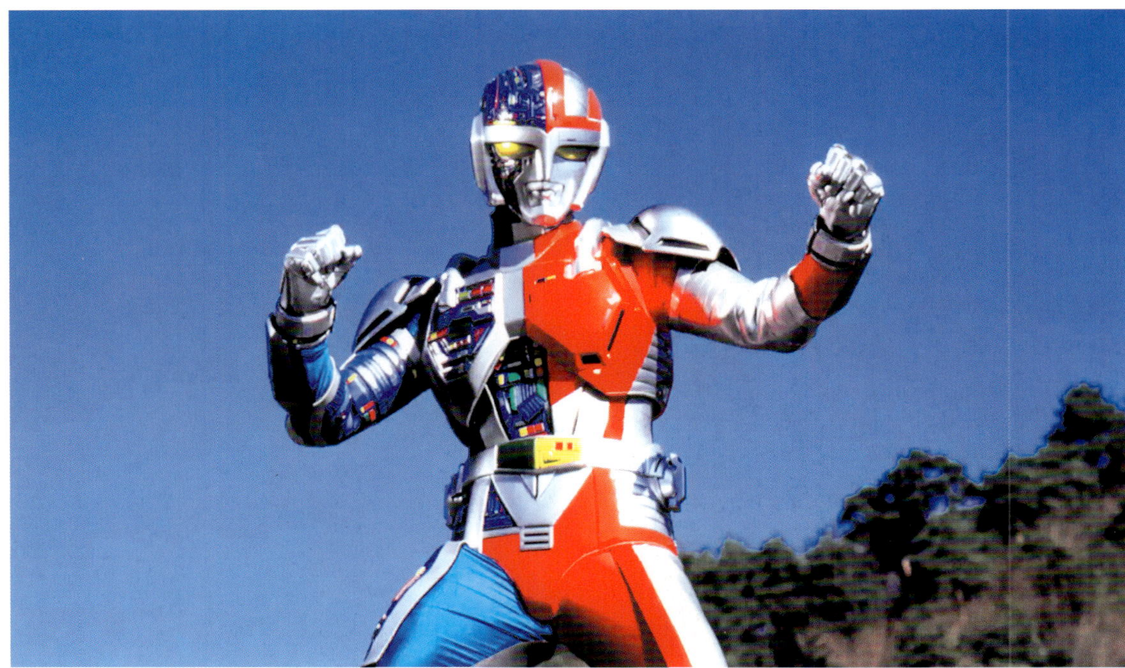

← **Left:** Choujinki Metalder *(1987) introduced a superhero tortured by his android identity.*

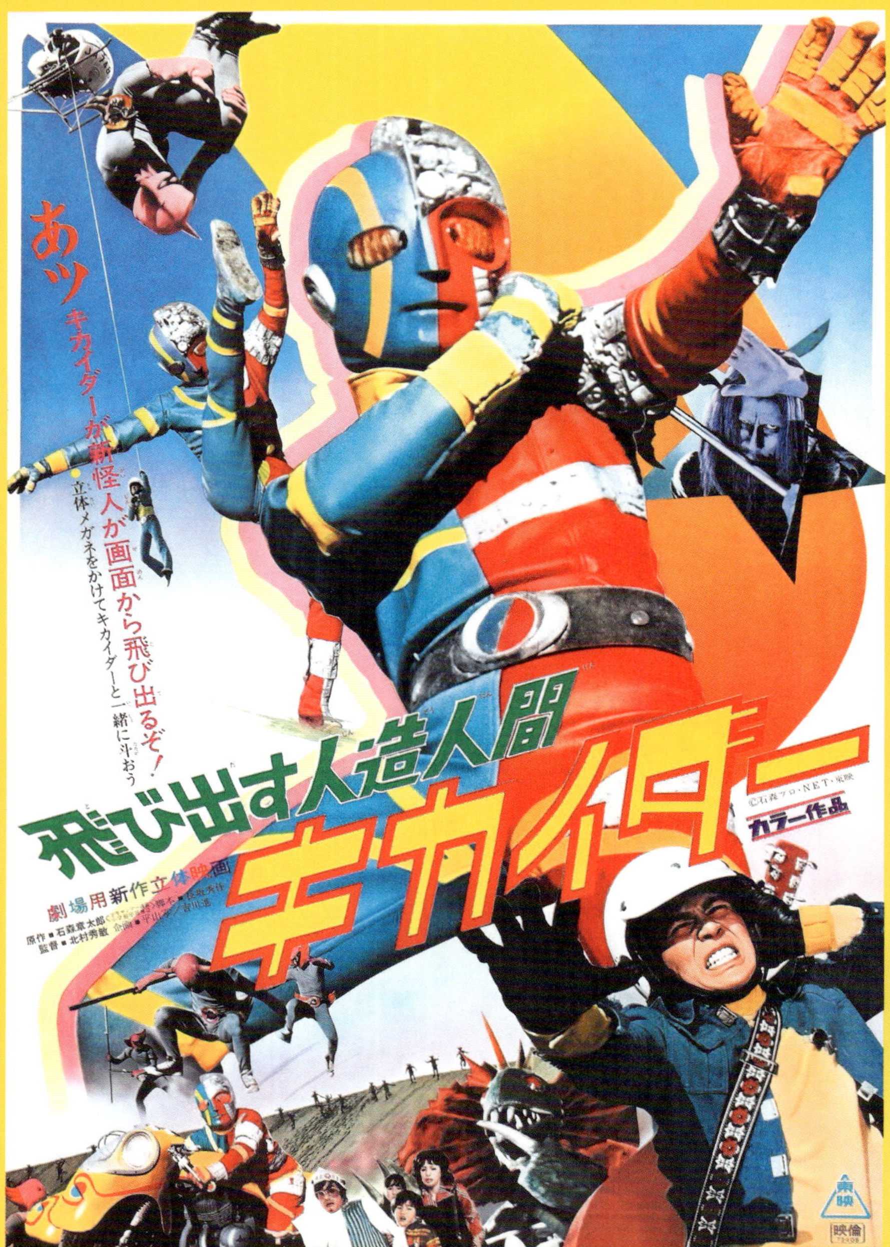

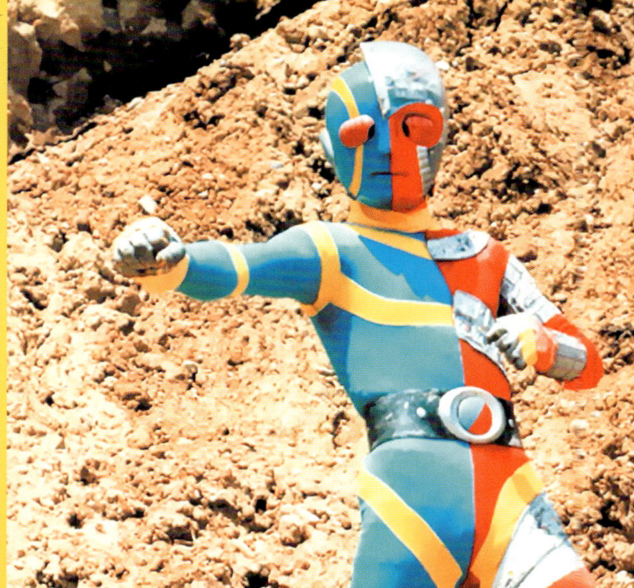

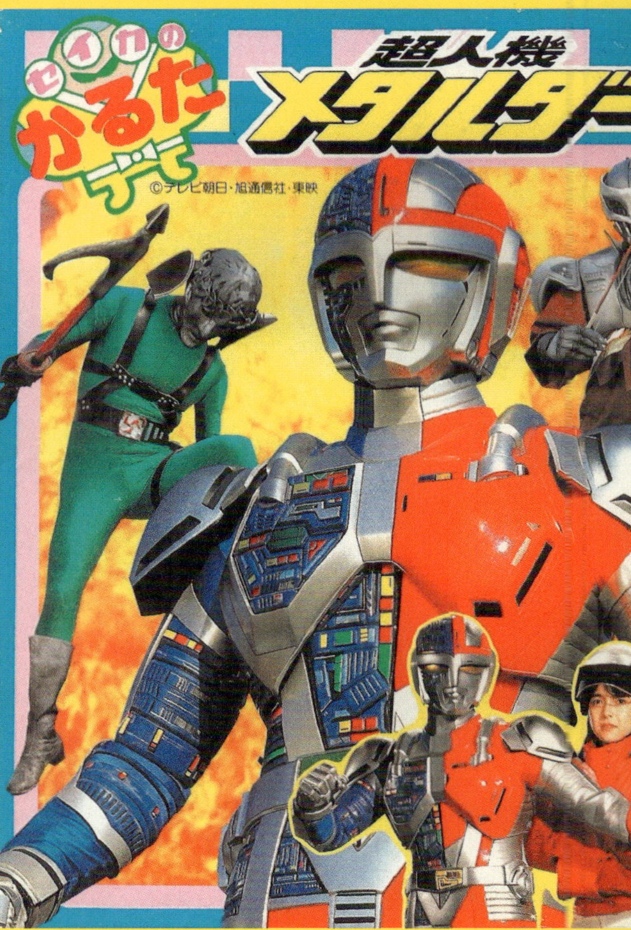

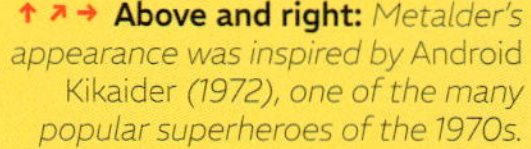
↑↗→ **Above and right:** *Metalder's appearance was inspired by Android Kikaider (1972), one of the many popular superheroes of the 1970s.*

superheroes, tropes from Westerns, and Zorro-inspired themes.

This rich period also created a biased image of *tokusatsu*. The genre is often associated with low-budget productions made with limited resources and tired concepts. Though not entirely untrue, this image was mainly formed in the 1970s, a time of frantic production that prioritized quantity over quality. The goal was to fill television airtime and simply to experiment with the still-new medium. Despite many iconic, high-quality works, even the Japanese acknowledge that the outdated image is merited and continue to find humor in it today through lighthearted tributes and parodies of a bygone era. This foundation has defined part of *tokusatsu* and contributes to its unique charm.

GARO: SUPERHEROES FOR ADULTS

Let us now move away from the retro style of the 1970s and turn our attention to Garo, a franchise with a radically different style that fully embraced modernity and breathed new life into the genre. We've mentioned Keita Amemiya, who worked on the *Kamen Rider* series, but the concept artist, who became a director out of necessity, ultimately created his own vision of the superhero in 2005, carving out a new niche and targeting the often-overlooked audience of adults.

The series' full title, *Golden Knight Garo*, speaks for itself. The show follows the adventures of Kouga Saejima, a Makai Knight and member of a warrior caste tasked with protecting humanity from Horrors, creatures born from and feeding on the darkness within humans. Featuring golden armor and an aesthetic reminiscent of Western chivalry but set in a modern (and sometimes futuristic) Japan, the franchise subverts expectations of a typical Japanese superhero.

Garo blends the spirit and aesthetics of chivalry with dark, eerie imagery that had never been seen before, even outside the *tokusatsu* genre. The juxtaposition of the alternative, almost timeless society of the Makai with the human world created a peculiar mix of styles. From urban settings to baroque locations and visions, right down to the grandiose appearances of some characters, the franchise served up an astonishingly unique blend.

Of course, the show still retained other designs typical of *tokusatsu*. Under Amemiya's unbridled creativity, viewers are treated to a spectacle of dazzling creatures and knights in all their forms. The monsters range from classic horned demons to giant, nightmarish or misshapen visions, some humanoid in appearance and others far less so. In contrast, every effort was made to ensure the heroes shone. Once transformed, they exhibited a rare beauty and embraced the image of the heroic figure without cynicism.

To assert its strong artistic identity and deliver a particularly solid action series, the franchise had to break free from some of the traditional constraints of *tokusatsu*. Though the series never shied away from the conventional, with its stunning costumes

Below: *Zaruba is a sentient ring that aids the hero Garo in his fighting.*

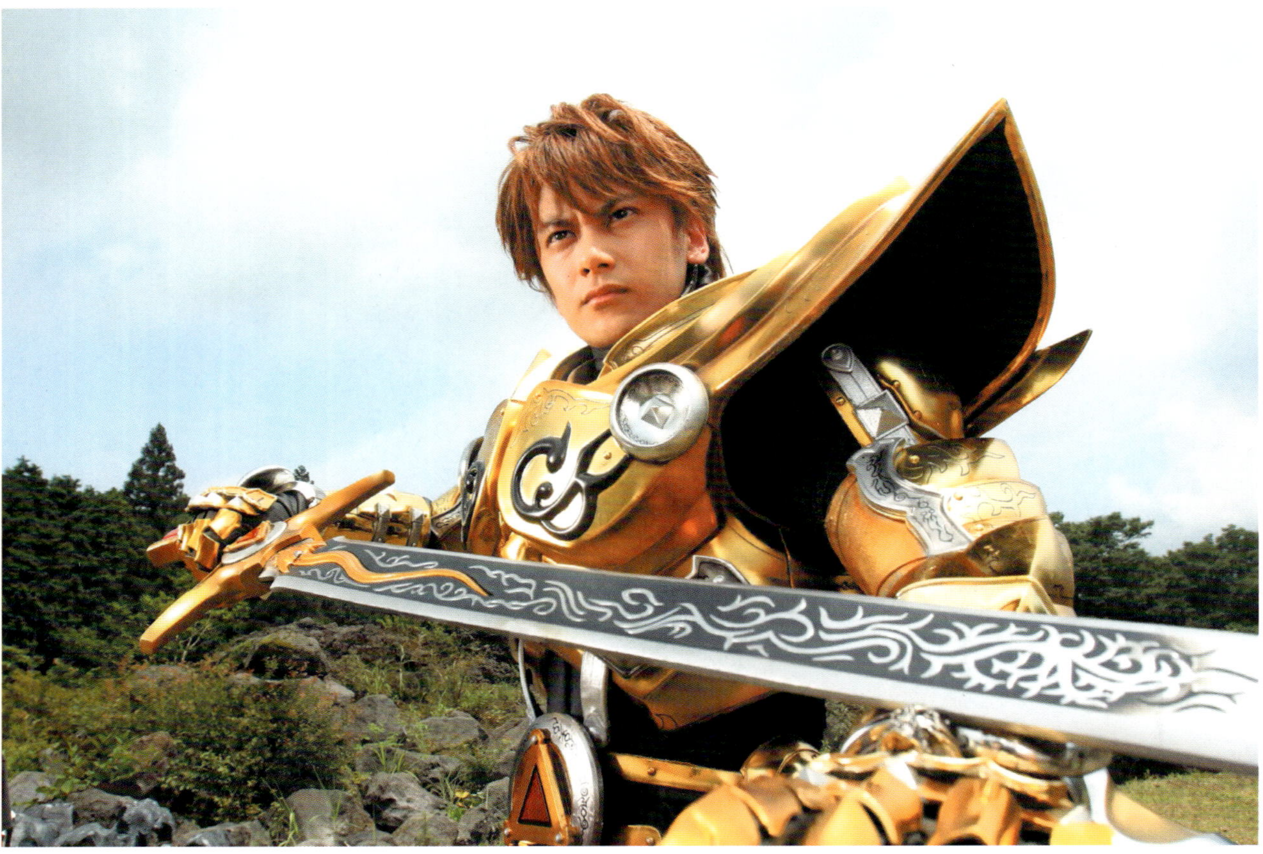

→ **Right:** *Kouga Saejima,* Golden Knight Garo *(2005).*

and makeup, it fully embraced digital effects to create impactful, larger-than-life moments over the course of the series. These finely choreographed battles helped *Garo* establish a unique identity within the genre.

Additionally, the series broke from the standard yearly renewal cycle adopted by competitors, instead opting for shorter series or films released several years apart. This approach ensured that newcomers were not left behind while also allowing for continuity across multiple series, allowing fans to watch the heroes grow and age. This served as a way to connect with longtime *tokusatsu* enthusiasts seeking a more relatable experience.

The franchise managed to remain fresh and innovative, finding new angles to explore, such as *GARO: Versus Road* (2020), a new iteration and a departure from previous paths. It ventured into the realm of virtual reality while deconstructing some traditional tropes.

Still alive and well today, *Garo* has become a reliable staple and a standout alternative in the genre, boasting an inimitable, captivating style and serving as the perfect gateway to the world of *tokusatsu*.

WONDROUS WOMEN: THE FEMALE SUPERHEROES OF TOKUSATSU

As you might have guessed, the world of Japanese superheroes is predominantly male. The reality is unfortunately simple. Solo or majority-led female superheroes are rare, but they do exist. It's time to introduce you to these wondrous women of *tokusatsu*.

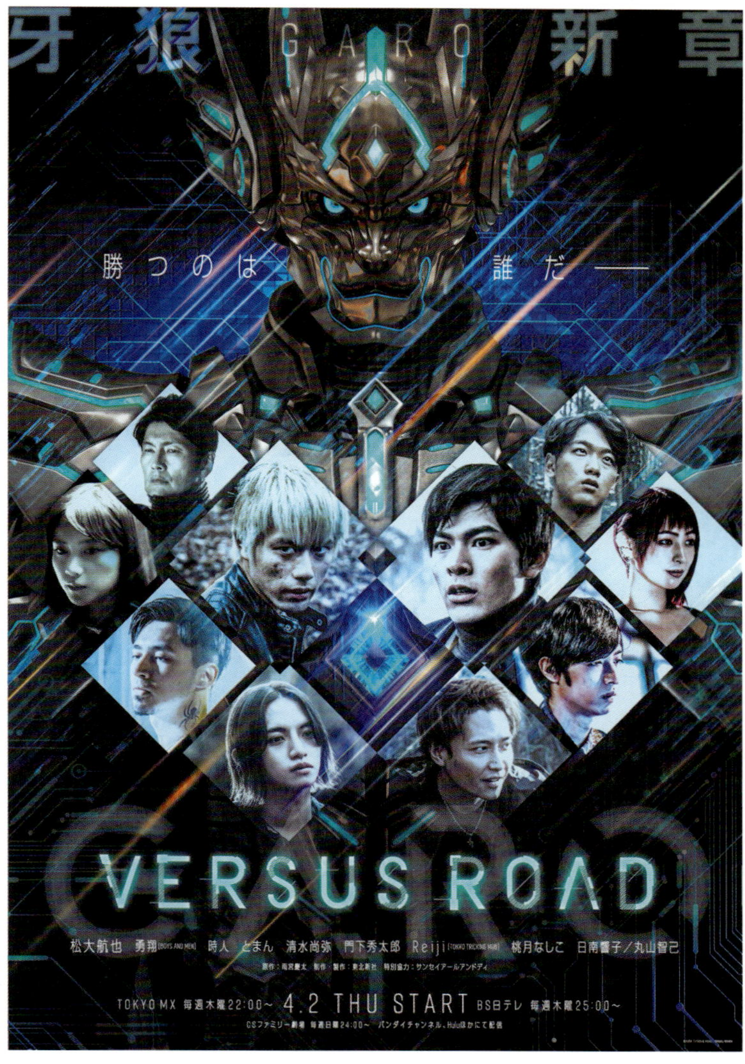

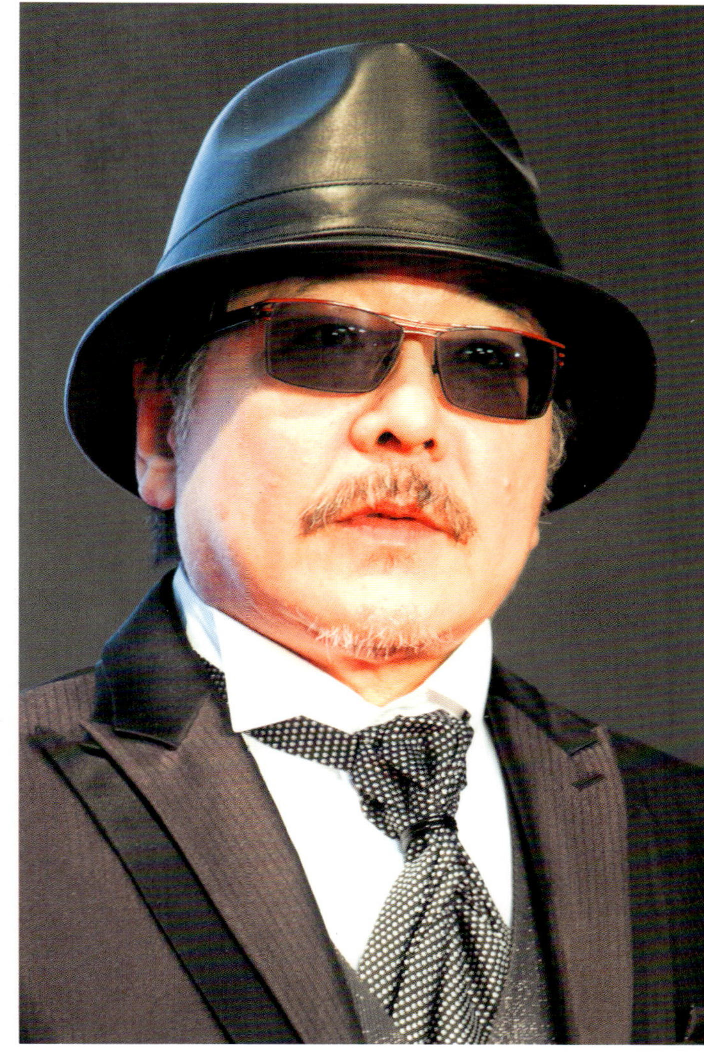

↖ **Above left:** *Japanese poster for* GARO: Versus Road *(2020).*

↑ **Above:** *Keita Amemiya, creator of the franchise.*

↓ **Below:** *Poitrine, one of the best-known magical girls in* tokusatsu.

The very first female *tokusatsu* superhero dates back to 1971, the year *Kamen Rider* began. *We Love You!! Witch Teacher* was inspired by the early days of the magical girl genre, kicked off in 1966 with the anime *Sally the Witch*. *Witch Teacher* combined *tokusatsu* conventions (such as transformations into costumed superheroes) with the slice-of-life charm of *Bewitched*. The magical main character and the setting were taken from the Japanese folktale *The Tale of the Princess Kaguya*, and the series was a Toei production conceived by the indefatigable Shōtarō Ishinomori.

After that, it would be some time before solo female superheroes reappeared on the scene. Alongside the *Metal Hero* series, Toei launched the quirky *Toei Fushigi Comedy Series* (*fushigi* means "mystery") aimed at younger audiences. After several series featuring tiny creatures and cute robots, and some detective-style stories reminiscent of *The Famous Five*, the world was finally treated to no fewer than six pure magical girl titles. They drew inspiration from Chinese mythology (*Magical Chinese Girl Paipai!*, 1989), Egyptian mythology (*Mysterious Nile Girl Thutmose*, 1991), and Japanese folklore (the character Urashima Tarō in *Sing! Great Dragon Palace*,

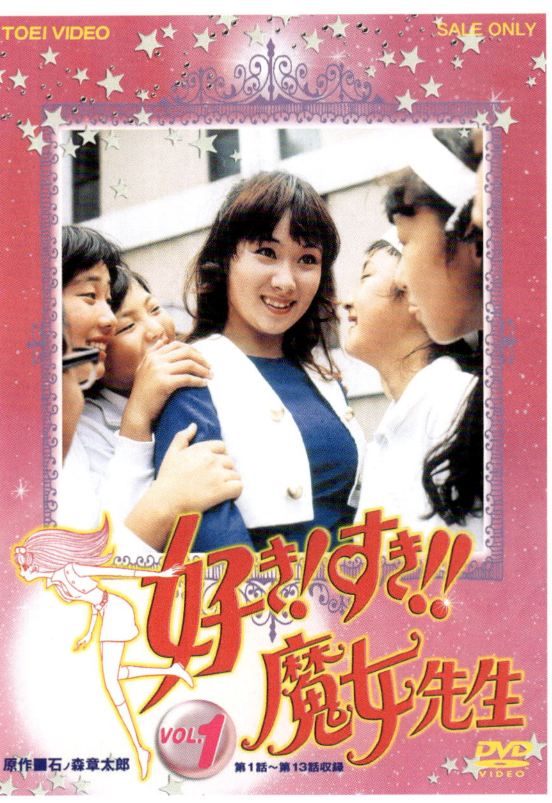

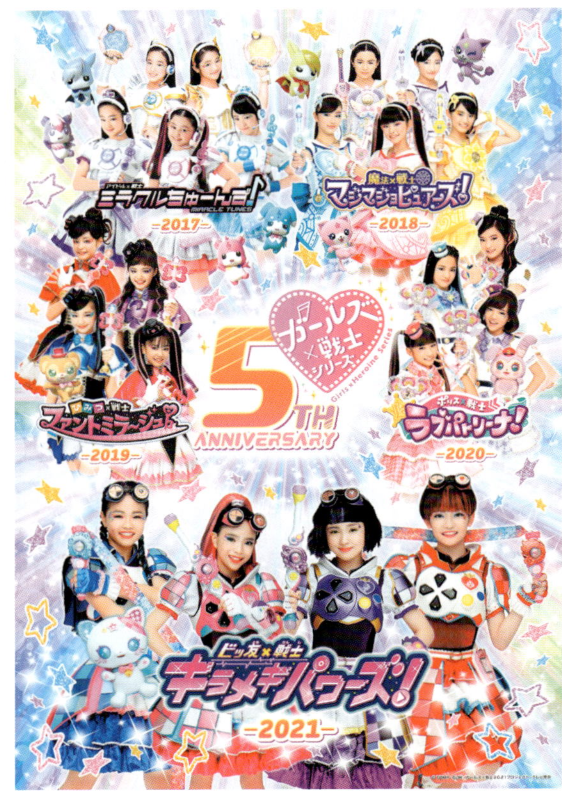

→ **Right:** *Cover of the Japanese DVD for the series* We Love You!! Witch Teacher *(1971).*

→ **Far right**: *Commemorative poster of the five series in the* Girls x Heroine *franchise.*

↓ **Below:** *The series* Mysterious Nile Girl Thutmose *(1991) drew from Egyptian mythology.*

1992). The series were impressively creative in their concepts. However, even with popular entries like *La Belle Fille Masquée Poitrine* (1990), the franchise ended in 1993 with *Yuugen Jikkou Sisters Shushutorian*.

It's worth noting that in 1992, Toei struck gold with its launch of the anime *Sailor Moon*, which incorporated the conventions of *Super Sentai* (colorful teams, weekly monsters)—tropes much beloved by the author of the original manga, Naoko Takeuchi. For a while, it seemed the genre would focus on animation instead of live-action productions—until the 2003 *Sailor Moon tokusatsu* series. Adapting the first part of the manga before forging its own path for a single broadcast year, *Pretty Guardian Sailor Moon* was a modest but heartfelt adaptation, supervised by Takeuchi herself.

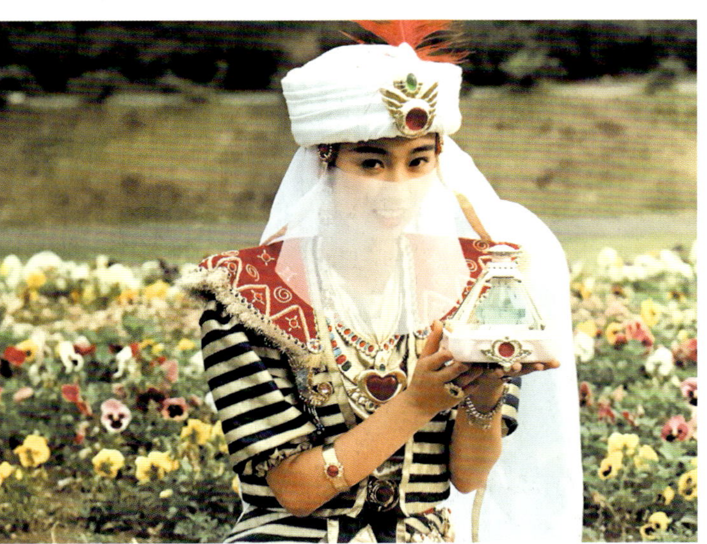

Despite these efforts, magical girls in the *tokusatsu* style have struggled to regain popularity, their appeal remaining primarily rooted in anime.

Yet, the itch to produce series with strong female superheroes never truly went away. *Lady Battle Cop* (1990), the female counterpart of *The Mobile Cop Jiban* (and thus *RoboCop*), shone in an explosive TV movie and held its own against its cousin, *Metal Hero*.

richness. Each era has its trends, obsessions, successes, failures, and surprises that have shaped the genre's history—a history that extends well beyond Japan. We'll also take a look at the influence of *tokusatsu* on the rest of the world and its impact on productions from Asia and the United States.

Tokusatsu is more prevalent than you might think. It's everywhere, lending its weight and popping up in the most unexpected places. Let's take a look at these multifaceted, captivating, sometimes surprising universes of whimsy to help you understand the history and evolution of Japanese television and cinema as a whole.

Below: Tokusatsu *has much more to offer than superheroes and kaijū.*

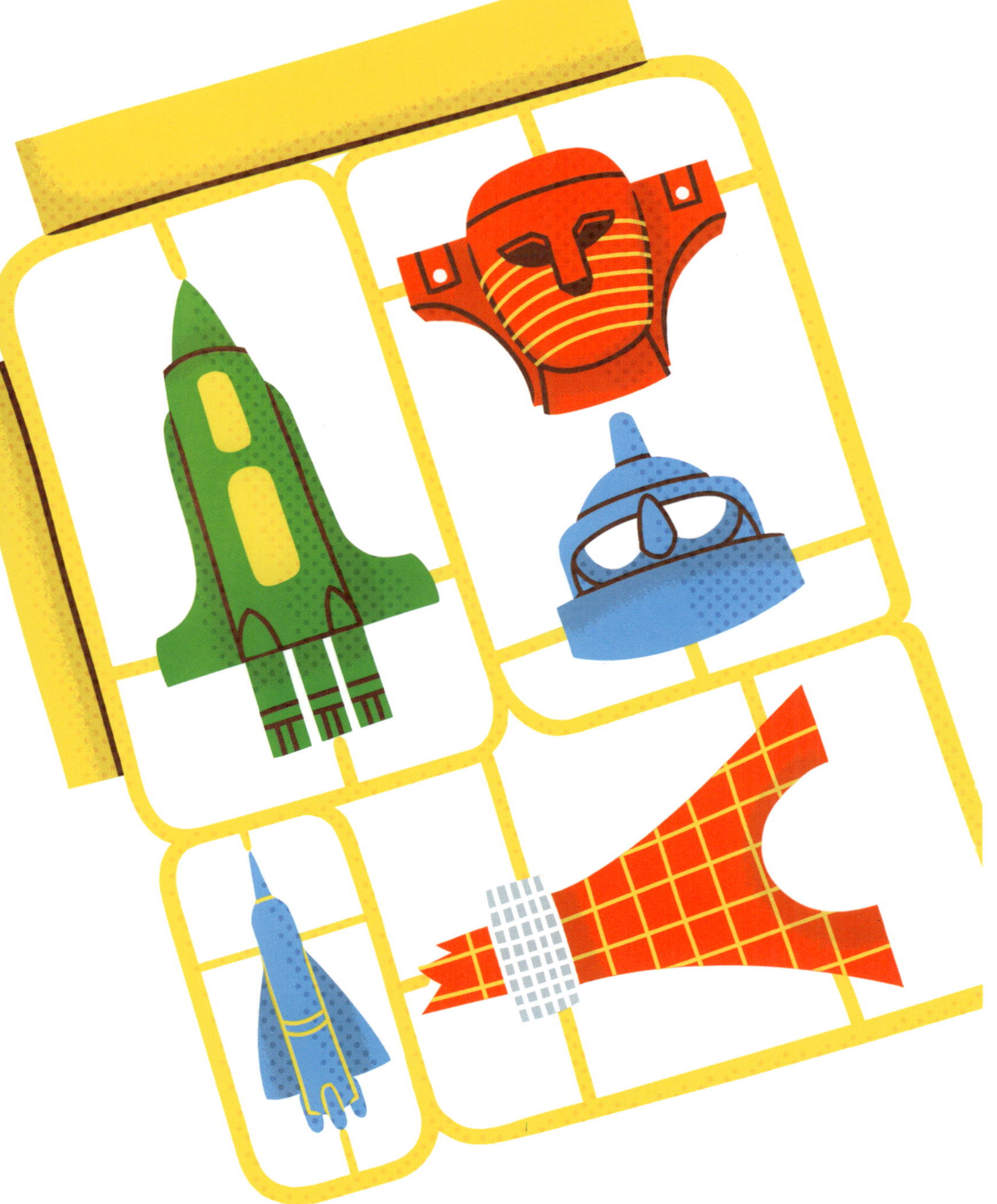

SCIENCE FICTION IN JAPAN

SPACE EXPLORATION

When you think of the vast realm of science fiction, you might immediately think of space exploration. Stories about humanity venturing to conquer the stars and discover the unknown—or conversely, tales of invasion by creatures from another galaxy—are central to the genre. Though space themes are touched upon in *kaijū* and superhero stories, many productions have explored different sci-fi themes.

One of the first Japanese sci-fi films in this vein was *Warning from Space* in 1956 by Daiei Studios. At the time, American theaters were dominated by movies about alien invasions, and Japan hopped on the bandwagon. *Warning from Space* featured starfish-shaped aliens who come to Earth to warn humans of an impending asteroid collision. The film exploited fears of the unknown, both alien threats and ineluctable cosmic disasters.

Toho responded in 1959 with *Battle in Outer Space*. This time, the story was more straightforward. Facing a series of strange events caused by lunar aliens, humans launch a mission to stop them. The simplistic, one-dimensional narrative was merely a pretext for Ishirō Honda and Eiji Tsuburaya to create impressive

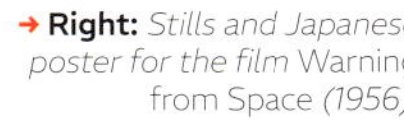

Right: *Stills and Japanese poster for the film* Warning from Space *(1956).*

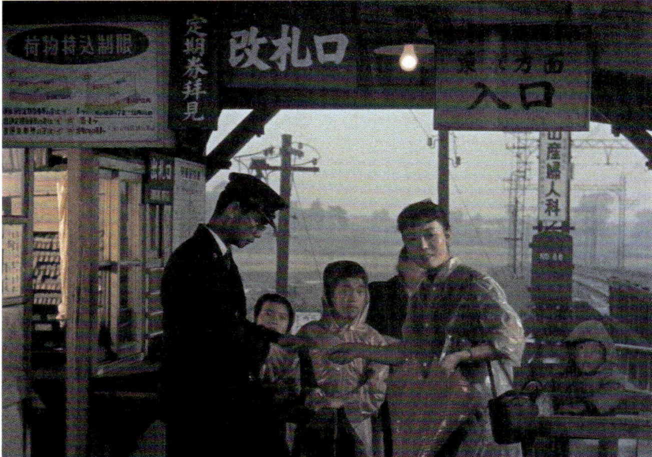

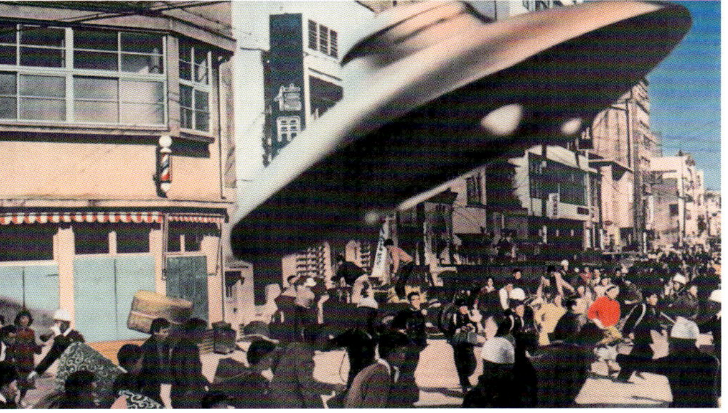

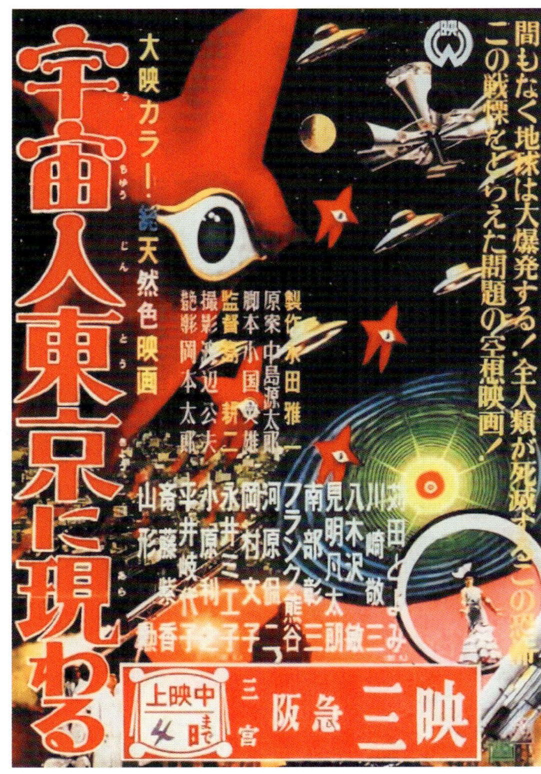

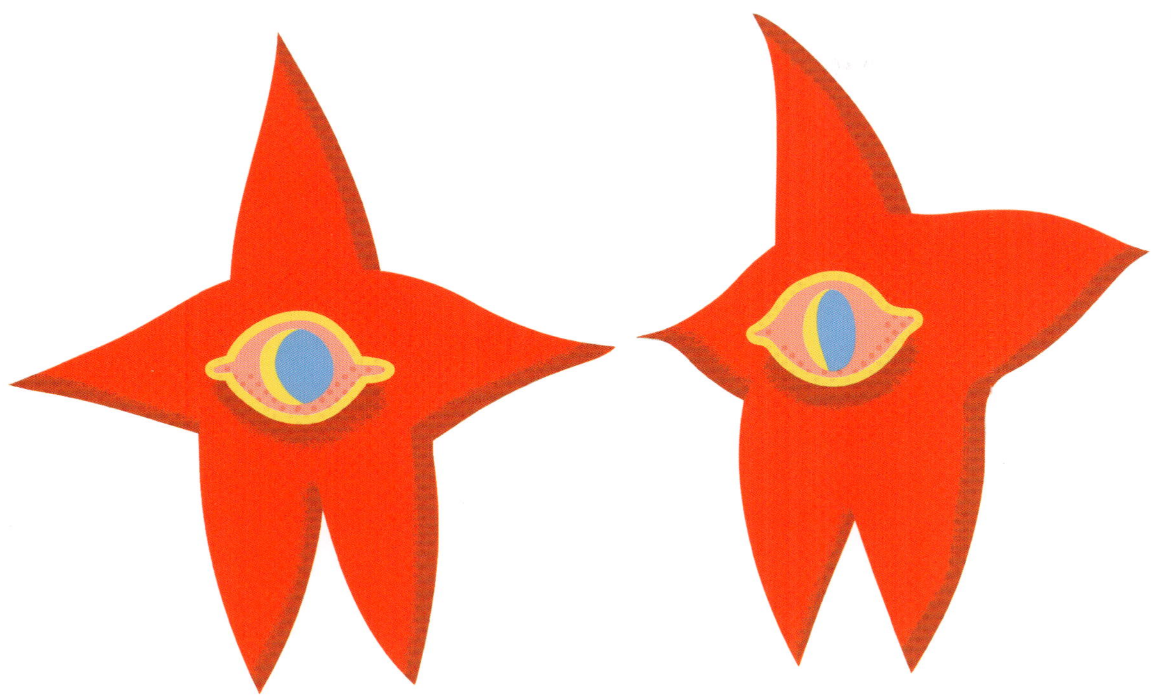

← Left: *The aliens in* Warning from Space *were designed by Tarō Okamoto.*

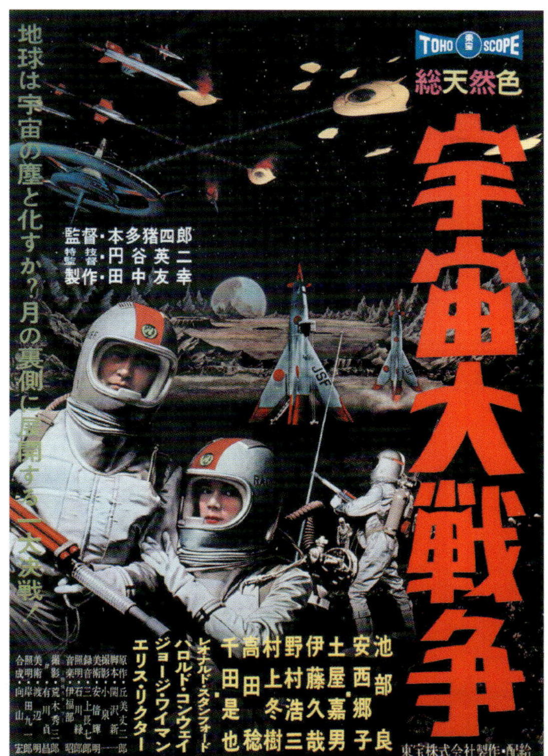

← Left: *Japanese poster for the film* Battle in Outer Space *(1959).*

↓ Below: *The dream team from the* Captain Ultra *series.*

scenes of space travel and exploration and large-scale attacks on Earth—scenes that still hold up today.

In 1966, *Ultraman* brought science fiction to Japanese television, marking a new era. Toei went on to experiment further with *Captain Ultra* in 1967, the adventures of a space patrol team protecting the solar system. Though the emerging *Star Trek* franchise also explored space themes on TV, *Captain Ultra* had a more retro aesthetic reminiscent of the pulp fiction of the 1930s to the 1950s, as well

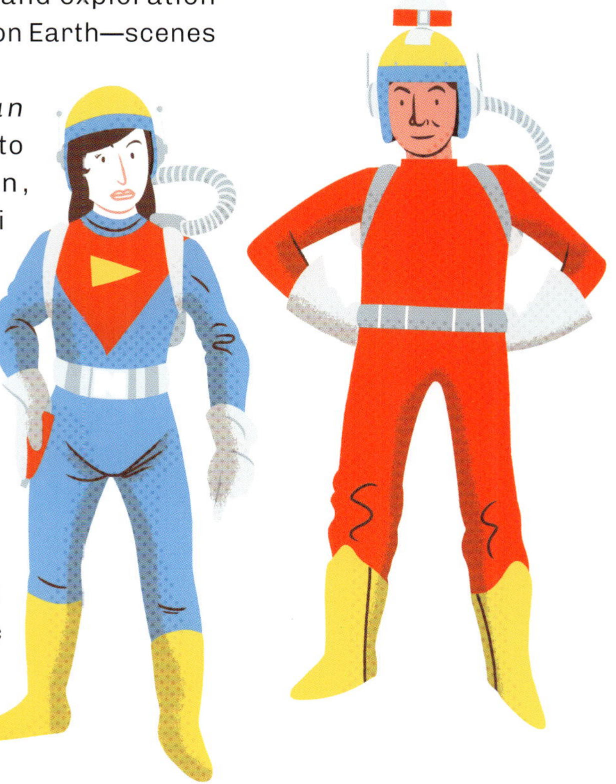

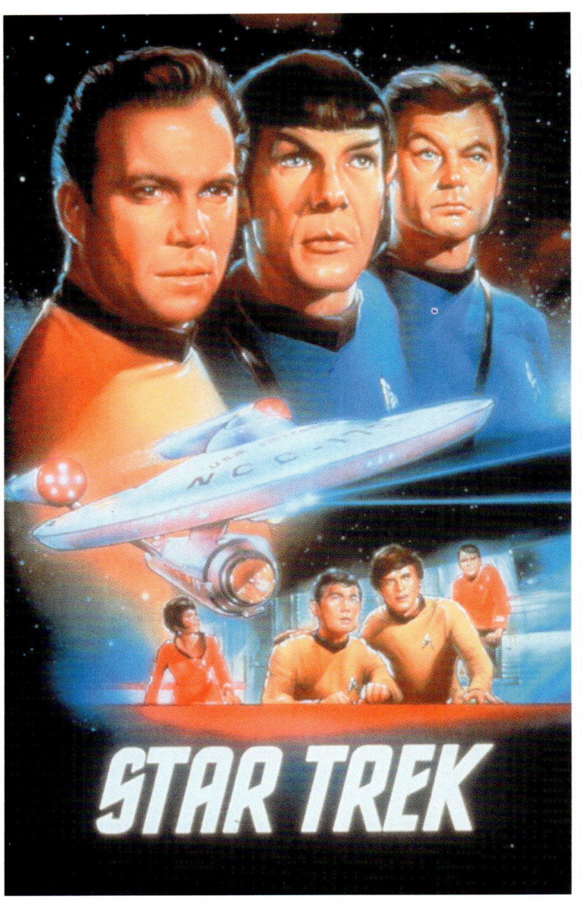

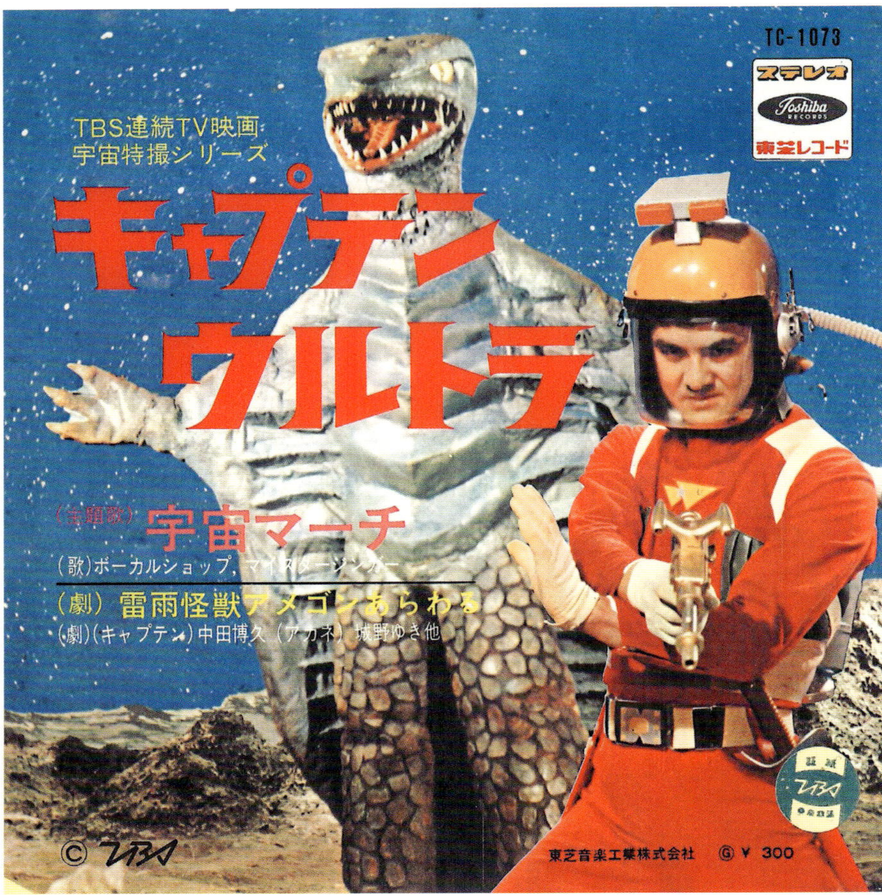

Above: *While* Star Trek *(1966) was breaking ground in science fiction,* Captain Ultra *(1967) went retro.*

Below: *The drill ship from* The War in Space, *ready to pierce the skies and travel into the far reaches of space.*

as robots and other aliens encountered in battle, rendering it unique for its time.

The arrival of *Star Wars* in 1977 reshaped science fiction worldwide, not least in Japan. In an ambitious response, Toho released *The War in Space* under the direction of Jun Fukuda (also the director of *Ebirah, Horror of the Deep* in 1966 and *Godzilla vs. Mechagodzilla* in 1974). The film featured flying submarines, evil galactic empires, warlike creatures, and ray guns. The final result was underwhelming, possibly due to a weaker script than its predecessors, but the special effects were astounding and the spaceship fight scenes well crafted.

The fascination with this side of science fiction continued in 1978 when Tsuburaya launched its own series in the genre with *Star Wolf*—inspired by Edmond Hamilton's novel of the same name—which took on the more measured tone of *Star Trek*. The real *Star Wars* facsimile would come from Toei later that year.

The explosion of Japanese anime across all media diminished the impact of the genre somewhat in its live-action film form. To stand out from the pack, productions needed a distinct, compelling formula, especially as the West continued to fuel theaters with regular releases, setting a blockbuster standard that more modest directing styles couldn't compete with.

Toho ventured back into the field in 1984 with *Bye-Bye Jupiter*, directed by Kōji Hashimoto and released the same year as *Godzilla*. The film is an epic space tale where humanity, fleeing an overpopulated Earth, seeks to conquer

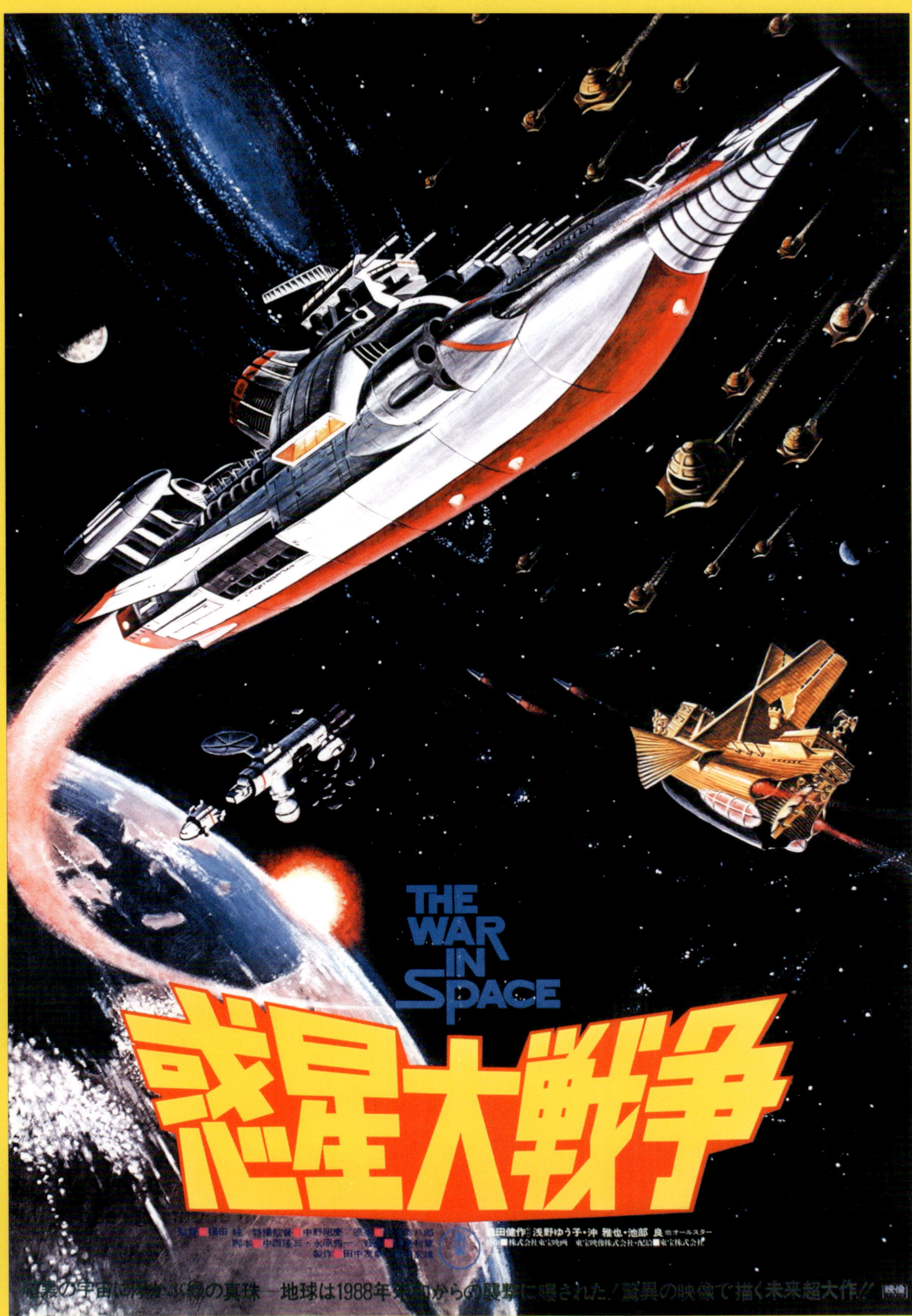

← **Left:** *Japanese poster for the film* The War in Space *(1977).*

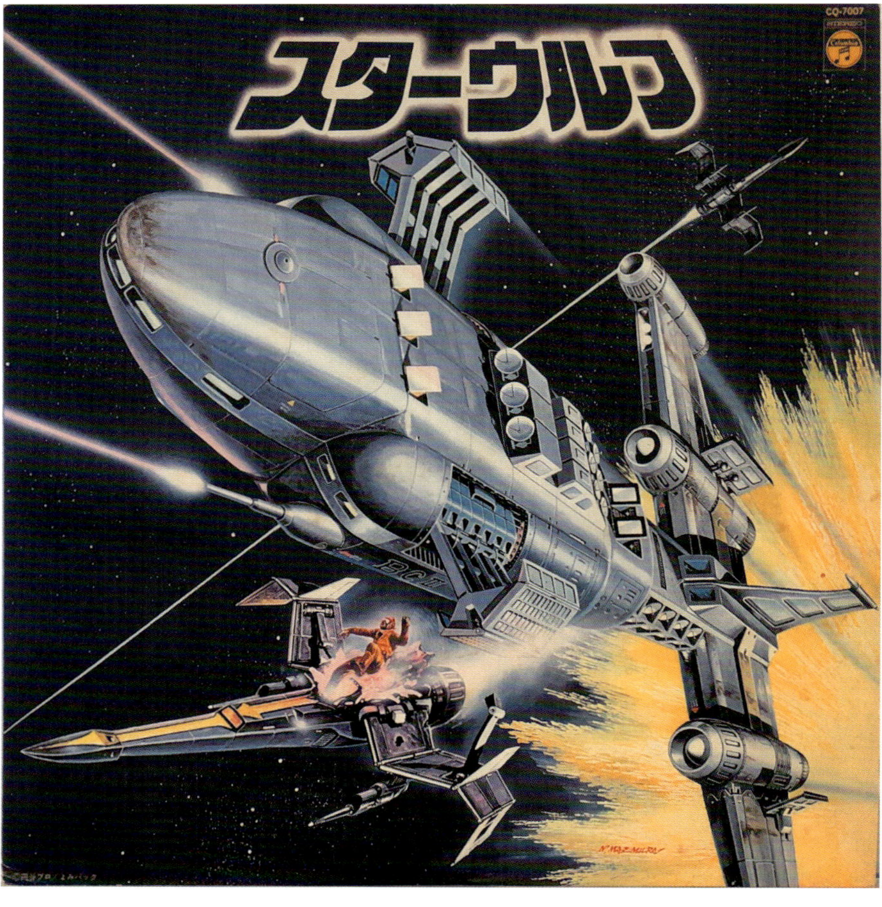

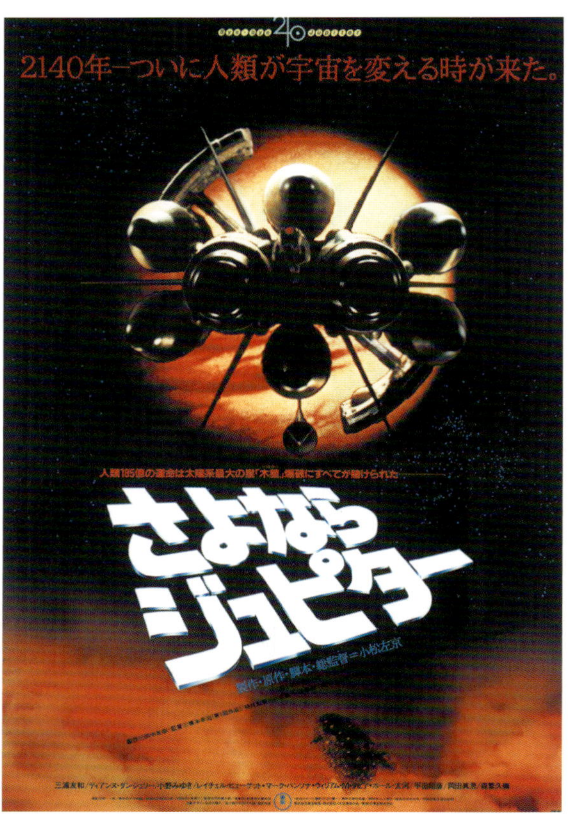

↑ **Above left:** *Promotional image for* Star Wolf *(1978).*

↗ **Above right:** *Japanese poster for the film* Bye-Bye Jupiter *(1984).*

space by transforming Jupiter into a second sun in order to terraform neighboring planets. Their efforts are soon threatened by the appearance of a black hole that endangers Jupiter's very existence. The ambitious film distinguished itself from its more fantastical predecessors, both by its screenwriting and its international cast.

Years passed before there was another production in the genre, as such projects grew increasingly expensive and demanding. One of the most recent examples is *Space Battleship Yamato* (2010), based on the eponymous manga and anime franchise and directed by Takashi Yamazaki. A specialist in digital effects, Yamazaki delivered a film that was technically impressive for both the genre and for Japanese cinema. Members of the technical team would even go on to work on *Godzilla Minus One* thirteen years later.

The film was a major box office success, but it polarized both critics and fans of the original work. Many saw it as a highly commercial story lacking originality, drawing heavily from successful American franchises such as *Star Wars*, *Star Trek*, and even *Battlestar Galactica*.

Thus, like many others to come, this branch of science fiction continues to be explored through *tokusatsu*, particularly in superhero series. *Ultraman* is a prime example, serving as both a true successor and an enduring relic of this pivotal era.

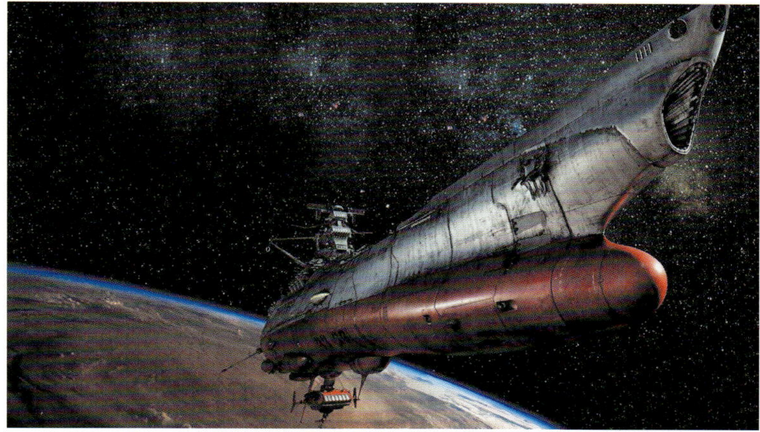

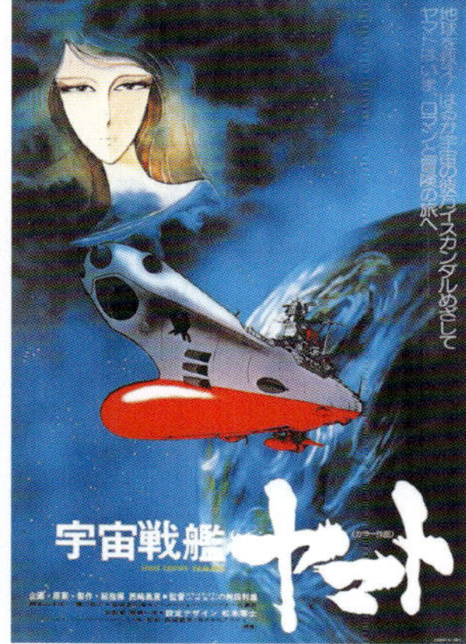

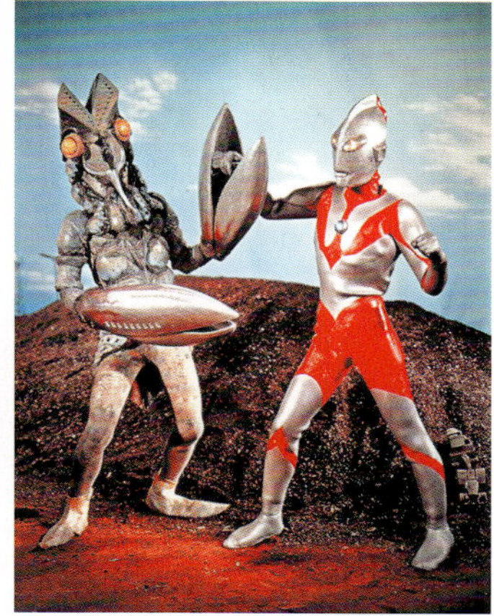

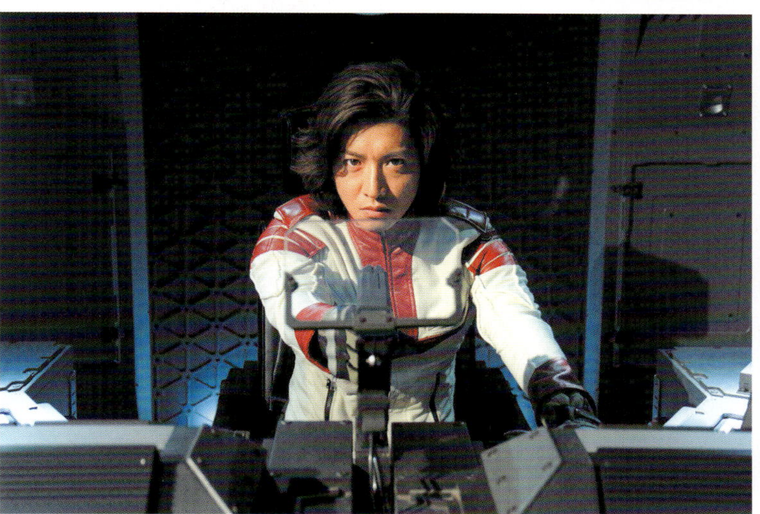

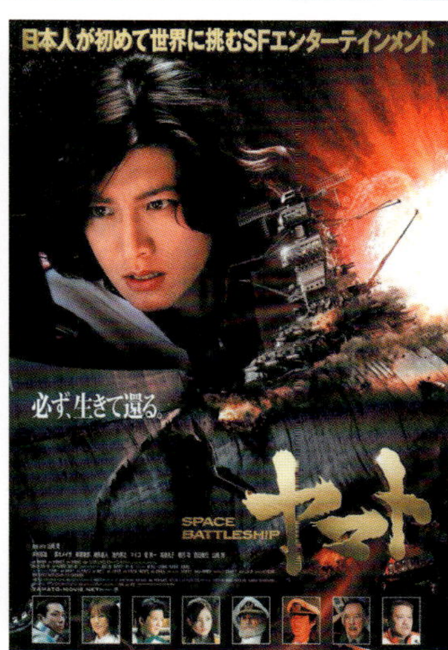

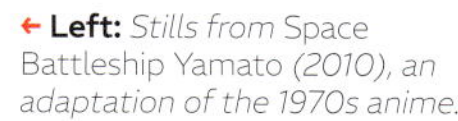
← Left: *Stills from* Space Battleship Yamato *(2010), an adaptation of the 1970s anime.*

THE JAPANESE STAR WARS

As we've seen, the 1970s saw a renewed interest in space travel, leading to a particularly notable and unique *tokusatsu* production. *Star Wars* premiered in May 1977 in the United States but didn't make it across the pond to Japan until July 1978. To bridge the sizable delay, and sensing an impending cultural shift, Toei seized the opportunity to launch its own project, *Message from Space*. Its goal was clear: to beat *Star Wars* to the punch with a homegrown space opera showcasing the studio's expertise.

Message from Space was directed by Kinji Fukasaku—renowned for his *yakuza* films, such as the *Battles Without Honor and Humanity* series, and later for the internationally acclaimed *Battle Royale* in 2000—and marked his first feature-length sci-fi film. Despite its aspirations of becoming a Japanese version of *Star Wars*, the film was no mere copy and paste of the original. Its plot and characters were plucked from Japanese fantasy literature, particularly the epic *The Eight Dogs of the Satomi Clan*. Like the novel, the film tells the story of eight characters chosen by fate to confront a common threat—in this case, the Gavanas Empire, which rules the galaxy with an iron fist.

Despite its initial premise, *Message from Space* unfolds as a lively, enjoyable adventure, featuring a charming cast of heroes, flamboyant villains, and thrilling space action sequences. These sequences were brought to life by the talented special effects director Nobuo Yajima, a luminary

➜ **Right:** *The helmet of an entire generation, worn by Hayato, who was played by Hiroyuki Sanada.*

↘ **Bottom:** *Japanese poster for the film* Message from Space *(1978).*

of Toei's *tokusatsu* projects who worked on most of the studio's major franchises and productions, including *Captain Ultra*, *Kamen Rider*, and the *Space Sheriff* trilogy, with its giant robot battles.

Filming took only fifty days, a remarkable feat for the time, and the film premiered in April 1978, less than three months before *Star Wars*. It was a resounding success, spawning a spin-off TV series, *Message from Space: Galactic Wars*, in July. The series was a loose reimagining of the film's story, shifting its focus more toward superheroes—a hallmark of Toei's productions, especially with Shōtarō Ishinomori contributing to designs, from the costumes to the spacecraft. The series is about two young men, Hayato and Ryū, and a monkey man named Baru who unite to fight the Gavanas Empire. Hayato and Ryū wear combat suits that conceal their identities, allowing them to operate under the superhero aliases Maboroshi and Nagareboshi, respectively. With this premise, the series offered a refreshing mix of Toei's *tokusatsu* superheroes (complete with monster-of-the-week battles), elements from *Message from Space*, and other genre staples.

The series was such a success that it was exported to Europe the following year, albeit with some changes to character names. It was even the first *tokusatsu* series to air on French television, achieving widespread acclaim and generating demand for such productions in France over the next fifteen years. *Message from Space: Galactic Wars* was followed by other iconic shows like *Space Sheriff Gavan*, *Spectreman*, *X-Bomber*, and *Choudenshi Bioman*.

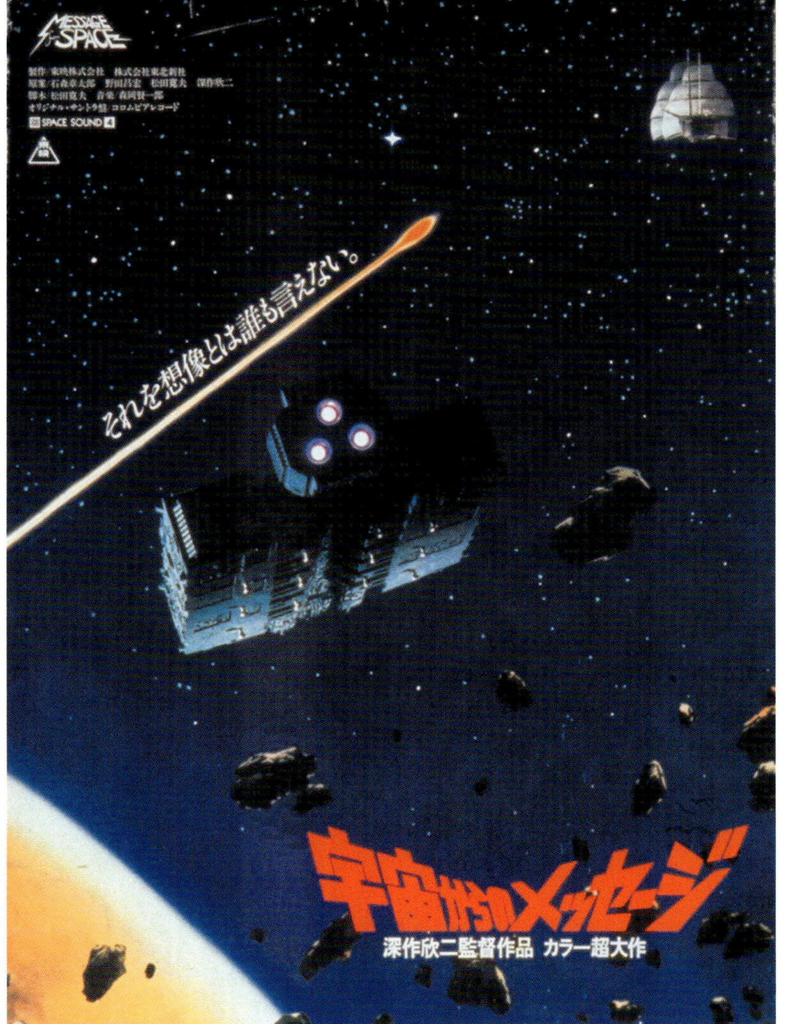

GIANT ROBOTS

Giant robots take pride of place among stories associated with Japanese pop culture. Iconic series and works like *Gundam*, *Macross*, *Neon Genesis Evangelion*, and even older titles like *Mazinger Z* and *UFO Robot Grendizer* need no introduction. But these are anime shows. What about giant robots in *tokusatsu*?

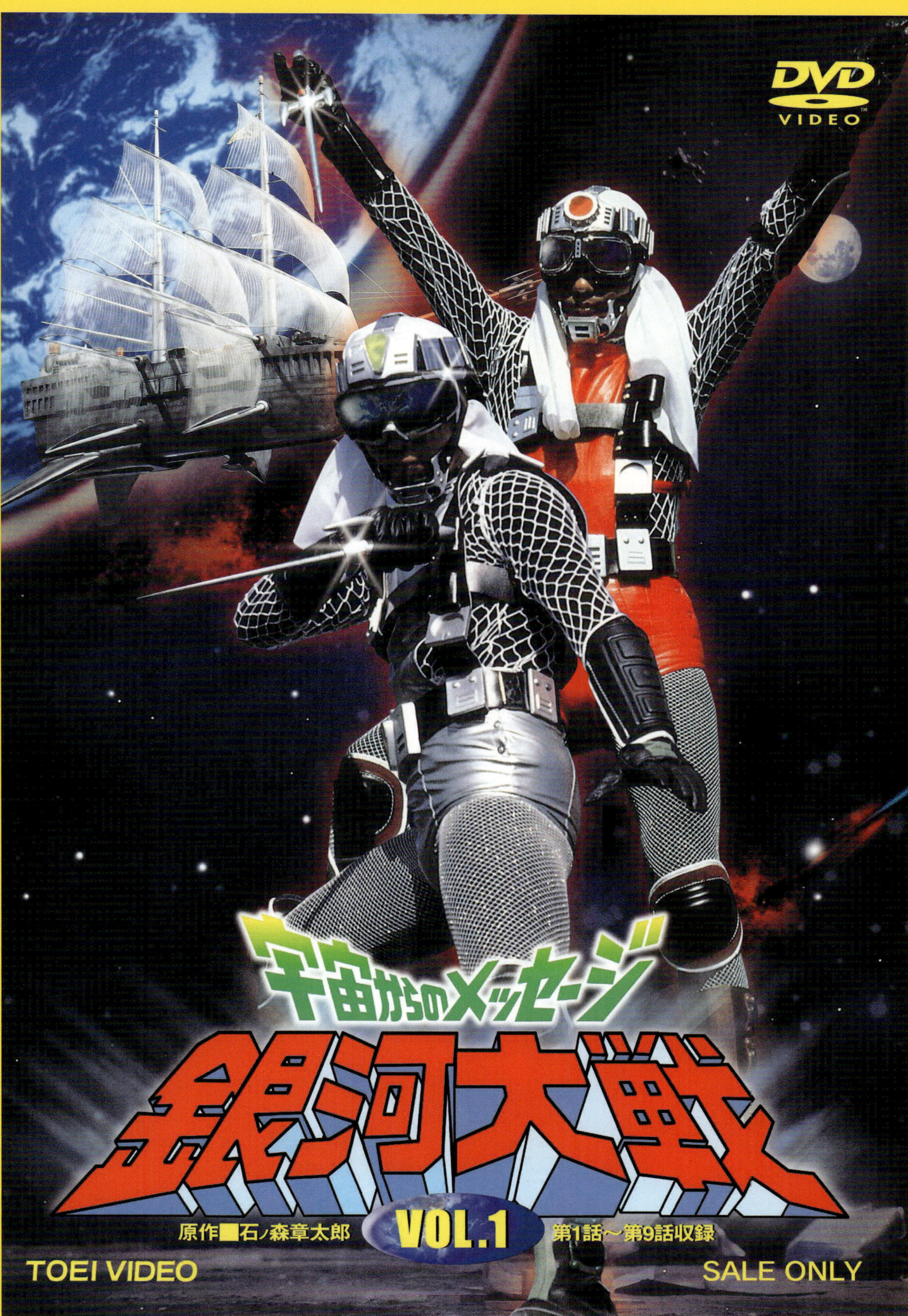

← **Left:** *Japanese DVD cover for the series* Message from Space: Galactic Wars *(1978).*

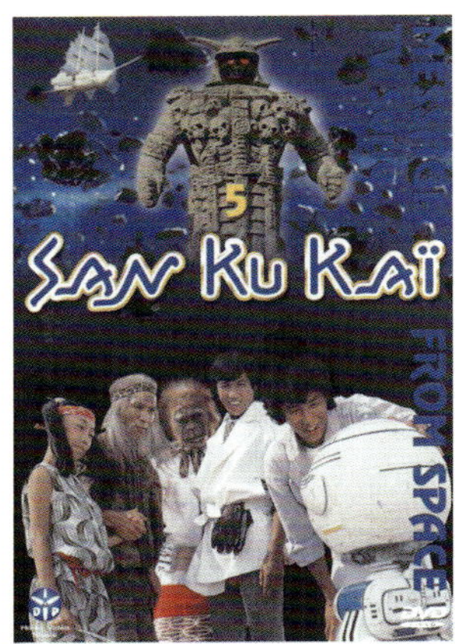

↑ Above: *French DVD cover for the series* Message from Space: Galactic Wars *(1978).*

→ Right: *Japanese poster for the film* The Mysterians *(1957).*

↓ Below: *The great* Daitetsujin 17, *an homage to* Tetsujin 28-go.

The first giant robot in *tokusatsu* history made its appearance in *The Mysterians* in 1957 and was remote-controlled. It was a pioneer of the mecha[4] genre and reminiscent of Mitsuteru Yokoyama's 1956 manga *Tetsujin 28-go*, in which the hero operates the robot using a remote control. The film employs a similar concept, with the robot Moguera serving as a weapon and deterrent to space invaders.

Shortly thereafter, *Tetsujin 28-go* made its first *tokusatsu* appearance in 1960 with its own series, though with one notable difference—no giant robots! Likely due to budget constraints, all the robots featured in the series were human-sized, though still remote-controlled. With a scant thirteen episodes, the series ended up as no more than a curious blip in the genre's infancy. But by the mid-1960s, manga adaptations were becoming more common, both in animated and live-action formats.

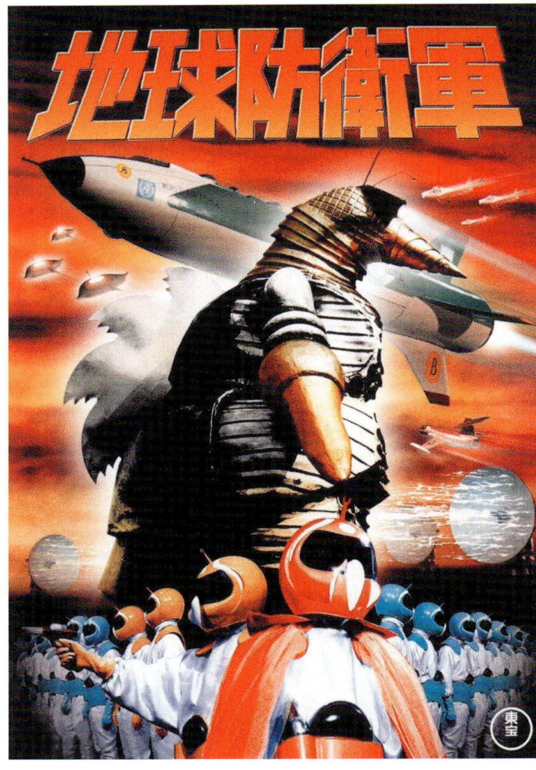

In 1966, the *Ambassador Magma* series by P Productions, based on the manga of the same name by Osamu Tezuka, became a notable entry in the history of giant TV robots. It introduced a sentient, autonomous gold robot from space capable of transforming into a rocket. The following year, Toei came out with *Giant Robo*, an adaptation of another manga by Yokoyama that one-upped *Tetsujin 28-go* by including a giant robot.

The pace quickened in the 1970s. Thanks to *Mazinger Z* and *Getter Robo*, which was published first as a manga and then as an anime, mechas evolved to be piloted from within, and multiple units could combine into one. The trend followed suit on the *tokusatsu* side. Senkosha Productions introduced its own take on the genre with *Super Robot Red Baron* (1973) and its sequel, *Super Robot Mach Baron* (1974), two series heavily inspired by *Mazinger Z*. Whereas Toei vacillated between safety and innovation—with *Daitetsujin 17* in 1977 (a clear homage to *Tetsujin 28-go*) and *Spider-Man* in 1978 (with an influence that continues to resound today)—Tsuburaya Productions acted more boldly, releasing its version of piloted robots with *Jumborg Ace* (1973), featuring a pilot seated in a cockpit and covered with sensors. His movements are replicated by the robot in real time. This technique would later resurface in *Pacific Rim* (2013), Guillermo del Toro's paean to the entire genre.

The evolution continued. By the late 1970s, the genre was dominated by animation, *Spider-Man* had left its lasting

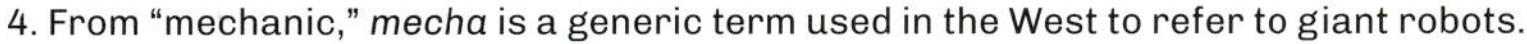

4. From "mechanic," *mecha* is a generic term used in the West to refer to giant robots.

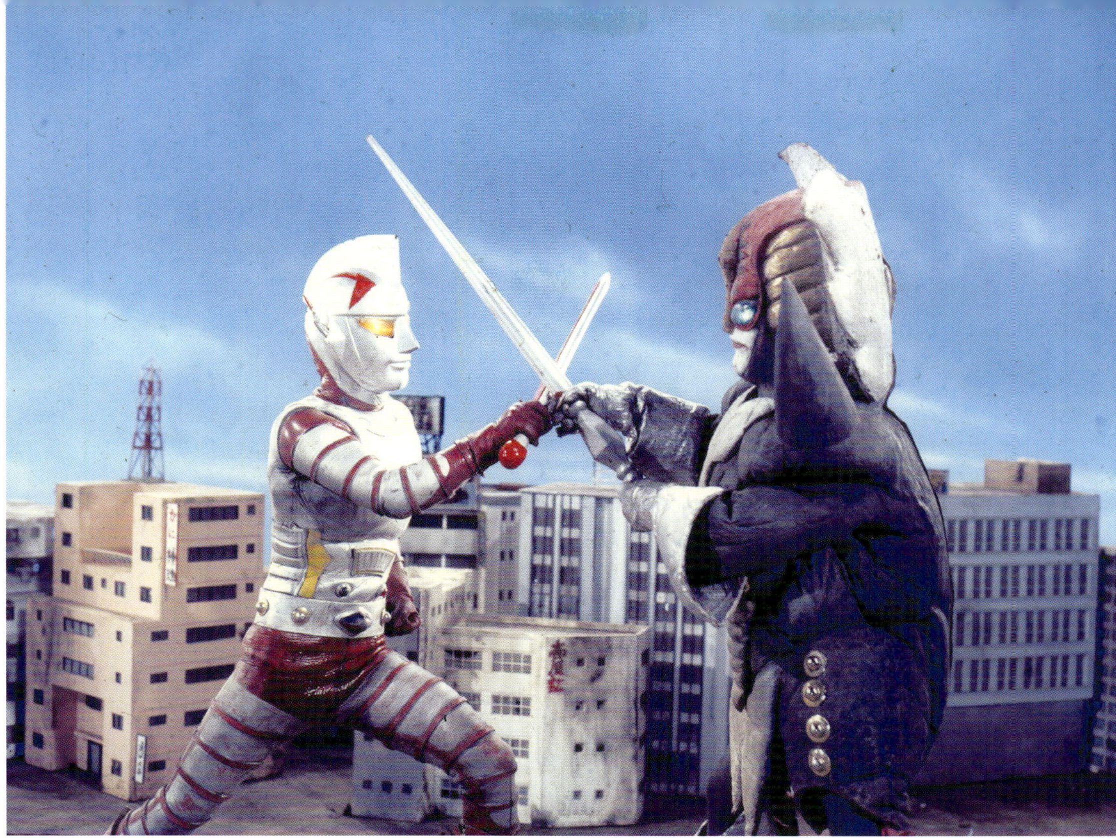

Left: *Still from* Jumborg Ace *(1973).*

Below: *The colorful aliens of* The Mysterians *foreshadowed the* sentai *to come.*

mark, and the *Super Sentai* series had taken up the mantle left behind by giant robots in *tokusatsu*. Mecha remained ever present, but it had become infused with superhero conventions. Still, there were a few exceptions over the years, in both cinema and television, reflecting a desire to sustain the fading but compelling genre.

One such example was *Gunhed* (1989), directed by Masato Harada for Toho. The film is set in a futuristic, cyberpunk world where humanity is overpowered by machines, particularly Kyron-5, a supercomputer with artificial intelligence that becomes sentient and declares war on humans. The protagonists discover a Gunhed, a powerful battle robot that becomes essential to their fight. Though the screenplay has its flaws, the film remains notable for its premise, polished technical execution, and unique aesthetic, which was echoed later in *The Matrix*.

In the 2000s, Japanese pop culture experienced a wave of nostalgia. *Tetsujin 28-go* made its first theatrical appearance in 2005, remaining faithful to the spirit of the original without seeking to modernize the foundational mecha. A similarly remote-controlled robot appeared in the series *Tekkōki Mikazuki* (2000) by Keita Amemiya, the creator of *Garo*. *Tekkōki Mikazuki* paid tribute to *Tetsujin 28-go* by highlighting the bond between a boy and his robot but with Amemiya's signature aggressive, contemporary style.

Finally, much like the *kaijū* genre, mecha found a new lease on life in the 2010s with *BraveStorm* (2017) by the young studio Blast. A modest but ambitious production, the film reimagined the foundations laid by the *Super Robot Red Baron* series (1973) and the superhero *Silver Kamen* (1971) in a single movie, using CGI effects reminiscent of *Shin Godzilla*. The film earned critical acclaim and boosted the studio's reputation. Riding the wave of its success, in 2023, the studio announced a *tokusatsu* adaptation of *Getter Robo* for 2025—a project full of promise and hope for the mecha genre beyond animation and the superhero-driven *tokusatsu* productions.

Below: *Japanese posters for the films* Gorath *(1962) and* Nihon Igai Zenbu Chinbotsu *(2006), and the French poster for the film* Japan Sinks *(1973).*

DISASTER FILMS

Another genre that complements the ones we've discussed so far is disaster films, movies featuring dramatic, unstoppable natural disasters. Though *kaijū* films share some of the same characteristics (*kaijū* could be considered a type of natural disaster, after all), let us take a look at some stories where the conflict comes from Mother Nature or outer space.

One of the first modern examples of a disaster film was *Gorath*, released in 1962. In it, scientists discover that an asteroid is on a collision course with Earth and devise a way to shift the planet out of its orbit to bypass it. The story was both fun and an opportunity for Toho to demonstrate its technical prowess in special effects—including a surprise appearance by a walrus *kaijū* in one scene. It remains exemplary of its time and still holds up today.

The genre took a leap forward and gained prestige in 1973 with the film adaptation of the novel *Japan Sinks*. The film tells of a Japan plagued by tectonic shifts, causing the entire country to slowly but surely sink into the ocean, providing an opportunity to explore how such a crisis would be handled politically and socially. *Japan Sinks* impresses with its highly detailed, realistic, and chillingly brutal scenes of destruction while also offering a gripping and poignant narrative. Its success was so great that the following year, the studio produced a TV series based on the same story but with a different cast. The serial format allowed for more in-depth storytelling while still delivering spectacular special effects, thanks to a healthy TV budget.

Overall, Toho dominated the market for disaster movies, which were costly to make. In 1974, *Prophecies of Nostradamus* presented a more

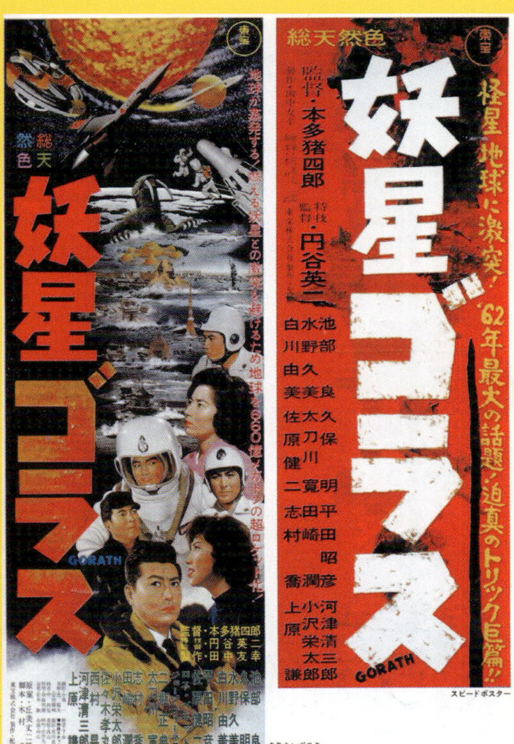

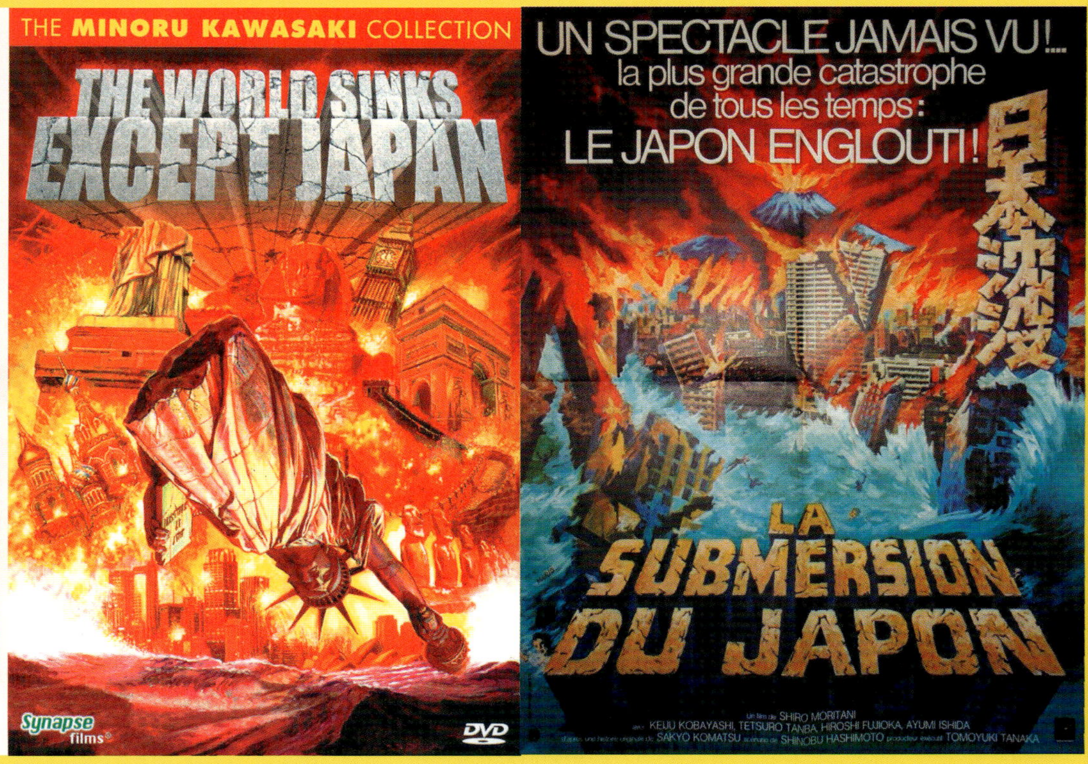

straightforward, violent depiction of the possible end of the world described by Nostradamus. Aside from the historical figure on which it was based, the story was primarily a pessimistic, urgent call to action against humanity's ecological recklessness. The film depicts multiple disasters in Japan and around the world: earthquakes, melting ice caps, environmental changes from nuclear fallout, and more. The film spares no one and remains as relevant as ever.

In the 1980s, a few minor films emerged, such as *Tokyo Daijishin Magnitude 8.1* and *Deathquake*, both centered on Tokyo in the midst of an earthquake. In 2006, Shinji Higuchi directed a new adaptation of *Japan Sinks*. The new version took a more conventional approach, heavily influenced by American disaster movies, resulting in a more melodramatic and less biting tone compared to the 1973 version, though with modern and relatively well executed special effects. The lampooning came instead from *Nihon Igai Zenbu Chinbotsu* (The Sinking of Everything Except Japan), a sharp critique of the Japanese government by *tokusatsu* comedy specialist Minoru Kawasaki.

From the original novel to the first film, *Japan Sinks* remains a significant work in the genre. It continues to inspire adaptations today (including *Japan Sinks: People of Hope* in 2021) and remains highly influential. Without it and its impact on Japanese popular culture, works like *Shin Godzilla* simply never would have come into being.

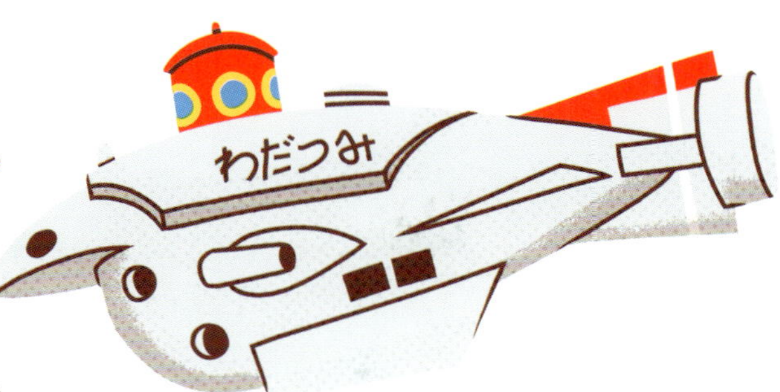

← **Left:** *The submarine from* Japan Sinks, *the first disaster film.*

↓ **Below:** *Promotional image for* Japan Sinks *(1973).*

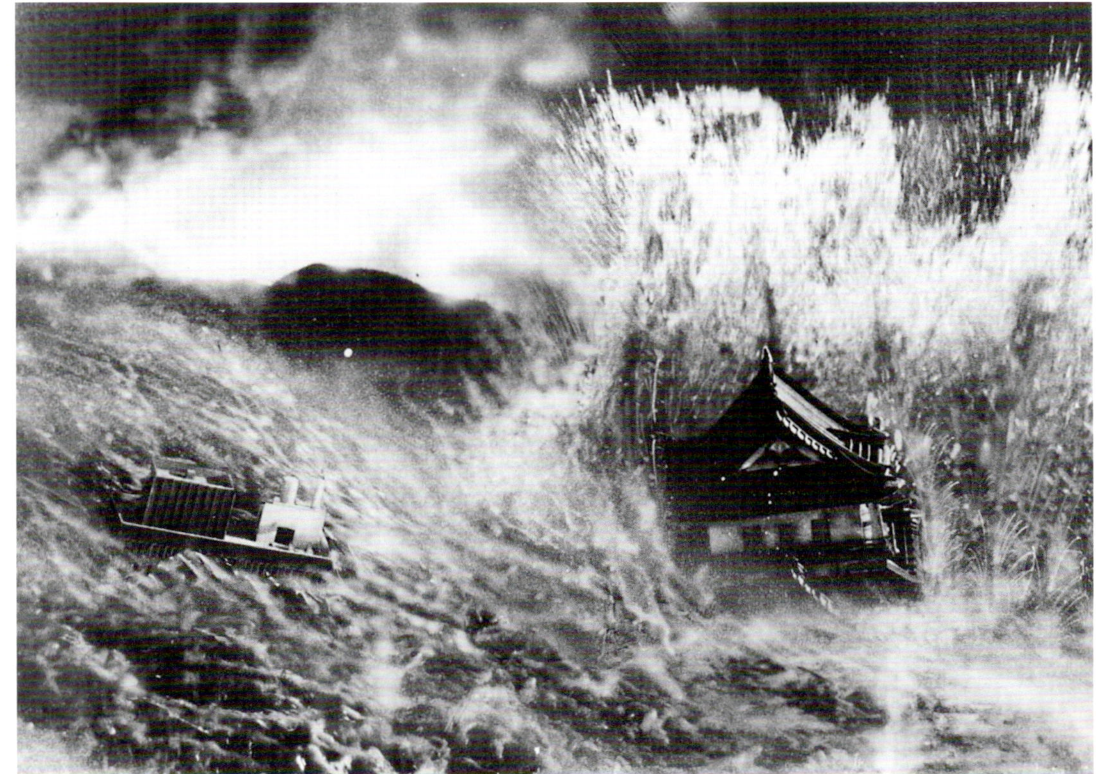

JAPANESE GIANT ROBOTS

BRINGING GIANT ROBOTS TO LIFE

People like Katsushi Murakami remind us of the significance of the toy industry on *tokusatsu*. In Japan, merchandising is seen as complementary, and it is natural to incorporate it into works of fiction. By contrast, it took many years for the West to follow suit, and even then, it was never entirely perceived as a positive thing. In Japan, a work and its derivative products are natural extensions of each other and work to promote each other mutually, a concept that *tokusatsu* has embraced exceptionally well. Companies like PLEX and Rainbow Zoukei were even established to manage both sides simultaneously, working alongside Bandai to design superhero costumes, monsters, and, of course, giant robots, a mainstay of Japanese pop culture.

Beyond their size and striking aesthetics, Japan's giant robots captivate audiences with their ability to transform from one combat mode to another or to combine multiple robots into one, popularized in large part by the *Super Sentai* series. Ideas for transformable giants can come from anything and anywhere. The constant challenge lies in balancing bold, original designs with practical concepts, ensuring they work both on-screen and in the hands of young viewers.

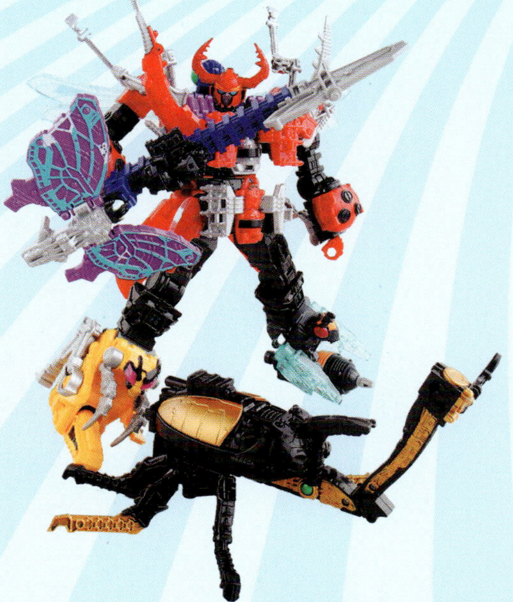

The physical realization of these robots is especially crucial for dedicated collectors. Designing these toys requires innovative engineering to capture the robustness and grandeur of the robots in physical form. Children must be able to re-create scenes from their favorite series, mimicking the same movements, iconic poses, and massive assemblies.

This balancing act extends to costume design as well, which faces inevitable physical requirements, such as movement and built-in mechanisms for the suit actor, as well as the assembly and transformation phases using models. Of course, with advances in technology and the advent of CGI, designers can make use of multiple types of media to take creative liberties while maintaining a coherent look.

One impressive example of this dual approach came in 2023 with the announcement of an

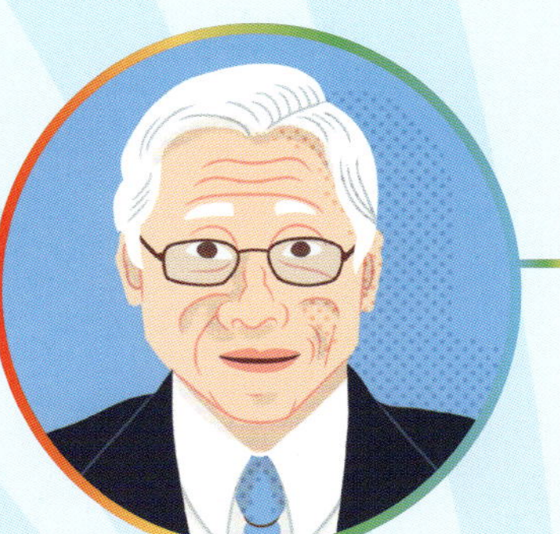

KATSUSHI MURAKAMI (1942–)

A prominent figure in *tokusatsu*, **Katsushi Murakami** is best known as an artist and toy designer for Bandai. He designed countless toys in the 1970s, with a particular fondness for anything mechanized, from terrestrial and space vehicles to the obligatory giant robots. In the world of tokusatsu, he was deeply involved in developing designs and bringing numerous superheroes and their mechanical sidekicks to the screen. He was the creator behind Leopardon, Spider-Man's robot, as well as Gavan and the robots of other *Metal Hero* series. He even redesigned *Mechagodzilla* for its reappearance in 1993.

Opposite: *One of the many possible robot combinations in the series* Ohsama Sentai King-Ohger *(2023), re-created exactly in toy form.*

Left: *Left: Leopardon, the giant robot from* Spider-Man *(1978).*

Below: *The robot from* Shin Japan Heroes Universe*, composed of Eva, Ultraman, Godzilla, and Kamen Rider on his motorcycle!*

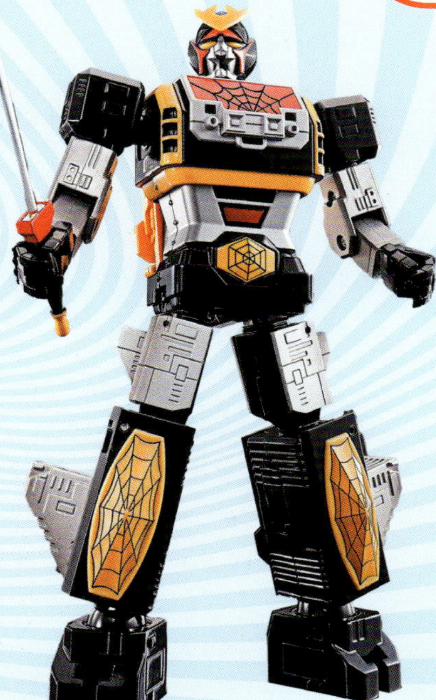

improbable toy, a giant robot formed from four well-known entities: Shin Ultraman, Shin Godzilla, Shin Kamen Rider, and Evangelion Unit-01 from the *Neon Genesis Evangelion* series. The off-the-wall idea was created in celebration of the Shin works and Hideaki Anno's influence. A promotional video—a short *tokusatsu* film in the classic style—was even produced, featuring a custom-made costume for the robot.

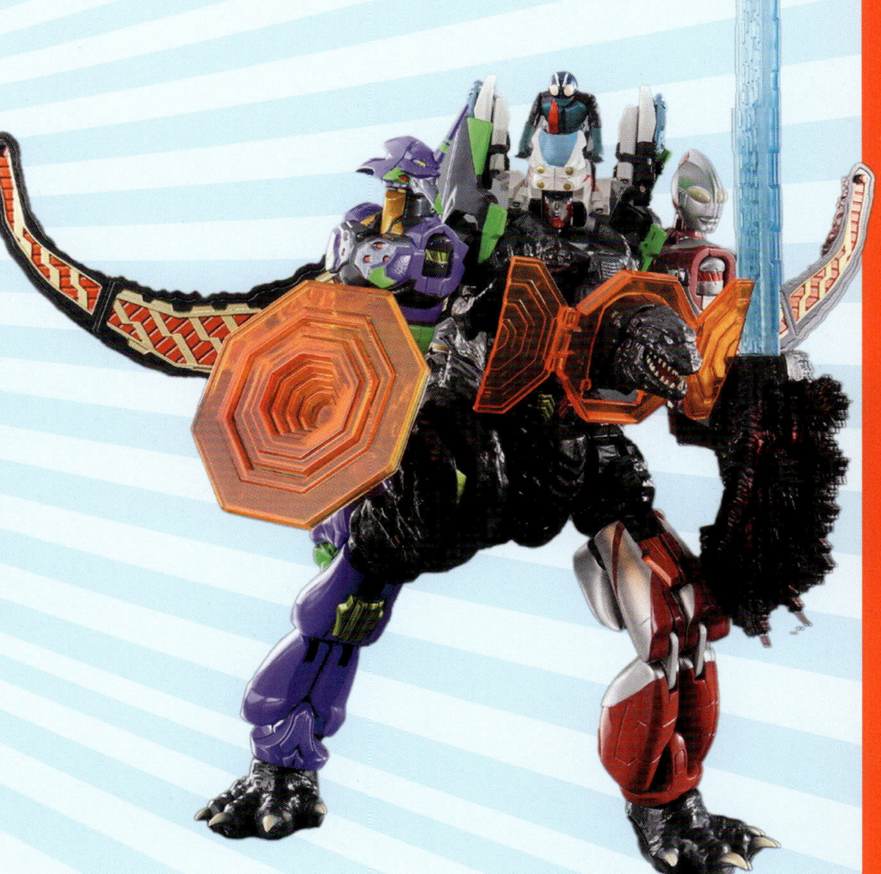

JAPANESE HORROR: CHILLS AND THRILLS

IN THE BEGINNING

Tokusatsu has also carved out a niche in the genre of horror movies. Though perhaps less colorful, the art of making monsters and special effects finds ample room for expression in horror. To uncover the early stirrings of Japanese horror capitalizing on the unique qualities of *tokusatsu*, we must travel back to the 1940s. Though the movies of that era were not yet full-fledged horror shows, they sowed the seeds for what would come in the years ahead.

Daiei, Toho's historical competitor, led the charge with its 1949 film *The Invisible Man Appears*. Like many Japanese films at the time (prime example: the original *Godzilla*), it was heavily influenced by the United States, Japan's occupier at the time. *The Invisible Man Appears* bears a striking resemblance to Universal Pictures' classic *The Invisible Man* (1933). The plot involves a scientist who develops a serum that grants him the power of invisibility, which he uses to commit theft. Though not genuinely terrifying, the movie represents an initial foray into horror tropes, featuring a "creature" (in this case, a human that turns invisible) that quickly becomes formidable and unpredictable, striking fear into those around him. With special effects once again crafted by Eiji Tsuburaya, *The Invisible Man Appears* marked a new era of suspenseful and tension-filled Japanese productions.

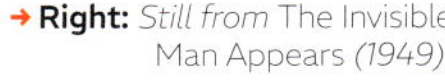

→ **Right:** *Still from* The Invisible Man Appears *(1949).*

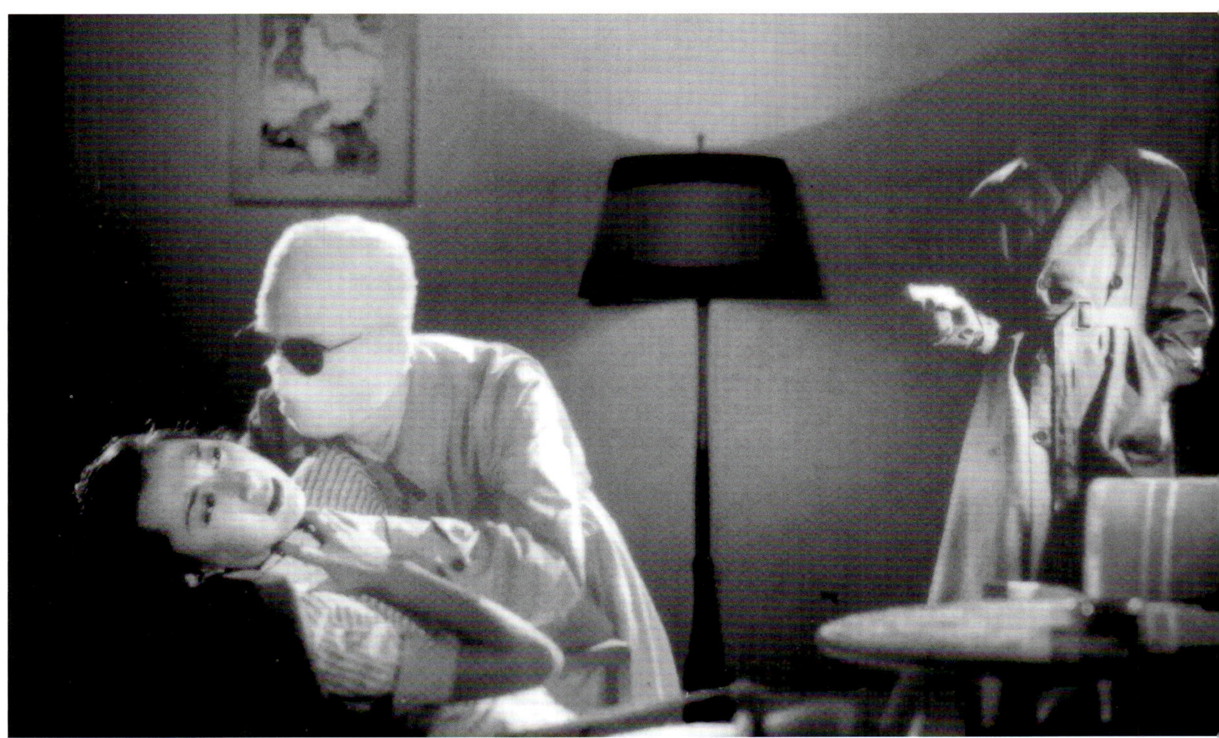

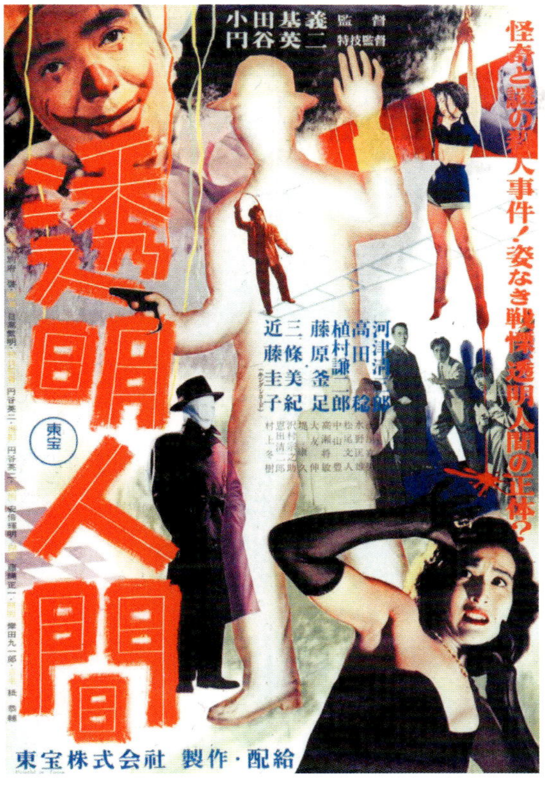

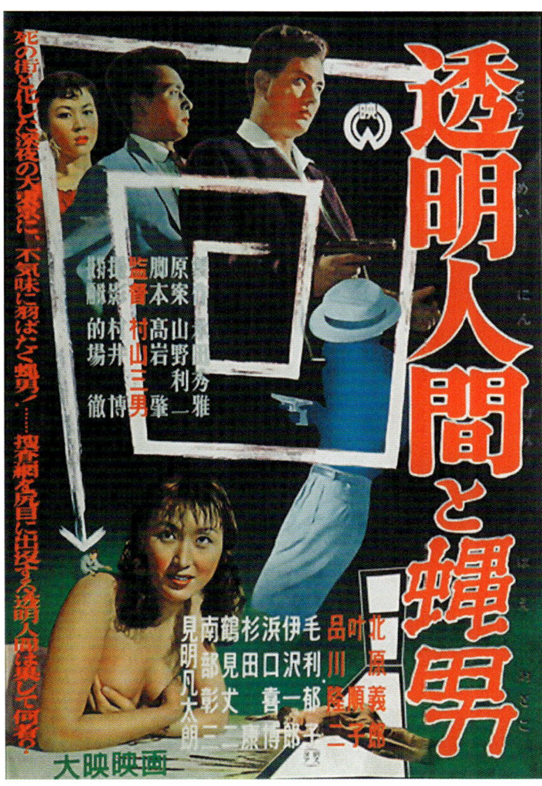

← Left: *Japanese posters for* The Invisible Avenger *(1954) and* The Invisible Man vs. The Human Fly *(1957).*

↓ Below: *As in the United States, early horror movies in Japan began with invisible men.*

Of course, Toho couldn't miss out on the chance of making its own invisible man, *The Invisible Avenger*, made in 1954 by Motoyoshi Oda, the man behind the *Godzilla* sequel in 1955. For something a bit more original, however, we turn back to Daiei in 1957 with its sequel *The Invisible Man vs. The Human Fly*. Behind this bizarre yet intriguing title lies the story of an invisible man facing off against a man with the power to shrink, with the two constantly growing and shrinking to escape various situations. Here, too, the horror is light, but the genre was on the cusp of a significant transformation.

Amid this fierce studio rivalry, Toho upped the ante, creating ever more chilling films. With *Godzilla* and a historical time period ripe with sources of inspiration, Japanese cinema began drawing from the country's past and its relationship with nuclear energy to fuel its sci-fi narratives. In 1958, Ishirō Honda directed *The H-Man*, the story of mysterious, green, semi-liquid humanoid creatures that dissolve their victims upon contact. The creatures are portrayed as victims of nuclear fallout in Japan, depicted as collateral damage seeking revenge and, ultimately, a form of eternal rest given what they've become. The film's success prompted the studio to produce two more in the same vein of horror and fantasy, forming an accidental trilogy of movies about humans in altered form.

The Secret of the Telegian (1960) took quite a different tack. In the plot, the threat comes from a man modified by science and capable of teleportation via a machine. He uses his ability to commit murder and take revenge for past events that left him presumed dead for many years. Directed by Jun Fukuda (*The War in Space*,

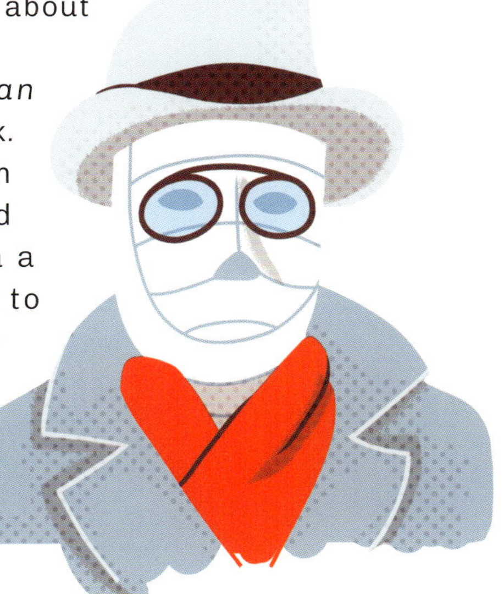

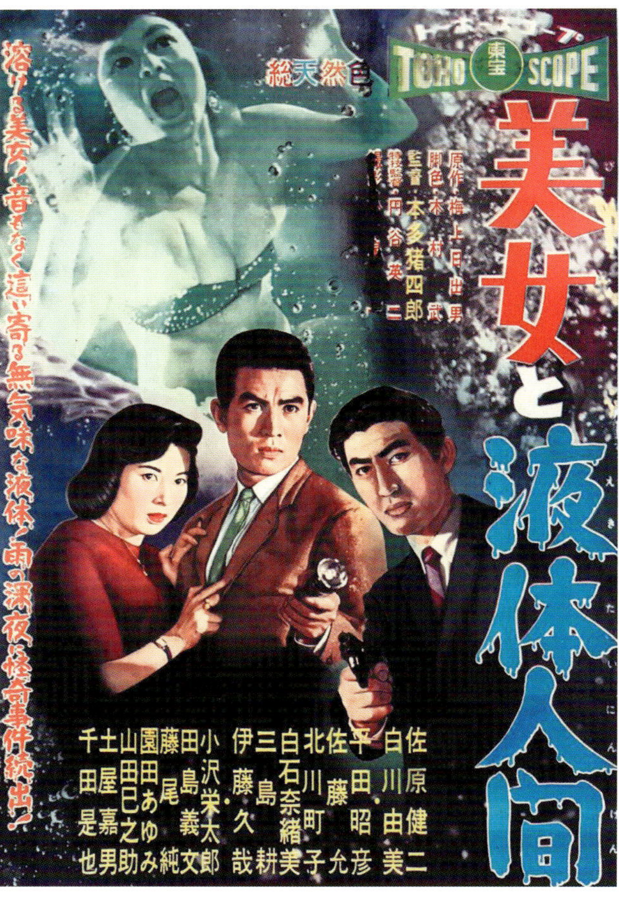

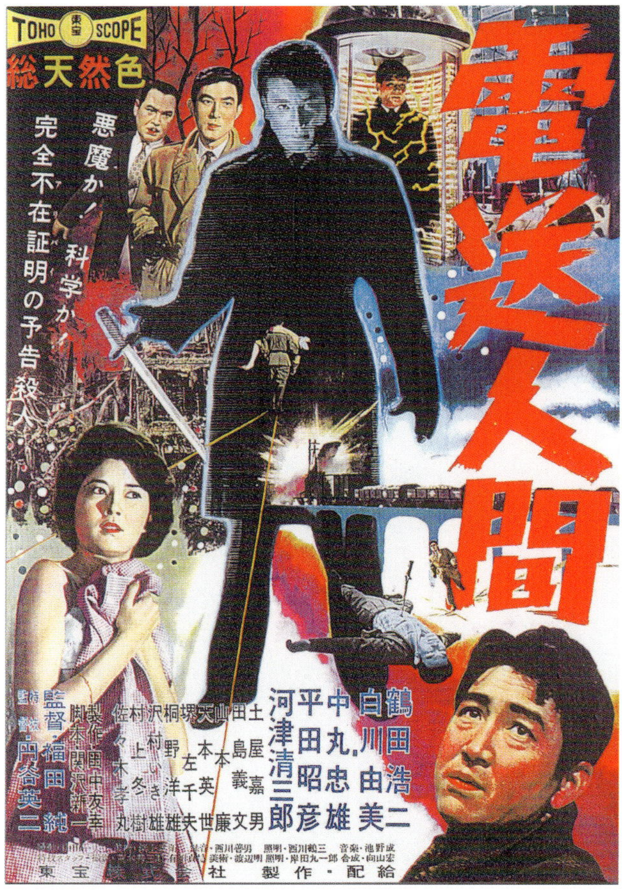

↑ Above left: *Japanese poster for the film* The H-Man *(1958).*

↗ Above right: *Japanese poster for the film* The Secret of the Telegian *(1960).*

Godzilla vs. Mechagodzilla), the movie reads as both a suspenseful thriller (with a race against time to stop a serial killer) and a tense horror film, in which a man for whom distance is no obstacle attacks his victims with ease, thwarting the authorities who are trying to stop him.

The third installment in the trilogy came the same year in the form of *The Human Vapor*, by Ishirō Honda. The movie stays in the same vein as *Telegian* and is, in a way, a compilation of the best parts of the *Telegian* and *H-Man*. In the film, the main character takes part in a scientific experiment that gives him the ability to transform into gas at will, but he doesn't use his power for good, of course. Instead, he robs banks and is quite violent, even murderous.

In the 1960s, storylines began to shift. Humans altered by science gave way to other, more popular genres (including *kaijū* films, naturally). The period ended with a bang with *Matango* (1963), once again by the tireless Ishirō Honda. The movie portrays the crew of a small cruise boat stranded on an unknown island after a storm. As they attempt to survive while awaiting rescue, paranoia sets in within the group, culminating in the arrival of aggressive, deformed humanoid creatures resembling mutated mushrooms. Instead of the usual urban backdrop, Honda sets the story in the jungle of a remote island, crafting a slow but pervasive atmosphere of horror where the true monster might not be the one you think it is.

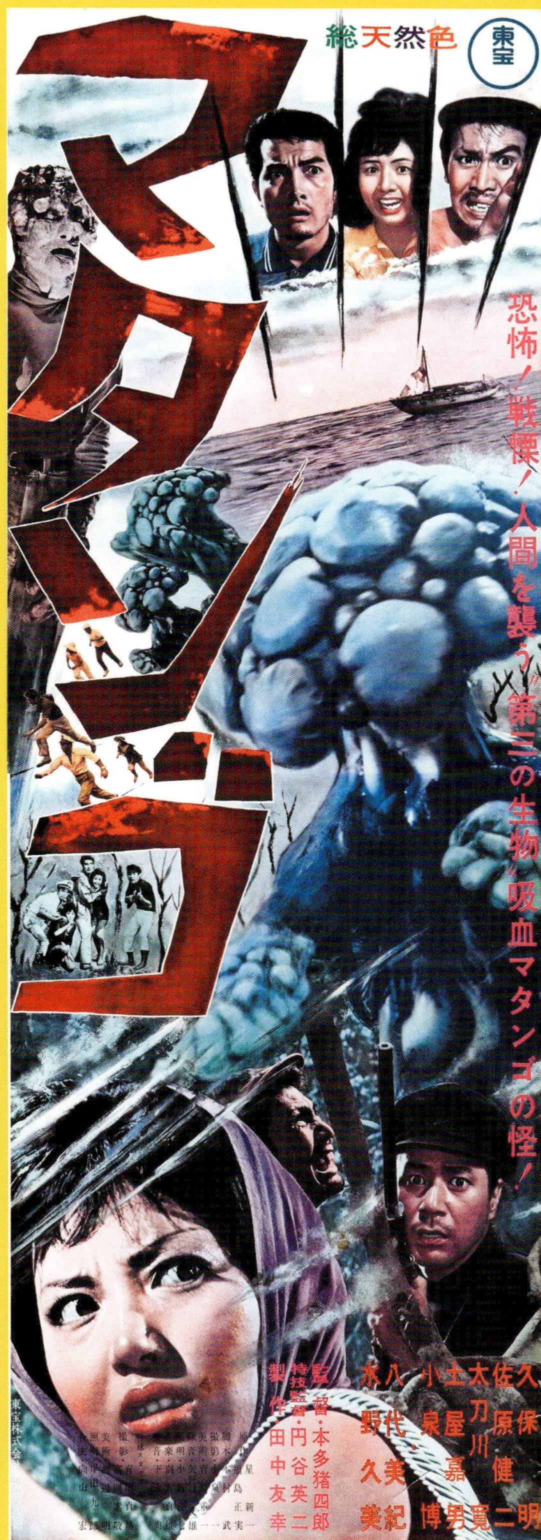

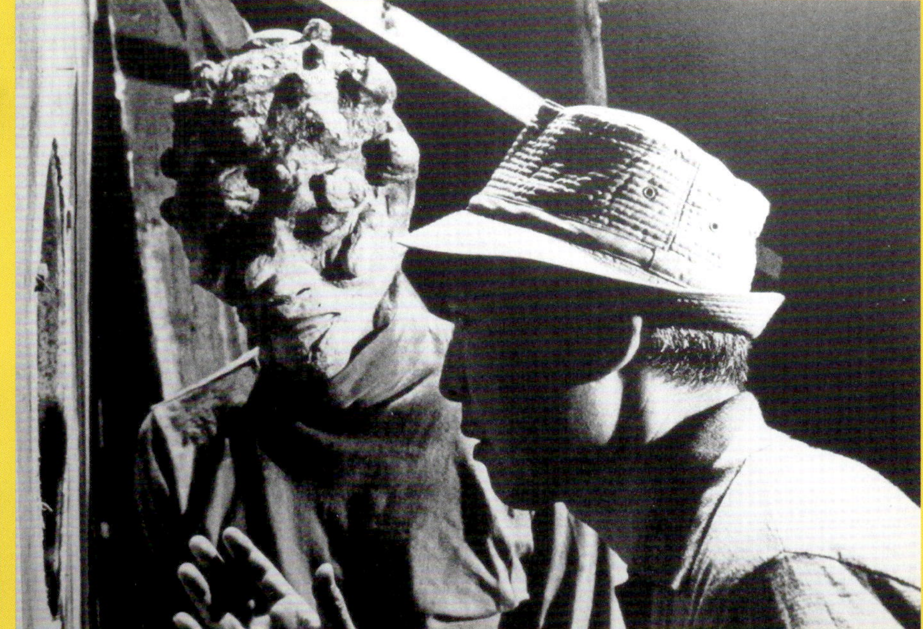

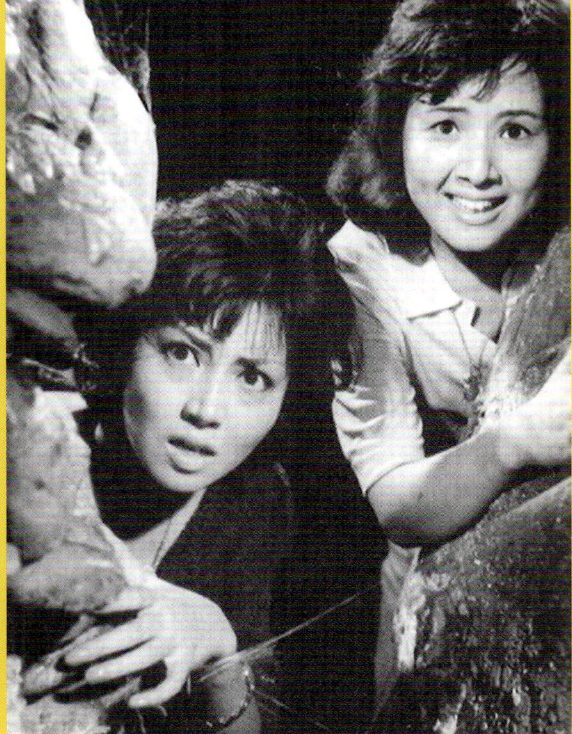

↑ **Above:** *One of the creatures on the set of the film.*

← **Far left:** *Japanese poster for the film* Matango *(1963).*

↙ **Below:** *The film's heroes.*

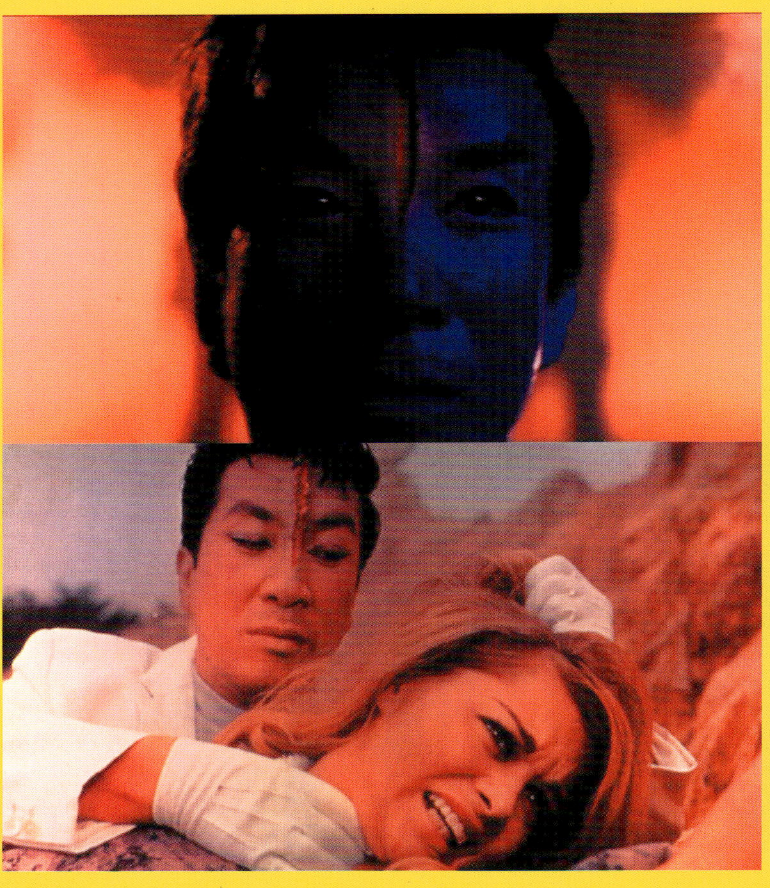

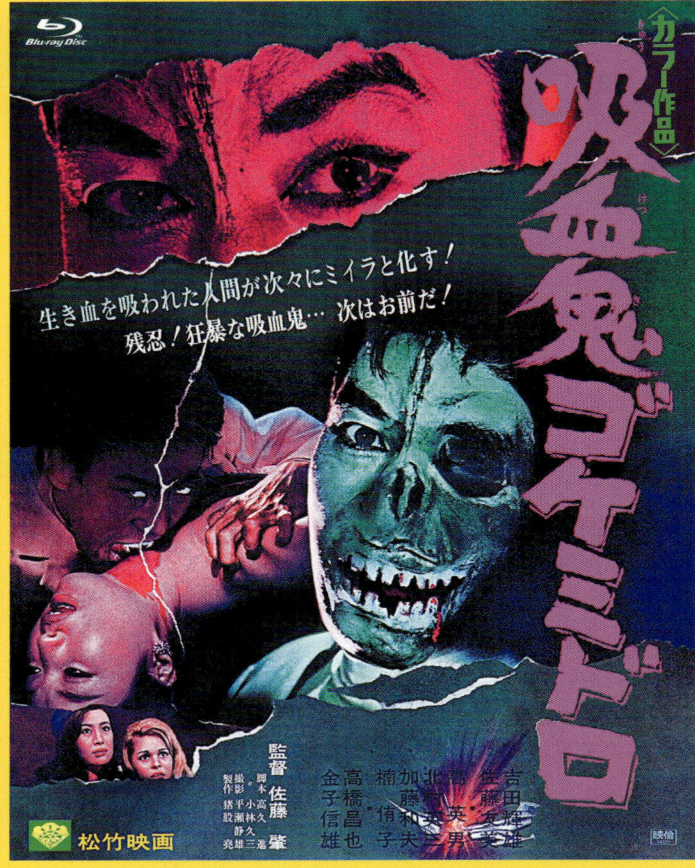

↑↗ **Above:** *Still and Japanese poster for the film* Goke, Body Snatcher from Hell *(1968).*

→ **Bottom right:** *US poster for the film* Goke, Body Snatcher from Hell *(1968).*

↘ **Bottom left:** *Japanese DVD cover for* The Vampire Doll *(1970).*

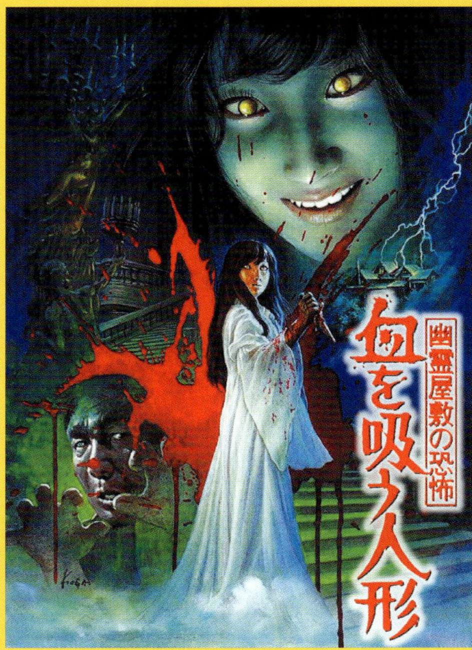

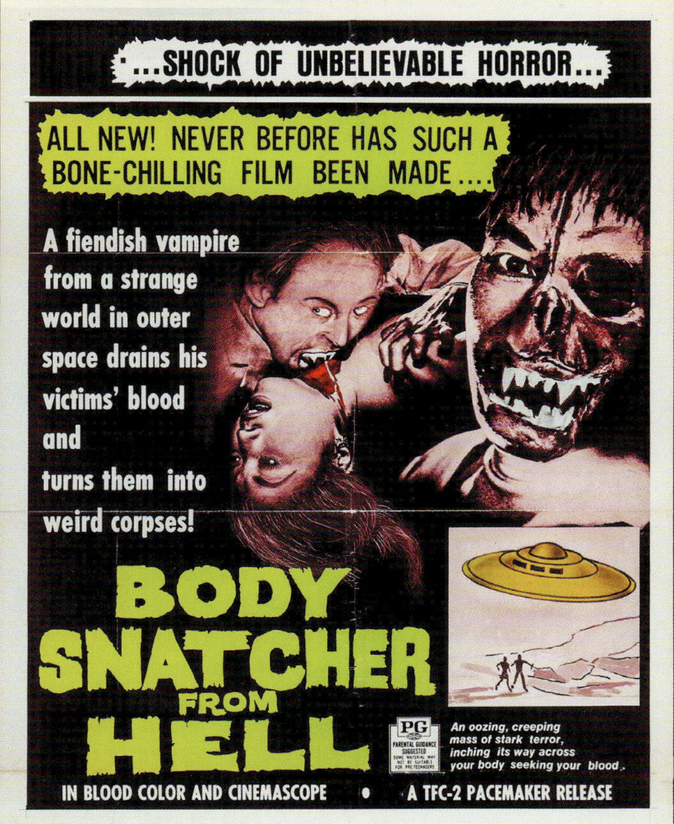

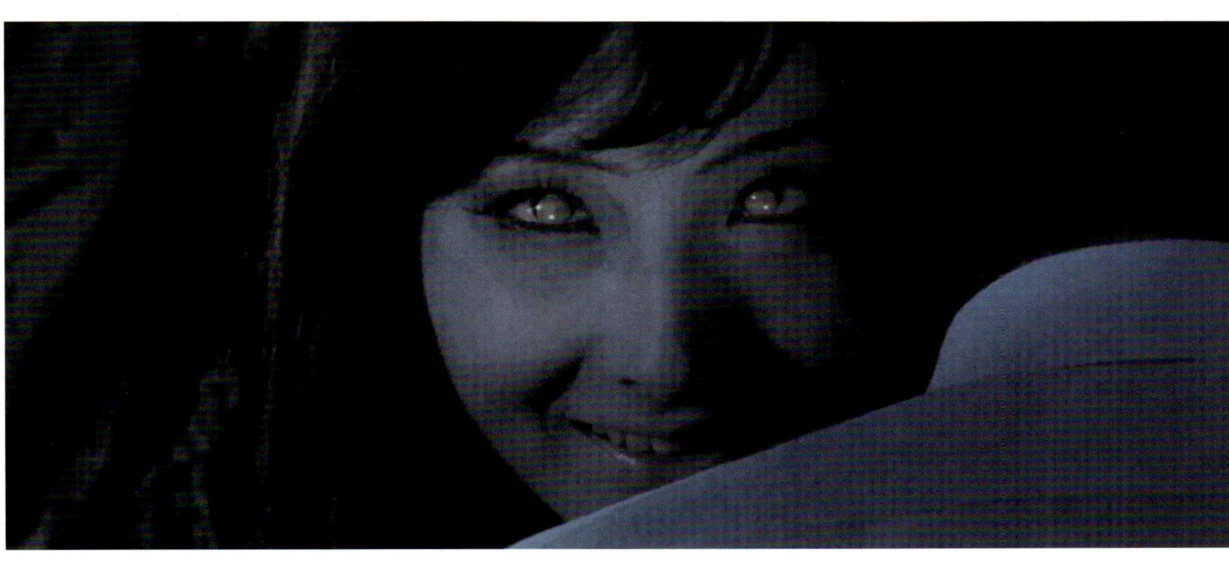

← Left: *Still from* The Vampire Doll *(1970).*

↙ Bottom left: *Vampires were popular in Japan, too!*

↓ Bottom right: *Japanese DVD cover for the film* Evil of Dracula *(1974).*

WESTERN INSPIRATION

Horror continued to play a role at the core of *tokusatsu*, taking inspiration from American movies while adding its own touch to create something truly unique. One part alien invasion, one part disaster movie, and one part vampire film, *Goke, Body Snatcher from Hell* was a 1968 horror movie produced by Daiei and directed by Hajime Satō (*Ōgon Bat*, 1966). A group of individuals survive a plane crash caused by an encounter with a flying saucer. As the survivors take stock of their situation, they discover that a gelatinous creature has infiltrated the aircraft. The entity begins to possess passengers by seeping through their skulls, turning them into vampires (the Japanese title, *Kyūketsuki Gokemidoro*, means "Vampire Gokemidoro"). The film rode the wave of *Matango*'s success by reusing the concept of an isolated group in a near-claustrophobic setting, fostering paranoia. However, its real genius lay in its distinctive aesthetic and sci-fi elements, resulting in a well-crafted piece for discerning enthusiasts.

Finally, we couldn't end a discussion on *tokusatsu* horror without mentioning *House* (1977). This cult classic and the first feature film by Nobuhiko Ōbayashi is about a girl who visits her aunt's house with a group of friends. Mysterious events unfold during their stay in the strange home, and the girls begin to disappear one by one.

House is a unique visual and narrative experience. The director's twelve-year-old daughter, Chigumi Ōbayashi, inspired many of the film's horrific scenes by sharing her personal fears, adding a surreal contrast between seemingly lighthearted situations and chilling, non-family-friendly horror. The film takes genuine comedic elements (absurd slapstick moments, despite the ominous setting) and contrasts them with pure, spine-tingling horror that veers into the grotesque in an instant.

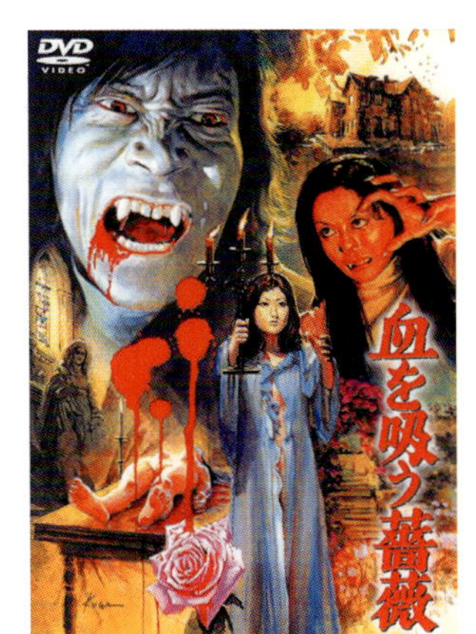

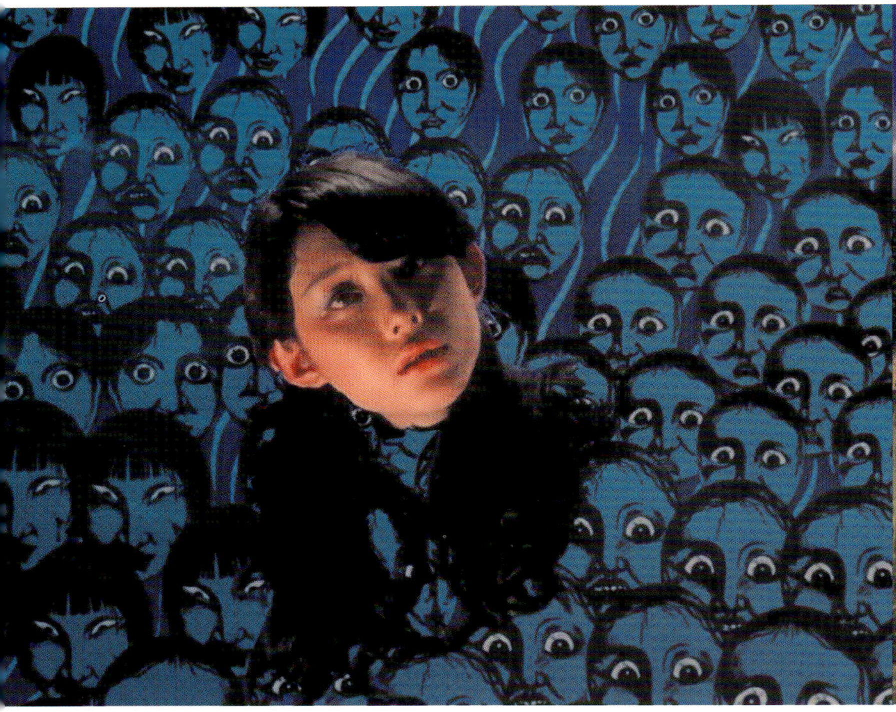

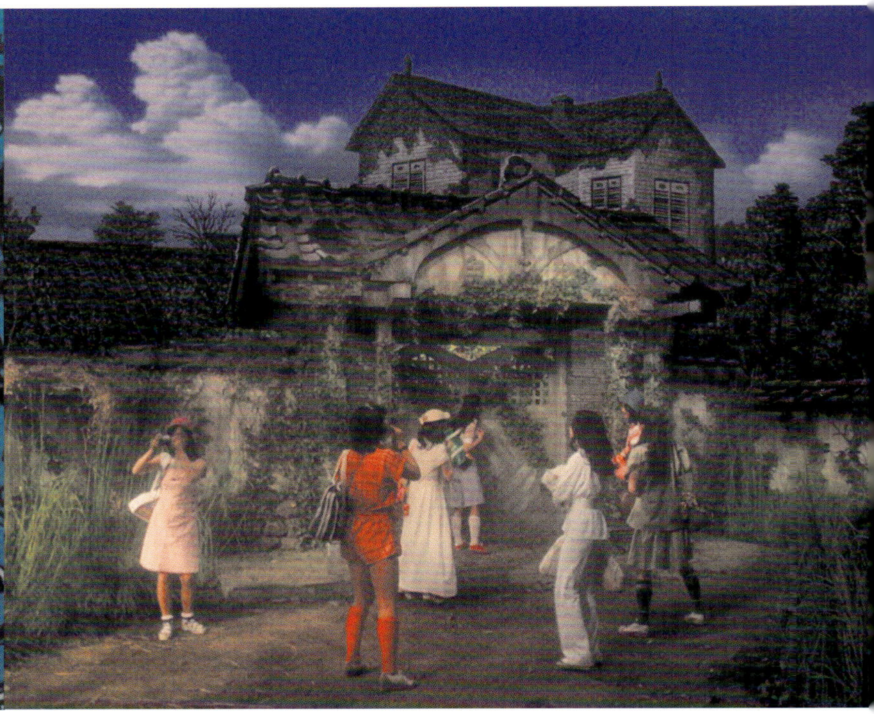

Above: *House redefined the concept of haunted houses.*

Below: *Japanese poster for the film House (1977).*

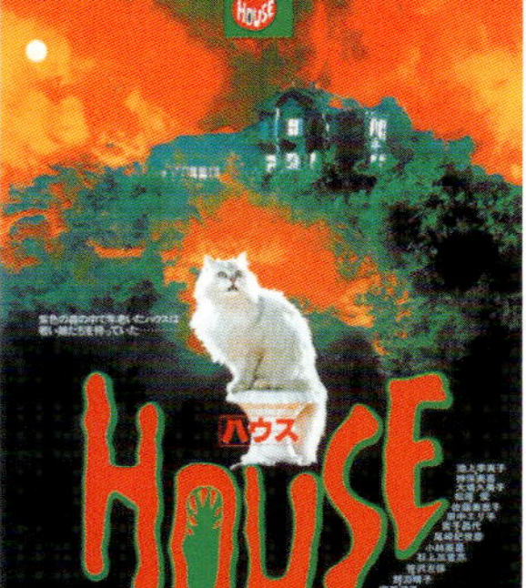

The direction and special effects revel in creating unforgettably inventive and psychedelic scenes that include elements such as a carnivorous piano, a ghost in a mirror, and a possessed cat. *House* leaves viewers feeling deeply unsettled—precisely the intended effect!

THE RISE OF SHOCK HORROR

By the turning point of the 1980s, horror had become firmly entrenched on TV and VHS. Small budgets and a thriving underground filmmaking scene proved a fertile combination, inspiring an entire generation of independent filmmakers. We'll now explore the realm of underground horror, home of some of the most peculiar works in the genre.

Gakidama (1985) is about a small forest creature similar in some ways to the monsters in *Alien* or *Gremlins*. The creature attacks a couple striving to start a family, with the story drawing a parallel between their desire and the creature's primal urge to multiply. Using a mix of puppetry and animatronics, the film still delivers some impactful scenes in an atmosphere suggestive of *The Exorcist* (1973).

Biotherapy, on the other hand, is a much more direct, no-holds-barred film from 1986 in which an alien from the future arrives on present-day Earth to steal a substance created by humans that could help its species survive—but it doesn't ask nicely. The creature knows only violence and kills anyone in its path. This extremely gory, half-hour slasher flick reflects a trend of the time: low-budget productions with short runtimes and shocking concepts, targeting a niche audience always eager for novelties that they can't get from the big screen.

Guzoo: The Thing Forsaken By God, another slasher released the same year, was a kindred spirit to *House* but even more violent. A group of young women spends a few days in a relative's home, only to discover the place is inhabited by

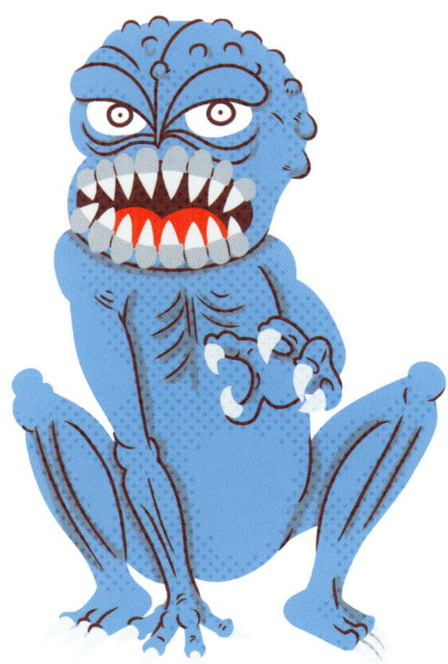

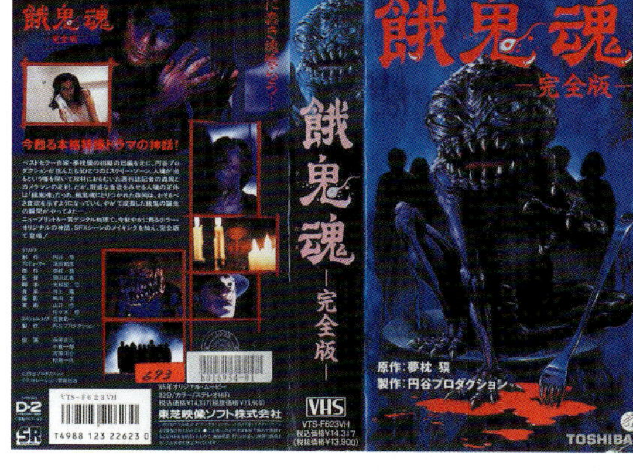

← Far left: *Gakidama, a forest creature seeking a host to help it breed.*

← Left: *VHS cover for the film* Gakidama *(1985).*

↙ Below: *VHS cover for the film* Biotherapy *(1986).*

a vicious creature. Again, due to its short runtime, the film gets straight to the point, serving up bloody carnage that showcases high-quality special effects in its monster, a giant carnivorous plant.

The trend continued, but some filmmakers pushed the envelope, as George Iida did in his debut film, *Cyclops* (1987). This mid-length movie produced for the direct-to-video market delved deeper into themes of human modification, exploring the aftermath of nuclear fallout, pervasive pollution, and its consequences. We see the tragic fate of several characters who, having grown up with mutations, are treated as outcasts by society. Though perhaps less flashy than its predecessors, the film stands out for its poignant themes and chilling atmosphere.

One work profoundly shaped Japanese cinema as a whole: *Tetsuo: The Iron Man* (1989), by Shinya Tsukamoto. Although Tsukamoto had already made waves with his short films *The Adventure of Denchu-kozo* (1987) and *The Phantom of Regular Size* (1986), *Tetsuo* was a full-length feature even stranger and more unpredictable. Disturbing and nearly impossible to summarize, the story revolves around two men, a car accident

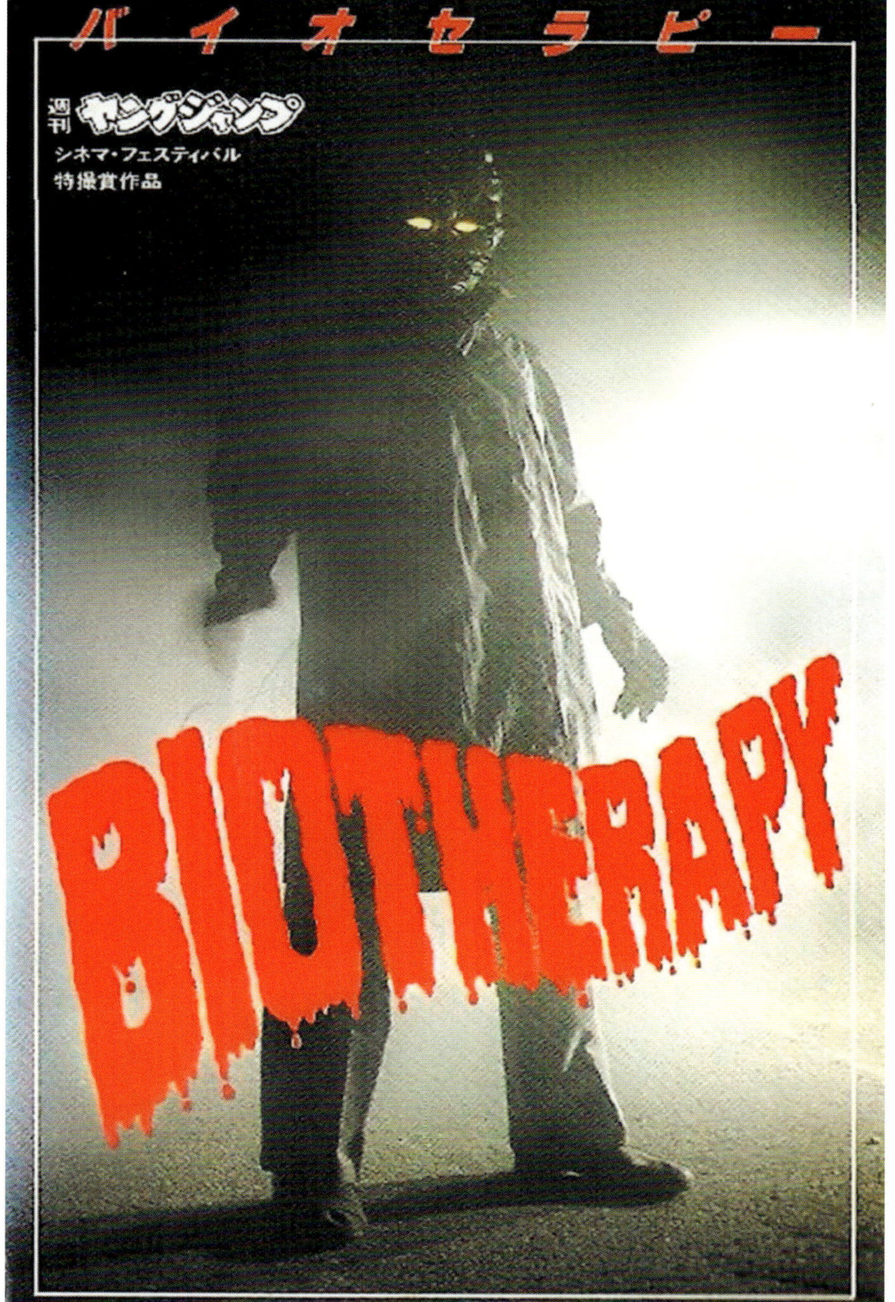

victim who develops an obsession with embedding metal objects into his body, and the driver responsible for the accident who gradually mutates into a creature made partially out of metal.

From this unusual premise, and building on themes glimpsed in *Cyclops*, Tsukamoto demonstrates his mastery of a fascinating experimental blend of body horror (physical deformities) and biopunk (mechanical elements incorporated into the human body). The film is a reflection of rising numbers of people sinking

➜ Right: *Watch out for Guzoo's tentacles, which will destroy anyone in their path!*

↓ Below: *Stills from Cyclops (1987).*

↘ Bottom right: *VHS cover for the film Guzoo: The Thing Forsaken By God (1986).*

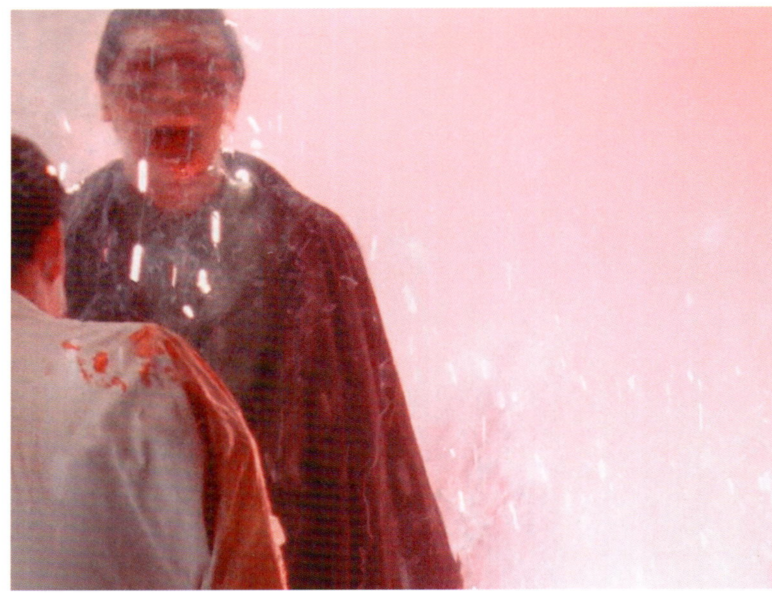

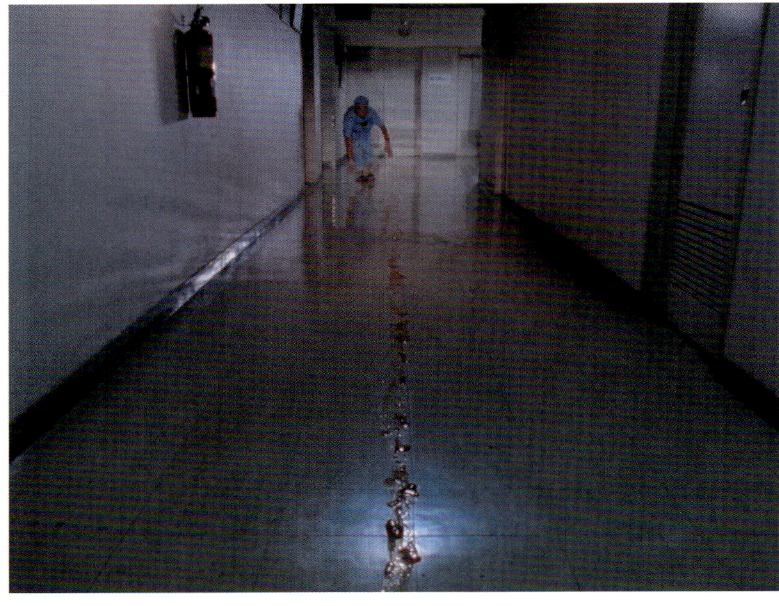

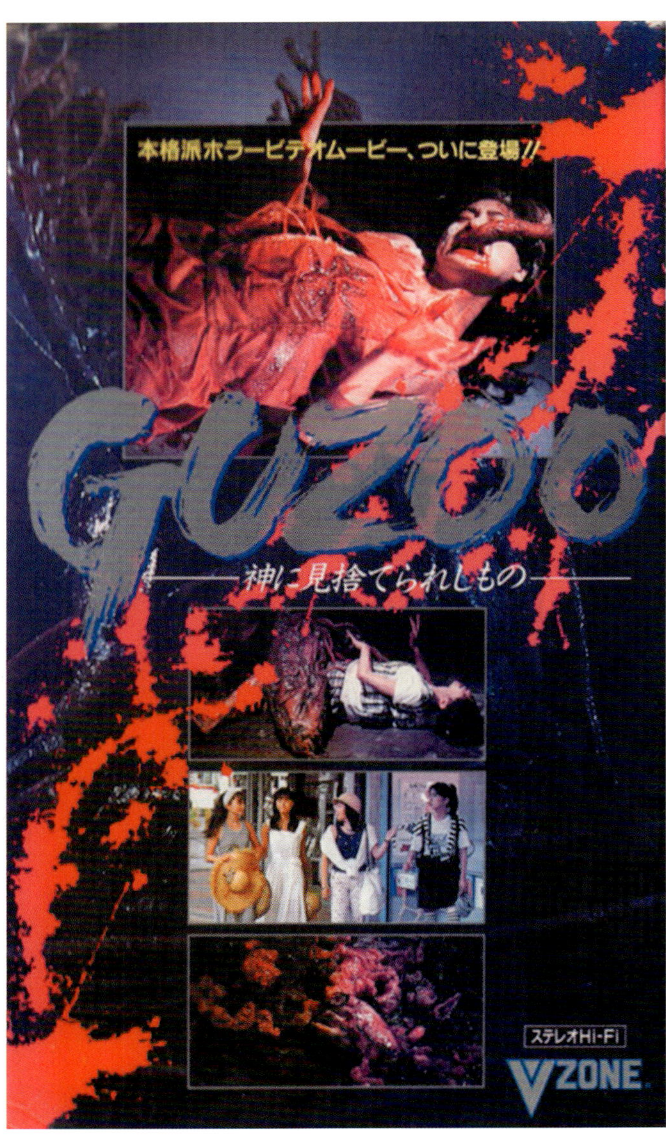

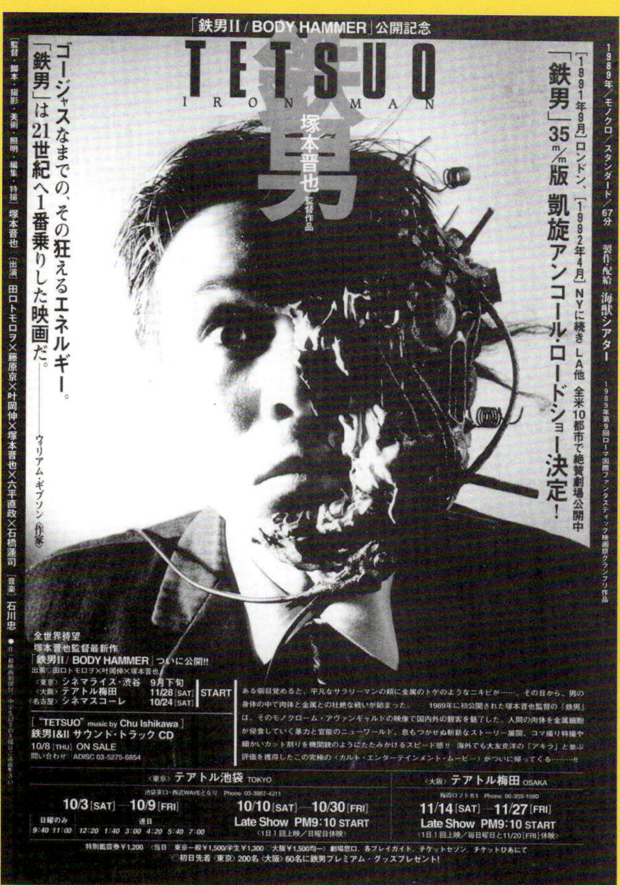

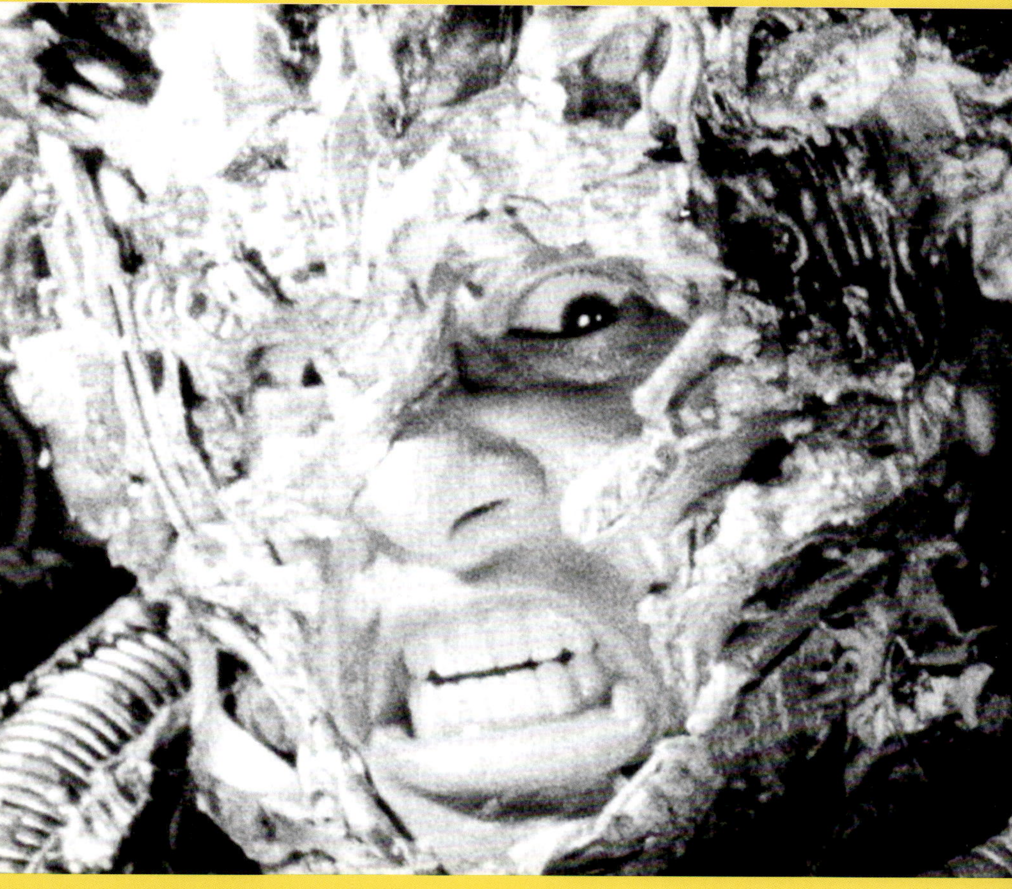

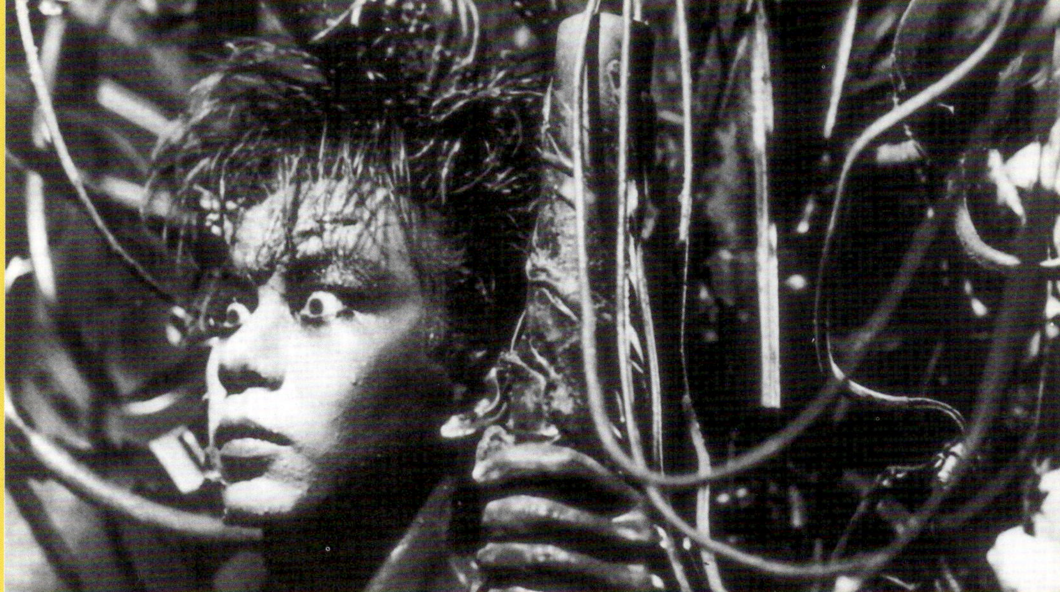

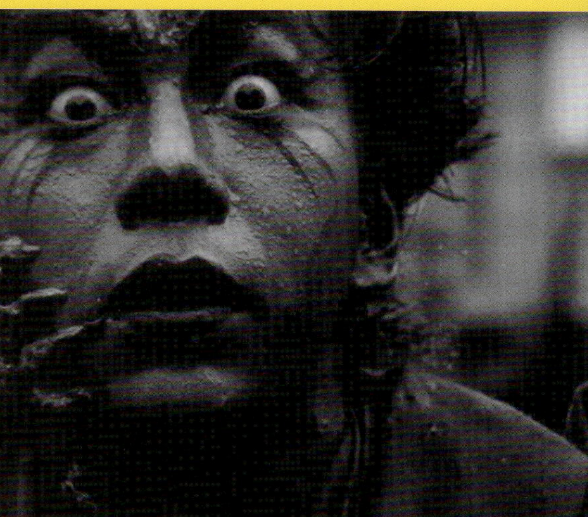

↖ **Above left:** *Japanese poster for the film* Tetsuo: The Iron Man *(1989).*

↑←↓ **Above right, left, and below:** *The main characters in* Tetsuo *mutate and slowly lose their humanity.*

↓ **Below:** Sweet Home *(1989) gave rise to a Nintendo video game, changing the survival horror genre forever.*

into poverty amid Japan's economic crisis, underscored by a gritty, industrial backdrop—a must-see in the genre.

J-HORROR COMES INTO ITS OWN

Tsukamoto made a significant impact, reviving a love of horror in both indie circles and on the big screen. The period from 1989 to the early 2000s marked an evolution, perhaps even a transformation, in how Japan approached horror, at times moving away from traditional *tokusatsu*.

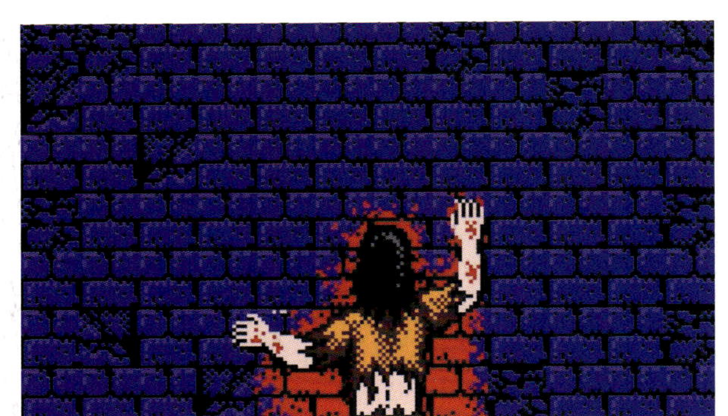

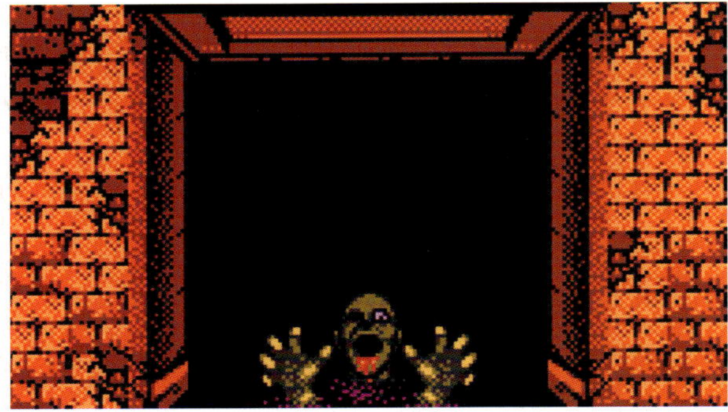

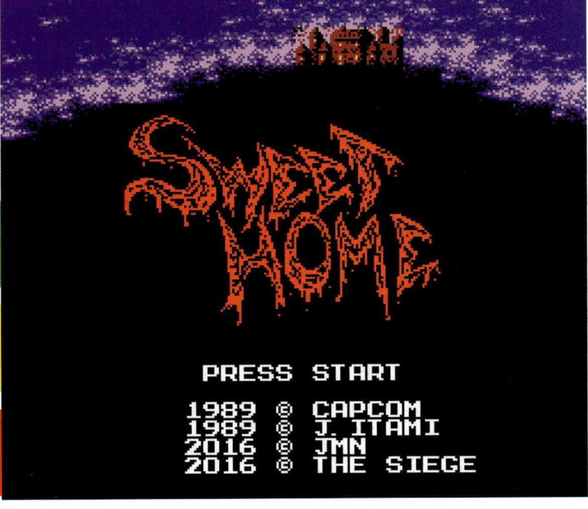

In theaters, 1989 was a landmark year for the genre. In addition to *Tetsuo*, audiences were treated to two cult classics, *Battle Heater* and *Sweet Home*. *Battle Heater* marked George Iida's first feature film on the heels of his success with *Cyclops*, though its tone was lighter and more humorous, comparable to Sam Raimi's *Evil Dead* series. The film features a haunted house, but the creature is a *kotatsu*, a traditional Japanese heated table, possessed by an alien that begins devouring everything in its path.

Sweet Home, on the other hand, is no indie film but rather a major Toho production in which a documentary crew investigates the life of an artist in his home. Predictably, the group finds itself trapped in an eerie house crawling with creatures and ghosts. The premise seems ordinary, but the execution is exemplary, with astonishing special effects, makeup, and visual tricks. The film's success spilled over into video games, starting with an adaptation for the original Nintendo console—one of the first survival horror games. *Sweet Home* would later go on to inspire iconic works like *Clock Tower* and *Resident Evil*.

Tsukamoto continued his career in the 1990s with a string of successes, the most relevant being *Hiruko the Goblin* (1991) and *Tetsuo II: Body Hammer* (1992). The latter succeeds both as a sequel and as a visceral cinematic experience, with a formula that remains just as impactful. Meanwhile, *Hiruko the Goblin*, though less well known, deserves attention for its *Evil Dead*–esque atmosphere. The film mixes lighthearted tones with gory horror when necessary. The goblins in the title are spiders with human faces relentlessly pursuing their victims.

Horror filmmakers scrambled to make their contributions to the genre. We can't list them all, but suffice it to say that even *tokusatsu* got in on the action. Tsuburaya Productions, through its Tsuburaya Eizo division, ventured into horror for the first time with *Mikadoroid* in 1991. Directed by Tomoo Haraguchi, the direct-to-video slasher featured a soldier genetically modified during World War II awakening to wreak havoc on 1990s Tokyo. Notably, Shinji Higuchi directed the special effects.

At this point, live-action horror began diverging into two distinct paths. *Tokusatsu* mainly stuck to one of them, paralleling the rise of J-Horror, a term used to define a particular vision of Japanese-style horror with a psychological bent, often featuring spirits and ghosts in tales of curses set in modern

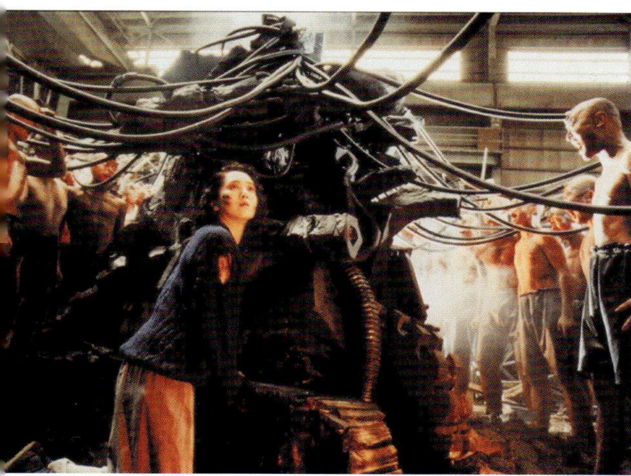

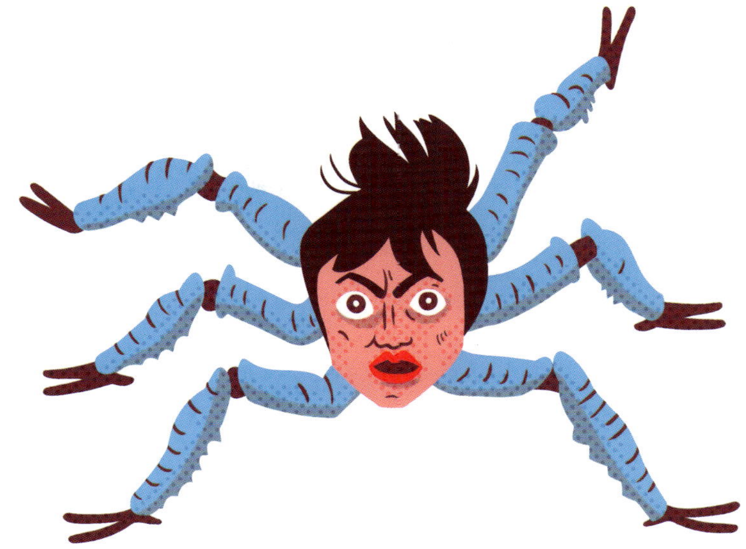

Japan. *The Ring* series (one sequel of which was directed by George Iida) and *Ju-On* are among the genre's most notable works. But how do *tokusatsu* and J-Horror differ? The boundaries may be blurred, but it's worth noting that *tokusatsu* is no longer considered true J-Horror, a category reserved for works that are more graphic in their use of special effects.

The *School Ghost Stories* films released between 1995 and 1999 are excellent examples. The series was adapted from the children's horror novel of the same name, which was popularized through countless adaptations (manga, animated series). The story involves various groups of children trapped in haunted schools where they encounter ghosts and a plethora of grotesque creatures (spider-men, dinosaur skeletons that come to life). The film series pushes the boundaries of horror, despite targeting a young audience, and presents a remarkable gallery of monsters of all kinds.

This type of horror gradually faded over time, becoming more diluted among the broader spectrum of Japanese cinema. However, some works stand out as a legacy of the "trash horror" era of the 1980s. *Meatball Machine* encapsulates the desire for a raw, low-brow, yet exuberant film with simple, straightforward concepts. From the 1999 short film to the 2005 movie and its 2017 sequel, the *Meatball Machine* series is little more than an excuse to revel in gore, featuring humans mutated by aliens whose only desire is to battle their own kind to the death. It also gave the special effects crew a chance to revisit the aesthetics of *Tetsuo*, with its wildly mutated bodies and extreme biopunk.

Tokusatsu horror is less prevalent today, but its influence remains palpable. J-Horror continues to be popular, whereas the "trashier" visual version also persists, with underground successors that likely wouldn't exist without the divide between the two subgenres. The films of Noboru Iguchi, with all their tasteless and utterly uninhibited gore, stand as testament to this legacy.

← **Left:** *Still from* Tetsuo II: Body Hammer *(1992).*

↑ **Above:** *The human-faced spider from* Hiruko the Goblin. *Its appearance was as disturbing as its movements were dangerous!*

↓ **Below:** *Still from* School Ghost Stories *(1995).*

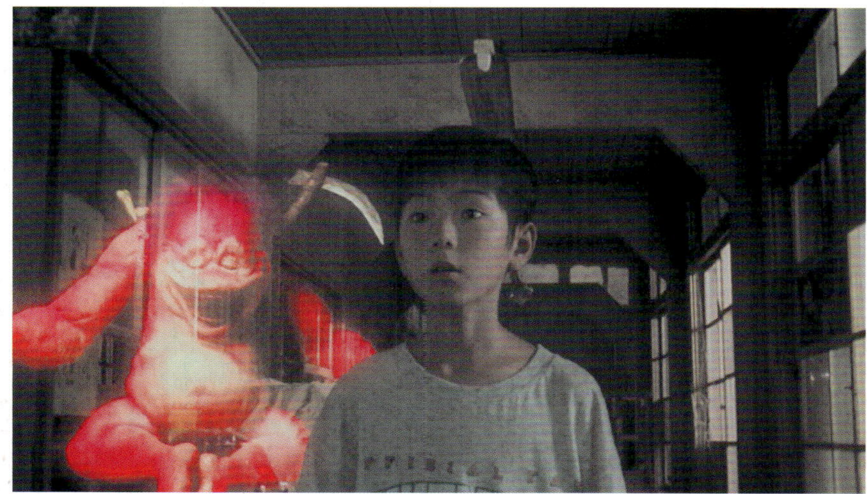

CREATURES & GHOSTS

THE YŌKAI TRILOGY

Midway between horror and giant monsters lies the world of *yōkai*, Japanese creatures that can be highly mischievous. Though they have appeared in numerous films and series throughout the history of *tokusatsu*, in this section, we'll focus on the studio Daiei and its multi-film *yōkai* series that blends family adventure, eerie tales, and epic coming-of-age stories.

The series began in 1968, a year after the success of *Daimajin*. The studio's Kyoto division was known for producing more ambitious films than its Tokyo counterpart (see *Gamera*). The concept was similar to *Daimajin*, a trilogy of standalone movies, all released within a year, featuring stories set in ancient Japan. The three films were *Yōkai Monsters: 100 Monsters*, released in March 1968 and directed by Kimiyoshi Yasuda (who also directed the first *Daimajin*); *The Great Yōkai War*, released in December 1968 and directed by Yoshiyuki Kuroda (assistant director of special effects on *Buddha* in 1961); and *Yōkai Monsters: Along with*

↑ **Above:** *The* rokurokubi *is a* yōkai *that lurks in the shadows with its horrifying long neck.*

→ **Right:** *The* kasa-obake *is a sweet-natured, one-legged umbrella* yōkai.

↘ **Below:** *Promotional image for the film* Yōkai Monsters: 100 Monsters *(1968).*

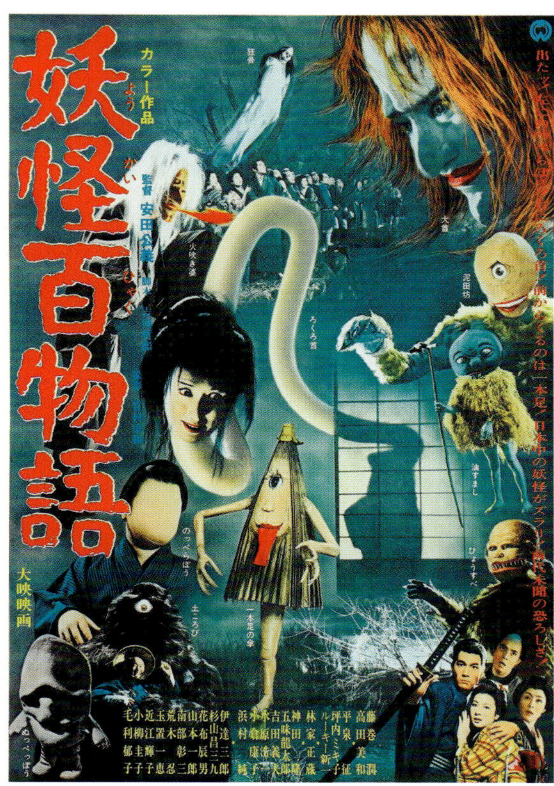

Far left: *Japanese poster for the film* Yōkai Monsters: 100 Monsters *(1968).*

Left: *A* noppera-bō, *one of the strangest* yōkai. *It takes human form but can cause its face to disappear.*

Ghosts, released in March 1969 and led by two co-directors.

Yokai Monsters: 100 Monsters recounts the tale of a wealthy landowner's unsuccessful attempt to seize a vast piece of land containing a sacred temple. Ignoring warnings, he snatches the land illegally, awakening the *yōkai* who show him the error of his ways. The film is Daiei's way of reminding audiences of a fundamental aspect of *yōkai*: that they share a deep connection to humans, living among them and influenced by their actions. Supernatural elements weave seamlessly into daily life throughout the film, sometimes playfully, through the umbrella *yōkai* called *kasa-obake*, and other times more chillingly, as with the snake-necked *rokurokubi* or the giant *ōkamuro* with the face of a woman. The nail-biting climax depicts a swarm of *yōkai* storming the main character's home.

The Great Yōkai War is the most popular installment in the series, in which a *kappa*, a humanoid *yōkai* resembling a turtle, and its companions face the arrival of Daimon, a malevolent creature from the distant lands of Babylon. The tone is lighter, emphasizing the noble and heroic nature of the *yōkai* who protect humans from supernatural threats. The studio enthusiastically brought the mythical creatures to life through costumes, puppetry, and delightfully crafted visual effects.

The final film, *Yōkai Monsters: Along with Ghosts*, strikes a balance but is more of a samurai story, with the *yōkai* relegated to supporting roles. In the story, Hyakasuro is a swordsman tasked with protecting a girl who has witnessed a murder in a sacred place by criminals that are now pursuing her. But as with all sacred places, *yōkai* are nearby to wreak vengeance. Although more modest in its technical achievements, the third entry in the series successfully delivers a captivating atmosphere.

The trilogy left a lasting mark on Japanese cinema and set the bar for years to come. However, as we've seen time and again throughout the history of *tokusatsu*, the franchise saw a resurgence in the 2000s, once again shining brightly.

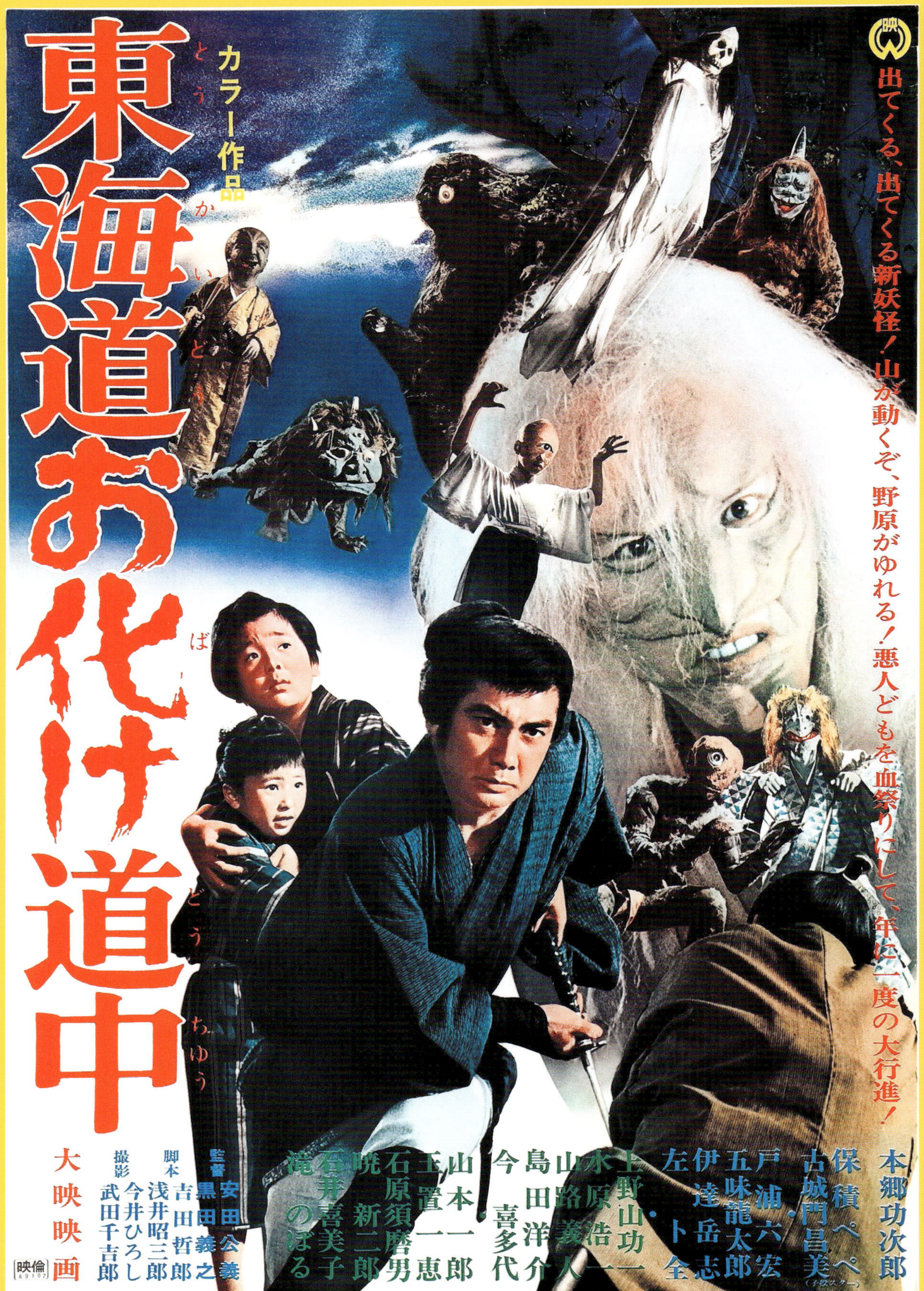

Right: *Japanese poster for the film* Yōkai Monsters: Along with Ghosts *(1969).*

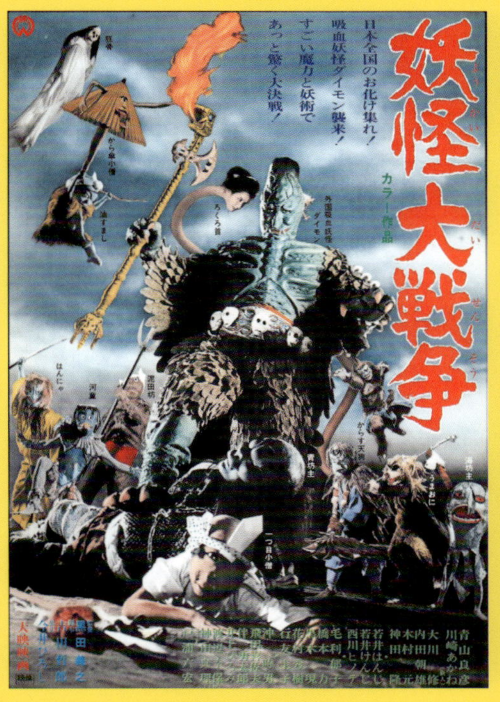

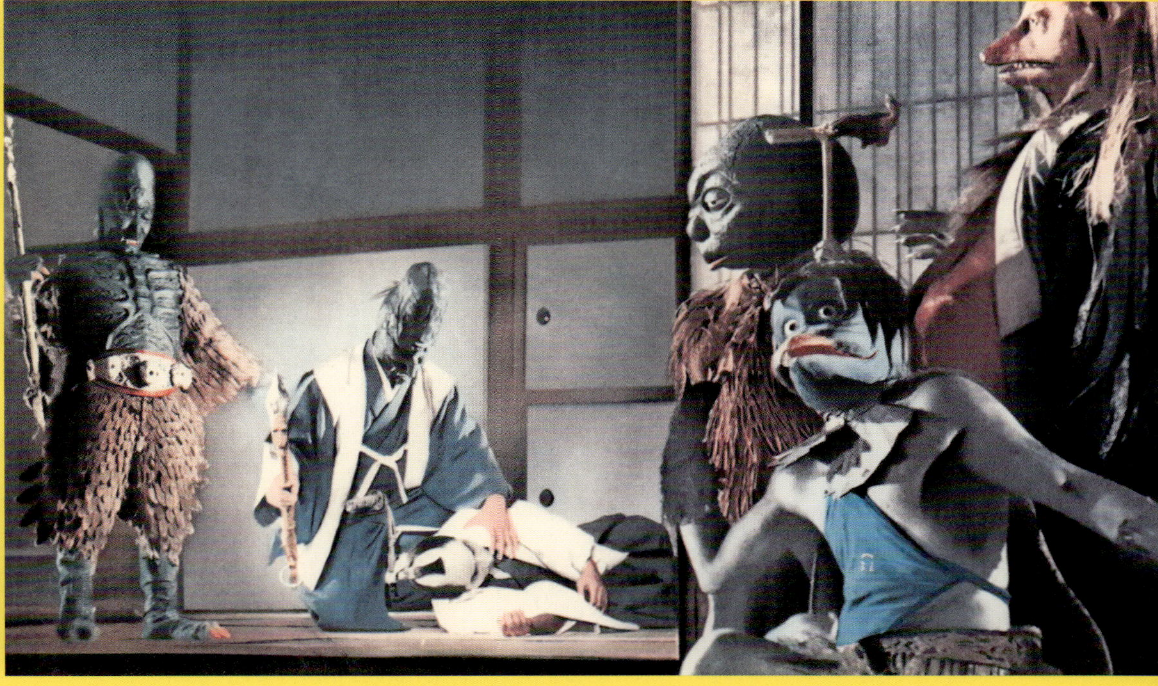

↖ ↑ **Above:** *Japanese poster and promotional image for the film* The Great Yōkai War *(1968).*

MODERN YŌKAI

After Daiei was acquired by Kadokawa in the early 2000s, and following the success of the *Gamera* trilogy in the 1990s, the studio began to think seriously about reviving some of its other franchises. Though *Daimajin* productions came and went until its full reboot in 2010, *yōkai* experienced a resurgence in 2005 with a project led by Takashi Miike, a rising figure in modern Japanese cinema.

Miike arrived on the scene in the 1990s with direct-to-video films, as well as critical theatrical successes (notably his *yakuza* film *Dead or Alive* and horror flick *Audition*, both released in 1999), and quickly became a versatile, inquisitive director. He would go on to create *The Great Yōkai War*, a very loose reinterpretation of the 1968 original, primarily retaining the concept of a grand battle of *yōkai* around an unknown force. The remake is the story of Ino Tadashi, a boy swept up by a group of *yōkai* on a quest for a sword that can transform him into a hero and that is his only means of fighting the army of monsters assembled by the demon Katō.

The Great Yōkai War simultaneously renders homage to the original film and modernizes it through its young protagonist and his adventures in the *yōkai* world. The film was inspired in part by Shigeru Mizuki's manga *GeGeGe no Kitarō*, whose main character is Yasunori Katō, an iconic, demonic figure from the massive dark fantasy literary work *Teito Monogatari*. The story was also adapted into a *tokusatsu* film, 1988's *Tokyo: The Last Megalopolis*, which traces Katō's attempt to destroy Tokyo in the 1920s. Katō is depicted somewhat differently in *The Great Yōkai War* but remains a sort of spiritual descendant of the earlier version of himself, targeting Tokyo once again with his legion of monsters.

The Great Yōkai War serves up a delightful family adventure that diversifies its director's filmography with flair. It features a host of *yōkai*, brought to life on-screen either through

➜ **Right:** *DVD cover for the film* The Great Yōkai War *(2005).*

➜ **Far right:** *Japanese poster for the film* The Great Yōkai War: Guardians *(2021).*

➘ **Below:** Kappa, *mischievous* yōkai, *appear in both of Daiei's series.*

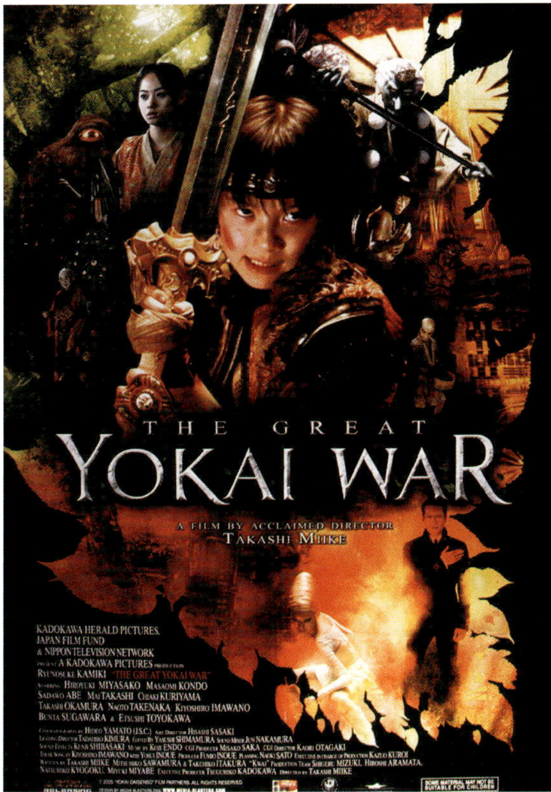

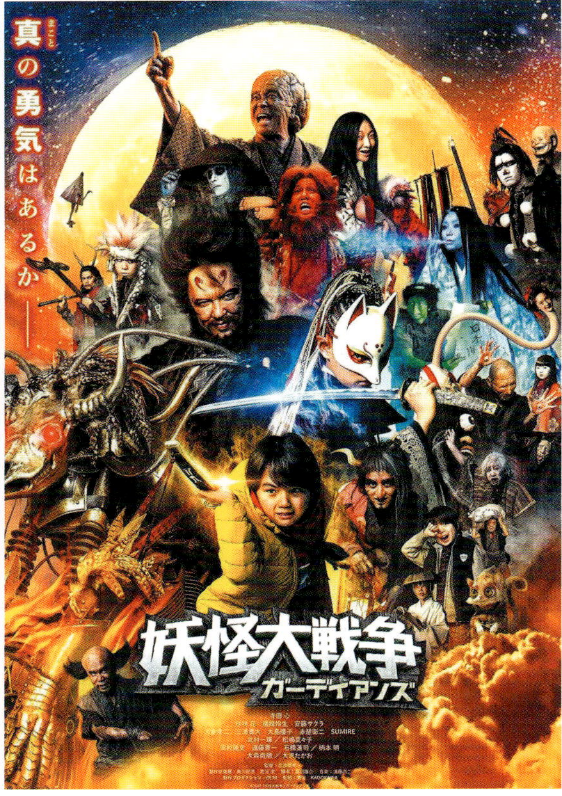

marvelous costumes and makeup (including the *kappa*, *tengu*—winged *yōkai* with long noses—and *nurikabe*, a wall-shaped monster) or through CGI, which opened up new possibilities and more ambitious scenes than ever before.

Despite the film's critical success, a sequel would not be made until 2021 with *The Great Yōkai War: Guardians*. The formula remained somewhat similar, featuring another young boy, Kei Watanabe, who is entangled in a new *yōkai* battle with the arrival of the Yōkaijū, a massive mystical creature destroying everything in its path. During his journey, Kei encounters the stone giant Daimajin, who assists him in his fight.

Although the premise is similar, Miike's sequel is no mere carbon copy. Despite its *yōkai* and Daimajin's promise, the second film is less warlike in spirit than the first, featuring scenes that are occasionally deeply poetic and pacifist in their view of war, including a surprising and moving musical scene.

The film's ending hints at a third installment that would connect the first two and form a trilogy with a single story arc. Though nothing has been announced at this time, we can only hope for a conclusion crafted by an ever-inspired Miike.

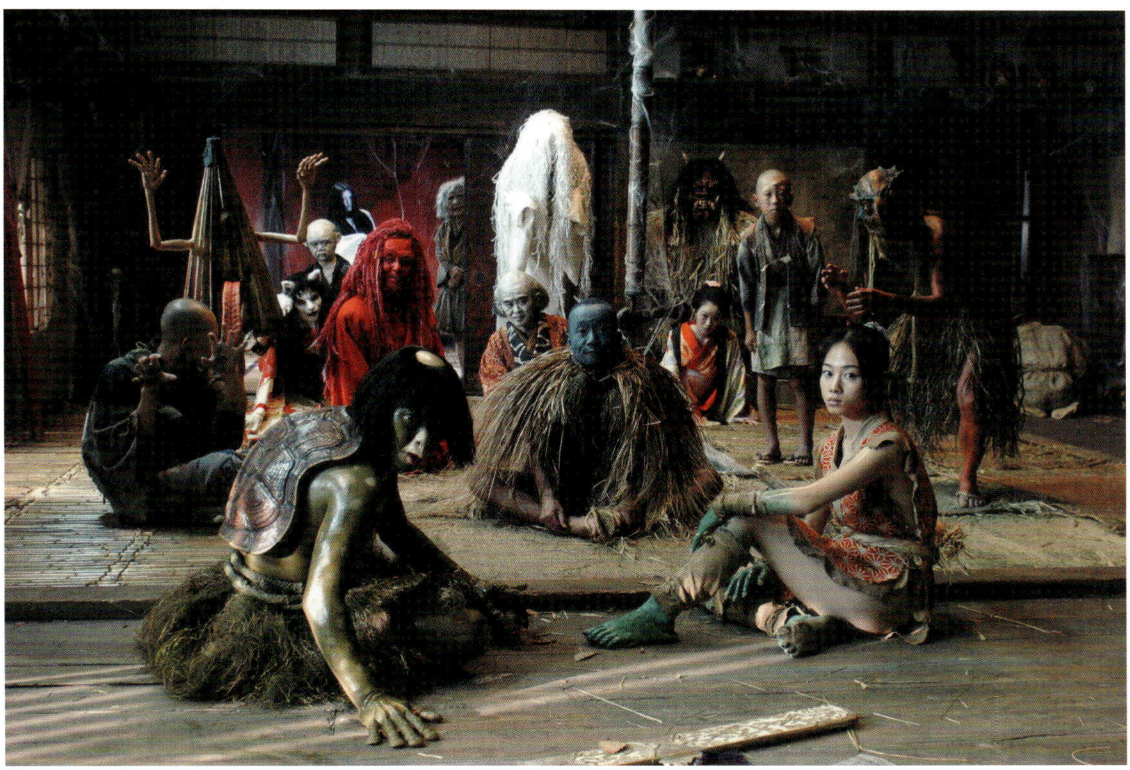

← **Left:** *Still from* The Great Yōkai War *(2005).*

THE WORLD OF SHIGERU MIZUKI

When talking about *yōkai* in Japanese culture, we have to include Shigeru Mizuki and his two flagship works, *GeGeGe no Kitarō* and *Akuma-kun*. These two significant productions have inspired an entire imaginary world around *yōkai* and, naturally, have been adapted into shows teeming with special effects.

Kitarō was originally a hero popular in *kamishibai*, a form of Japanese street theater, created in the 1930s alongside *Ōgon Bat*. In 1959, the character Kitarō, a *yōkai* child that maintains the balance between the human and spirit worlds, was transferred to Shigeru Mizuki to develop his own manga. It met with great success. With its dark atmosphere and reinterpretation of Japanese folklore, Kitarō revived interest in stories about *yōkai* and other fantastical monsters.

Riding the wave of his success, in 1963, Mizuki created a similar hero, a boy nicknamed Akuma-kun, meaning demon, for his powers, which allow him to summon demonic creatures. Alongside his mentor, Mephisto, who wears a top hat, they embark on adventures in the world of *yōkai* and other creatures from across the globe.

Akuma-kun's popularity led to the first *tokusatsu* adaptation of Mizuki's works. Produced by Toei in 1966, during the boom of *tokusatsu* productions for television, the TV series consisted of twenty-six episodes. Although some elements were adapted to better suit the new medium, the series remained true to its concept, showcasing a wide array of creatures of all shapes and sizes in a "monster of the week" format. This allowed the studio to refine its craft, paving the way for the *tokusatsu* explosion of the 1970s.

Kitarō and Akuma-kun returned to the *tokusatsu* genre in the 1980s via

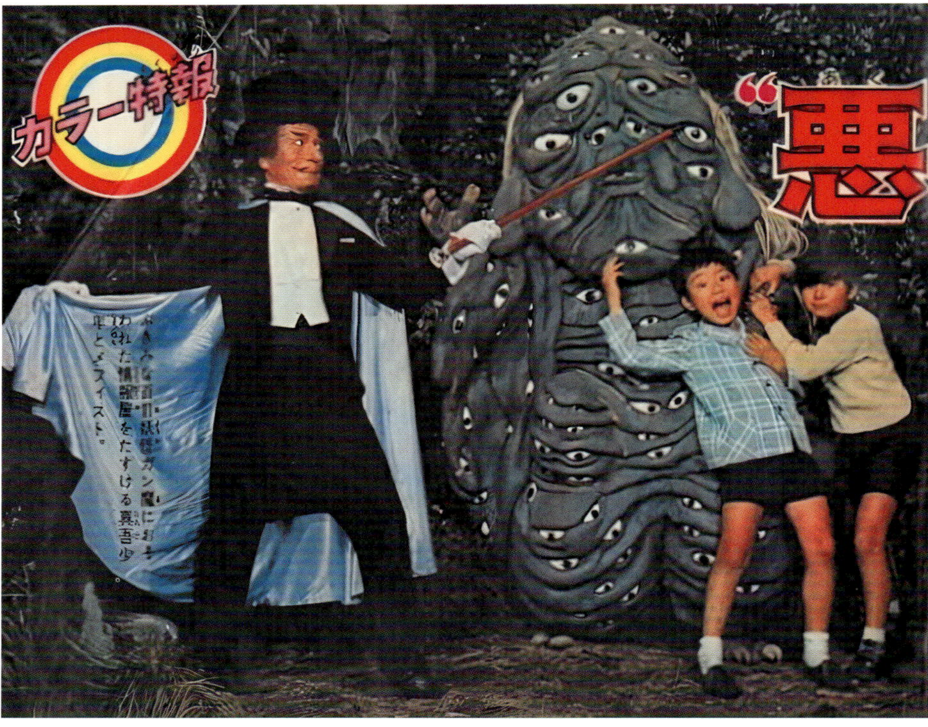

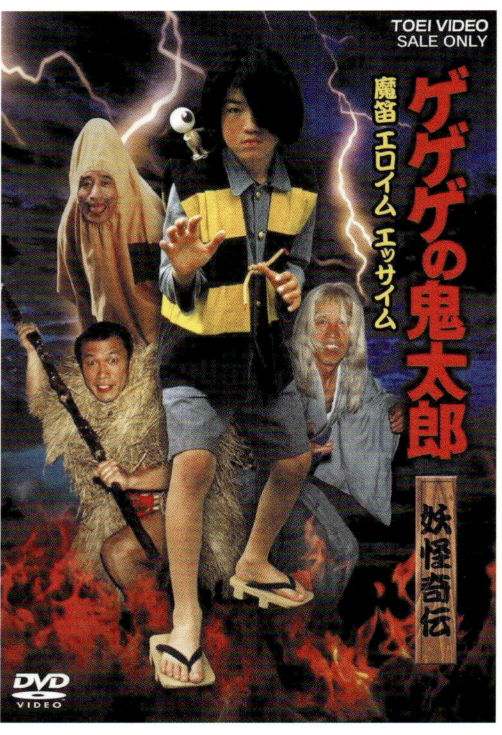

Above left: *Magazine spread for the series* Akuma-kun *(1966).*

Above right: *Japanese DVD cover for the film* GeGeGe no Kitarō Yōkai Kiden: Mateki Elohim Essaim *(1987).*

made-for-TV movies produced by Toei. Though not the best-known works in its repertoire, the first was *GeGeGe no Kitarō* in 1985, followed by *Akuma-kun* in 1986, and concluding in 1987 with a direct-to-video crossover film featuring both characters.

The productions were quite modest for their time (and occasionally somewhat ridiculous due to certain costume designs, like the rat man Nezumi Otoko), but their execution was spirited, thanks in part to Toei's expertise in *tokusatsu* TV franchises such as *Metal Hero*. The crossover featured unmitigated action with inventive *yōkai* battle scenes.

Despite these attempts, both works remained deeply tied to the worlds of manga and anime, the latter more conducive to portraying fantastical creatures. Kitarō and Akuma-kun continued to thrive in anime series in the following years, and the popularity of the series showed no signs of waning. Nevertheless, a live-action Kitarō, complete with special effects, wouldn't appear until the late 2000s. On the other hand, despite Akuma-kun's enduring popularity (including a Netflix animated series in 2023), he has yet to receive the live-action treatment.

Kitarō left Toei for the studio Shochiku (known for *The X from Outer Space* in 1967, its satirical sequel in 2008, and *Big Man Japan* in 2007) to join a more ambitious production, a movie version of *GeGeGe no Kitarō*, which hit theaters in 2007. The film features the adventures of an adult Kitarō alongside other key characters from the franchise, including Nezumi Otoko, Neko Musume (a cat girl), and Medama-Oyaji (Kitarō's father, who has an eyeball for a head). It was the franchise's first theatrical release and was directed by Katsuhide Motoki.

The story focuses on an item with the power to manipulate both the human and *yōkai* worlds. It becomes targeted by *kitsune*, mischievous fox *yōkai* that can transform into humans. The film echoes *The Great Yōkai War* with its relatively well-executed special effects, which use both CGI and actors in costume and makeup, including the *wanyūdō*, a *yōkai* in the form of a flaming wheel with a human face at its center. The result might not exactly rival Takashi Miike's work, but it is an honest introduction to Kitarō on the big screen.

The following year, in 2008, the franchise achieved significant success with its second film, *Kitarō and the Millennium Curse*. The direct sequel featured the same director and cast but was a more ambitious production, taking the first film and turning it into a vibrant, charming adventure. The plot was more engaging this time around, with entertaining scenes, such as a concert by *tanuki* (Japanese raccoon dogs, which are also considered *yōkai*) and more dynamic sequences showcasing Kitarō's energetic combat skills. Additionally, making their debut were new, more visually striking *yōkai*, including the *gashadokuro*, a giant skeleton.

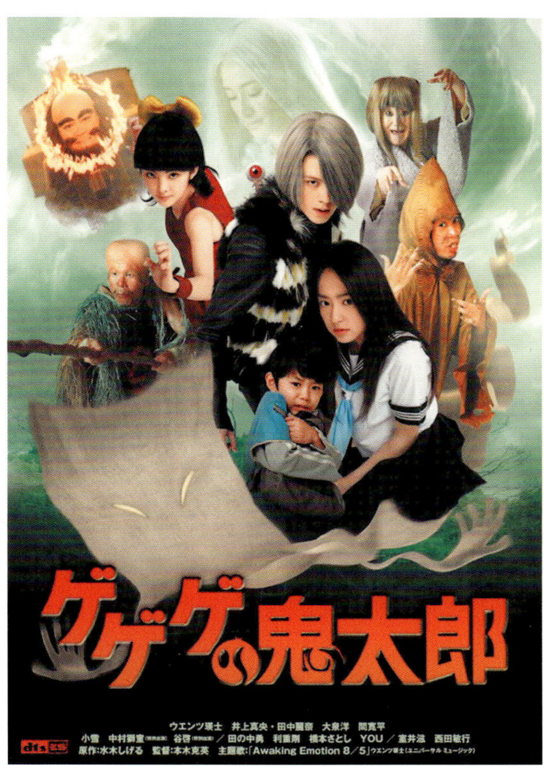

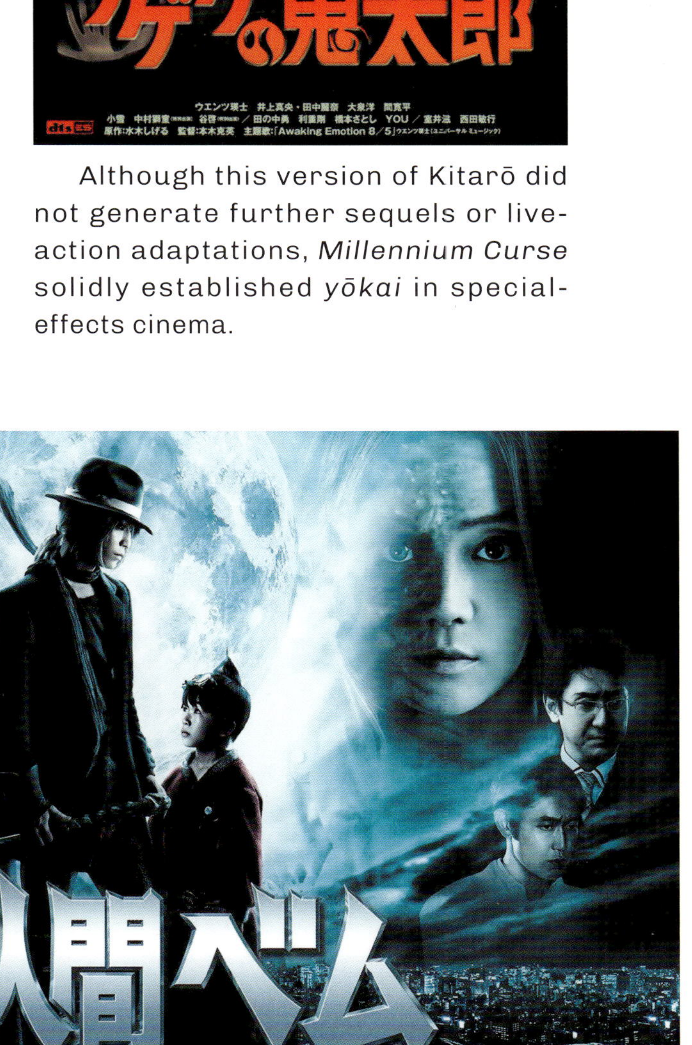

Although this version of Kitarō did not generate further sequels or live-action adaptations, *Millennium Curse* solidly established *yōkai* in special-effects cinema.

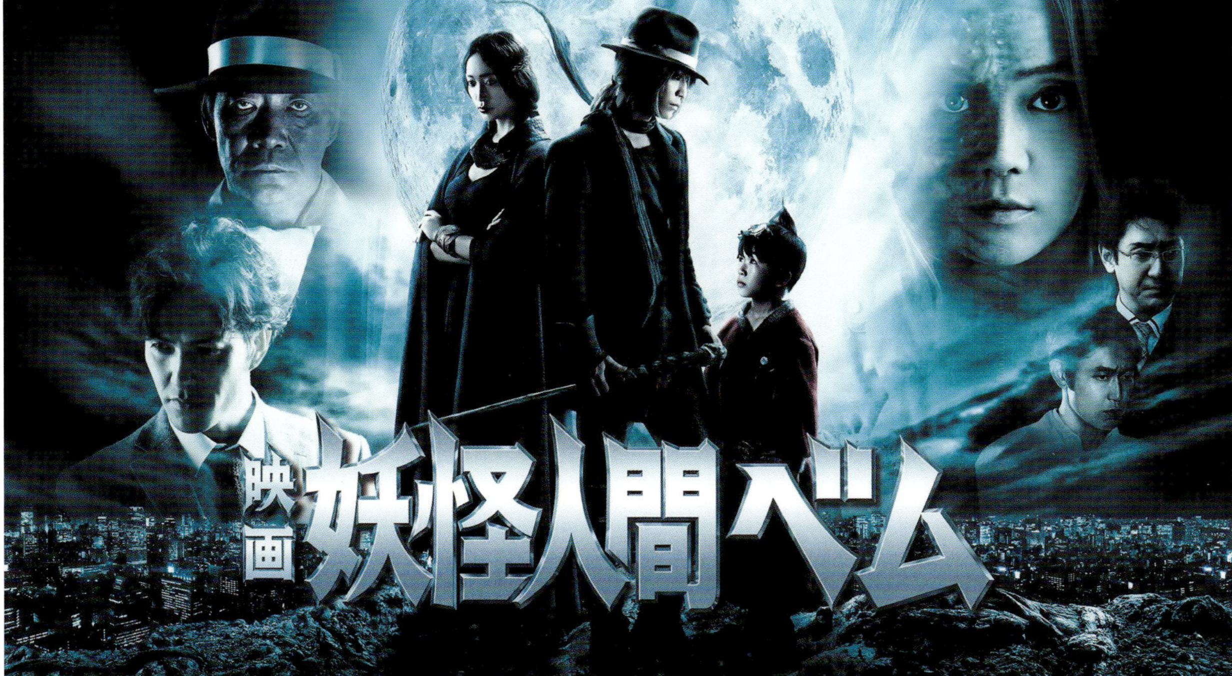

← **Left:** *Poster for the film* GeGeGe no Kitarō *(2007).*

↓ **Below:** Humanoid Monster Bem *(2011).*

Right: *The three main characters from the series* Humanoid Monster Bem *(2011).*

Below: *Japanese poster for the series.*

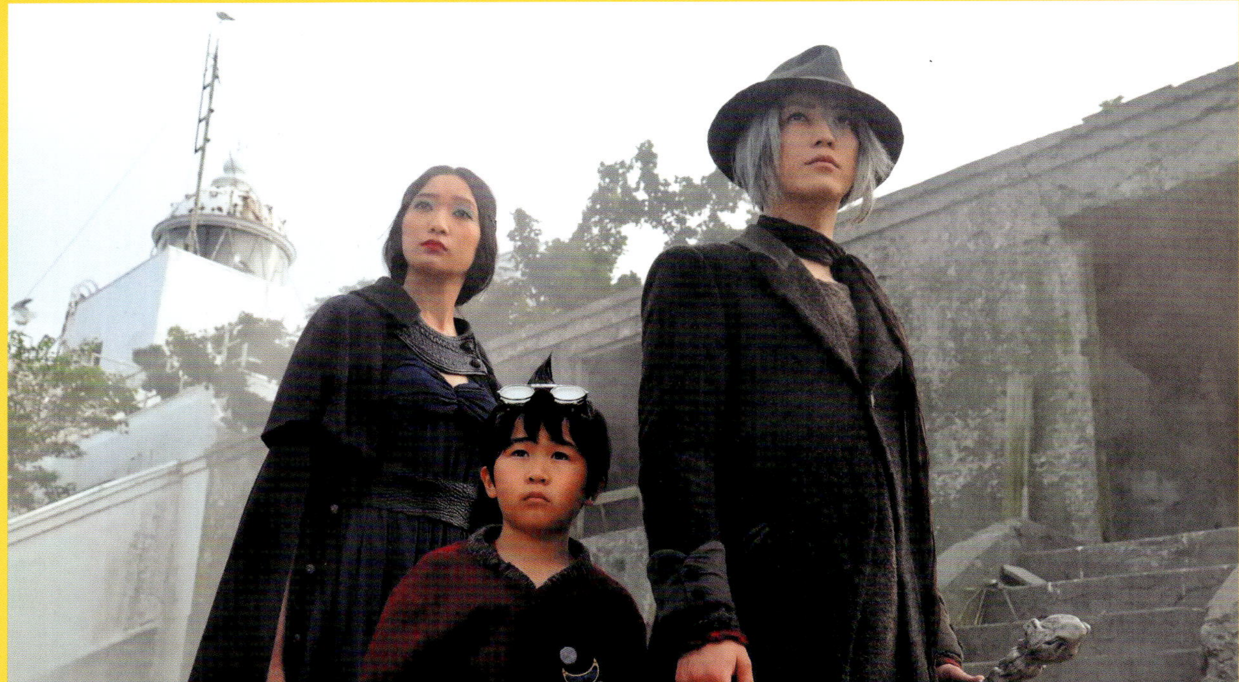

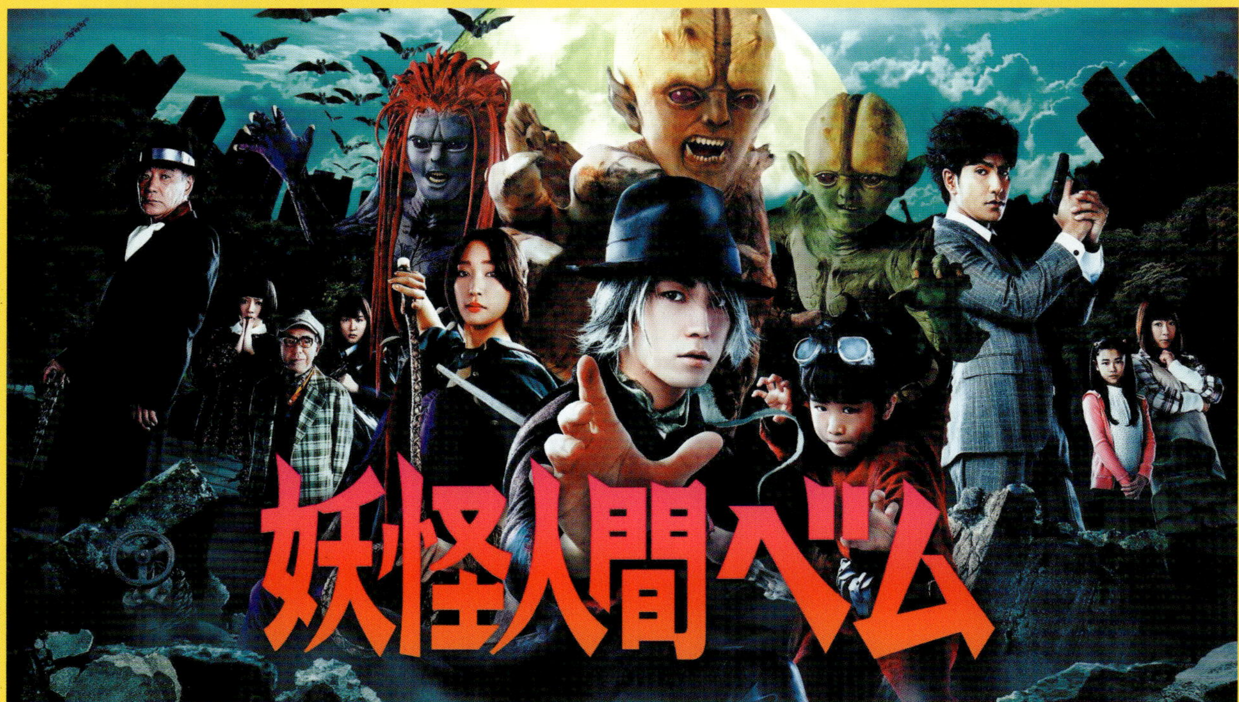

DEMON-SLAYERS

Yōkai are well rooted in both film and television. Now that we've seen the major works in the genre, let's look at some lesser-known productions that explore *yōkai* in their own way—for example, the idea of *yōkai* in human society.

Like Kitarō and Akuma-kun, the 1968 anime *Humanoid Monster Bem* received its first live-action adaptation in 2011. This series features three *yōkai* who take human form in order to blend in. Despite being rejected when they reveal their true selves, the ragtag family aspires to become human by rescuing people threatened by other *yōkai*. Though modest in technical execution, the series combines supernatural elements with a cop show format, one of the most popular genres on Japanese television. The trio teams up with a police officer to face off against a common threat. The show achieved notable success and even sparked a renewed interest in the franchise, leading to subsequent films (one in 2012 and another spin-off in 2020) and new animated adaptations.

In 2000, there was a resurgence in fantasy stories involving both samurai and spirits. Director Tomoo Haraguchi, known for his debut film *Mikadoroid* (1991) and his *kaijū* modeling in the *Gamera* films of the 1990s, delivered his second feature, *Sakuya: Yōkaiden* (literally Sakuya: Slayer of Demons, never officially released in the United States), set in a fantasy version of feudal Japan. After the death of her father, the powerful *yōkai* hunter Sakuya must prevent the rebirth of an occult force inside Mount Fuji. She takes over her father's mission, wielding the legendary Muramasa sword, all while caring for her adopted brother, a young *kappa*—thus becoming a demon-slayer in her own right.

Made for the Towani Corporation, *Sakuya* was Haraguchi's first theatrical production and the studio's first film. (The short-lived corporation would be best known for the 2004 film *Cutie Honey*, directed by Hideaki Anno.) *Sakuya* delivers a rich, engaging action film with a simple but classic story of a teenage girl embarking on an epic adventure. The film features a wide array of *yōkai*, such as *tsuchigumo* (spiderlike *yōkai*) and *bakeneko* (cat *yōkai*), enhanced by Shinji Higuchi's signature special effects and the expertise of Tokusatsu Kenkyūjo studio.

Higuchi and Haraguchi were longtime collaborators, working together frequently throughout their careers, especially at the start, when they were both struggling to make it big in the major

↓ Below: *Japanese poster for the film* Kibakichi *(2004).*

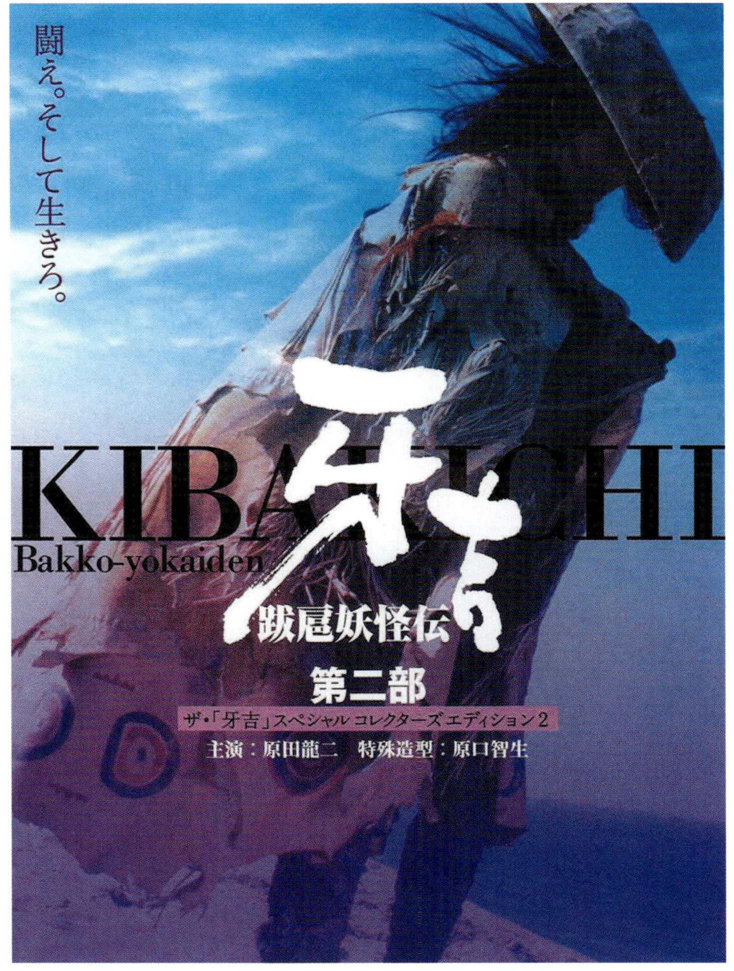

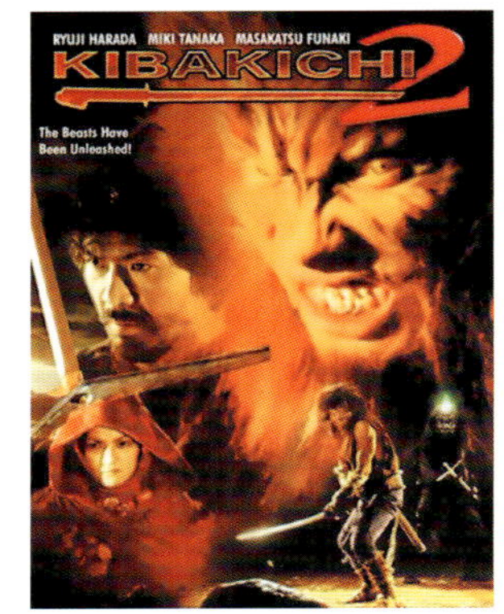

studios. For example, Haraguchi worked on visuals and special effects for Higuchi's early films, such as *Lorelei: The Witch of the Pacific Ocean* (2005) and *Sinking of Japan* (2006).

Haraguchi continued making *yōkai* stories in 2004 with *Kibakichi: Bakko-yōkaiden* and *Kibakichi: Bakko-yōkaiden 2*—unique in that they featured a werewolf, a Western character rarely found in Japanese pop culture. The story is of a samurai who wanders about in a world where the relationship between *yōkai* and humans is fraught, if not outright hostile. The *yōkai* are not a threat, but a microcosm seeking peace in a world that despises them and hunts them for sport. Burdened by his werewolf identity, Kibakichi roves the land, restoring balance between the two worlds however he can.

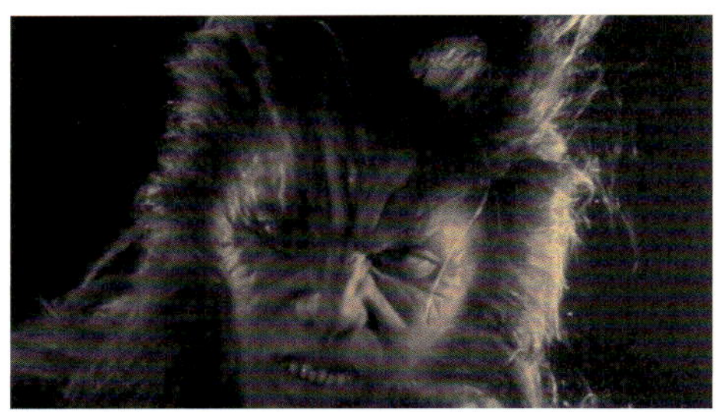

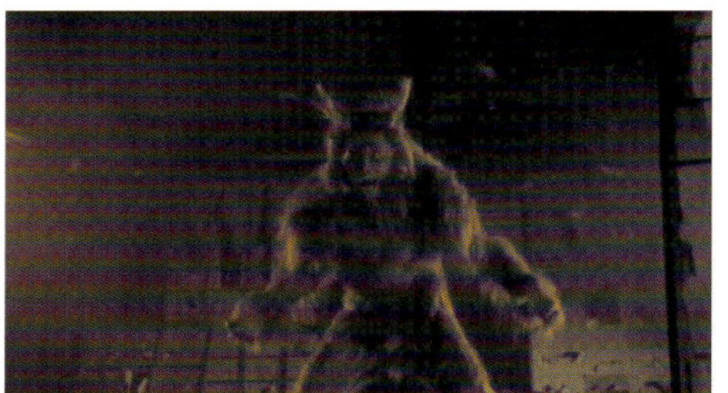

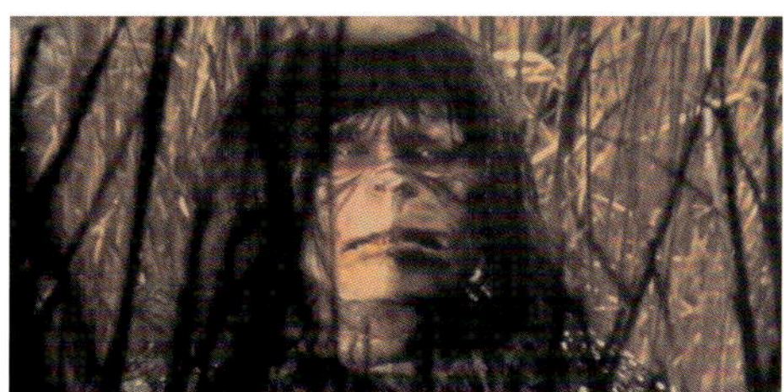

The ambiance of the two films is more subdued, the pacing more measured than *Sakuya*. The action scenes are also more tempered, resembling the swordplay epics that defined Japanese cinema in the 1960s (and that remain popular today). Kibakichi himself is a man of few words, but he acts decisively to protect the weak. Both films—but particularly the first, the more successful of the two—focus on building tension throughout the story, culminating in moments of heroism and turning the spotlight on a ferocious, agile samurai werewolf.

Haraguchi remained deeply involved in special effects, often collaborating with Higuchi and contributing to the *Ultraman* franchise. He returned as a director in 2010 with *Death Kappa*, mentioned previously, commingling *kaijū* and *yōkai* themes in quirky fashion and reflecting his passion for recurring themes he has explored throughout his career in *tokusatsu*.

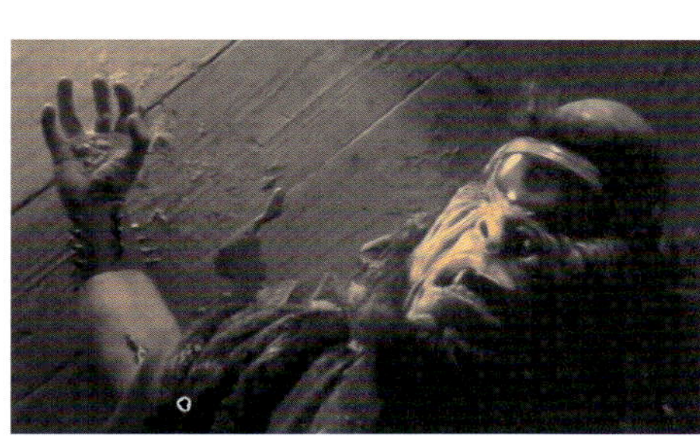

↑ **Above:** *Poster for the film* Kibakichi: Bakko-yōkaiden 2 *(2010) and stills from the first film.*

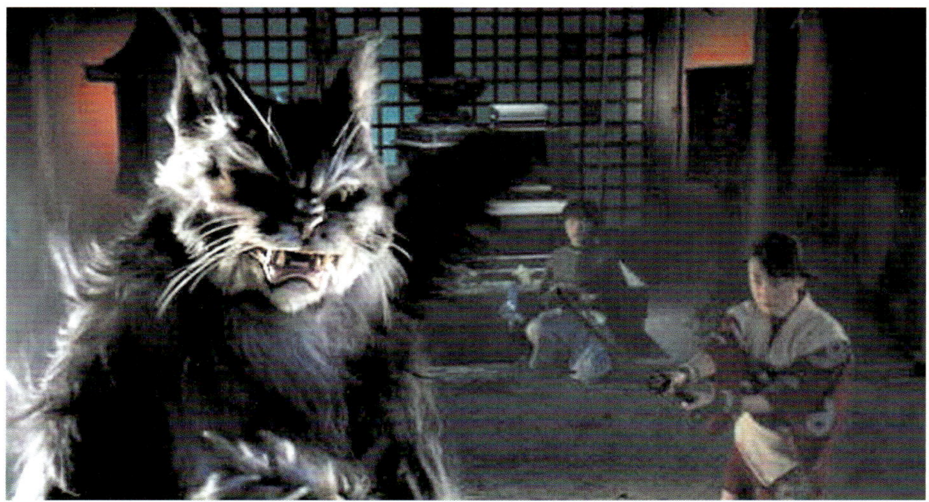

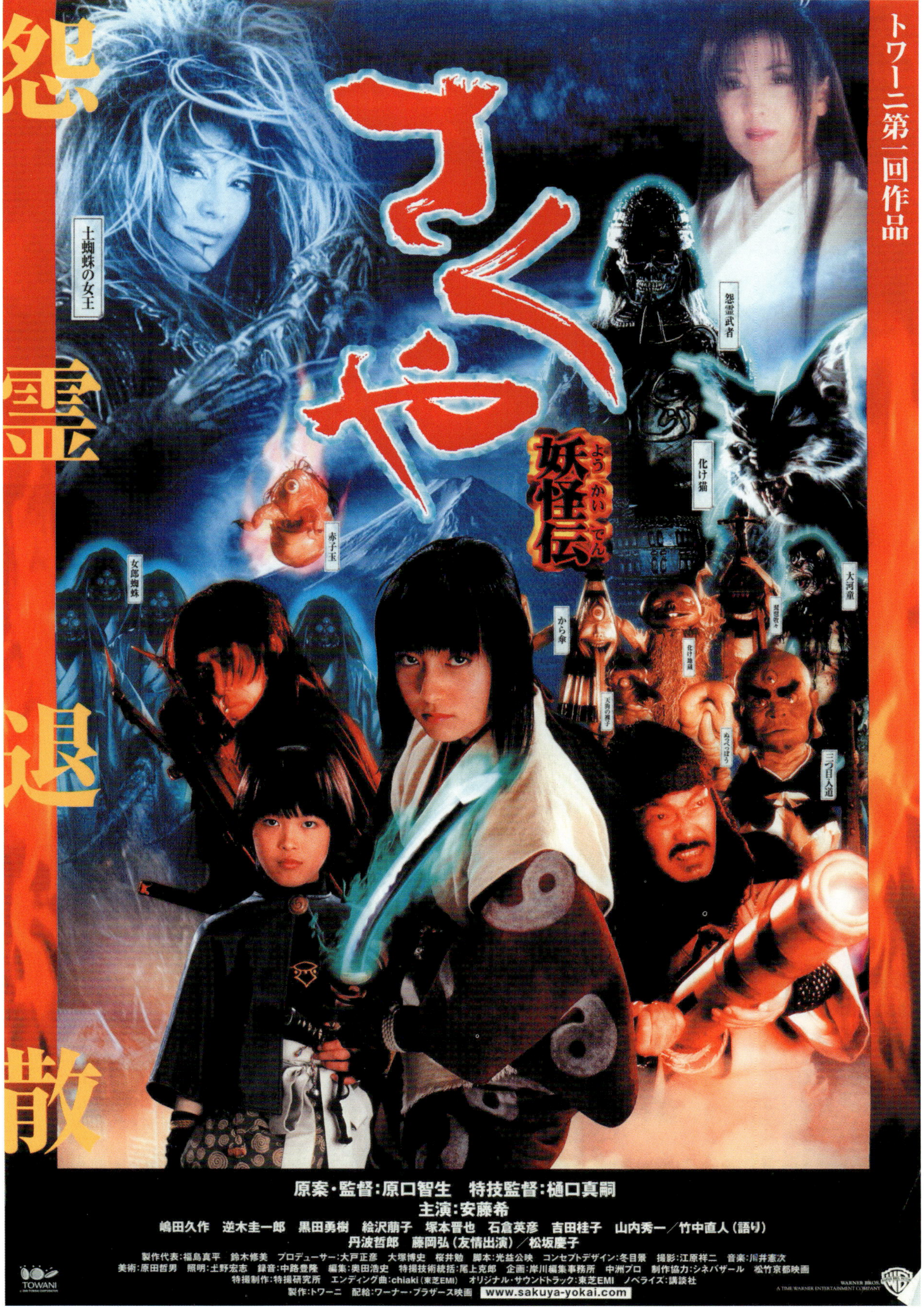

← **Left:** *Poster for the film* Sakuya: Yōkaiden *(2000).*

DIGITAL EFFECTS

CGI IN TOKUSATSU

Even today, *tokusatsu* continues to evolve in both form and substance. Though purists remain deeply attached to the old-school approach to special effects, the genre has been forced to up its game in response to Western influences. It has had to reinvent itself. It took a while for Japan to fully embrace digital effects and even longer for its historical *tokusatsu* icons to adapt to it. But will CGI erode or erase the genre's unique identity? Far from it.

CGI is ubiquitous nowadays, even in simple TV series, but that doesn't mean throwing out the baby with the bathwater—on the contrary. There might be fewer series today, but they are being produced by historic studios that are masters of the genre, allowing them to incorporate new technologies gradually. These series have been renewed annually, uninterrupted, for decades, requiring significant resources and working on tight deadlines—the ultimate opportunity to experiment with new special effects techniques.

All of *tokusatsu* benefits from technological advancements to varying degrees (and vice versa). However, franchises like *Super Sentai* and *Ultraman* benefit the most, incorporating CGI and motion capture to create their iconic characters and monsters. These techniques are particularly effective at conveying a sense of scale.

To the uninitiated, these shows might seem somewhat outdated. Yet, it's worth noting that behind the scenes, things are continuing to evolve. Nothing is set in stone. Taking a broader perspective of the genre helps fans appreciate what these shows have to offer, as well as their natural limitations.

Even *tokusatsu* movies, with their fatter budgets and greater scope, remain unchanged at their core. There is a deep desire to honor the genre's foundations while infusing modern elements, creating a persistently unmistakable style. *Tokusatsu* has come to describe the technical side of production as much as the aesthetic, seen in formats that are almost exclusively found in Japan!

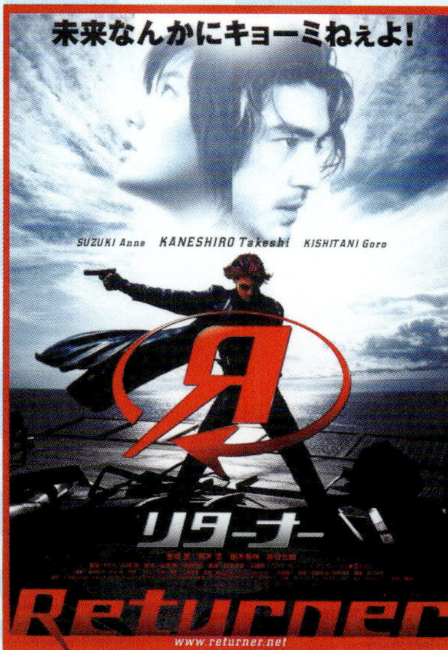

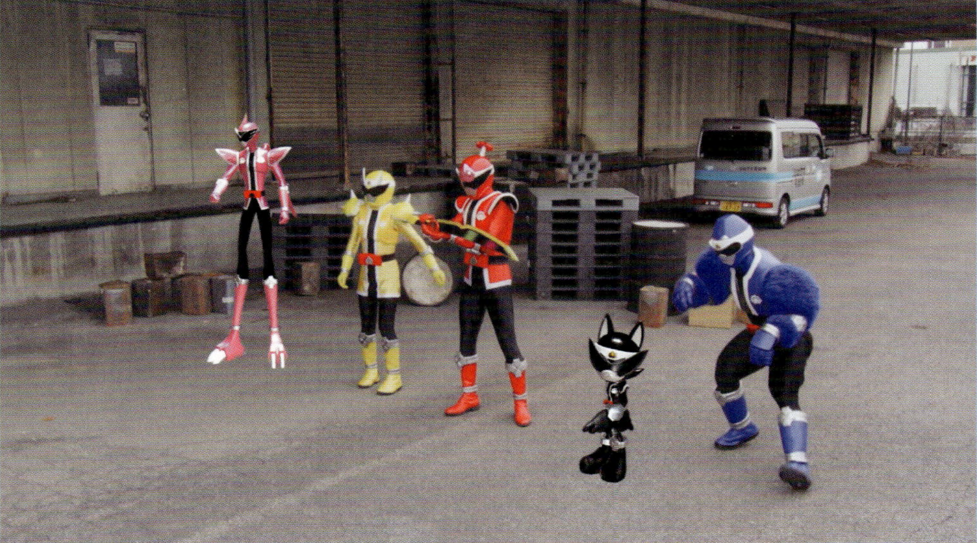

↑ **Above:** *Japanese poster for the film* Returner *(2002).*

↑ **Above:** *Still from* Avataro Sentai Donbrothers *(2022) and its CGI characters.*

TAKASHI YAMAZAKI (1964–)

Takashi Yamazaki dove right into special effects at the very beginning of his career, notably working on *Sweet Home* (1989). He quickly transitioned to directing, with films such as *Juvenile* (2000) and *Returner* (2002), two fantasy movies that showcased CGI heavily. He has worked on many sci-fi and fantasy projects throughout his career, affirming his passion for modern digital imagery while also exploring dramas set in postwar Japan, exemplified by his *Always: Sunset on Third Street* series. Animated films such as *Lupin III: The First* (2019) further boosted his reputation. Ultimately, he had the opportunity to direct *Godzilla Minus One* (2023), which earned an Oscar for its special effects.

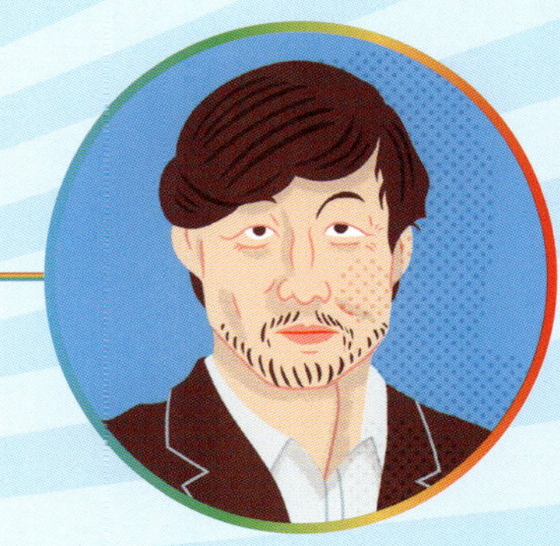

← **Opposite:** *The little robot from* Juvenile *(2000), Takashi Yamazaki's first film.*

↓ **Below:** *Bin Furuya reprises his role of Ultraman in 2022, thanks to motion capture technology.*

↓ **Below:** *Godzilla is reborn yet again through CGI in* Shin Godzilla *(2016).*

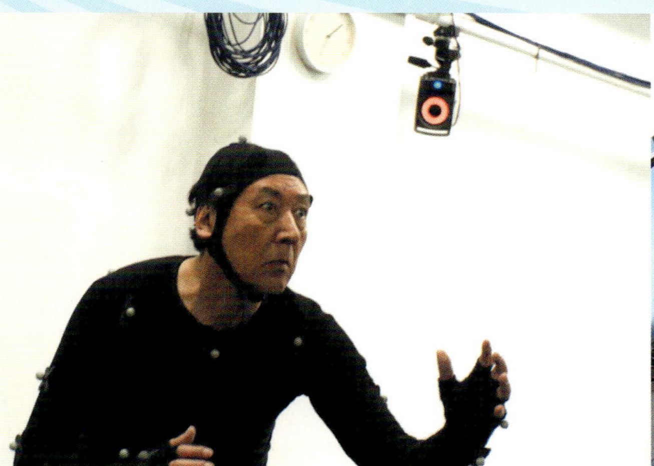

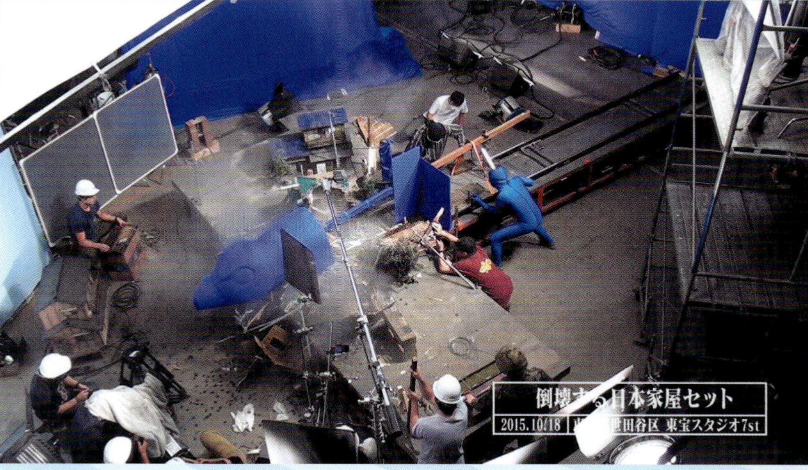

THE GENRE OF ENDLESS POSSIBILITIES

WAR FILMS

Now we'll go on to explore the next layer of *tokusatsu*, finding it where you might least expect it. To do so, we turn to an era of Japanese war films with special effects, specifically those from the period spanning the 1940s to the 1960s—a pivotal time for the genre for obvious historical reasons.

The first examples of the category all stem from the work of director Kajirō Yamamoto. His career began in the 1920s, but he didn't begin making a name for himself until the 1930s, notably by becoming a mentor to Akira Kurosawa (*Rashōmon* in 1950, *The Hidden Fortress* in 1958). When World War II began in 1939, he continued doing film work for Toho, focusing primarily on making propaganda.

↓ **Below:** *Photo from the set of* The War at Sea from Hawaii to Malaya *(1942).*

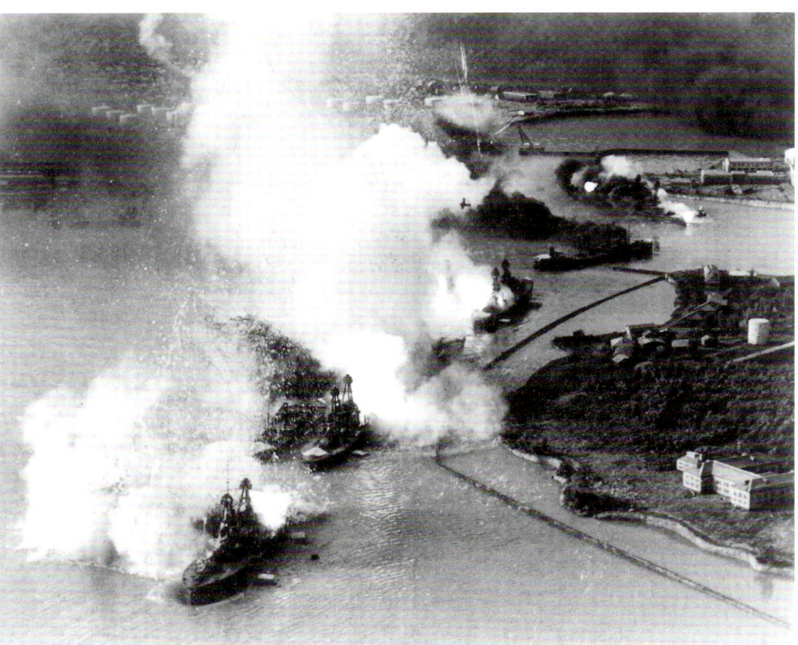

Until then, Yamamoto had been accustomed to comedies, dramas, and samurai films. However, in 1942, he directed the grand war epic *The War at Sea from Hawaii to Malaya*. The film primarily served as propaganda for the events of Pearl Harbor, the attack by the Japanese on the American naval base in December 1941, and was released a year after the attack to "celebrate" the victory.

Technically, the film is part documentary, part romanticized storytelling. For its time, it featured impressive re-creations of naval and aerial battles, using models and miniatures on large sound stages for the scenes taking place at sea.

Behind it all was Eiji Tsuburaya, who had already succeeded in establishing an entire special effects department at Toho in 1939. Tsuburaya was given carte blanche and a substantial budget to work with. As the story goes, his impressively meticulous re-creations were so convincing that not only were the Americans convinced he had gained access to classified military documents, but the combat scenes were also later reused in documentaries and billed as genuine archival footage.

The War at Sea from Hawaii to Malaya was overwhelmingly successful and encouraged the studio to produce other similar (propaganda and special effects) films in following years. Kajirō Yamamoto responded with *Kato hayabusa sento-tai* (literally, Colonel Katō's Falcon Squadron) and *Battle Troop*, released in March and December 1944, respectively.

In 1953, after being controlled for years under US occupation, Japanese cinema and its spectacular war stories made a comeback, aiming to restore the image of a wounded nation. Examples included *Operation Kamikaze* in 1953 and *Storm Over the Pacific* in 1960. Tensions left over from the war even led to alarmist war and sci-fi stories, such as *The Last War*, a 1961 film that explored the potentially catastrophic effects of a World War III on humanity.

Even today, postwar stories continue to inspire and provoke reflection in Japan about its past and fears. From the original 1954 film to *Godzilla Minus One* in 2023, Godzilla demonstrates how, having been born as a direct result of war, the conventions and themes of these war stories have inspired and will continue to inspire it.

NINJAS AND OTHER ADVENTURES

A world away from the realistic drama of war, we find a more playful subgenre, one that requires a colorful, fantastical imagination. Welcome to the era of *tokusatsu*-style adventures filled with kindhearted adventurers, ninjas, and samurai.

The Chinese novel *Journey to the West*, with its monkey hero and band of companions embarking on adventures, needs no introduction. Many a fan of the manga *Dragon Ball* knows that the series borrowed heavily from the classical Chinese work to build its world. But Japan had begun adapting Chinese tales long before that.

After several attempts in the 1940s and early 1950s, the 1959 film *Monkey Sun* stood head and shoulders above the rest. A Toho production, the movie was a charming and ambitious adaptation of the monkey king's adventures. It was directed by Kajirō Yamamoto, previously known as a master of war stories, and oscillated aesthetically between live sets and matte paintings, with a deliberately more colorful and whimsical touch, giving it the feel of an animated film. As always, the special effects were handled by Eiji Tsuburaya. (One scene, in particular, featured Goku's famous flying nimbus). The costuming crew tasked with designing the main character's primate features included a young Keizō Murase, a master of the craft.

The film was so popular in Japan that another adaptation emerged in 1978, this time for television. *Monkey Sun* had fifty-two episodes and was produced by the station NTV, with Tsuburaya Productions

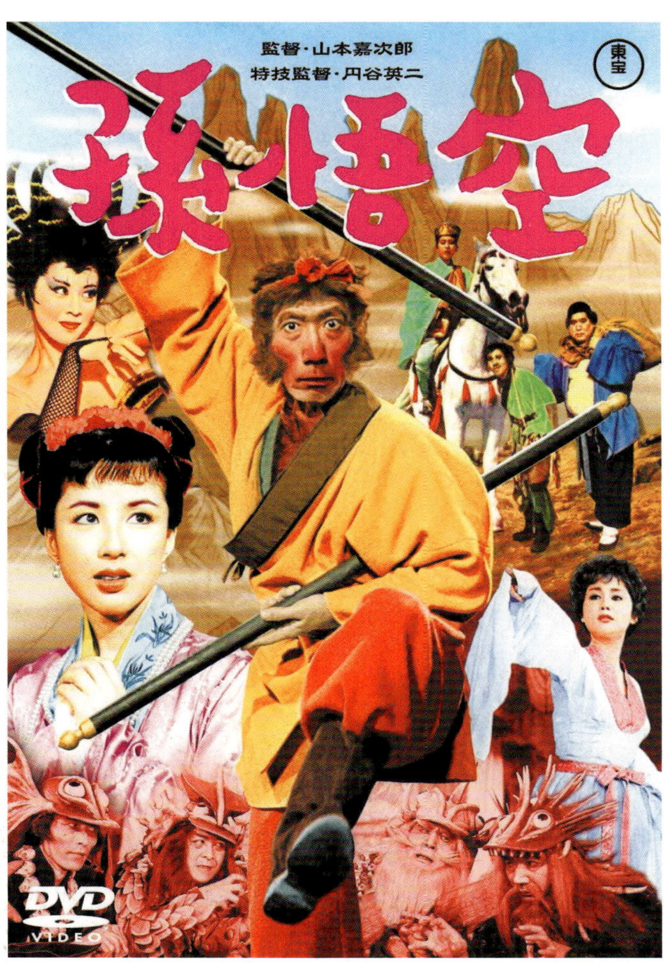

Below: *Japanese DVD cover for the film* Monkey Sun *(1959).*

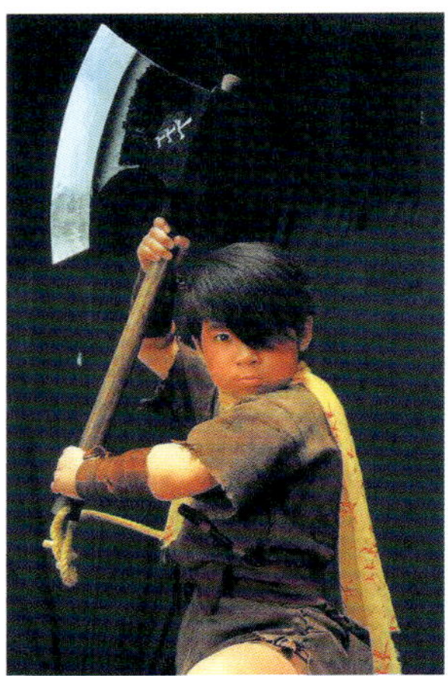

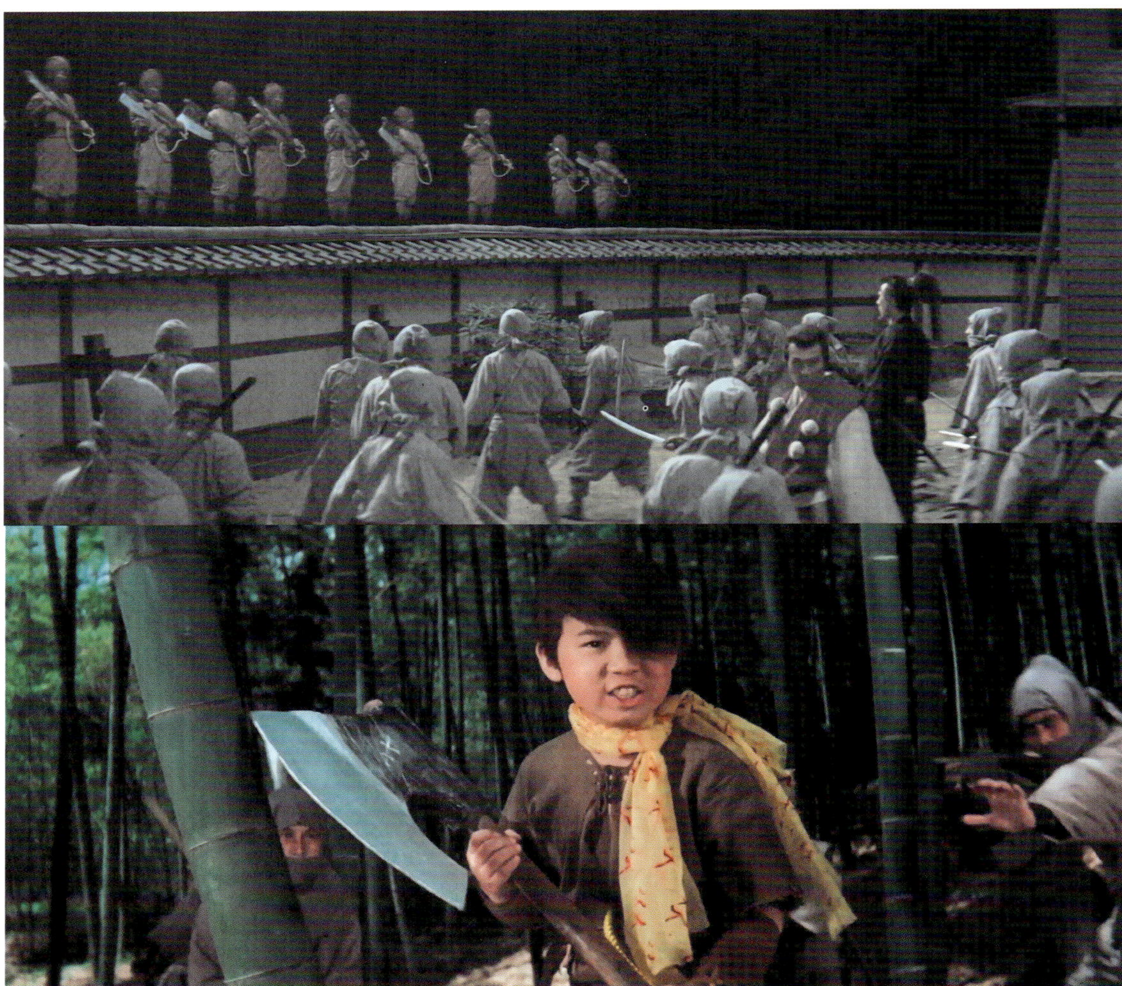

↑ → **Above and right:** Watari, Ninja Boy *(1966)*.

↓ **Below:** *Young Watari, the big-hearted ninja. Watch out for his axe!*

overseeing special effects. The series remains a classic to this day.

Other types of adventure stories also sprouted up in the 1960s. *The Lost World of Sinbad* is a 1963 tale with a distinctly Middle Eastern vibe, evoking occidental adaptations of *A Thousand and One Nights*, starring Sinbad, among other characters. In the film, Toshirō Mifune plays Sukezaemon Naya, a real-life Japanese merchant, in a wild adventure that blends fantastical elements (a sorcerer who can transform into a fly) with grandiose scenes, including a famous one where the hero soars over a castle dangling from a giant kite.

Grandiose also describes the adventures of *Watari, Ninja Boy*. Originally a manga by Sanpei Shirato, renowned for his ninja and samurai manga (*Kamui* is one of his most famous), the story was adapted into a movie in 1966, produced by Toei. The movie showcases boundless creativity in its direction. Armed with his axe, Watari faces not only a clan of ninjas but also a giant cat, a cyborg, and other beings with supernatural powers, all in battles that emphasize ninja techniques—including teleportation, where Watari replaces himself with a piece of wood.

The film boasts remarkably rich visuals, blending all sorts of special effects, including illusions of scale and animation techniques to depict certain feats of magic. One iconic scene shows the hero surrounded by a swarm of butterflies.

The following year, after *Watari* and its sequel *The Magic Serpent*, Toei rode on the momentum of its success by sticking with the ninja theme with a live-action TV adaptation of *Kamen no Ninja Akakage*, a manga by Mitsuteru Yokoyama (*Tetsujin 28-go*, *Giant Robo*, *Sally the Witch*). In fifty-two episodes, the series offered up a potpourri of every element we've mentioned so far: feudal Japan, ninjas, fantasy, magical powers, clan wars, and even giant monsters. Some of the monster costumes used were even taken directly from the set of *The Magic Serpent*. The series contributed to the popularization and liberation of *tokusatsu* on television alongside *Ultraman*, setting the stage for the golden age in the following decade.

Audiences continued to be captivated by special effects, the clash of swords, and the flight of *shuriken* on both the big and small screens, thanks to the enduring appeal of ninjas and samurai. One notable example in film is 1983's *Legend of the Eight Samurai*, directed by Kinji Fukasaku, a quintessentially Japanese take on heroic fantasy, bursting with grandeur in its scope, sets, and special effects. Fukasaku's involvement is no coincidence. The story is a retelling of the novel *Tale of Eight Dogs*, mentioned in the section on his other film, *Message from Space*, which took a fantastical feudal Japan and placed it in a distant galaxy.

As is often the case, the various subgenres and themes eventually began to overlap and intermingle. Some works were inspired by *kaijū* (*Takeru Yamato*, *The Magic Serpent*, *The*

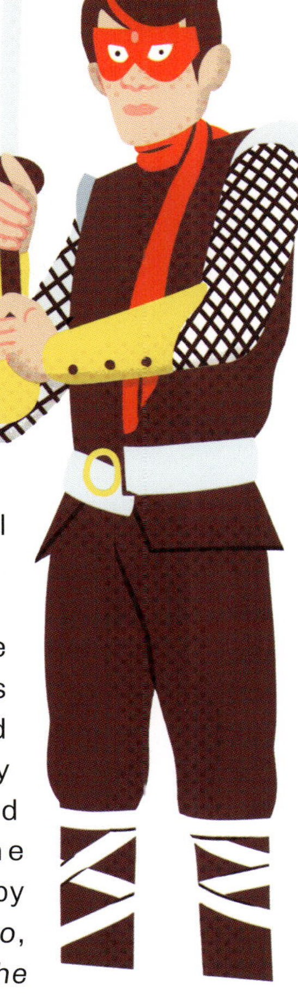

← Left: *Akakage from the series* Kamen no Ninja Akakage, *one of* tokusatsu's *first TV ninja heroes.*

↓ Below: *Still and Japanese poster for the film* Legend of the Eight Samurai *(1983).*

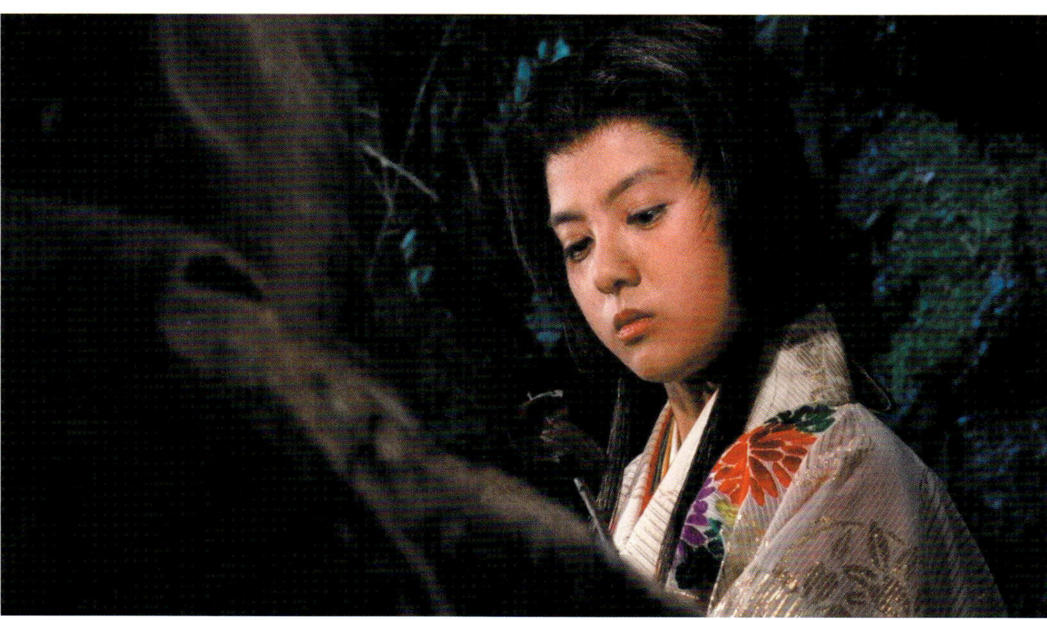

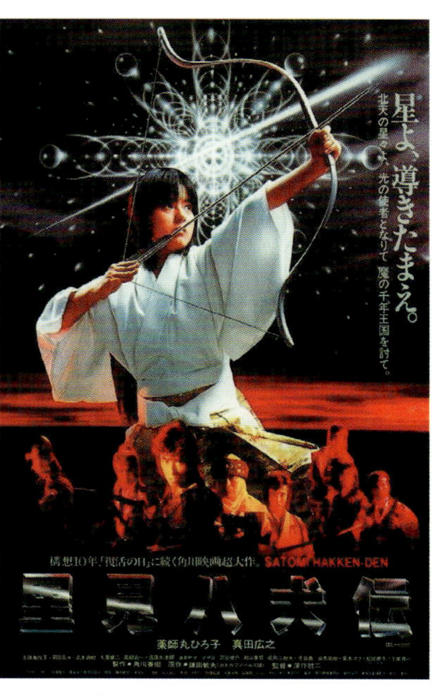

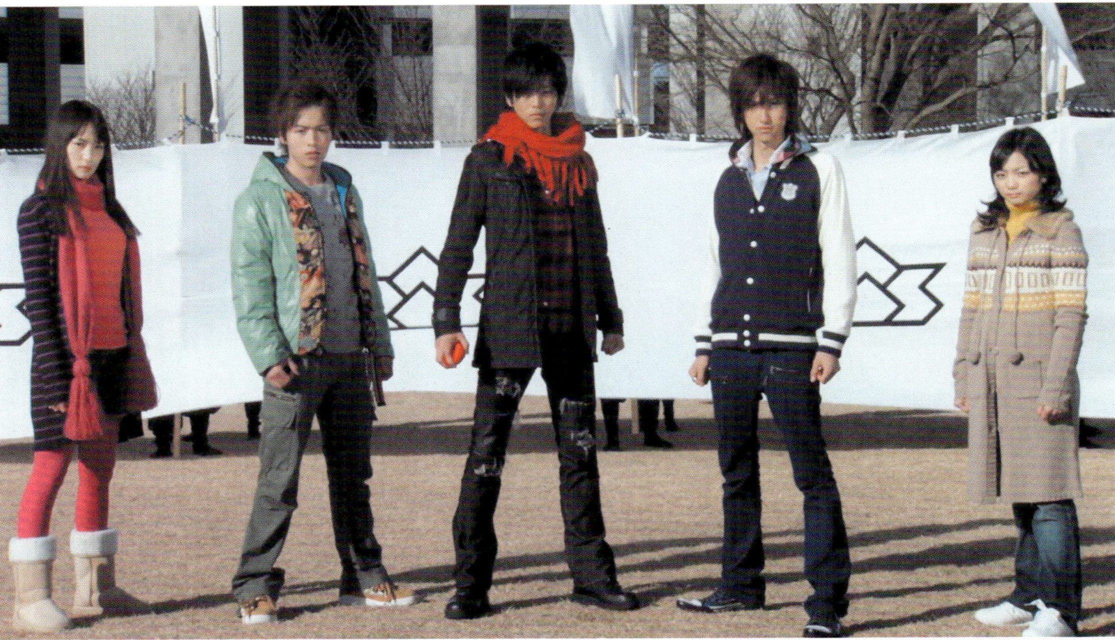

Right: *Still from* Samurai Sentai Shinkenger *(2009).*

Three Treasures), Japanese ghosts (*Sakuya: Slayer of Demons*, *Kibakichi*), and even the ever-present superheroes, exemplified by series like *Ninja Sentai Kakuranger* in 1994 and *Samurai Sentai Shinkenger* in 2009 (among many others), described by their titles.

THE WORKS OF KEITA AMEMIYA

All these many and varied genres have one thing in common: Keita Amemiya, a creator whose distinctive style has left an indelible mark on these imaginative universes. Primarily a concept artist, Amemiya began his career in *tokusatsu* by designing characters and creatures for a number of *Metal Hero* series, from *Spielvan* to *The Mobile Cop Jiban*. Frequently associated with Toei (even contributing to *Kamen Rider Black RX*), his role as a designer soon led to his directorial debut with the 1988 film *Cyber Ninja*.

Cyber Ninja was a feature-length promotional film for the video game *Mirai Ninja*. Both the film and the game used traditional ninja elements in a futuristic, cyberpunk setting, where giant bipedal robots and cyborgs reign supreme. Though the film was merely a direct-to-video promotional project with a commensurately modest budget, it was enough to offer a glimpse of Amemiya's potential as a director, evident in his striking visual designs and compelling cinematic execution.

Amemiya was ubiquitous in the 1990s. He served as chief director of *Chōjin Sentai Jetman* (1991), contributed to the horrific transformation scene in *Shin Kamen Rider: Prologue*, and directed *Kamen Rider ZO* (1993) and *Kamen Rider J* (1994). In addition to these Toei productions, Amemiya also ventured into independent filmmaking with *Zeiram* in 1991, his first feature-length film for the big screen.

The premise was simple. Zeiram is a terrifying creature greatly feared across the galaxy. He is thought to be contained but escapes and arrives on Earth. A bounty hunter named Iria sets out to capture him, resulting in a high-stakes

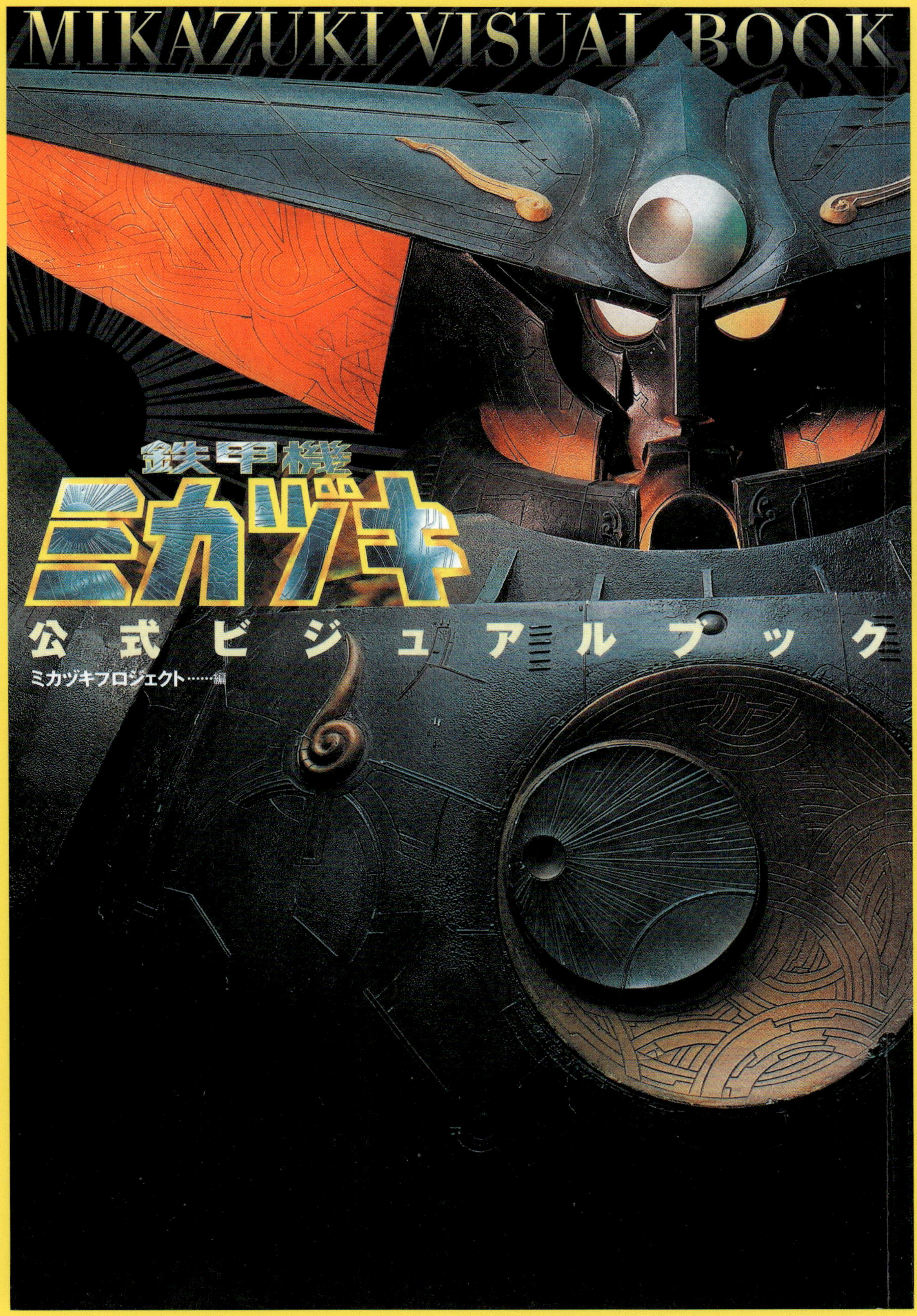

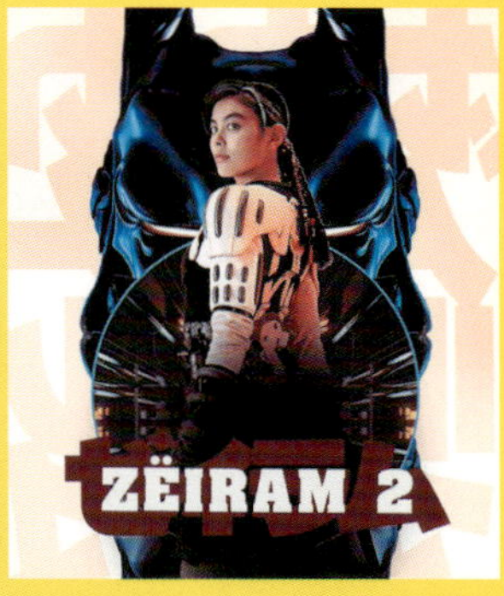

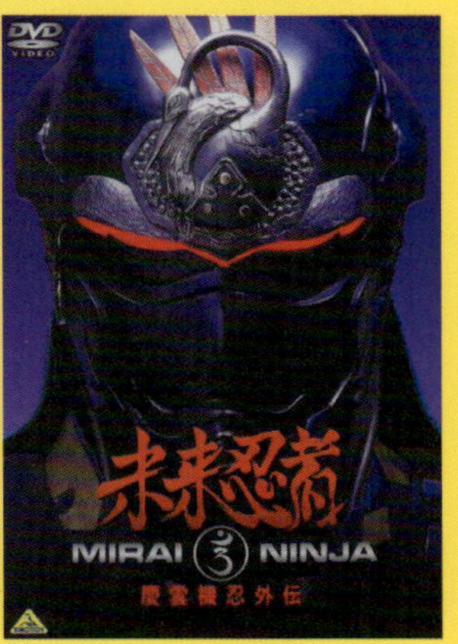

↑ **Above:** *Japanese poster for* Zeiram 2 *(1994) and Japanese DVD cover for* Cyber Ninja *(1988).*

← **Left:** *Cover of a coffee table book on the series* Tekkōki Mikazuki *(2000).*

urban hunt, a sort of Japanese *Predator*. Amemiya flexed his creativity to the fullest. The action scenes are explosive, Zeiram is visually striking both in design and technical execution, and Amemiya takes the opportunity to utilize innovative special effects for the creatures, including stop-motion animation.

Amemiya expanded the universe in 1994 with the short animated series *Iria: Zeiram the Animation*, followed by a second film, *Zeiram 2*. The sequel followed a similar structure, with another confrontation against Zeiram, giving Amemiya the chance to refine his direction, enhance the special effects, and play with his signature creature design, which was further developed in the second movie. The result was an action film that perfectly encapsulated its era, to the delight of its audiences.

Toei's influence loomed large in Amemiya's career. In 1995, he directed *Mechanical Violator Hakaider*, a bold reinterpretation of the iconic villain from *Android Kikaider*, mixing and matching elements from *Mad Max* and *Terminator*. His final leap toward independence came in 1997 with *Moon Over Tao*. Though it may have appeared to be a straightforward samurai story, it incorporated elements of fantasy. The film's creature used a combination of CGI—a rare technique at the time but in line with Amemiya's penchant for experimentation—and a life-sized animatronic model standing thirteen feet tall.

Moon Over Tao may not be his most famous work, but it marked his transition into the 2000s, laying the foundations for his later creations, like the giant robot Mikazuki and the golden knight Garo. Amemiya continues to oversee the franchise today, now nearing its twentieth anniversary, leaving an indelible mark on *tokusatsu* and inspiring a new

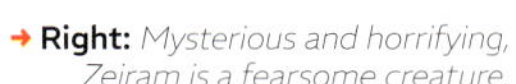

→ **Right:** *Mysterious and horrifying, Zeiram is a fearsome creature.*

↓ **Below:** *Stills from Zeiram (1991).*

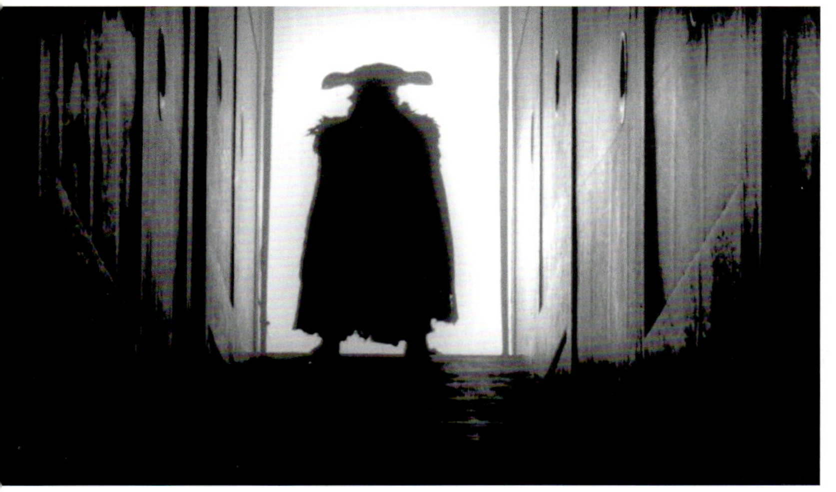

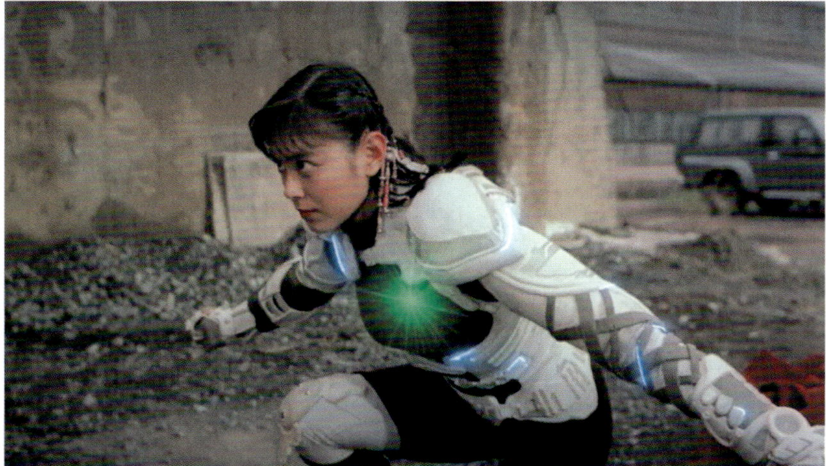

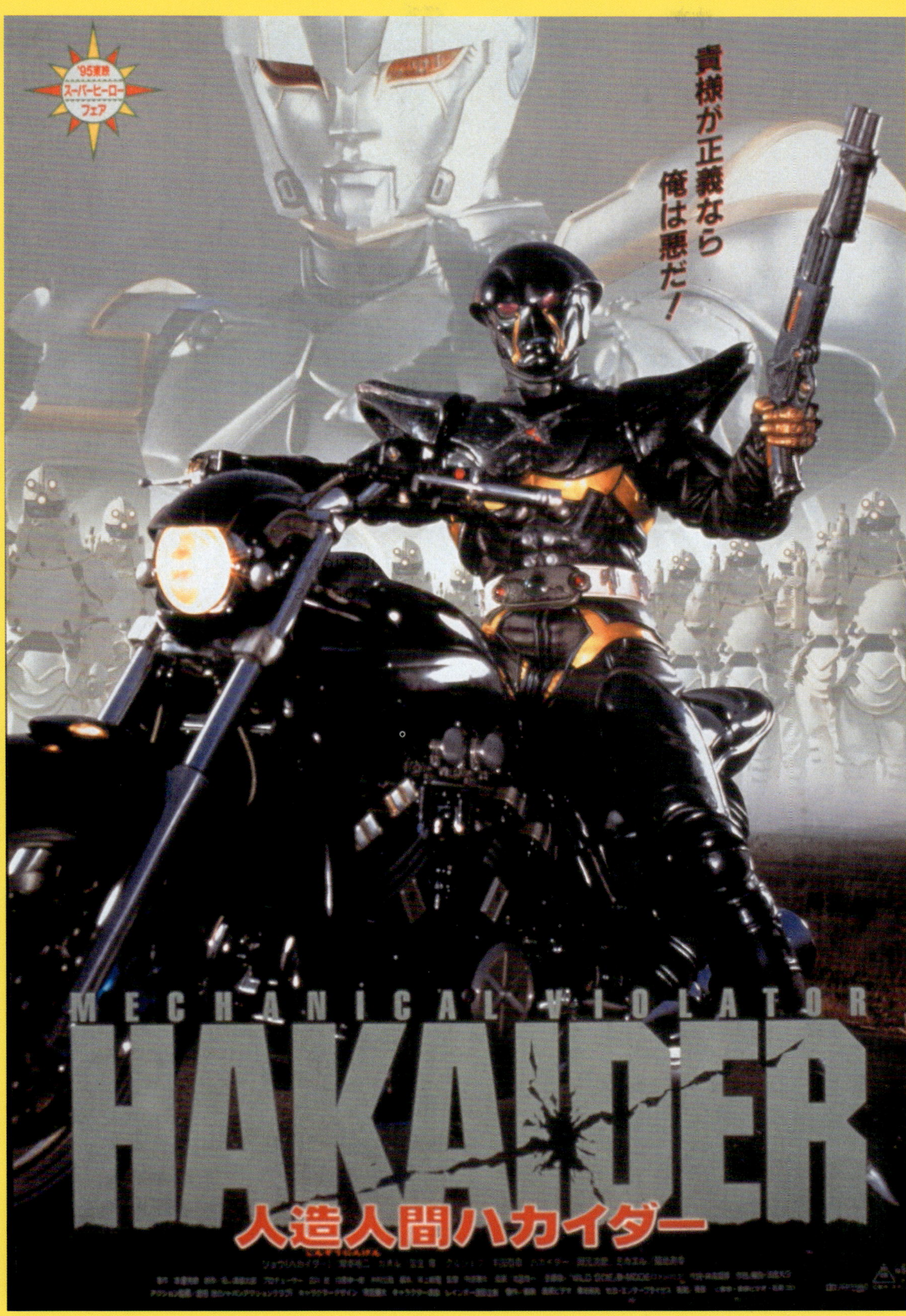

Left: *Japanese poster for the film* Mechanical Violator Hakaider *(1995).*

generation of fans with his unique approach to the genre.

OTHER WACKY WORKS

Upon entering the world of *tokusatsu*, one quickly realizes just how vast it is, almost dizzyingly so. There are a multitude of lesser-known works across every imaginable category, but we'll conclude with a small selection of "miscellaneous" gems, each unique in its own way. These examples showcase the incredible diversity and inventiveness of the genre.

During the 1970s—a wild time when superheroes, robots, and *kaijū* commingled, alongside the occasional space adventure—Tsuburaya Productions ventured into more unusual concepts. In 1974, Japanese audiences were introduced to *Army of the Apes*, a *tokusatsu* series that drew heavily from *Planet of the Apes* and the original novel by Pierre Boulle. The premise remained similar. Humans find themselves in a distant future (in the Japanese series, a group of humans is cryogenically frozen for nearly 2,000 years) where humanity has been replaced by a society of various ape species. The series came about during a period when Japan was producing speculative fiction, such as *Japan Sinks*.

In the early 1990s, the world was swept up in dinosaur fever, thanks in large part to *Jurassic Park*. In Japan, however, the theme took a different turn. A family's life is upended by the arrival of an adorable creature in the irresistible *Rex: A Dinosaur's Story* (1993), a film adaptation of Masanori Hata's novel. In the story, scientists discover an egg

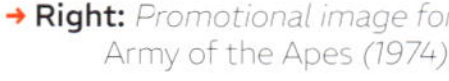

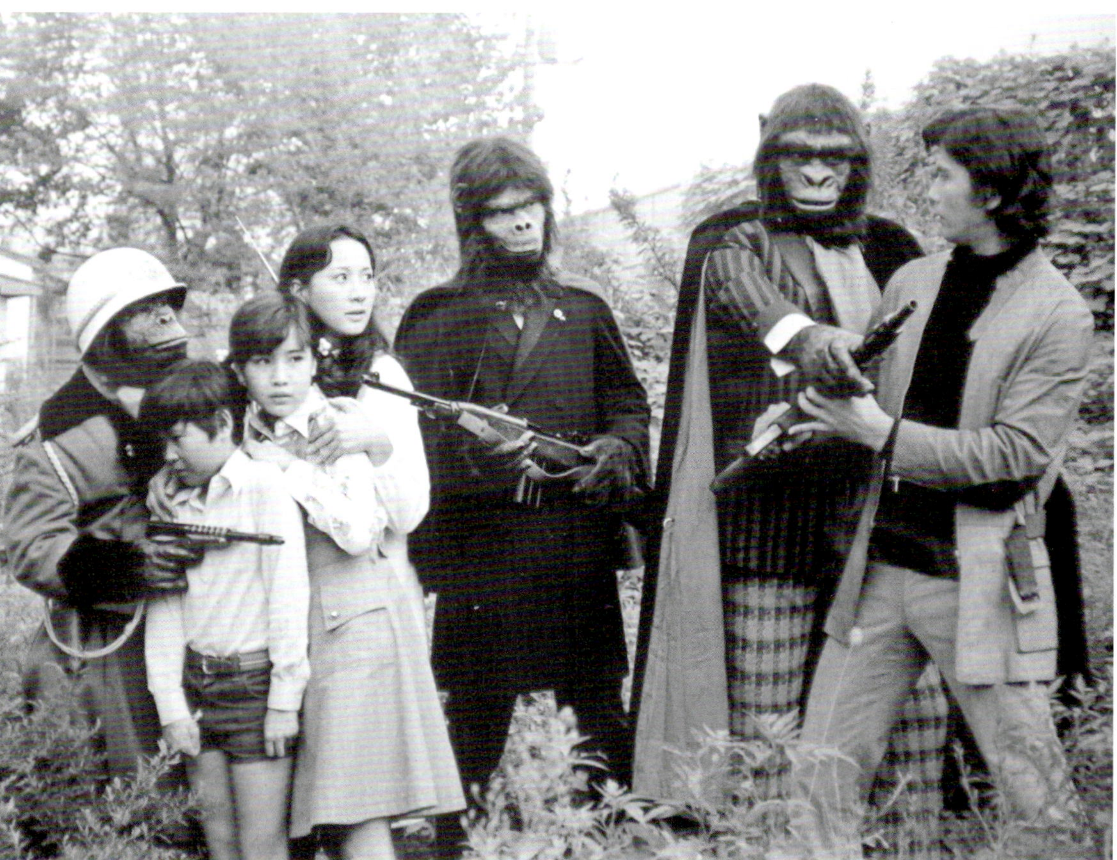

→ **Right:** *Promotional image for* Army of the Apes *(1974).*

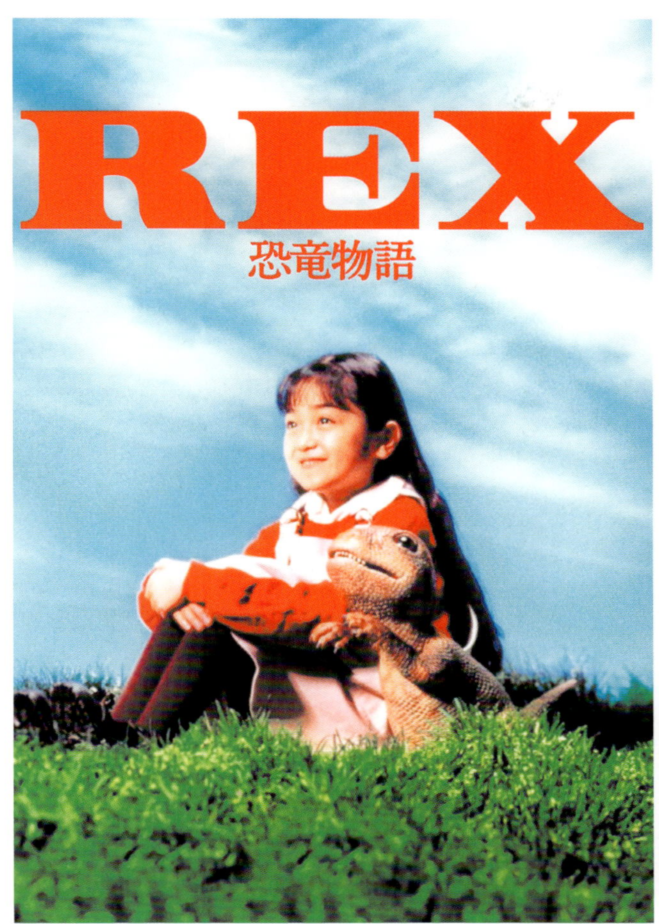

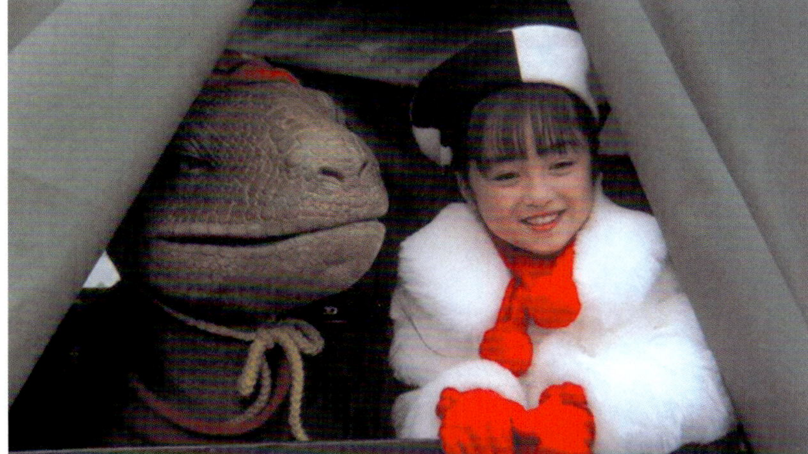

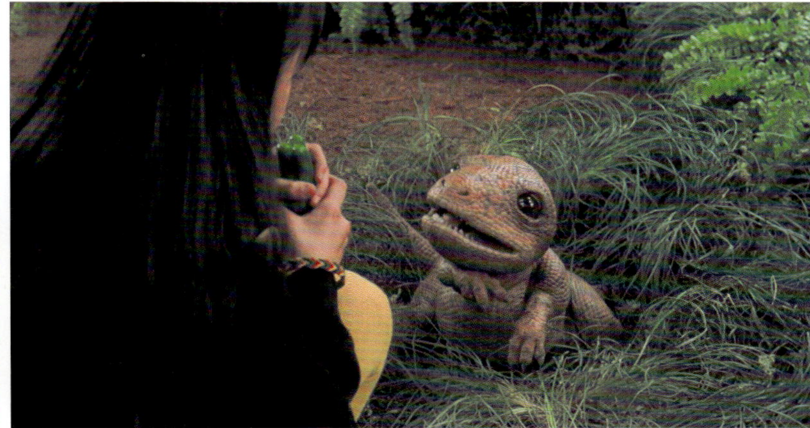

↑ **Above:** *Stills and Japanese poster for the film* Rex: A Dinosaur's Story *(1993).*

millions of years old in a cave in Hokkaidō. They study the egg, and thanks to the presence of Chie Tateno, daughter of one of the scientists, the egg hatches, giving birth to Rex, a baby dinosaur. Rex imprints on Chie and becomes inseparable from her, until an organization attempts to capture him for display as a sideshow attraction. This heartfelt film, set around Christmastime, features special effects (a mix of costume and animatronics) created by Carlo Rambaldi, the mastermind behind *E.T.* (1982) and *Alien* (1979).

The trend of endearing, human-sized, and sometimes outright bizarre creatures continued to persist in *tokusatsu*. Enter Minoru Kawasaki, the master of off-the-wall comedy, who delivered two highly recommendable works, *The Calamari Wrestler* (2004) and *Crab Goalkeeper* (2006). *The Calamari Wrestler* featured a humanoid squid embarking on a wrestling career. It was a hilarious yet surprisingly earnest parody of boxing films like *Rocky*, with a protagonist who surmounts adversity to reach the top. In *Crab Goalkeeper*, a human-sized crab is seeking purpose in life, ultimately excelling as a soccer goalkeeper. Absurd yet touching, the film served as an improbable but heartfelt pastiche of *Forrest Gump*.

The 2000s brought even more surprises brimming with creativity. In 2005, Toei introduced somethirg unusual alongside its superheroes, the peculiar, short-lived *Sh15uya* (pronounced "Shibuya Fifteen"). The story is set in a futuristic, eerie, threatening version of Shibuya, a district controlled by an entity named Piece. The amnesiac protagonist

→ **Right:** *Japanese poster for* Crab Goalkeeper *(2006).*

→ **Far right:** *Promotional image for* Sh15uya *(2005).*

↓ **Below:** *A human-sized crab finds its purpose in soccer.*

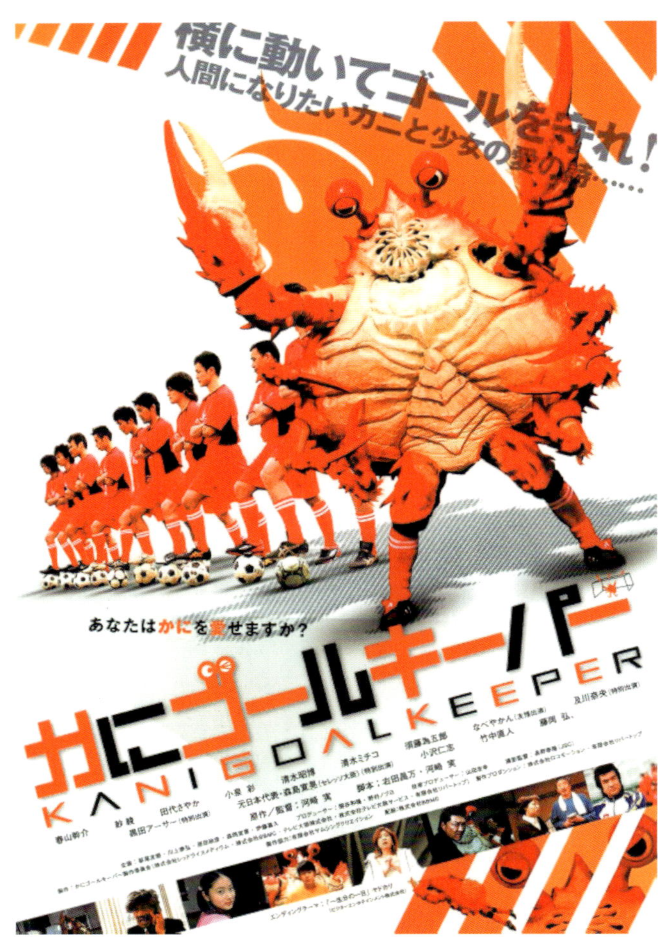

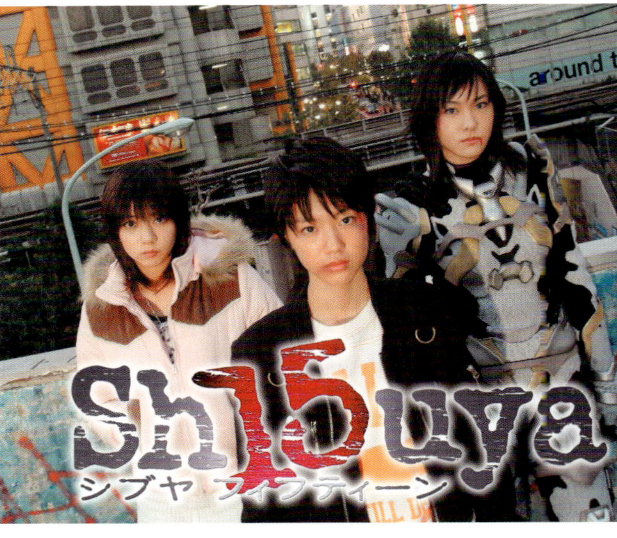

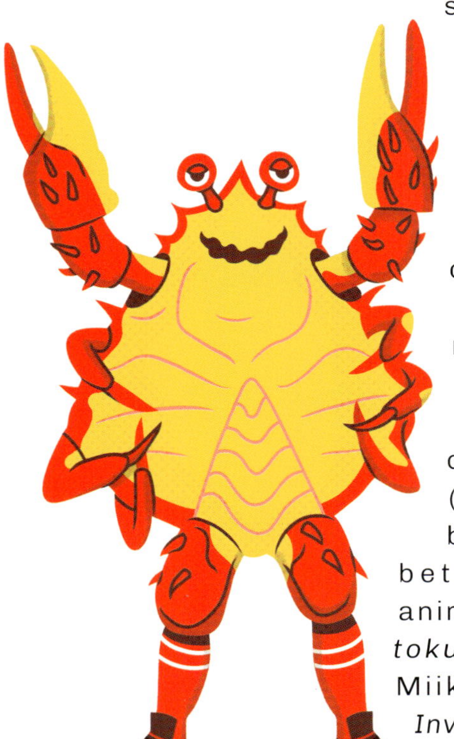

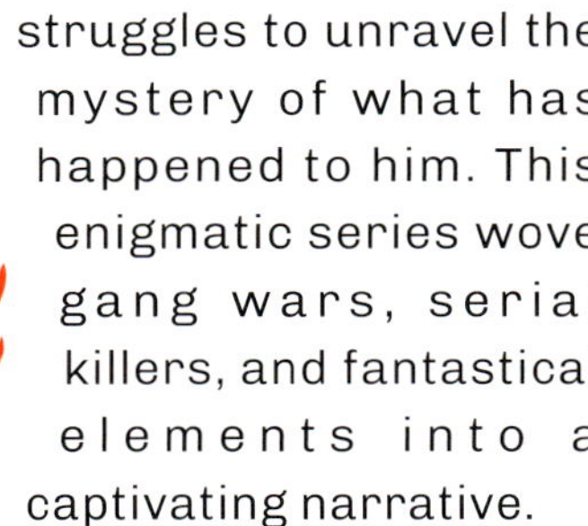

struggles to unravel the mystery of what has happened to him. This enigmatic series wove gang wars, serial killers, and fantastical elements into a captivating narrative.

For an investigative mystery with a lighter tone but still in the *tokusatsu* style, check out *K-Tai Investigator 7* (2008), the first foray by Production I.G—better known for its anime—into the world of *tokusatsu*, with Takashi Miike at the helm. *K-Tai Investigator 7* is the story of high school student Keita Amishima, who finds himself swept up in the clandestine activities of Under Anchor, an organization that fights cybercrime. Their secret weapon? Autonomous, sentient, flip-phone-shaped robots called Phone Bravers. Amishima teams up with Phone Braver 7, whose previous partner died during a mission. The series was a breath of fresh air for Japanese TV, blending elements of police procedurals with science fiction in cunning fashion and bringing the charming, walking flip-phones to life through phenomenal use of special effects.

Tokusatsu continues to showcase its variety today through the genres we've discussed thus far. A final notable example is the unique *Girl Gun Lady* (2021) by Bandai. The story is set in what seems like an ordinary all-girls high school, but the main character is unwillingly thrust into a team-based battle royale. Initially believing it to be a dream or a simulation, she discovers that each of the game's victims seems to vanish from reality entirely. The series was a mystery filled with dynamic combat sequences amid a vibrant, pop-colored world.

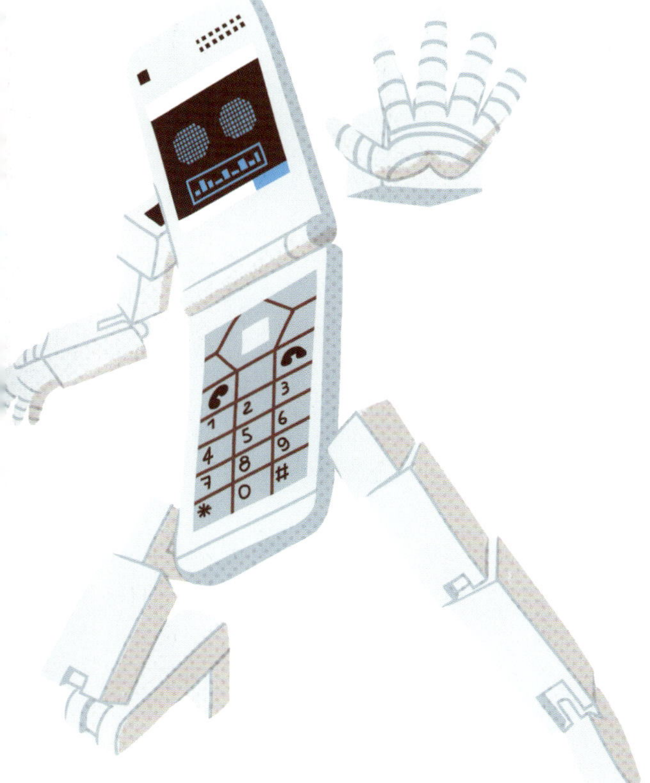

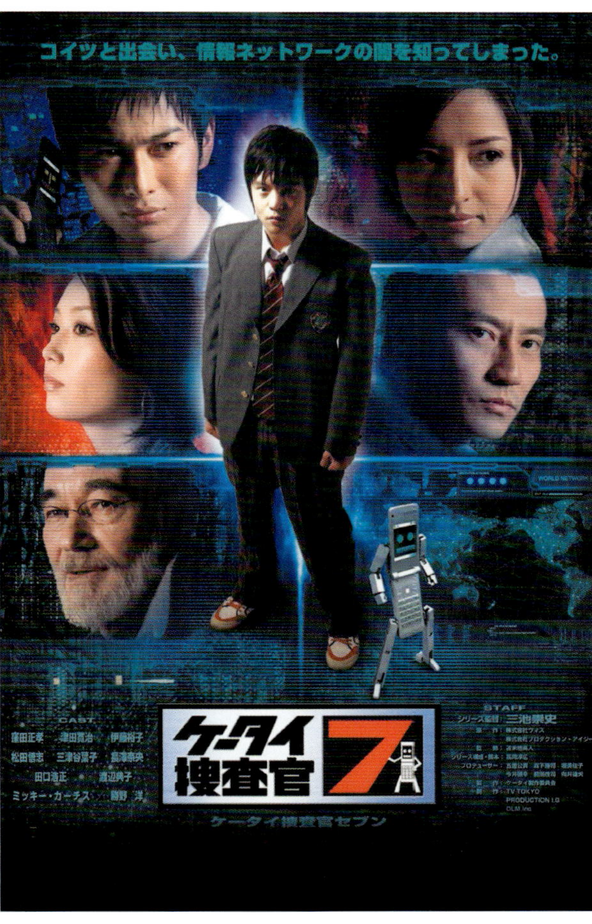

Far left: *The pocket-sized Phone Braver 7 plays the hero's sidekick in all his missions.*

Left: *Promotional poster for* K-Tai Investigator 7 *(2008).*

Below: *Stills from* Girl Gun Lady *(2021).*

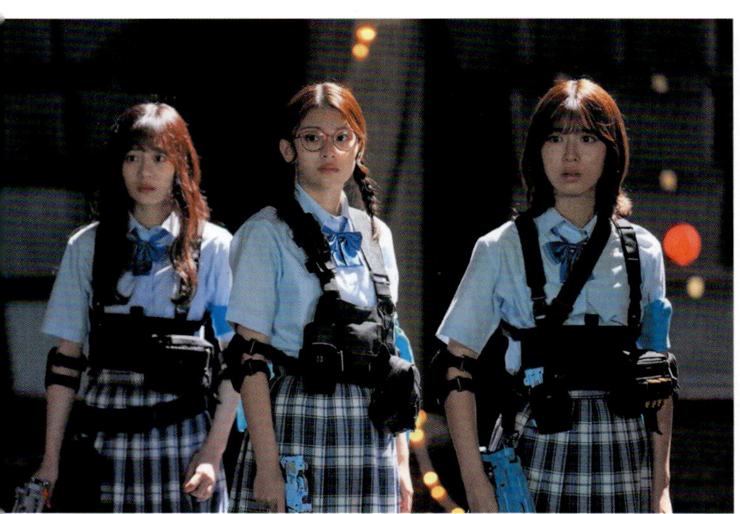

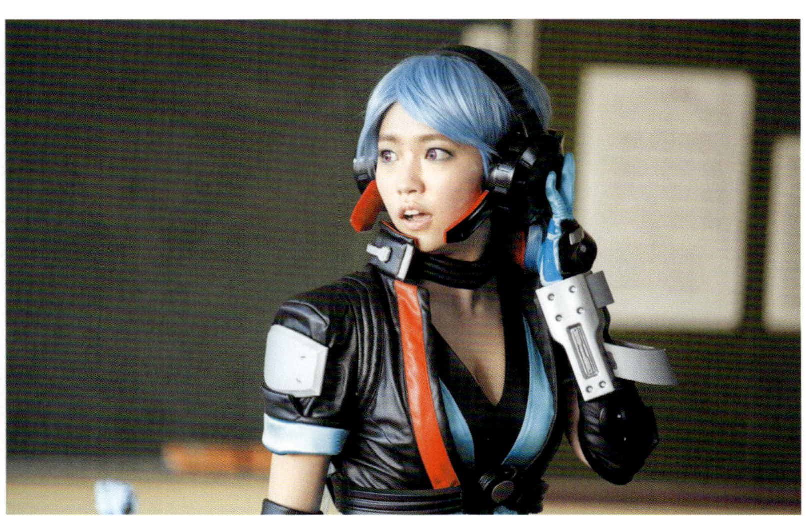

FRANCE FIVE

Now that we've explored the range of what *tokusatsu* has to offer, we'll conclude with a discussion on foreign productions. They may not be considered *tokusatsu* in the strictest Japanese sense, but the source of their inspiration is clear, and they appear to build on the same styles and vision.

Let's start with the French production *France Five*, an amateur production from 2000 by Alex Pilot. The series contained all the tropes of the *Super Sentai* genre: a colorful, five-member team (plus a sixth added later, as tradition dictates) defending Earth (specifically Paris and the Eiffel Tower) against the Lexos Empire with the assistance of a giant robot. The production followed in the footsteps of *Bitoman*, another amateur series by Alex Pilot that playfully embraced the tropes of *Sentai* and other *tokusatsu* superheroes popularized during the 1980s (such as *Space Sheriff Gavan* and *Choudenshi Bioman*).

But *France Five* achieved greater success, showing genuine respect for the genre and its conventions, from costumes to choreography, while incorporating French culture into its storylines. Each team member represented a well-known French stereotype. The red warrior represented cheese, the yellow was for croissants, blue for accordions, black for wine, pink for fashion, and the silver represented musketeers.

Despite the challenges of designing the costumes, crafting the giant robot, and performing the action scenes (all on a shoestring budget, as evident from the first episode), the series earned a solid reputation among fans, as well as at conventions like Cartoonist, in the early 2000s. The first four episodes aired

Bottom left: *The original France Five team.*

Bottom right : *Cover of the France Five DVD box set.*

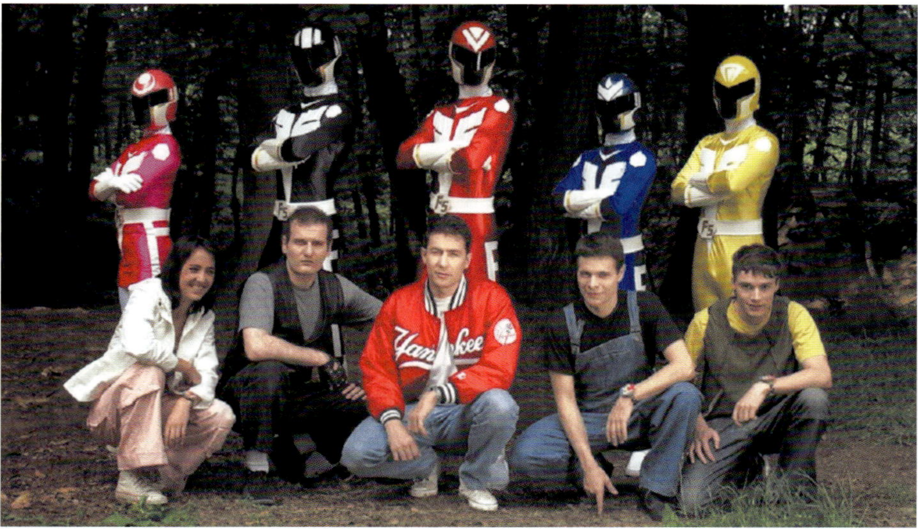

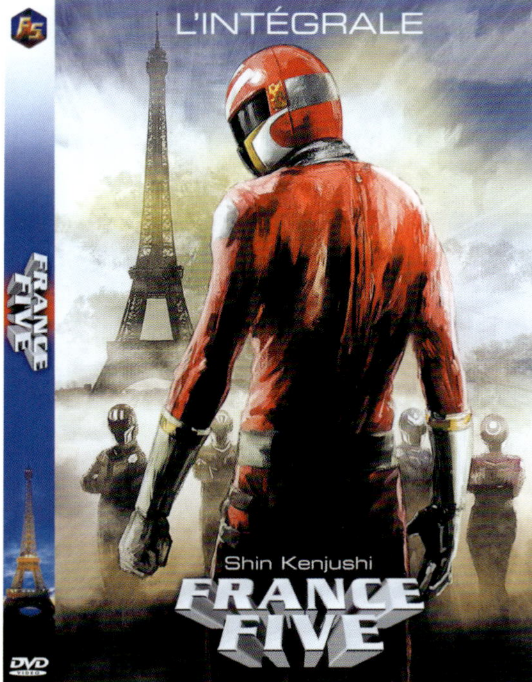

between 2000 and 2004. They demonstrated the producers' growing ambitions, with new and improved costumes and cinematography that became more polished and faithful to the original *Super Sentai* style.

The series gained such recognition that it caught the attention of Japan, was featured in programs on the station NHK, and developed a local fanbase able to appreciate the tribute. The *France Five* team even produced a theme song in Japanese sung by the legendary Akira Kushida (known for iconic *tokusatsu* theme songs for shows including *Space Sheriff Gavan*). It was at this time, with the airing of episode 4 in 2004, that the original title *Jushi Sentai France Five* was changed to *Shin Kenjushi France Five*.

However, the last two episodes were released only after nearly a decade of waffling, partly thanks to the creation of the TV channel Nolife by Alex Pilot and Sébastien Ruchet, who played the red warrior in *France Five*. In 2012 and 2013, they delivered a conclusion worthy of fan expectation, elevating the series from its amateur roots into a recognized work with genuine independence and acclaim.

Today, *France Five* holds a special place in global *tokusatsu* culture as an amateur production that perfectly understood the genre's tropes and created a dignified, captivating work that is more than a mere imitation. The series came full circle in 2021 with *Message d'Outre-Espace*, a medium-length prequel directed by Pilot that beautifully wraps up the story twenty years after it began.

POWER RANGERS

We touched on the *Power Rangers* franchise when we discussed *Super Sentai* in the 1990s, but its massive popularity deserves its own section. An adaptation of *Super Sentai* for the American market, *Power Rangers* replaced Japanese actors with an American cast but retained the Japanese action scenes featuring costumed heroes and robots. After an unsuccessful attempt in the 1980s with a pilot based on the *Bioman* series, TV producer Haim Saban—known for composing soundtracks for 1980s children's programs—tried again a few years later. In 1993, his persistence paid off.

The adaptation focused on *Kyōryū Sentai Zyuranger* and its dinosaur robots. It was released in 1993, just one year after the Japanese series and coinciding perfectly with the dinosaur craze sparked by *Jurassic Park* that same year. Saban swapped the original story of ancient warriors for a group of high schoolers in a low-budget sitcom-style setting. Despite minimal effort, the series became a massive hit in the United States and also found success in France, where *Sentai* had been struggling and was ultimately replaced by *Power Rangers* altogether.

The franchise plundered Japanese series like *Gosei Sentai Dairanger* (1993) and *Ninja Sentai Kakuranger* (1994) for their costumes and robots to cobble together three seasons of *Mighty Morphin Power Rangers* and *Mighty Morphin Alien Rangers*. It struck a balance by adapting each *Super Sentai* series annually into a corresponding *Power Rangers* series, mirroring Japan's schedule. It also introduced a unique twist drawn from superhero comic culture: interconnected stories and recurring characters and storylines across multiple seasons.

This refined formula helped the franchise thrive and leave its mark on

↓ Top: *Promotional poster for* Mighty Morphin Power Rangers *(1993).*

↓ Bottom: *Poster for the film* Mighty Morphin Power Rangers *(1995).*

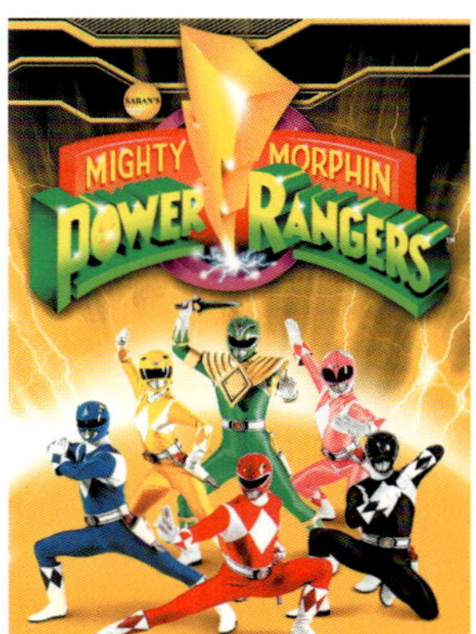

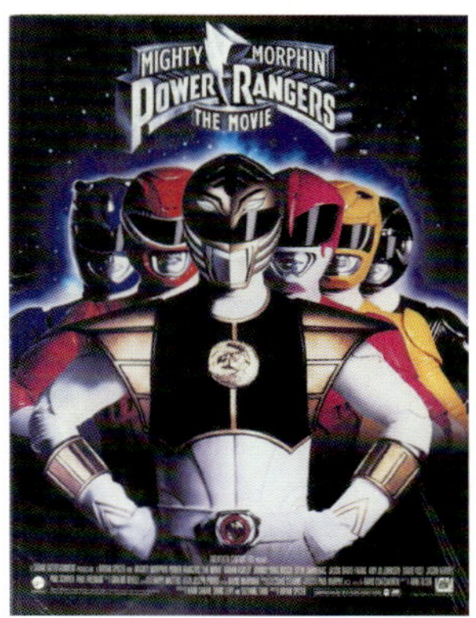

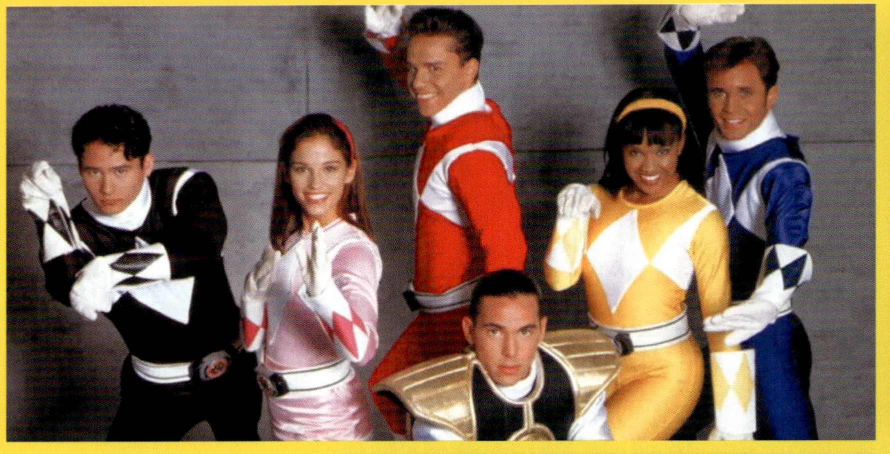

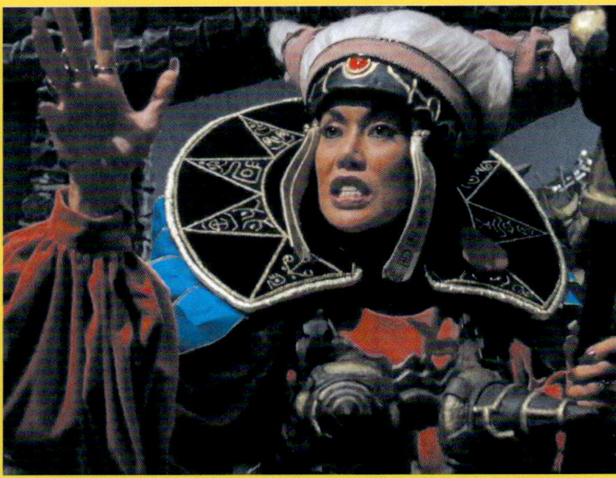

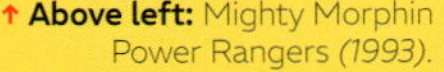

↑ **Above left:** Mighty Morphin Power Rangers *(1993).*

↗ **Above right:** *Rita Repulsa, the principal nemesis of the* Power Rangers.

→ **Right:** *Promotional poster for* Power Rangers RPM *(2009).*

→ **Far right:** *Promotional poster for* Power Rangers S.P.D. *(2005).*

↓ **Bottom left:** *The team from* Power Rangers RPM.

↓ **Bottom right:** *The team dressed in civilian clothing.*

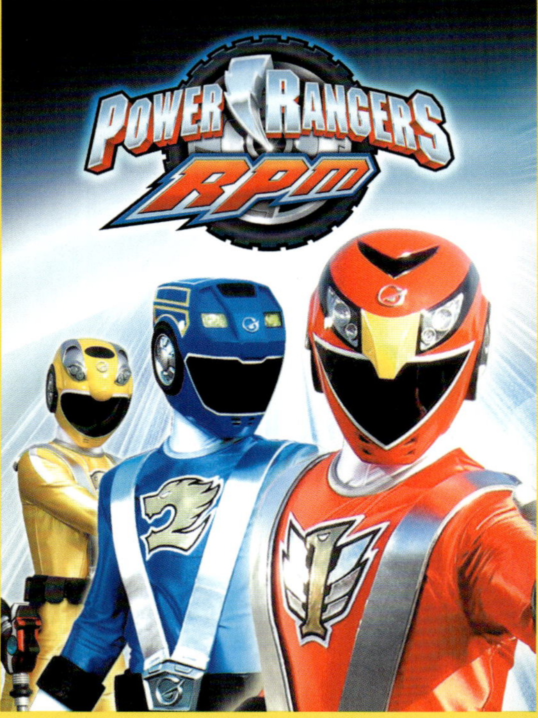

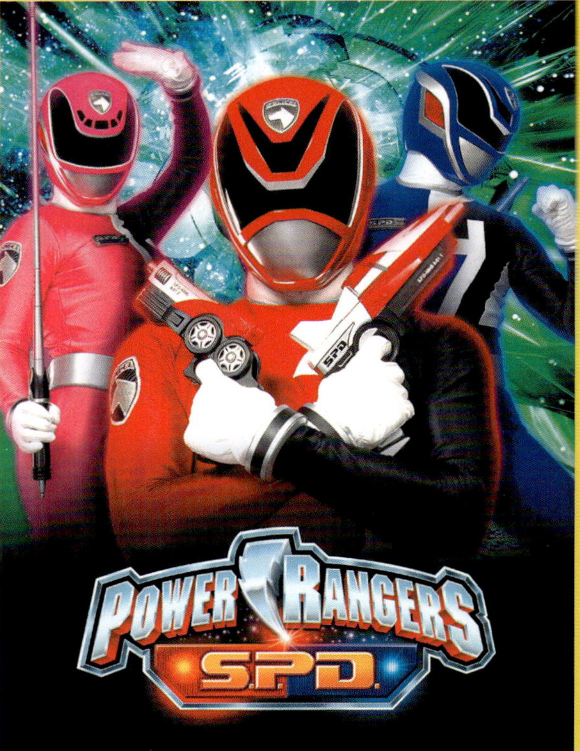

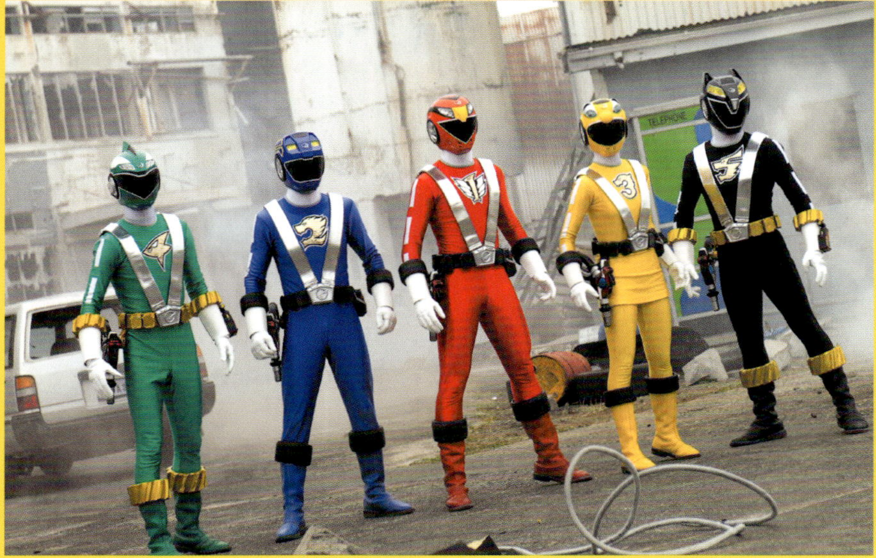

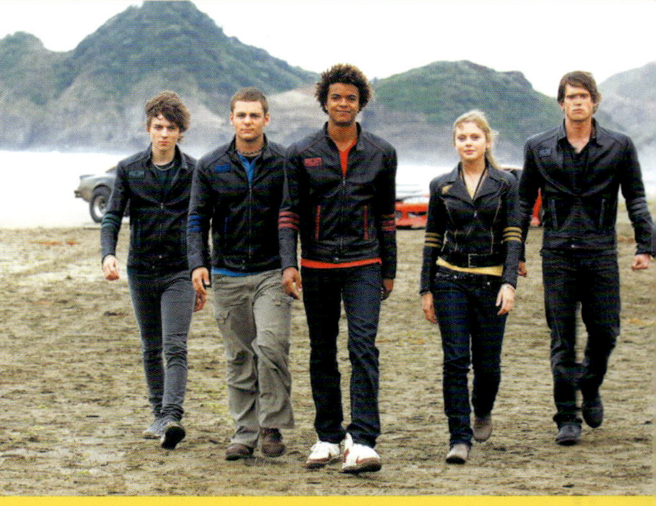

multiple generations of fans. However, occasional dips in popularity led to changes in ownership, from Saban to Disney in 2001, back to Saban in 2010, and finally to toy manufacturer Hasbro in 2019. Under Hasbro, success waned, raising questions about yet another—perhaps final—change of hands.

Power Rangers also raises inevitable ethical concerns. On one hand, it must be acknowledged that some seasons have outshone their Japanese counterparts, featuring stupendous new action scenes shot by Americans with help from Japanese directors (e.g., *Power Rangers S.P.D.* in 2005 by Kōichi Sakamoto). Others, like *Power Rangers RPM* (2009) and *Engine Sentai Go-onger* (2008), have offered unexpectedly rich storylines, diverging significantly from their *Sentai* roots. And Japan's lighthearted, kid-friendly series featuring wide-eyed robot vehicles akin to Pixar's *Cars* was reimagined by American producers as a serious, post-apocalyptic narrative à la *Mad Max*.

The concern is that the proliferation of such series cannibalizes *Super Sentai's* global audiences. Despite modern distribution channels like streaming, the original Japanese programs remain difficult to access, their image overshadowed by American interpretations of the genre. Should the American franchise step aside? Though it still has many fans, one can only hope for a compromise that allows *Super Sentai* to gain visibility and recognition as a legitimate pillar of the genre on the world stage.

OTHER SUPERHEROES FROM ASIA

The influence of *Super Sentai* and its counterparts has seemingly bypassed American filters and continues to radiate throughout Asia, where Japanese productions are popular, abundant, and inspire local adaptations. The spread of *tokusatsu* and its conventions and style to Japan's neighboring countries has created an entire microcosm virtually unknown in the West.

Interestingly, the name *Power Rangers* is also used in Asia. In South Korea, it serves as the name for the *Super Sentai* franchise. There's no American cast, but the Japanese series are dubbed in Korean and given a localized name derived from *Power Rangers*. South Korea's experience with *Super Sentai* began even before the *Power Rangers* phenomenon, with *Earth Protector Flashman* in 1989. However, the advent of Saban's powerhouse and Disney's involvement in 2001 solidified this unique middle ground.

Zyuden Sentai Kyoryuger (2013) became *Power Rangers Dino Charge* in the United States (2015), but in Korea, it was simply localized as *Power Rangers Dino Force* (2014), even though there was no relation between the two versions. Korean audiences were so enthusiastic that a sequel to the Japanese series was produced in 2017, featuring an entirely Korean cast, titled *Power Rangers Dino Force Brave*. This unusual blend is an example of a successful compromise in exporting a significant aspect of modern Japanese culture.

↓ **Below:** *Promotional poster for* Power Rangers Dino Charge *(2015).*

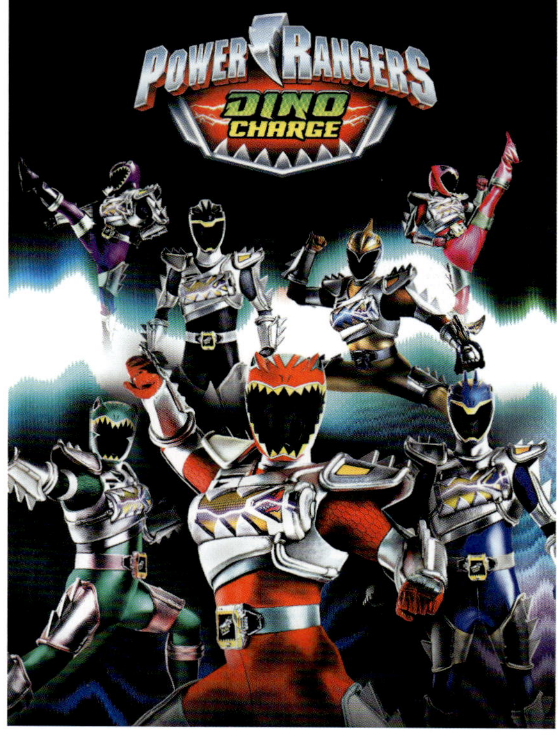

→ **Right:** *Still from* Zyuden Sentai Kyoryuger *(2013).*

↓ **Below:** *Stills and promotional poster for* Power Rangers Dino Force Brave *(2017).*

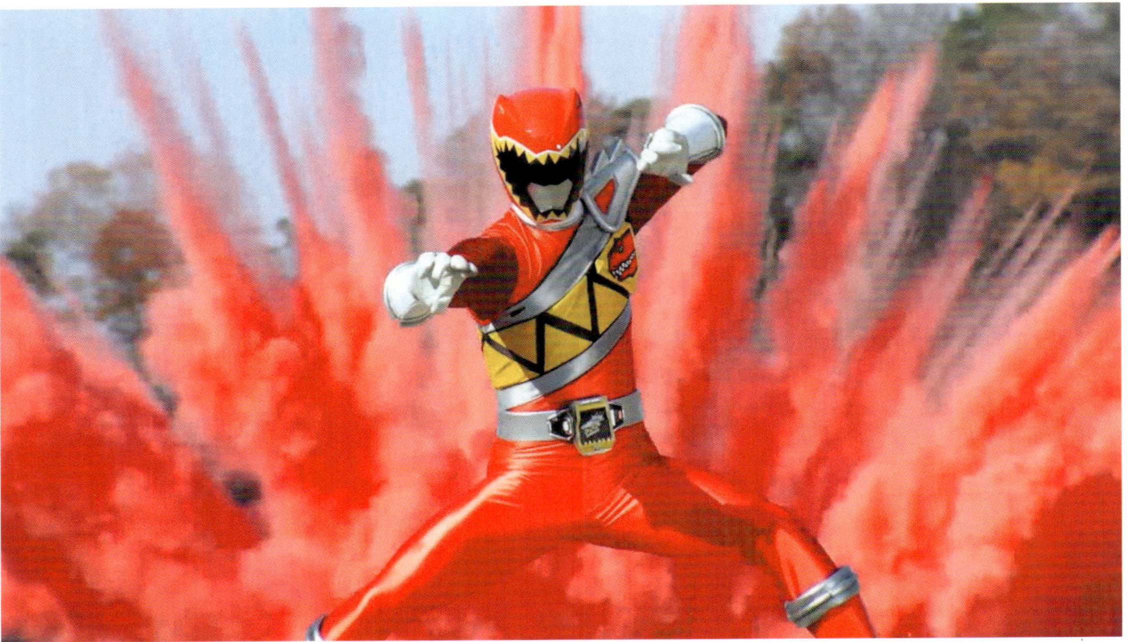

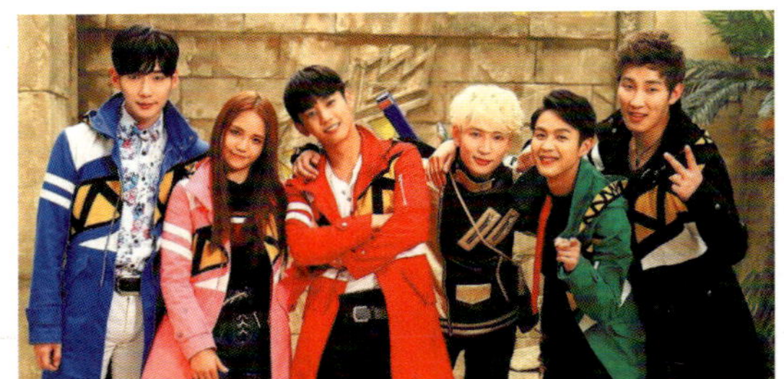

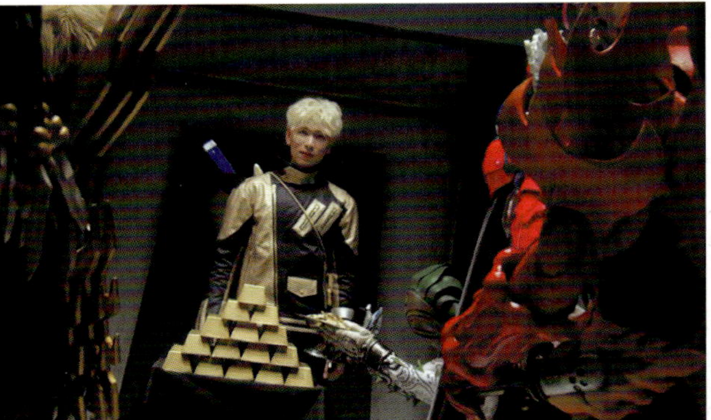

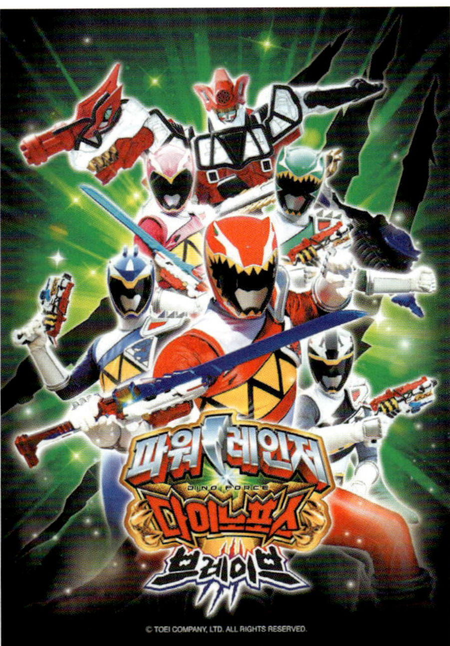

The still-recent success of *Super Sentai* in Korea has left a lasting impact, inspiring new series over the past fifteen years with no connection to Japan. For example, *Legend Hero Samgugjeon* (2016) made use of both Japanese tropes and Chinese culture. The plot and style were taken from the historical Chinese tale *The Three Kingdoms* but the characters were costumed superheroes and giant robots.

Riding on the success of exported Japanese series, neighboring countries have ventured into their own *tokusatsu*-style superhero shows. Between 2012 and 2016, China produced a three-series franchise named *Battle Strike Team* modeled after *Super Sentai*. Similarly, *Armor Hero*, launched in 2008 and still active today, was a blatant imitation of *Kamen Rider*. The franchise now includes six series and several films.

Toei productions remained the primary catalyst for these regional creations. After *Kamen Rider* aired in Indonesia, *BIMA Satria Garuda* was created in 2013 as an homage. *BIMA* and its sequel, *Satria Garuda BIMA-X* (2014), stayed faithful to the Japanese vision of the genre that they were based on (including 1987's *Kamen Rider Black* and 1988's *Kamen Rider Black RX*) while also incorporating creative superhero designs and distinctly Indonesian cultural elements. The series was even co-produced by Ishimori Productions,

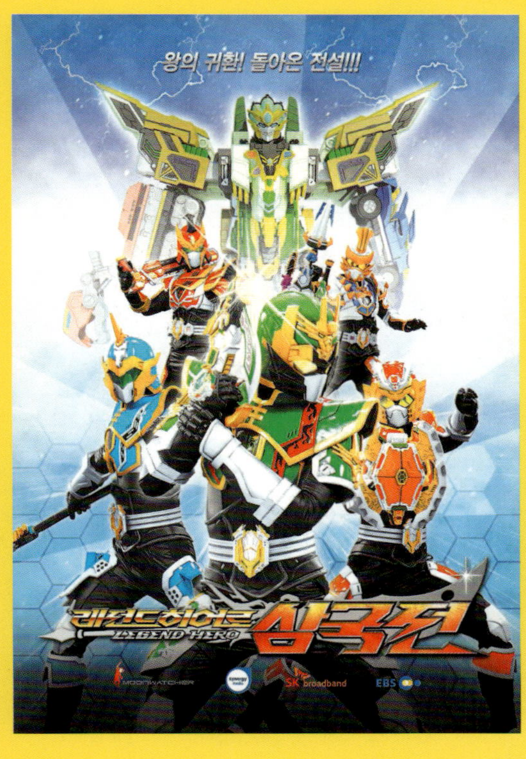

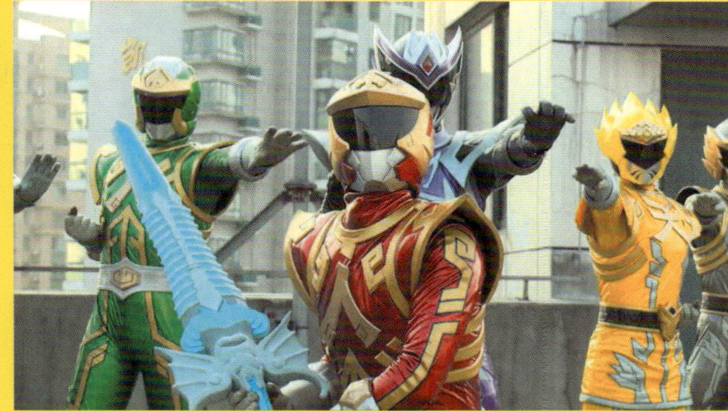

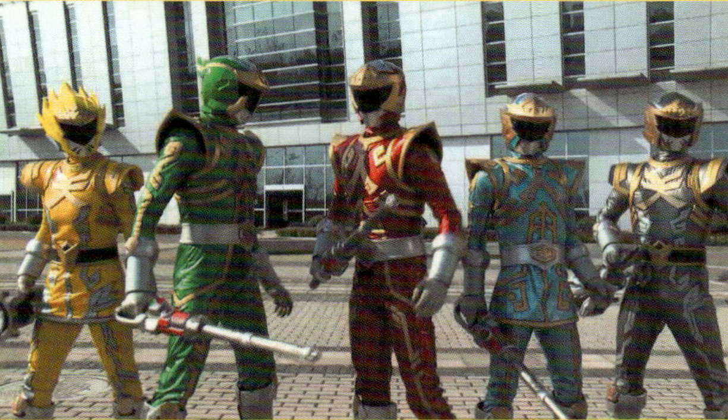

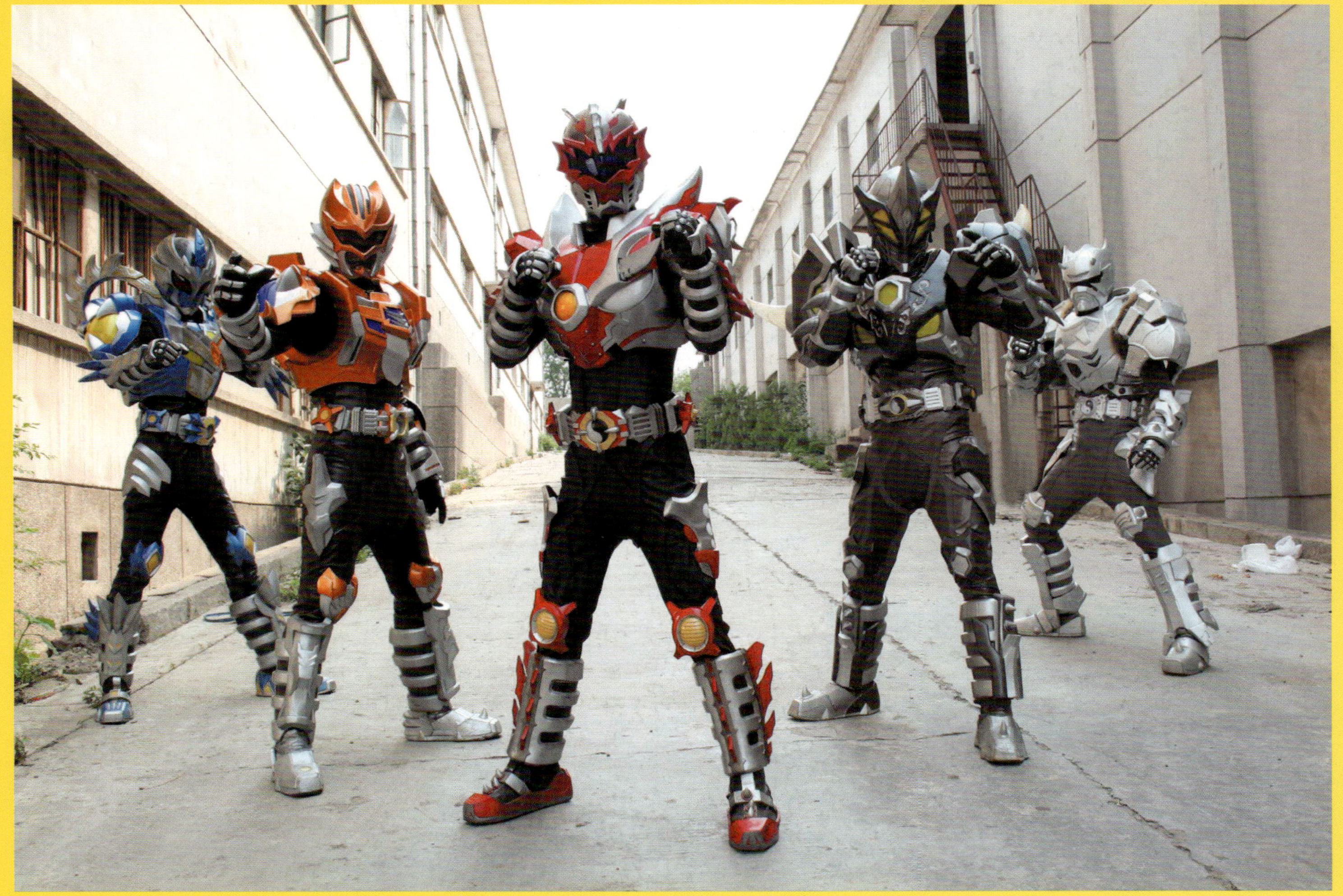

Clockwise from top left: *Promotional poster for* Legend Hero Samgugjeon *(2016), two stills from* Battle Strike Team: Giant Saver *(2012), and a still from* Armor Hero *(2008).*

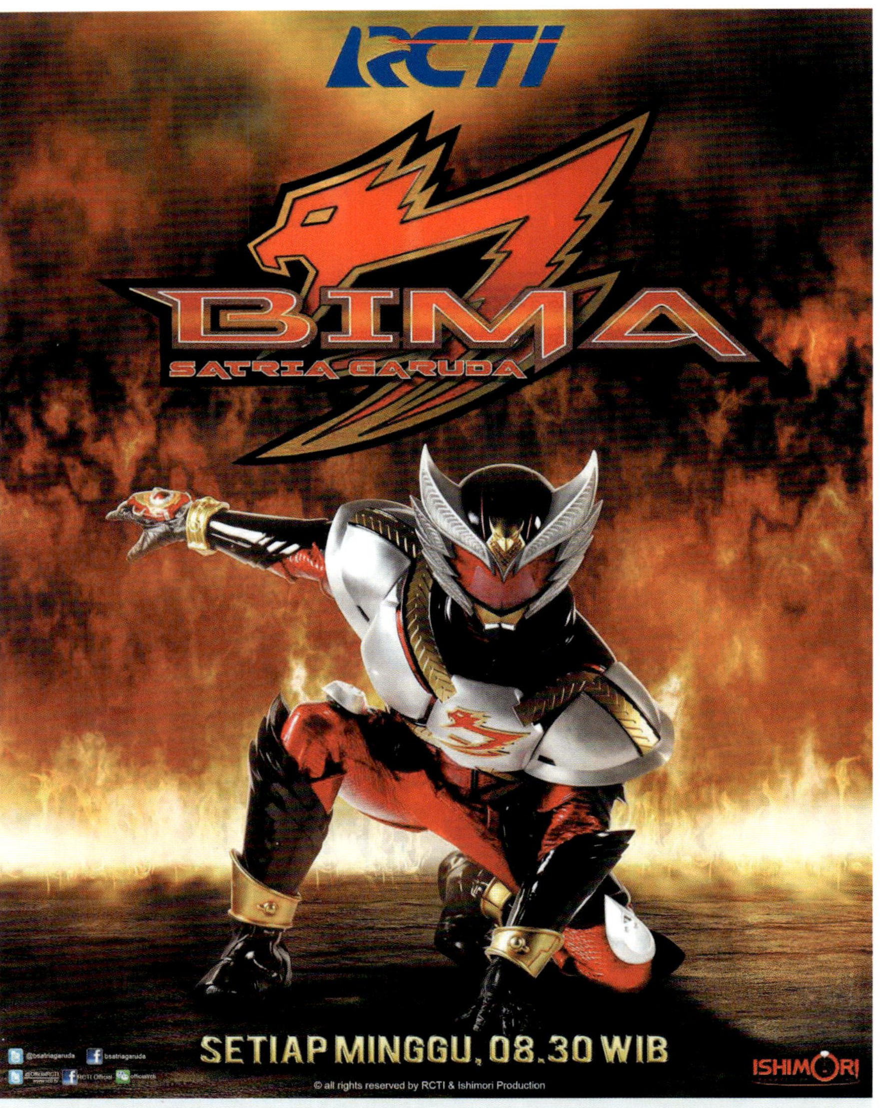

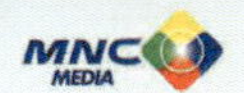

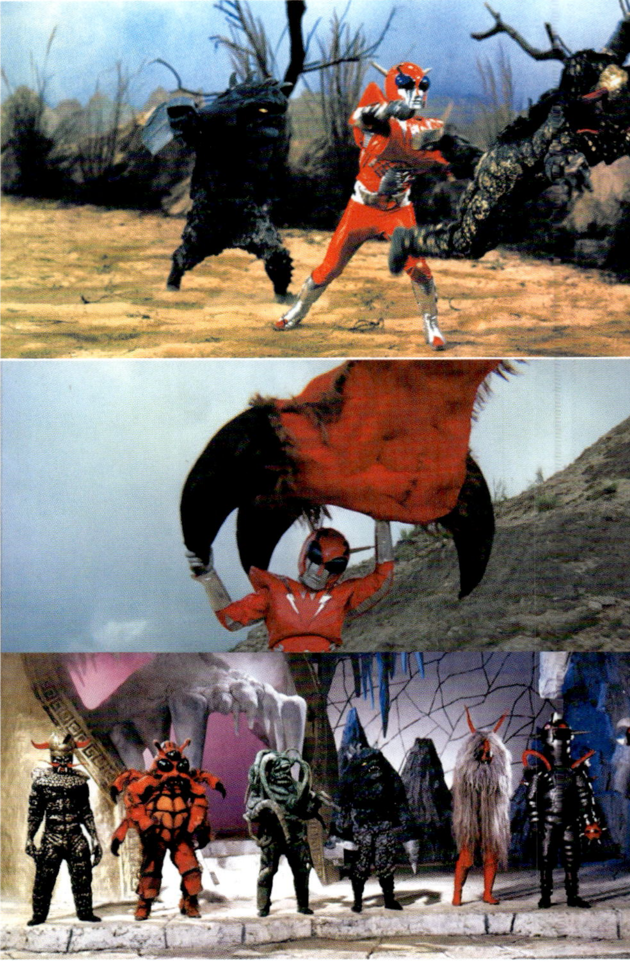

↑ **Above left:** *Promotional poster for* BIMA Satria Garuda *(2013).*

↗ **Above right:** *Stills from* Super Inframan *(1975).*

the company founded in 1967 by Shōtarō Ishinomori, who has overseen its creations and legacy ever since.

One of the wackiest examples of Japanese-influenced Asian superheroes was *Super Inframan* made by Hong Kong's Shaw Brothers Studio in 1975. The film echoes the spirit of *Kamen Rider*, but clearly displays Shaw Brothers' trademark lively kung-fu style. The result is a wild and spectacular adventure that is striking for its unique mix of influences.

GIANT ASIAN MONSTERS

There are many other works that share similarities with *tokusatsu*, from their underlying concept right down to their creative teams. Let's revisit another dominant Japanese genre, the *kaijū*, and look at how it has been reinterpreted throughout Asia.

In Hong Kong, the Shaw Brothers released *The Mighty Peking Man* (titled *Goliathon* in the United States) in 1977. Riding on the coattails of John Guillermin's American remake of *King Kong* the previous year, the film presented its own version of a giant ape wreaking havoc in

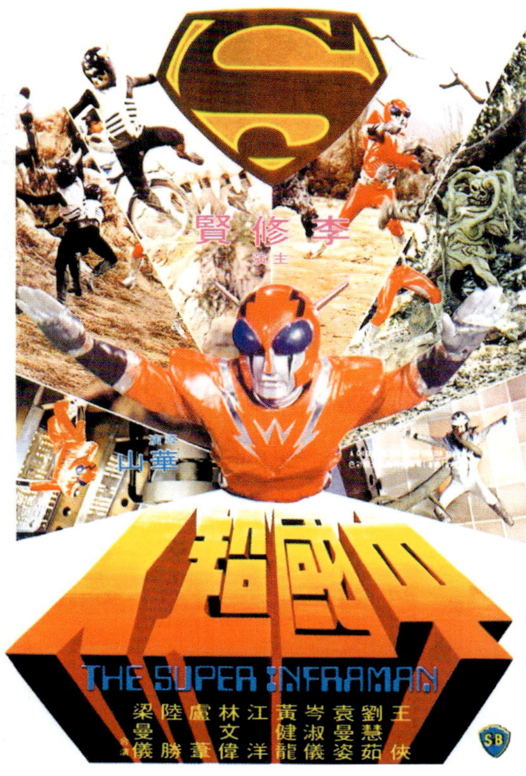

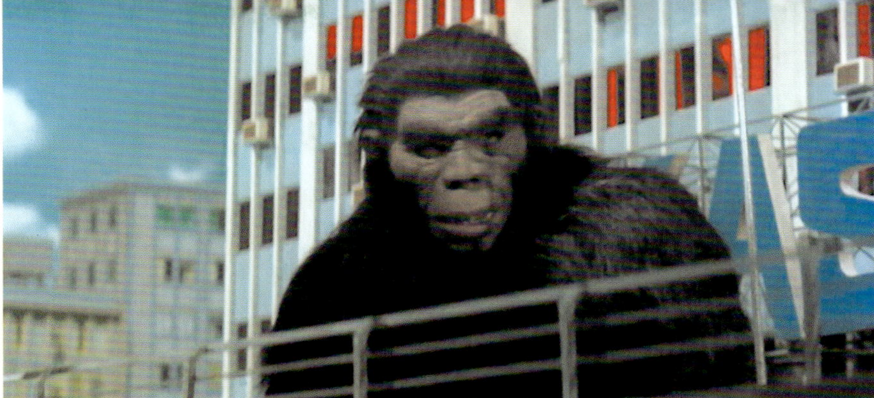

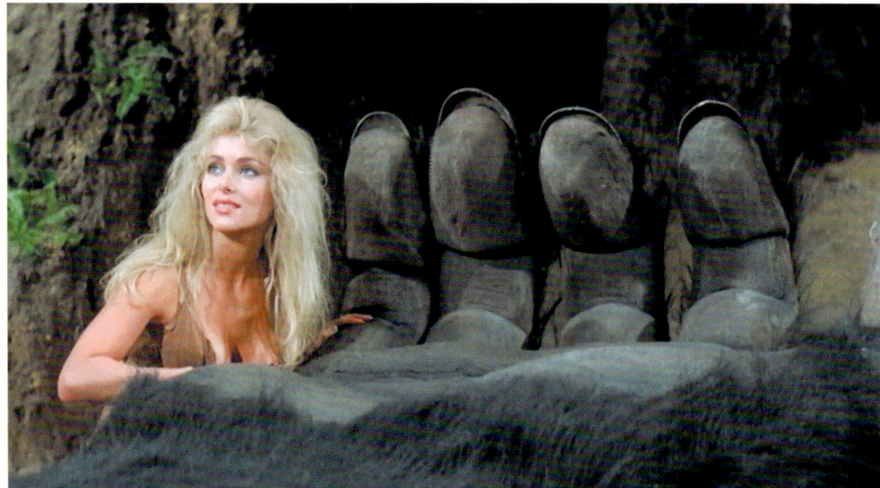

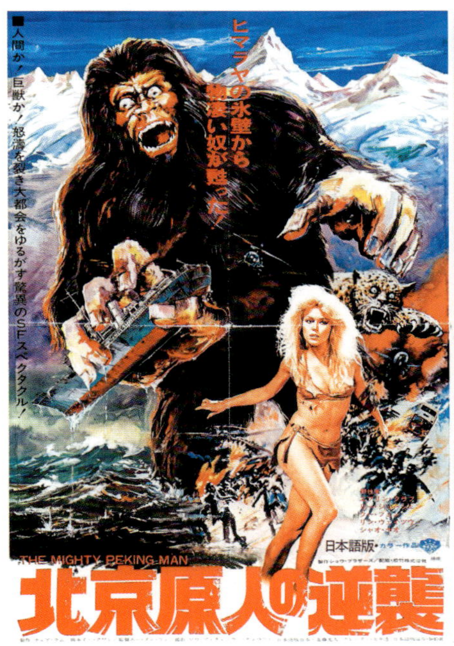

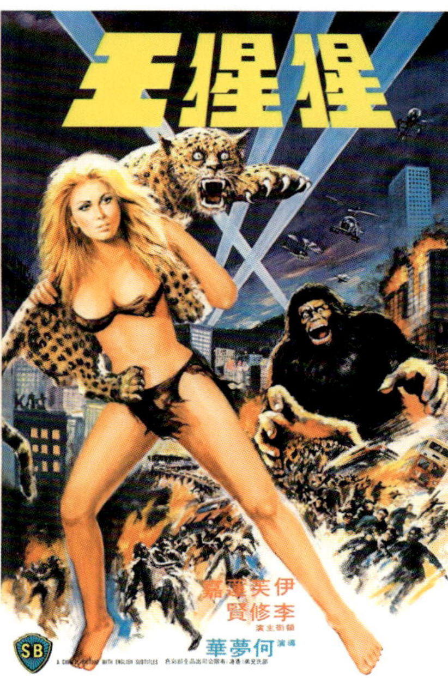

a city, complete with a damsel in distress. That premise alone, reimagined through the Shaw Brothers lens, was enough to ensure a noteworthy production, but it was the movie's technical aspects that truly stood out.

The special effects, including the giant ape costume and miniature cities, were crafted by a Japanese *tokusatsu* team led by someone we've already discussed: Keizō Murase, the renowned designer of monster costumes. Murase not only designed the ape costume but also supervised the impressive model scenes and even performed as the stuntman inside the suit. His deep involvement gives the film an additional layer of flair.

Kaijū culture extended throughout Asia to both North and South Korea. In the 1960s, *Godzilla* sparked some of South Korea's first projects in the genre, including *Yongary, Monster from the Deep* and *Space Monster Wangmagwi*, both released in 1967. *Yongary* took a classic approach, resembling *Godzilla* with its nuclear-awakened monster, whereas *Wangmagwi* veered into absurd, nearly surreal comedy with a uniquely grotesque creature.

Yongary received a peculiar remake in 1999. Although the film was Korean, the cast was entirely Western, as if the film

↖ **Above left:** *Hong Kong poster for the film* Super Inframan *(1975).*

↑ **Above:** *Stills and Hong Kong posters for the film* The Mighty Peking Man *(1977).*

→ **Right:** *Stills and promotional poster for the film* Space Monster Wangmagwi *(1967).*

↓ **Below:** *Korean poster for* Yongary, Monster from the Deep *(1967).*

↓ **Bottom:** *Still from* Yongary, Monster from the Deep *(1967).*

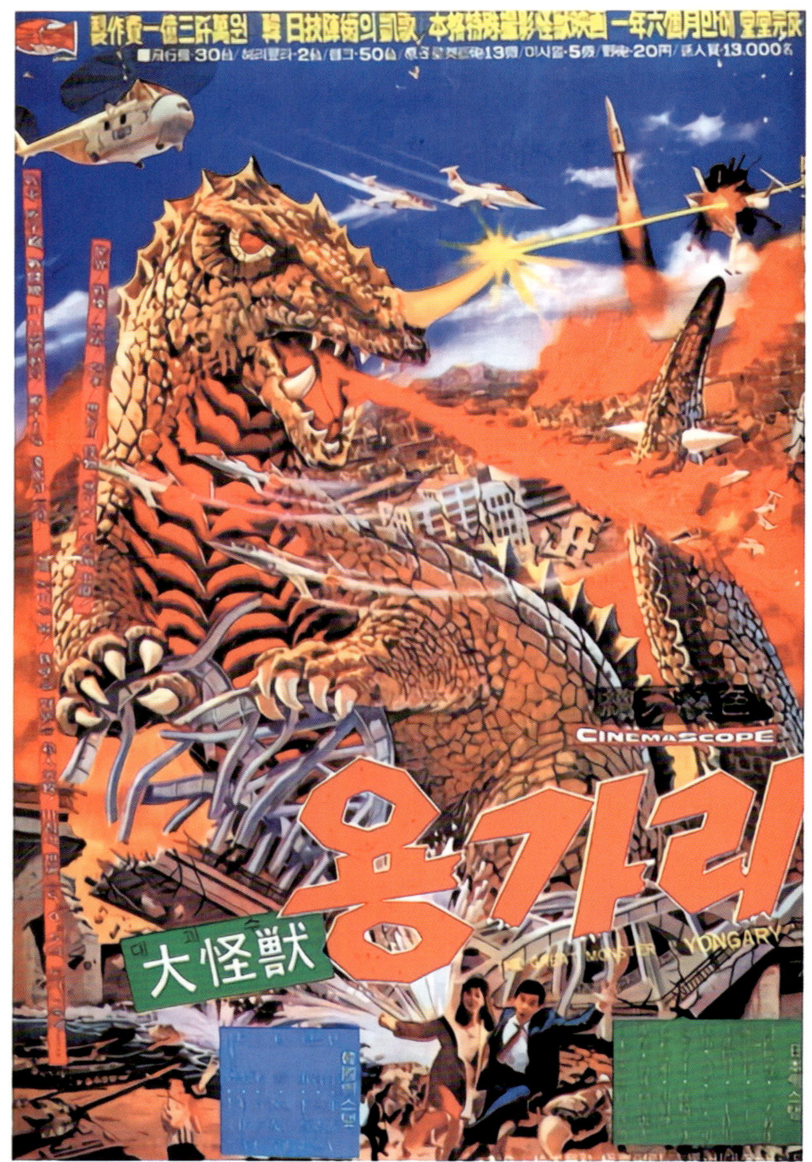

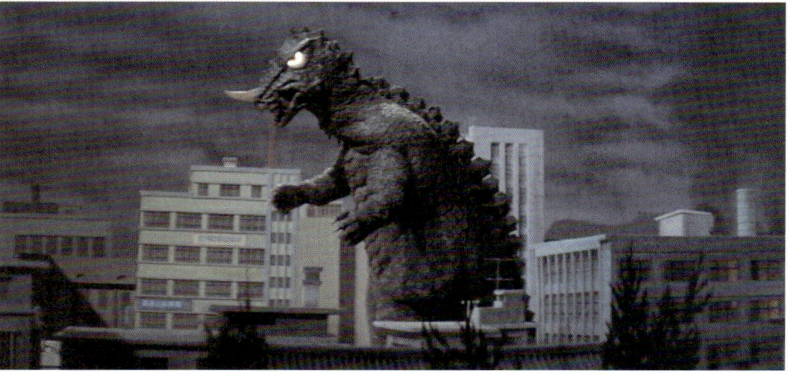

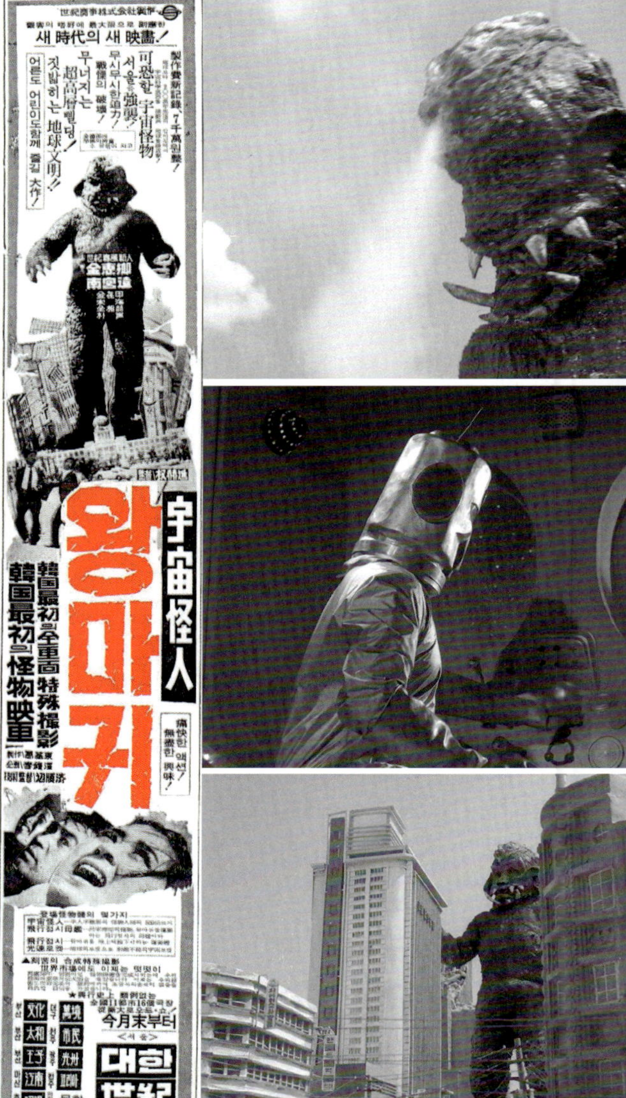

were aimed at an international audience—but it wasn't. The film was notable for its primarily practical special effects, using costumes and miniatures. However, the movie flopped, prompting a complete overhaul for the 2001 release, replacing everything, including the monsters, with poor-quality CGI. The 2001 version was titled *Yonggary: 2001* (or *Reptilian* in the USA), while the 1999 cut appears to have been buried forever.

North Korea also created its own unusual kaijū tale. *Pulgasari* (1985) was a fantasy set in ancient Korea where a creature aids villagers in overthrowing a tyrannical king. However, the film's backstory is even more fascinating. Its director, Shin Sang-ok, was a South Korean national kidnapped by dictator Kim Jong-il to produce propaganda films! The special effects team was brought in from Toho (creator of Godzilla), but as the story goes, they believed they would be filming in China. Most incredibly, Shin Sang-ok managed to escape during shooting, leaving the film to be completed with limited resources.

The final result bears the scars of this tumult. Considering its country of origin, the film has a strangely anti-dictatorship message, and Toho's craftsmanship was evident in the scenes of miniature destruction. Other scenes were rather clumsy and patched together. In the end, the work was remarkable for its unlikely history more than for its actual quality.

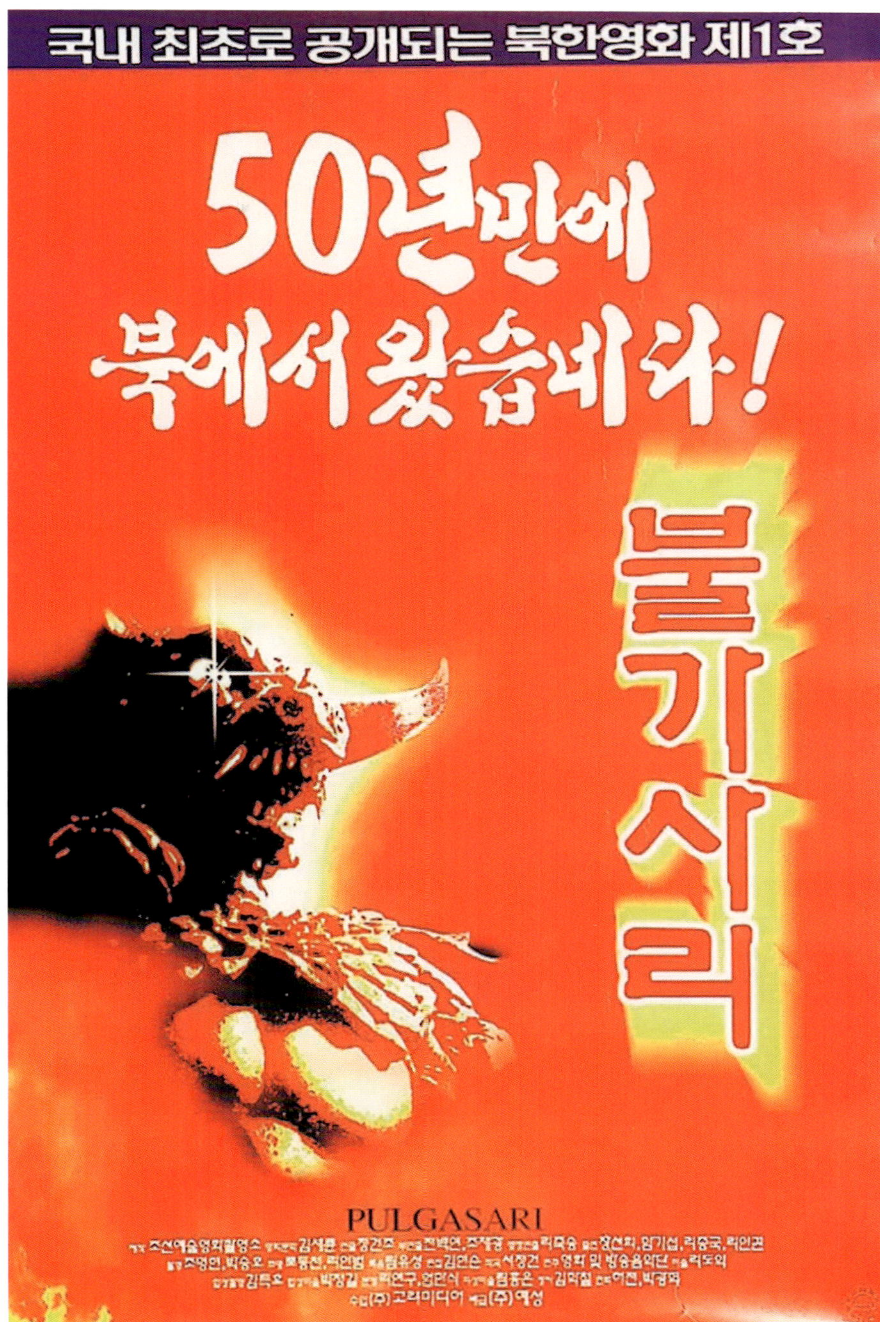

↑ Above: *North Korean poster for the film* Pulgasari *(1985).*

PILI & TAIWANESE PUPPETRY

For our final stop on our tour through *tokusatsu*-inspired productions near Japan, we turn to Taiwan and the world of Pili puppetry. Puppet shows are a cornerstone of popular culture in Taiwan, where for centuries they have narrated epic adventures using intricately carved wooden figures dressed in richly detailed costumes. The art form evolved post–World War II, transitioning from street performances to television in the 1970s as TVs became more common.

The transition gained momentum in the 1980s with the establishment of Pili studio and its early TV programs. Under the leadership of Huang Wen Chang, Pili elevated puppet shows by incorporating spectacular action, special effects, and *wuxia*-style choreography.[5] Large-scale puppets were manipulated by one or more puppeteers, depending on the complexity of the scene, filmed amid detailed

5. *Wuxia* are Chinese fantasy stories featuring exaggerated aerial fight scenes. *Crouching Tiger, Hidden Dragon* (2000) is a prime example.

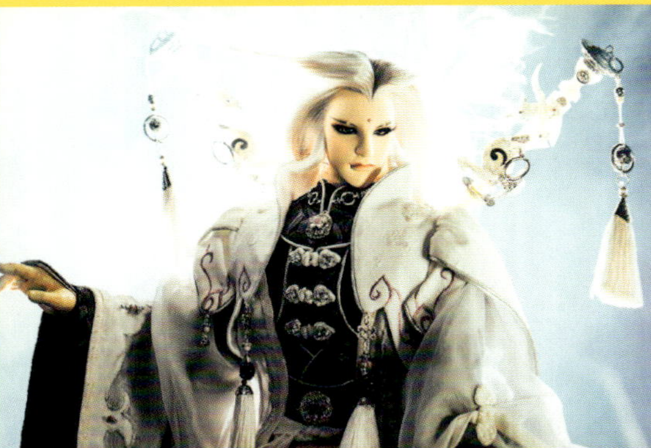

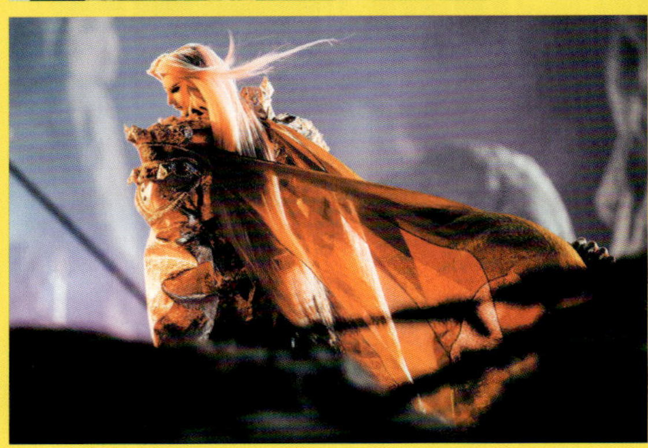

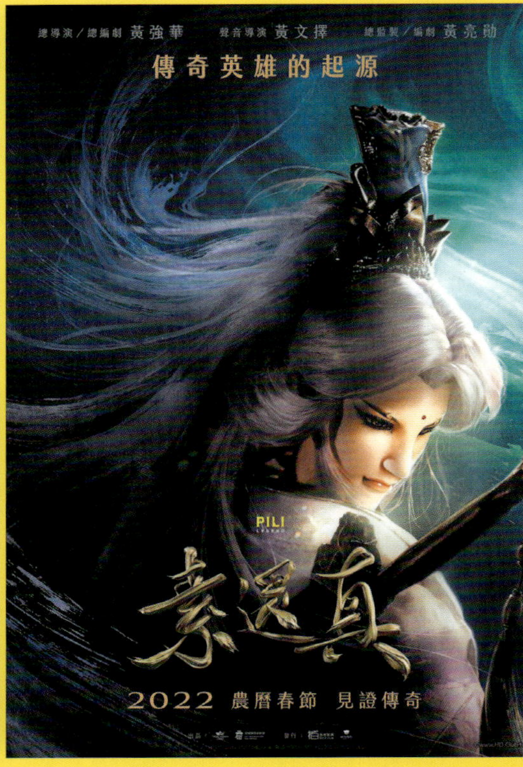

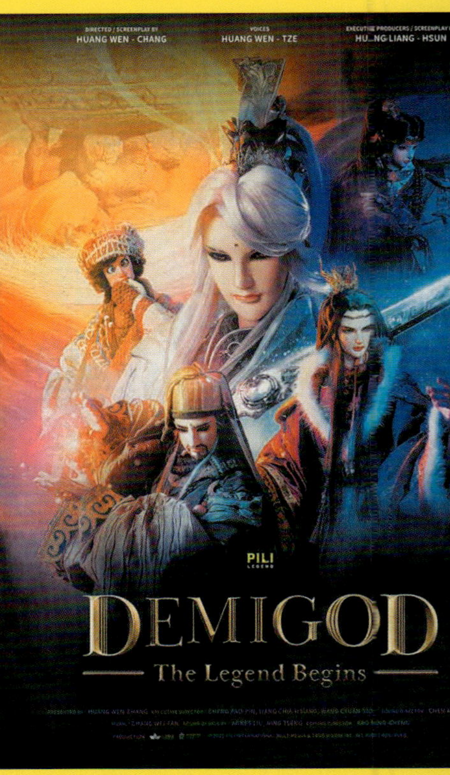

↑ Above, from left to right: The Broken World *(2024) series and the film* Demigod—The Legend Begins *(2022) feature the same hero.*

→ Right: *Puppets also arrived in Japan via the series* Thunderbolt Fantasy *(2016).*

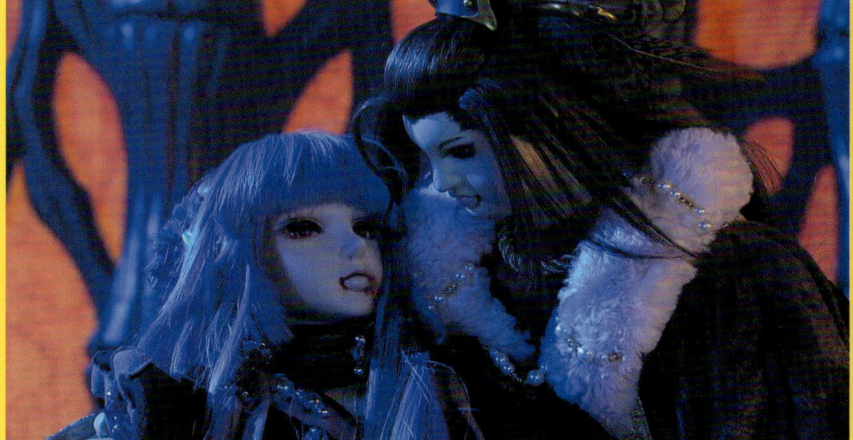

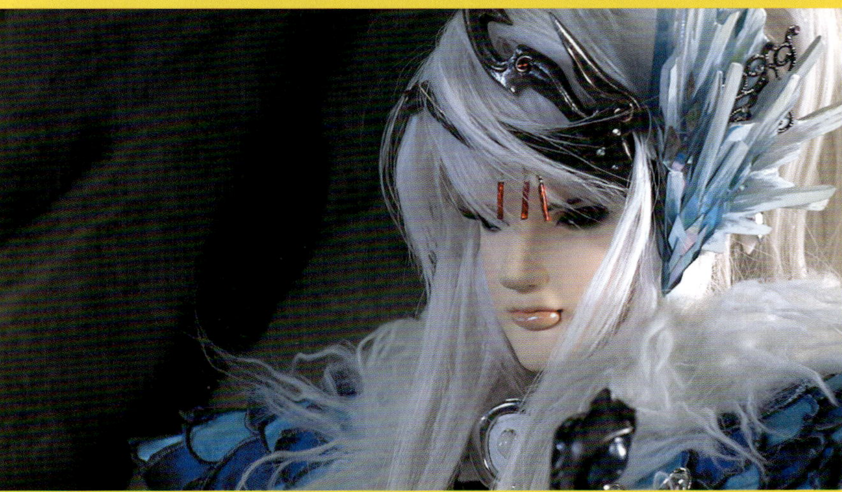

miniature sets. Action sequences featured explosions, destructible props, and flying dust, and the puppets themselves were even battered about, forming an impressive spectacle.

The new approach brought instant success in Taiwan, becoming a staple of the culture. New series continue to be released annually, with recurring series and an ongoing story arc. The latest installment, *Broken World*, premiered in April 2024.

For two decades, the Huang family has sought to take Pili global. In 2016, they collaborated with Japanese screenwriter Gen Urobuchi (*Kamen Rider Gaim*, 2013) to produce *Thunderbolt Fantasy*. Featuring a new storyline and a universe aimed at international audiences, the series was streamed worldwide, including on Crunchyroll. The Japanese-Taiwanese spin-off runs parallel to the main series and will conclude in 2025.

It seemed the studio had hit its stride. In 2022, the film *Demigod—The Legend Begins* marked a new chapter in the franchise, reaching international markets. Though the film's story is a conventional epic adventure, the production itself is significant for Taiwan's collaboration with Japan. In a behind-the-scenes feature, Huang Liang Hsun, who succeeded his father as studio head in 2015, described Taiwanese puppet productions as closely related to *tokusatsu*. As such, he even bolstered the project by enlisting Japanese technical experts to design the movie's giant creatures. The monster suits were devised by Kakusei Fujiwara, a thirty-year veteran of *tokusatsu* creature design (*Godzilla*, *Ultraman*, *Shin Kamen Rider*). The movie was a fascinating fusion of charming cultures and styles, a compelling showcase of a segment of Taiwanese culture.

CONCLUSION

You now have a solid foundation in *tokusatsu* culture, from the countless Japanese works that defined it to the global creations it has inspired. *Tokusatsu* is everywhere, often without us even realizing it. Paradoxically, though, the genre remains relatively obscure outside of its home country. This is understandable to some extent, as the productions are primarily made for Japanese audiences. At best, they may find a market elsewhere in Asia, but rarely beyond.

Furthermore, promoting *tokusatsu* internationally presents significant challenges. Its style is as unique as it is niche when compared to anime, which is ubiquitous and easy to export—which likely dissuades Japan from changing its processes. But things are gradually evolving, both in terms of distribution methods and audience perception.

Though you may have to dig a little, some *tokusatsu* works and franchises have begun breaking out of Japan and Asia to reach wider audiences, becoming easier to find—not a lot easier, mind you, but all signs point to progress being made. Nevertheless, there's still work to be done, both by Japanese studios to facilitate international exposure for their productions, and by fans worldwide, who can play a vital role in amplifying the reach of such shows and movies on a larger scale.

Thanks to the tireless efforts of earlier generations to pass down their knowledge, a new generation of *tokusatsu* enthusiasts is growing every day. Behind the camera, among actors, and even in front of screens, a community is thriving.

Although Japanese special effects—including the more modern approaches (as seen in *Godzilla Minus One* and crowned by a coveted Oscar)—remain relatively unknown in many regions, overshadowed as they are by Hollywood's style, the art continues to draw attention, spark intrigue, and fuel passion. Will *tokusatsu* finally have its day in the sun?

There's never been a better time in history to dive into *tokusatsu* and all its rich, varied offerings that are easier to access than ever before, bolstered by active and increasingly vocal communities. This is a golden opportunity to explore productions that remain exciting, inventive, and captivating, some of which have endured for over forty years.

From superheroes—the ultimate embodiment of technical and narrative possibilities—to iconic giant monsters, as well as the countless lesser-known productions that have punctuated the history of *tokusatsu*, we hope this overview has given you a deeper understanding of the evolution of Japanese film and television, will guide you in your exploration of their themes across eras, and has gifted you with a newfound appreciation for its underappreciated range.

TIMELINE

Kaijū
(Super)heroes
Other
Foreign productions
1921
Jiraiya the Hero
Tōmei Ningen Arawaru
1949
1950
1954
Godzilla
1956
Rodan
1959
Battle in Outer Space
1960
Mothra
1961
King Kong vs. Godzilla
1962
Ghidorah, the Three-Headed Monster
1964
Gamera, the Giant Monster
1965
1966
Ultraman
Ultra Q
1967
The X from Outer Space
Ambassador Magma
The Magic Serpent
The Golden Bat
Daimajin
Akuma-kun

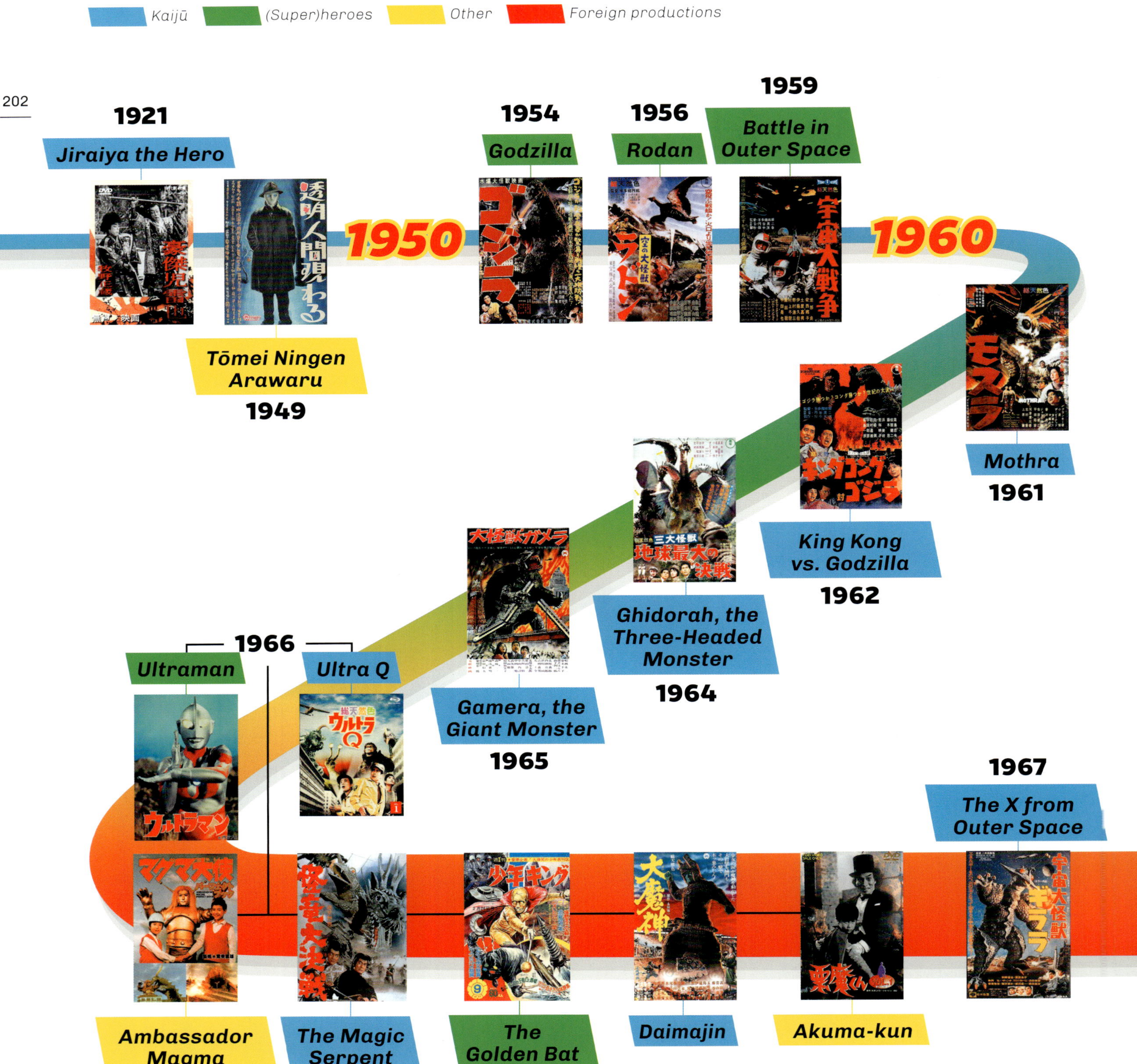

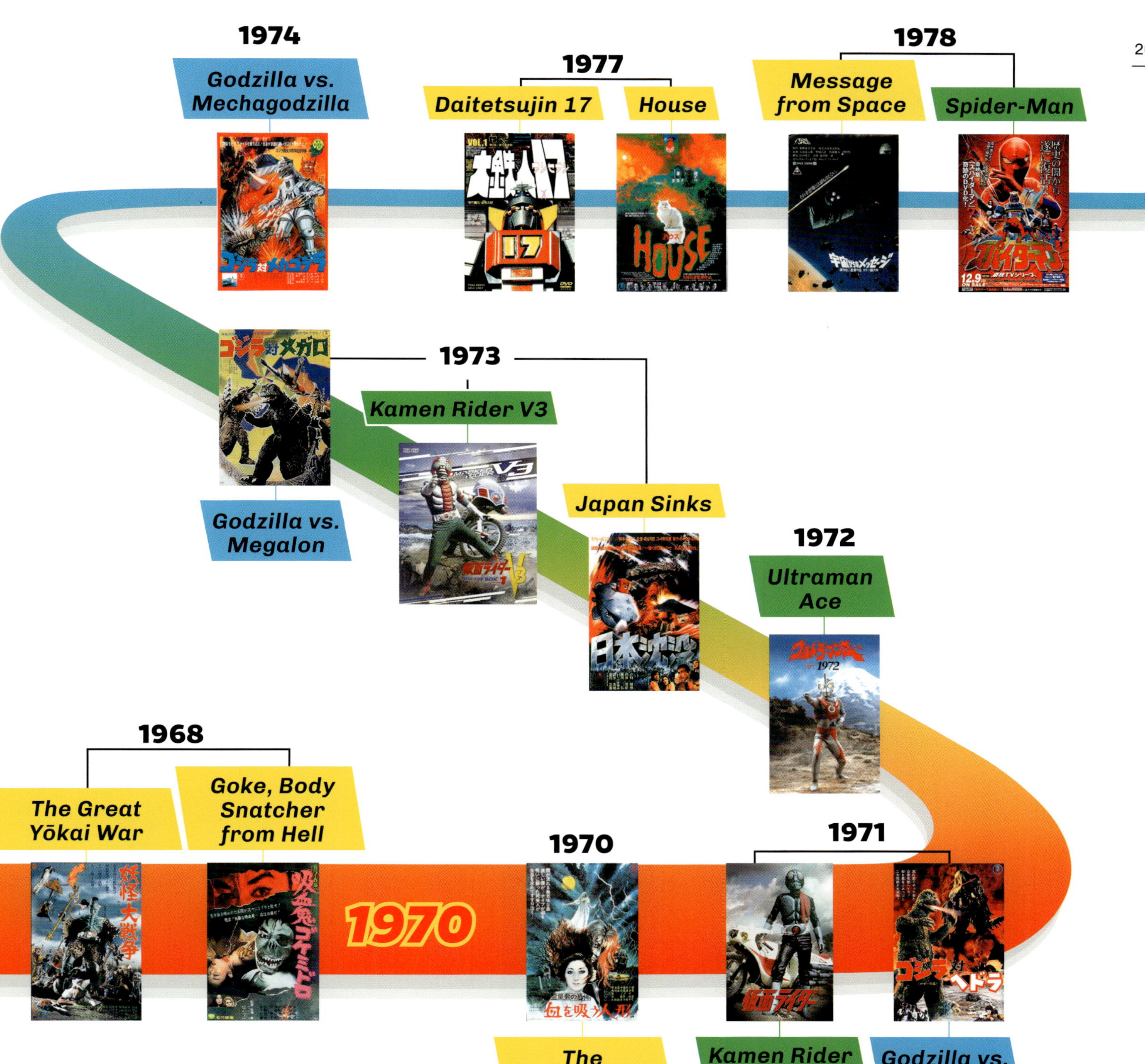
1974
Godzilla vs. Mechagodzilla
1977
Daitetsujin 17
House
1978
Message from Space
Spider-Man
1973
Kamen Rider V3
Japan Sinks
Godzilla vs. Megalon
1972
Ultraman Ace
1968
The Great Yōkai War
Goke, Body Snatcher from Hell
1970
1970
The Vampire Doll
1971
Kamen Rider
Godzilla vs. Hedorah

TIMELINE

Kaijū (Super)heroes Other Foreign productions

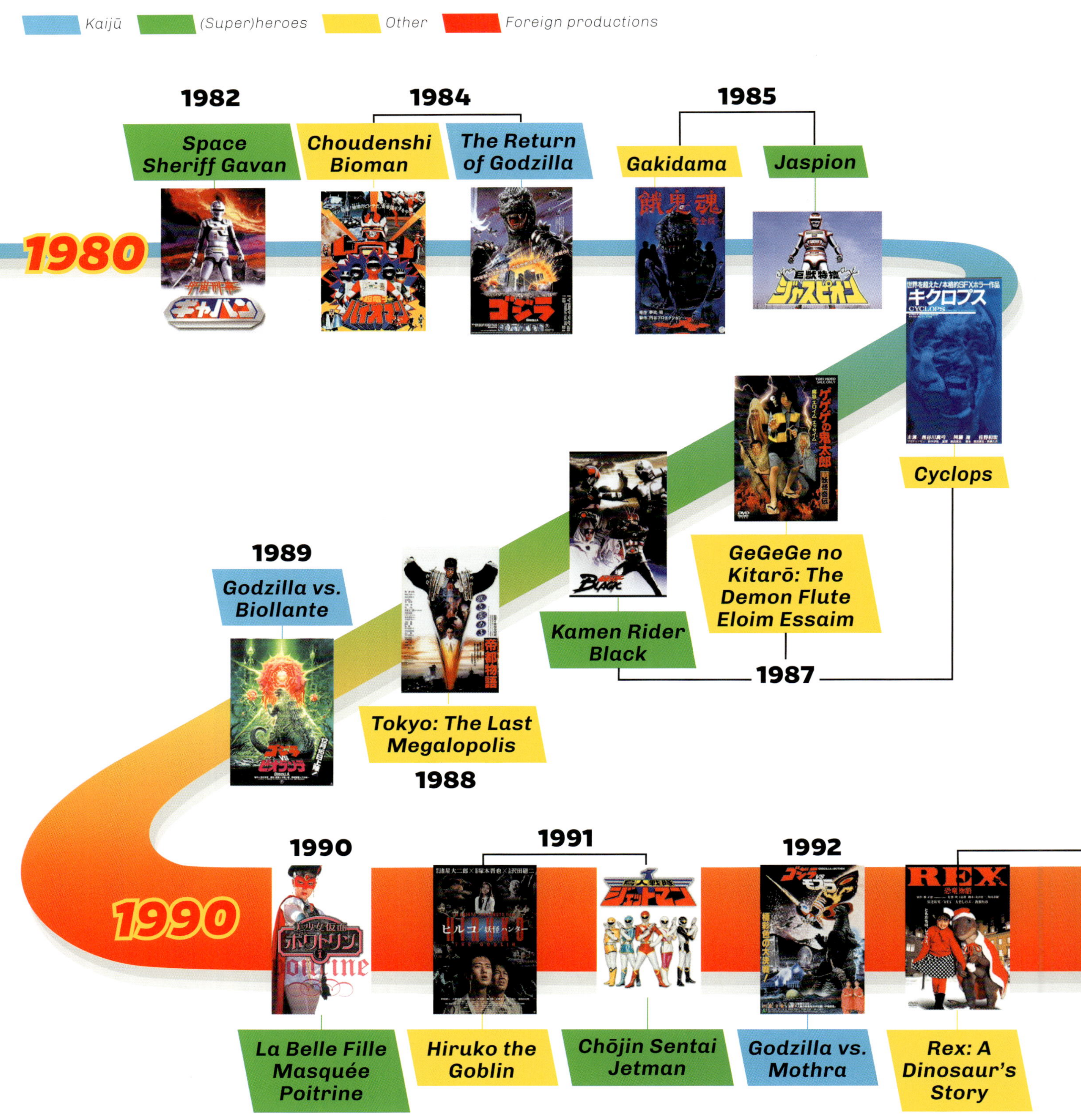

2006 Crab Goalkeeper

2007 Big Man Japan

2007 GeGeGe no Kitarō

2009 Samurai Sentai Shinkenger

2010

2010 Death Kappa

Garo 2005

Sailor Moon 2003

2000

Meatball Machine 1999

1998 Ultraman Gaia

1996 Rebirth of Mothra

1993 Godzilla vs. MechaGodzilla

1993 Mighty Morphin Power Rangers

1994 Ninja Sentai Kakuranger

1995 School Ghost Stories

1995 Gamera: Guardian of the Universe

TIMELINE

Kaijū
(Super)heroes
Other
Foreign productions
2012
Giant God Warrior Appears in Tokyo
2013
BIMA Satria Garuda
2015
Attack on Titan
2016
Shin Godzilla
2017
Idol × Warrior Miracle Tunes!
Uchū Sentai Kyuranger
2020
Monster Seafood Wars
2020
2021
Nezura 1964
The Great Yōkai War: Guardians
2022
Kamen Rider Black Sun
Shin Ultraman
What to Do with the Dead Kaijū?
2023
Godzilla Minus One
MINUS ONE

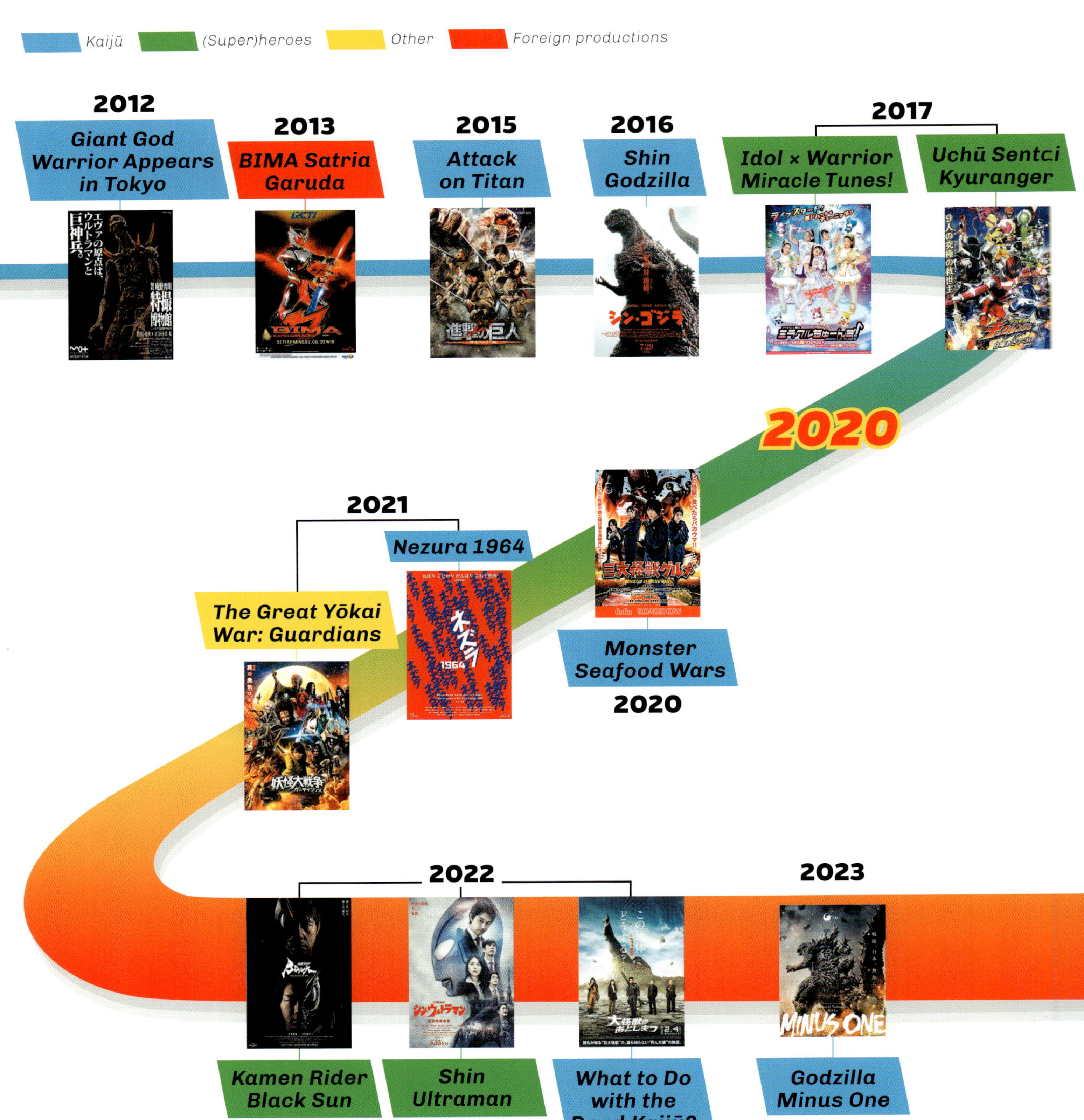

ACKNOWLEDGMENTS

MARVIN RINGARD, AUTHOR

There are so many people who made my first book, on a subject so near and dear to my heart, possible. First, I'd like to thank my friend Bastien Auguste, who initially urged me to watch the *Kamen Rider* franchise sometime in the early 2010s. I was hesitant at first, as its bizarre style was new to me, but I eventually fell in love with it, leading me to where I am today.

I am deeply grateful for everyone I've met along the way and all the people with whom I continue to share my newfound passion. Special thanks to Vincent Marcantognini, friend and fe low *tokusatsu* expert in France, without whom I wouldn't know half of what I do today. And, of course, a huge thank-you to Romain Taszek for suggesting this (probably) wild idea, and to all the publishers at Ynnis for their support throughout this project.

ROMAIN TASZEK, ILLUSTRATOR

I want to express my heartfelt gratitude to Marvin Ringard, who jumped into this project with both feet. An enormous thank-you goes to Mathilde as well, whose unwavering and invaluable support was essential throughout this endeavor.

CREDITS

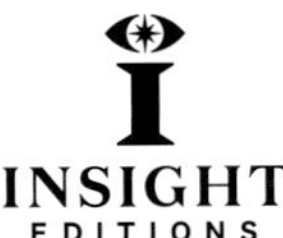

PO Box 3088
San Rafael, CA 94912
www.insighteditions.com

Find us on Facebook: www.facebook.com/InsightEditions
Follow us on Instagram: @insighteditions

Originally published in French as *Le guide du tokusatsu: kaijû, sentai et effets spéciaux japonais des origines à nos jours* by Ynnis Editions, France, in 2024.

English translation by Andie Ho.

ISBN: 979-8-3374-0122-5

Publisher: Raoul Goff
SVP, Co-Publisher: Vanessa Lopez
VP, Creative: Chrissy Kwasnik
VP, Manufacturing: Alix Nicholaeff
Editorial Director: Lia Brown
Art Director: Matt Girard
Designer: Lola Villanueva
Senior Editor: Stephen Fall
Editorial Assistant: Audrey Salo
Executive Managing Editor: Maria Spano
Senior Production Manager: Greg Steffen
Strategic Production Planner: Lina s Palma-Temena

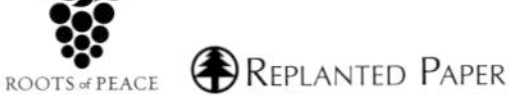

Insight Editions, in association with Roots of Peace, will plant two trees for each tree used in the manufacturing of this book. Roots of Peace is an internationally renowned humanitarian organization dedicated to eradicating land mines worldwide and converting war-torn lands into productive farms and wildlife habitats. Roots of Peace will plant two million fruit and nut trees in Afghanistan and provide farmers there with the skills and support necessary for sustainable land use.

Manufactured in China by Insight Editions

10 9 8 7 6 5 4 3 2 1

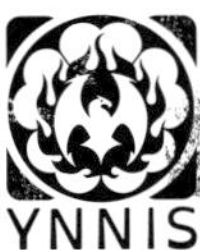

President: Cedric Littardi
Editorial and Art Director: Sébastien Rost
Editor: Charlotte Thomas
Editorial Coordinator: Jeanne Bucher
Corrections: Mélissa Veludo
Graphic Design: Cécile Chatelin
Illustrations: Romain Taszek
Images: Jeanne Bucher and Marvin Ringard
Cover: Sébastien Rost
Manufacture: centSucres
Marketing & Communications: Célia Bourrel

Ynnis Éditions
38 rue Notre-Dame-De-Nazareth
75003 Paris, France
www.ynnis-editions.fr
Instagram: @ynnis_editions
Facebook: Ynnis Éditions
X: @YnnisEditions